Obeah, Race and Racism

Obeah, Race and Racism

Caribbean Witchcraft in the English Imagination

Eugenia O'Neal

The University of the West Indies Press
Jamaica • Barbados • Trinidad and Tobago

The University of the West Indies Press
7A Gibraltar Hall Road, Mona
Kingston 7, Jamaica
www.uwipress.com

© 2020 by Eugenia O'Neal
All rights reserved. Published 2020

A catalogue record of this book is available from the
National Library of Jamaica.

ISBN: 978-976-640-759-9 (paper)
978-976-640-760-5 (Kindle)
978-976-640-761-2 (ePub)

Cover illustration: iStock.com/ilbusca, stock illustration ID: 658584394
Book and cover design by Robert Harris
Set in Adobe Garamond Pro 11/14. x 24

The University of the West Indies Press has no responsibility for the persistence or accuracy of URLs for external or third-party Internet websites referred to in this publication and does not guarantee that any content on such websites is, or will remain, accurate or appropriate.

Printed in the United States of America

This book is dedicated to
my aunt Linda O'Neal, who considered Obeah
an odd subject for me to be interested in but,
nevertheless, grew interested in my findings.
Obeah, Race and Racism is also dedicated to my father, Eugene O'Neal, who
founded the first museum in the British Virgin Islands
and whose interest in history is, no doubt, responsible for mine;
to my aunt Gertrude O'Neal, without whom the foundations
of my scholarship would not have been set;
and to my mother, Antonia Jimenez de O'Neal,
who, I hope, would have been proud.

Contents

    Introduction / 1

1. Strange Encounters: Christian Captains and African Fetish Masters / 10

2. The Black Thread of Mischief Crosses the Atlantic: Egyptian *Aub* or Ashantee *Obayifo* / 38

3. "Prophet, Priest and King of His District": The Obeah Man in His Society / 91

4. Challenging Order and Inspiring Resistance / 125

5. Obeah, Race and Racism / 177

6. The Early Literary Response / 200

7. The Case of Three-Finger'd Jack / 222

8. Credulous Blacks and Faithful Mulattoes / 253

9. Black Sorceresses and Mulatto Vampires / 314

10. Fictional Adventurers and Real-Life Travellers: Obeah in Boys' Papers and Travel Narratives / 355

    Conclusion / 397

    Selected Bibliography / 405

    Index / 419

Introduction

BRITISH SLAVE SHIPS TOOK MORE THAN THREE million captive Africans to the plantations of the New World. Naked, without belongings, the captives would have appeared utterly bereft, carrying nothing, owning nothing. But this was not quite true. Something powerful and dread came with them: a belief in magic that would grow among the cane, taking root in soil seeded by blood, sweat and tears. This belief would sustain and empower Africa's sons and daughters in a way that nothing else could. It came to be known as Obeah.

Nobody can be very sure exactly from where Obeah came, but some scholars have traced it to the region of the Gold Coast now known as Ghana and to the Ashanti and Fanti people of the area. The Ashanti term *obi okomfo* refers to a priest, but this is countered by the Igbo *dibia*, a title whose meaning can range from "master of knowledge" to "herbalist". Richard Allsopp in his *Dictionary of Caribbean English Usage* also mentions *o-bayi-fo*, the Twi word for witchcraft, and the Efik word *ubio*, signifying "a charm put in the ground to cause sickness". Thus, the only thing one can be certain of is that the people of these and other ethnicities took across the Atlantic beliefs and practices which they reshaped to meet their physical and spiritual needs.

The practices and beliefs of the various peoples overlapped, and even within a single language grouping the meaning of the terms was fluid, depending on context. A *dibia* is an Igbo priest who, then and now, acts as an intermediary between the gods and humanity. Always a male, he can perform acts such as divination, foretelling the future and interpreting signs from the gods. Using knowledge passed from father to son, the *dibia* can tell a supplicant if he or she has offended one of the gods or can put the supplicant under divine protection, thus making him or her immune to bad magic. But the word *dibia* can also take on the meaning of "one who heals" when used in conjunction with certain other words. A *dibia*, then, could be not just a priest but also a medicine man, possessing a deep knowledge of the medicinal uses of plants, and also of their toxicity.[1] Africans, like Europeans, considered witches as being quite distinct

---

[1] Ogunyemi Steven Oluwatosin, personal communication, 30 August 2017.

from priests. Witches were evil, and all their works were considered evil. They had no other purpose but to wreak evil, by sucking out a person's soul; visiting sickness, poverty, bad luck and infertility on their enemies; causing drought or raising a storm.

In many African societies, the roles sometimes overlapped, however. Witches and priests could be distinct from sorcerers, like the *bokonons* of Benin, who are able to wield either bad or good magic and who, like priests, can also offer protection to victims of evil. Even today, they rely mostly on magic to aid them in their works, while the priests rely on help from the relevant god or gods. But all witches, priests, and sorcerers use powerful objects to do their work. So, for example, a priest of the Fon people might use a *bo* made of human bones to protect the innocent from the wrath of the gods and from the magical attacks of witches. Similarly, a sorcerer might keep a bottle of protection, decorated with beads and cowry shells and containing items of magic, which might include feathers, leaves and bones.

Yet there were important distinctions that were known to Africans. Priests oversaw your acceptance into the society as a baby and presided over your rites of passage. They helped you navigate the pitfalls of life by consulting the ancestors and the gods and protected you from harm. Should you break a divine law, say, by murdering someone, it was the priests who would put you to the test to determine your guilt or innocence, in much the same way that Catholic priests would test suspected witches in Europe. Sorcerers were different from priests, but they protected you from harm and could also help cure what ailed you or bring your desires to life. The difference was that they did not have the assistance of the gods but they offered good-luck charms and amulets to preserve your health, and could send magic after your enemies.

All these activities took place within the framework of religions no less complex than those of the Hindus and the Vikings. Gods and ancestors in the pantheons of the various tribes either held themselves aloof, mingling little in human affairs, like Obatala of the Yoruba, or meddled so much that humans became exasperated with them, as in the case of the trickster god Anansi, son of the Sky Father, Nyame, and the fertility goddess, Asase Yaa.

But most of this was closed to the European captains and company men who sailed down the coast of Africa. Amazed and excited by all they were seeing and, of course, by the possibility of great wealth and power, they carefully took time to record navigational routes, their impressions of the land, the crops grown, trading opportunities, and the minerals available. They also sent back descriptions of the peoples they encountered, their hospitality or lack thereof, their appearance, their habitations, and their religious and other customs. This last – their descriptions of the poorly understood religious beliefs of the Ashantee, Koromantyn, Quoja, Mandingo and other peoples they met – created a racialized impression of Africa and Africans that had an impact which arguably lasts to this day.

Ignorant of the rich and complex theologies that supported the religious rites they witnessed, their breathless accounts centred instead on cannibal kings, human sacrifices and devil-worshipping fetish men and women, painting a picture of Africans as primitive and barbarous, ferocious and bestial. Their frank refusal to understand the cultures they came across resulted in depictions of Africans as subhuman, existing in darkness, immoral and vile, desperately in need of the light brought by Christianizing Europeans. For centuries, this image of black people as inferior to the European, as a brutal, superstitious and savage Other, dominated European writings. It was an image which provided many British intellectuals with the foundation for their development of racist theories of black inferiority and savagery. These theories first justified a transatlantic slave trade on a scale so massive it had no precedent, and then, after abolition, supported imperialist ambitions around the world while fostering a virulent racism at home in Britain.

Yet, despite the hard work of the missionaries and others who launched themselves at Africa with the aim of Europeanizing the natives and removing them from "their savage ignorance and superstition",[2] the natives proved strangely resistant. Even those who made an outward show of adopting the values of Europeans, mimicking their habits and embracing their faith, often practised the traditions of their ancestors in secret. This was a vexing problem for the whites in Africa, but it took slave dealers and slave owners some time to realize that the men, women and children being exported to the plantations of the New World were bringing Africa's traditional religions with them. Nobody, not even the Africans themselves, had any way of knowing just how that legacy would shape interactions between whites and blacks and form their perceptions of each other and of themselves for centuries to come.

In the English colonies of the Caribbean, the religious practices of the various African peoples and their systems of magic melded and became known as Obeah. No other single word caused as much fury and dread in the hearts of both abolitionists and anti-abolitionists, plantation owners and missionaries.

---

2   John McLeod, *A Voyage to Africa, with Some Account of the Manners and Customs of the Dahomian People* (London: Frank Cass, 1820), 57.

In fact, the missionaries had no higher aim than eradicating the transplanted Africans' trust in their witch doctors and supplanting it with faith in the "white Obeah" of Christianity. Blacks could no more be allowed to retain their belief in the traditions of their ancestors than they could be allowed to keep their original names, so Methodist, Baptist, Moravian and other missionaries set to with a will in the different islands, converting hundreds of thousands of Africans and their descendants to Christianity.

Not content with conversions alone, however, Caribbean missionaries and planters, the representatives of officialdom, confronted the supposed Obeah men and women wherever they found them and destroyed their charms and even their houses. When Obeah was criminalized, Obeah men and women were taken to court, and several were sentenced to burn at the stake or be hanged until dead. Some were flogged and many transported to other colonies.

Missionaries and plantation owners inveighed against Obeah at every opportunity, but the belief in it became woven into the fabric of black life on the plantations and in the new societies. Away from the prying eyes and condemnation of whites, Obeah helped to balance the scales of justice and put the power of the supernatural on the side of its devotees. On any given night a woman might knock on the Obeah man's door to request a love potion, or a man might come wanting to "set" Obeah for whoever had robbed his plantation ground.

Some whites speculated about harnessing this power on the side of plantation owners. "As in all other countries, so in Guinea, the conjurers, as they have more understanding, so are they generally more wicked than the common herd of their deluded countrymen; and as the negroe-magicians can do mischief, so they can also do good on a plantation, provided they are kept by the white people in proper subordination", wrote Dr James Grainger in 1764.[3] The Maroons "believed, as I have observed, in the prevalence of Obi (a sort of witchcraft of most extensive influence), and the authority which such of their old men as had the reputation of wizards, or Obeah-men, possessed over them, was sometimes very successfully employed in keeping them in subordination to their chiefs", Bryan Edwards declared,[4] no doubt wishing planters could find a way to add it to their existing means of control over their slaves.

---

3 James Grainger, "The Sugar Cane", in *On the Treatment and Management of the More Common West India Diseases, 1759–1802*, ed. E. Hutson (Kingston: University of the West Indies Press, 2005), 71n8.

4 Bryan Edwards, "An Introductory Account Containing Observations on the Disposition, Character, Manners and Habits of Life of the Maroons", in *Proceedings of the Governor and Assembly of Jamaica in Regard to the Maroon Negroes* (London: John Stockdale, 1796), 29.

As it was for their counterparts back on the continent, the Obeah man or woman was a healer as well as a person who commanded the allegiance of spirits. Their knowledge of healing herbs was said to be at least equal to their knowledge of poisons. Blacks who fomented rebellion resorted to Obeah men and women for charms to protect the rebels from the bullets of the militias, as well as for the administration of oaths swearing the conspirators to secrecy and to action. In fact, whatever the conversion numbers of the missionaries, for centuries Obeah was central to the lives of blacks in the Caribbean. Even those blacks who professed not to believe in it were sometimes found to have had some dealing with it, however slight. Belief in Obeah was not restricted to black people alone, either; some whites also believed in the practice, and all were aware of it.

The hold that Obeah had on the minds and hearts of blacks in the Caribbean was mirrored by the horror, fear and disgust it engendered in the plantation owners and in those with a keen interest in the West Indies. Given the strength of feeling against it and the pervasive nature of belief in it, it is no surprise that Obeah frequently featured in reports on plantation conditions made to the British Parliament, but as great as official interest in Obeah was, it was no match for the fascination it held for British writers and travellers. As Eden Phillpotts, a bestselling writer in his day, noted in his *In Sugar-Cane Land* "a fair sprinkling of literary people" visited the Caribbean and wrote about the islands. Several wrote about the islands without having visited at all, their stories influenced by the accounts of Long, Edwards and others. Few failed to mention Obeah. In fact, from the early 1800s to the middle of the twentieth century, Obeah enthralled succeeding generations of British writers who devoted considerable ink and column inches to the phenomenon. All made much of the supposed credulity of blacks and the pervasiveness of Obeah superstition, as most termed it.

"In every British West Indian colony, the obeah superstition permeates the social order and is a ruling impulse in the lives of nine negroes out of ten", wrote a correspondent for the *Manchester Guardian* in 1907.[5] He could well have added that there was probably no prominent English writer of the nineteenth century who had not heard of Obeah, even if he or she had not written about it. In fact, the more popular the writer, the greater the chance that he or she had written a story that made, at the very least, a passing reference to

---

5 C.B., "Obeah and Vadoux: The Magic of the West Indies", *Manchester Guardian*, 12 March 1907, 8.

Obeah. Commercially successful novelists as diverse as Maria Edgeworth and Mayne Reid wrote entire stories around Obeah, while others such as Charles Dickens edited literary magazines which were not immune to the charms of Obeah-themed stories.

Not to be outdone by fiction writers, every travel writer worth his salt did his best to produce Obeah stories almost as fearful and outlandish as those found in novels and boys' adventure papers. Travel writers also took avid note of previous works and referred to them often. Patrick Leigh Fermor, for example, refers to Coleridge's *Six Months in the West Indies,* Pere Labat and Lafcadio Hearn; Hearn himself frequently mentions Labat, while Coleridge refers to Bryan Edwards and Richard Ligon. These writers and others like them participated in an unbroken literary line that fed on itself, consuming and regurgitating the stories and accounts that shaped racial theories about black people.

For more than a hundred years, Stephen Fuller's 1789 report to the House of Lords was a rich source of material for several writers and novelists, but few of the later writers acknowledged their sources. Most readers in the late 1800s would have been unaware that a considerable portion of what they were reading about Obeah was recycled information that had originated in the 1700s. A few writers, such as Hesketh Bell and Benjamin Moseley, covered all the bases, penning popular works of fiction as well as official reports. Some, including Edwards and Moseley, were considered the definitive authorities on Obeah, their pronouncements as likely to be quoted in government reports as in novels.

The very incestuousness of the English intelligentsia, where writers leapt to read and sometimes plagiarize each other's works, ensured that an awareness of Obeah spread like fire within literary, scientific, political and other circles and passed from generation to generation. Many of the leading historians, botanists, scientists, writers and poets of the day who wrote about the West Indies shared a similar background and knew and corresponded with one another. For example, the historian Edward Long, author of *The History of Jamaica,* was friends with the botanist Thomas Dancer, while Revd Charles Kingsley, author of *The Water Babies,* was a friend to such eminences as Thomas Carlyle and James Anthony Froude. Maria Edgeworth was the good friend of Sir Humphrey Davy, brother of Dr John Davy, who spent several years in the West Indies and wrote about Obeah in his non-fiction work. Many of these people (they were predominantly men) quoted liberally from each other's works on the issues of slavery and race, shaping and reinforcing their own ideas on those subjects and often using stories about Obeah to support their arguments.

When I began researching the subject, I was surprised by how much Obeah figured in arguments for and against abolition in England. In a way that Obeah men and women never understood or realized, Obeah was employed by both the pro-abolition and pro-slavery lobbies to support their respective positions. The books and stories written by nineteenth-century novelists, such as Edgeworth, Reid, Phillpotts and others, often reinforced negative images of black people and accustomed new generations to thinking of blacks as inferior human beings (if they even conceded that they were human at all) who needed to be controlled and civilized by the superior whites. Thus, racist ideology, founded upon centuries of propaganda about superstitious, cannibalistic, credulous, devil-worshipping Africans in works written by European captains and explorers, paved the way not just for the division of Africa among the European powers and for European control of that continent well into the twentieth century, but also for the adoption and solidification of stereotypes which continue to exist to this day.

Over and over again, writers made the point that Obeah was intertwined with blackness, was synonymous with black people; the blacker (or more African) the Negro, the more savage and superstitious he was and the more removed from the restraints of white civilization. According to whites, all blacks believed in Obeah, and this supposedly innate belief symbolized their inferiority – the blackness outside was mirrored by an interior spiritual darkness that would confound all efforts at racial advancement. Obeah men and women in literature were almost always Africans direct from Africa, even in works set long after the abolition of the slave trade.

In addition to novels, boys' adventure papers and travellers' narratives, Obeah often found its way into newsprint, ensuring it as wide an audience as possible. "The negroes, who are superstitious in the extreme, are the credulous dupes and tools of a few artful men, called Obeah-men, who pretend to regulate the dispositions, feelings, and actions of their fellow-creatures, and even cause their deaths at pleasure" went the introduction to a short story in the 1851 edition of *Bentley's Miscellany*, edited by Dickens. Obeah was a "singular species of African superstition", the writer explained, adding

> the profound belief in [Obeah men's] supernatural powers operates strongly on the imaginations of the negroes: hence the practice of their art is full of mischief, and thence considered in the West Indian Islands a criminal offence. A negro

guilty of it may be summoned before a slave court, and if found guilty, sentenced to transportation or death. The art is, notwithstanding, extensively practiced, chiefly by a few cunning old negroes, who thereby acquire no small gains.[6]

"Obeah, as everybody knows, is an African fetich of the very lowest type", claimed William Rutherford Trowbridge in the first line of his chapter on Obeah in the 1893 *Gossip of the Caribbees*.[7] Yes, thanks to the continuous stream of books, short stories and newspaper articles, everybody in Great Britain did know about Obeah. *The Graphic* of 2 July 1898 carried a sketch of "a Jamaica Obeah man", complete with his cuttacoo, while the succeeding page showed an illustration of "evidence of an Obeah man's work". The caption reads:

> a little coffin . . . stands on trestles, with a broken-necked bottle on it, in the middle of a yam "piece", placed there because the man's yams had been stolen and effectually prevented any further thefts – so it is said. "Obeah" is said to be derived from the Greek, meaning "a serpent", snakes being indispensable to the Obeah man. It is a religious superstition of the negroes, and is still much practiced chiefly among the Haytian settlers.[8]

Obeah was an enduring fascination. The 8 September 1937 issue of the *Manchester Guardian* carried a story by W.G. titled "Obeah Man", about a young boy, Egbert, who was struck dumb at a prayer meeting. His mother resolved to take him to the "new Obeah man" who "had come from Haiti not long before, no doubt for good and sufficient reasons" and was already getting "plenty of custom". At the Obeah man's hut "a skull grinned over the doorway and another hung down from the roof". The Obeah man asked for a shilling and a bottle of rum in payment before he began work, uttering incantations in French and a mixture of English and "gibberish". He held a skull in one hand and in the other a supple-jack, with which he struck the boy, who still did not speak. When the Obeah man lifted the supple-jack to strike the boy again, the boy begged him not to hit him and was considered cured.[9]

Fetish worship had made its own triangular voyage; starting from Africa, Obeah crossed the Atlantic to the West Indies, then made the journey back across the ocean, in the form of traveller's narratives and plantation reports, to

---

6   Richard Bentley, *Bentley's Miscellany* 30 (1851): 195.
7   William Rutherford Trowbridge, *Gossip of the Caribbees: Sketches of Anglo–West Indian Life* (London: T. Fisher Unwin, 1895), 63 [emphasis added].
8   "Jamaica and the War", *The Graphic*, 2 July 1898, 20–21.
9   W.G., "The Obeah Man", *Manchester Guardian*, 8 September 1937, 18.

Great Britain, where it was incorporated into the plots of scores of books and stories which went on to inform the world view of explorers and colonial officials in Britain's far-flung empire. In this book I will trace some parts of that journey, paying the greatest attention to Obeah itself, its definition and the uses for which it was employed by black people, before moving on to discuss some of the travel narratives that described it and the novels and stories in which it figured as a significant plot device. Because I am examining what British or European writers had to say about Obeah, I have not looked at writing on the subject by Caribbean writers. Works by people such as Herbert G. de Lisser, Jean Rhys, Derek Walcott, Aidonia and Mavado in which Obeah is mentioned are important for what West Indians have to say on the subject, but they do not fall within the ambit of this study. Similarly, works by Jerome S. Handler, Diana Paton and others that examine Obeah within the context of modern Caribbean society and law also do not come within the scope of this project, but they do point to the ramifications of all that negative literature of the past three hundred years. Laws created two hundred years ago by colonial administrators remain on the books in the region precisely because of fears fanned by writers who kept the attention on Obeah long after slavery had ended.

In the same vein, what Obeah men and women themselves had to say about Obeah would not have been included in this study even if they had left more of themselves behind than we can glimpse from accounts of court trials and from exchanges with them related by missionaries and others. Of the scores of books and stories and reports written on the subject, none were authored by an actual practitioner; but again, though regrettable, for the purposes of this study that was immaterial. What I have really sought to understand, examine and relate is what British writers had to say about Obeah and how that in turn shaped racial perceptions of blacks in the wider British society that continue to resound today.

Where I have quoted from primary sources I have adhered to the original text, which I believe grants us an insight into the language of the day while allowing us to see the evolution of words and ideas. For example, nowadays *Obeah* denotes both the noun and the verb, but certain writers from the seventeenth and eighteenth centuries were likely to use a variety of spellings, including *Obi* and *Obia*, to indicate the difference. Similarly, readers will recognize that while some scholars today make distinctions between myalists, herbal healers and Obeah practitioners, past observers perceived them all as merely different facets of Obeah.

CHAPTER 1

Strange Encounters
CHRISTIAN CAPTAINS AND AFRICAN FETISH MASTERS

OBEAH IN THE WEST INDIES WAS A product of the culture, religion and experiences of enslaved Africans brought over on the Middle Passage, and the reaction to it in the United Kingdom reflected the culture, religion and experiences of Britons. Europeans were just then emerging from the dark Middle Ages, but superstition and belief in magic remained strong. It was, in fact, this mindscape – strewn with good-luck charms, the bones of saints and the words of scripture – which formed the fertile ground on which the fear of Obeah and of black people was planted, and flourished. As we will discover in this chapter, Europe's theological and other writers had, over the centuries, prepared their readers to identify black people, and especially the black man, with the Devil and to view him with fear and loathing. This was the narrative that found its full expression during the encounter between Africans and Europeans on the "Dark Continent", and it was to inform the reactions of Britons to Obeah.

FAMILIAR MAGICKS

If Africa had not existed, Europeans of the Middle Ages would probably have had to invent it, if only as a way to escape the upheavals and uncertainties afflicting the continent. Famine and war were common, life expectancy hovered around age thirty, and diseases such as the Black Death and bubonic plague carried off millions as they swept through the unhygienic towns and cities. To save themselves, people turned to magic and religion. Indeed, some religious practices of the time, such as the veneration of relics, looked a lot like magic. The church condemned the man who placed a magical stone or written charm on his chest as a cure for his persistent cough but blessed the woman who used a phial of holy water or a quotation from the Bible in the same way and for the same purpose.

Each year, thousands of people crisscrossed Europe on pilgrimages to the cathedrals, abbeys and priories which made a brisk business of selling relics: bits of bone, hair and nails said to come from various saints and guaranteed to cure whatever ailed the faithful pilgrim. Sick true believers placed the Gospel of John or a relic under their bed in the expectation that they would wake up healed the next morning. And these religious articles were not just expected to have curative properties; they were also thought to be able to protect their owners from fire and floods, to assure the safety of their crops and animals, to bring them safely home from the sea and to assist in the recovery of lost or stolen valuables. In fact, the demands placed on religious relics were much the same as those placed on the charms provided by Europe's witches and wise men and wise women.

If the herbs and charms of the wise woman did not work, believers simply used another weapon from the medieval arsenal. For example, "the priest of Ramsholt in Suffolk tried to cure his daughter with 'charms and medicines' before appealing to the spirit of [Thomas] Becket. Such charms were freely used along with herbs and semi-precious stones, sometimes self-applied or tied round the neck of the sufferer – often by a parent."[1] But the church (for most of the Middle Ages this meant the Roman Catholic Church) was quick to stamp out any rivals to its supremacy, and it did not often see any differences between folk-healers and witches. To the church, someone versed in herbal lore was probably also a spell-caster, a shape-shifter, a storm-maker, a diviner and maker of poisons.

Belief in magic permeated the society, affecting not just the poor but royalty too. Queen Elizabeth I, for example, employed the services of John Dee, who, whatever his contributions to astronomy and mathematics, was also a firm believer in divination and the potency of crystal balls. Though nothing was ever proved against her, Madame de Montespan, the courtesan, was famously associated with Catherine Monvoisin, also known as "La Voisin", who was alleged to have given her love philtres aimed at attracting and keeping the affection of Louis XIV. Meanwhile, the Holy Roman Emperor Rudolf II employed several alchemists and astrologers in his court.

---

[1] Ronald C. Finucane, *Miracles and Pilgrims* (London: J. M. Dent & Sons, 1977), 62.

But, according to the church, where there was magic there could also be found witches and sorcerers acting in concert with the Devil, their master:

> A renowned midwife, Amy Simpson, affirmed that she in company with nine other Witches . . . the Devil their Master being present, standing in the midst of them, a Body of Wax shapen and made by the same Amy Simpson, wrapped within a Linen Cloth, was first delivered to the Devil, who after he pronounced his Verdict, delivered the said picture to Amy Simpson, and she to her next neighbour, and so round about, saying, this is King James the Sixth, ordered to be consumed at the instance of a Nobleman, Frances, Earl Bothwel.[2]

James VI was not the first or only member of royalty to suffer the murderous attentions of witches. The nobles of sixth-century France were scandalized when one of their number was accused of obtaining poisons from Paris witches to kill King Chilperic's infant son. In 1419 Henry V of England accused his stepmother of attempting to kill him by witchcraft. Two decades later, the Duchess of Gloucester was prosecuted for trying the same thing with his son, Henry VI. Sometimes the assistance of witches was required for other purposes. In 1483 Richard III charged his sister-in-law with seducing his brother into marriage with the aid of witchcraft. And so it went. Every screech owl was a witch in disguise, and everyone who was not a witch was busy buying either love potions or poisons, and sometimes both together!

As we have seen, the fear of witches was real and present at all levels of society. Everyone knew that witches could spoil crops, kill children with a glance, poison water and milk and generally ruin the lives of anyone who incurred their ire. It was agreed in many quarters that witches ate children and had access to diabolical poisons. If somebody died in mysterious circumstances or was suddenly afflicted with a strange sickness, witchcraft was inevitably blamed. The hysteria of the witch hunts that took place in most European countries between the fifteenth and eighteenth centuries heightened the fear. Witches did not act alone but served their master, the Devil, church leaders said, and anyone who had not been afraid before trembled. A belligerent old crone living on her own in a wretched hut could be avoided or ignored, but not so the Devil. And it was this alleged concourse between witches and the Devil that most occupied the men obsessed with rooting out witchcraft.

---

2 James Melville, *The Memoires of Sir James Melvil of Hal-Hill* (London: George Scott, 1683), 194.

"Satan's prevalency is most clear in the marvelous number of Witches abounding in all parts. Now hundreds are discovered in one shire; and (if fame deceive us not) in a village of 14 houses in the North are found so many of this damned breed", claimed one bishop.[3] Most (but not all) of the people imprisoned or burned at the stake for witchcraft were women. Women were feebler in body and mind, more credulous and more given to carnal lust, wrote the inquisitors Heinrich Kramer and James Sprenger in their landmark work, the *Malleus Maleficarum* ("Hammer of Witches"). "All witchcraft comes from carnal lust, which is in women insatiable", they wrote. Like Eve, women were sinful and weak, vulnerable to temptation – so the church leaders said, and everyone hearkened to their words. Naturally it followed that women, prone to infidelity, ambition and lust, were also highly susceptible to superstition and witchcraft. "Those women are chiefly apt to be witches who are most disposed to such acts", Kramer and Sprenger thundered, and their voices resounded down through the ages.[4]

Adulterers and whores were not the only ones who faced the rack; old women were another favourite target for accusers. Poverty-stricken women living alone and long past their childbearing years were often the first to be identified as witches, not least because, in an age of early mortality, the long-lived were inevitably suspect. The anonymous author of *Poems Chiefly on the Superstition of Obeah* includes a poem about an Irish witch who goes out to "meet the Devil upon the Western hill". When they meet her on the road, "old men bless themselves and children run from her", but the poet argues that she was probably nothing more than a "lonely, alienated, scorned and isolated old woman".[5]

Briggs contends that "many old women levied blackmail on their neighbours; and where they bore a grudge, the terror of their charms produced the evil they desired; or if these failed, poison was often at hand".[6] In fact, accord-

---

3   Richard Baxter, *The Practical Works of Richard Baxter* (London: George Virtue, 1838), 3:115.
4   Heinrich Kramer and James Sprenger, *Malleus Maleficarum* (1487; New York: Dover, 1971), 47–48.
5   *Poems Chiefly on the Superstition of Obeah* (London: Gale and Fenner, 1816), 78. That the author chose to include a poem about an Irish witch in a book about Obeah is illustrative of the association many made between the superstition of the Irish and that of Africans. In fact, many English people considered the Irish close to blacks on the evolutionary scale and thought of them as almost equally uncivilized. Charles Kingsley, for example, referred to the people he saw during a visit to Ireland as "white chimpanzees."
6   Katherine Mary Briggs, *Pale Hecate's Team: An Examination of the Beliefs on Witchcraft and Magic among Shakespeare's Contemporaries and His Immediate Successors* (London: Routledge and Keegan Paul, 1962), 220.

ing to the *Malleus Maleficarum*, witches were so depraved that they deliberately provoked others to hostility in order that they might have a reason for working witchcraft on them.

Quarrelsome old women who had outlived their husbands and perhaps had no other living relatives, far from inspiring kindness, could hope for nothing better than neglect. They were a burden on communities and families struggling to feed themselves, their very wretchedness a reproach. Friendless and thus justifiably grudgeful, at least to the medieval mind, they were highly blameable if someone's baby died of no apparent cause, if a sudden tempest destroyed crops or if a valuable farm animal sickened.

People were not entirely without recourse, however. "Salt consecrated on Palm Sunday and some Blessed Herbs . . . enclosed together in Wax and worn around the neck" was a remedy against the illnesses and diseases caused by witches, while sprinkling holy water and invoking the Holy Trinity and saying a Paternoster could protect dwellings. "But the surest protection for Places, men or animals are the words of the triumphal title of our Saviour, if they be written in four places in the form of a cross: IESUS † NAZARENUS † REX † IUDAEORUM †. There may also be added the name of the Virgin MARY and of the Evangelists, or the words of S. John: The Word was made Flesh."[7]

If all of this failed and the witch was still able to wreak havoc or, at the very least, to annoy her neighbours, she could be brought to trial and, upon conviction, burned at the stake. Thousands were. The following account of a Martinique witch trial in 1657 is fairly typical, for all that it took place in the West Indies, far from the European theatre of operations.

> It was almost impossible to doubt of her guilt; for they proved, that the moment she touched infants, they became languid, and died in that state! That she sent a sort of unknown caterpillar to the houses of those with whom she quarrelled, which destroyed the best of every thing they had, while none of the neighbouring houses suffered any injury from these insects, and other similar things! The judge having put her in irons, to get the truth from her, had her examined, to see if she had any mark, such as they say that the devil puts upon all sorcerers, but not finding any he resolved to try if the remark which, he said, he had read in several authors worthy of credit, was true: it was that sorcerers never cry while they are in the hands of justice! He therefore begged one of our fathers without discovering his design to him, to go and see this poor unfor-

---

7   Kramer and Sprenger, *Malleus Maleficarum*, 91–92, 228.

tunate, say every thing the most touching that he could, to make her sensible, and weep for her fault.

This good priest did not fail to go, and in the guard-room, which served her for a prison, he said every thing he could to affect her, but in vain. The judge, having now this further proof, had her conducted to a magazine, where he requested the same priest to speak to her again; but scarcely had he opened his mouth when she began to cry, and shed so many tears, that she made all those who saw her cry likewise. The judge, not satisfied with this proof, followed the counsel of a Mr Jacques, a surgeon, an Italian by birth, and called the Roman, who told him that he had seen the trial by water practised in Germany and in Italy, and he was allowed to use it. This "good man", without taking the advice of the Jesuit fathers, or ours, condemned this poor wretch!

The next day, they carried her to a tolerably deep river near the "Carbet", where they stripped her. M. Jean, who upon this occasion acted more like an executioner than a surgeon, tied her two thumbs to her two great toes, and having fastened a great rope round her waist, which was across the river, she was pushed into the water, and hauled to the deepest part, where she floated like a balloon, without their being able to sink her, although she herself made several efforts to go to the bottom! More than 200 persons were present at this sight, and would have gone away sufficiently convinced; but this Roman sent a little boy to swim to her, who, having fastened a sewing needle in her hair, she sunk, like a piece of lead, to the bottom: in the space of a good "miserere", they saw her motionless: and when they had taken her out of the water, were obliged to give her something to quench her thirst! These three circumstances, of not being able to sink her without a little morsel of iron – of her being under water without breathing, and without having swallowed any water, determined the judge to condemn her to death the next day!

But while he was preparing the sentence, this Roman thought proper, during the evening, to give her the trial according to his plan; and he burnt her so severely upon the sides and flanks, that she died the same night, without having confessed the crime of which she was accused![8]

This trial took place in the West Indies but followed conventions already established over the preceding centuries in Europe, and all the principals, including the witch, were almost certainly Europeans, since there is no mention made of her being black. For most Europeans of the time, it was an article of faith that the Devil was very real and acted in the world through the malevo-

---

8   Thomas Southey, *Chronological History of the West Indies* (London: Longman, Rees, Orme, Brown and Green, 1827), 21–22.

lence of witches, whose wickedness knew no bounds and who could as easily affect a farmer as a king. This, then, was the situation on the continent from which the captains sailing down the coast of Africa set out.

BLACK DEVILS AND WILD MEN

Blackness was associated with evil in the Christian world view from a very early time. Russell points out that by "about 120 AD, the *Epistle of Barnabas* designated Satan as *be meal*, the black one, and by the time of the *Apostolic History of Abdia* and the *Acts of Philip* he is completely limned as black, winged and reeking of smoke".[9] In around AD 360, Bishop Athanasius widely publicized the story of Saint Anthony's confrontation with the Devil and described how

> the dragon, seeing that he could not overthrow Anthony, was seized by rage. He appeared to Anthony as he is in reality, that is, in the form of a black child. . . . Anthony asked him, "Who art thou?" The Devil replied in a groaning voice, "I am the friend of fornication. I lay my snares before the young to make them fall into this vice and I am called the spirit of fornication. . . . It is I who have tormented thee so many times and have always been repulsed." Anthony after giving thanks to God, replied to his enemy confidently: "Thou art utterly contemptible; thy spirit is black and thou art like a child without strength. Henceforth I will disturb myself no more because of thee for the Lord is my help and I can despise my enemies." When he heard these words, the black man fled at once and did not even dare come near this man.[10]

In fact, the medieval Devil was regularly described as a black man. In the seventeenth century, Jean Grenier, a French boy who thought himself a werewolf, declared during his trial that he had killed several girls at the behest of "Monsieur de la Forest, a black man of gigantic stature". This Monsieur de la Forest was thought to be the same tall black man known elsewhere as *Le grand veneur* ("the Great Huntsman"). Similarly, the demon said to have appeared

---

9 Jeffrey Burton Russell, *Satan: The Early Christian Tradition* (London: Cornell University Press, 1981), 247.
10 Peter Stanford, *The Devil: A Biography* (London: Heinemann, 1996), 105. More recently, a poster for the 1982 movie *The Devil and Max Devlin*, by Walt Disney Productions, depicted a horned Bill Cosby in a cape standing behind Elliott Gould, a white man, indicating a continued association between black men and the Devil.

in the early 1300s to the wealthy Irish witch Lady Alice Kytele often took the form of a black man and was accompanied by other black men. A young girl, thought to be safe in a convent, nevertheless reported seeing "an evil spirit, in the form of a blackamoor, foul and hideous".[11]

It is no surprise that Satan and his minions were imagined in this way, as illustrations to religious and other stories depicted them as black. For example, a page from Gerard d'Euphrates' *Livre de l'histoire*, printed in 1549, shows several black figures bearing witches to Satan's court. Paintings and miracle plays under the sponsorship of the church also drove the point home, depicting the damned as black so that even an illiterate peasant could understand the message. Conversely, when the Devil wanted to fool people, he disguised himself as a "white man" so they would think him good. In John Bunyan's *Pilgrim's Progress*, written in 1678, pilgrims on their way to Zion are led astray by a black man clothed in white who is denounced as the "Flatterer, a false Apostle that hath transformed himself into an Angel of Light". White was beautiful and pure, the colour of the holy; black was ugly and frightening, the colour of evil and of the damned. Blackness was associated with the void, with blindness, mental depression, intellectual stupidity, religious despair and moral sin, with dirt, poison and plague.[12]

But by the Middle Ages, black men and women were not a completely uncommon sight in Europe. A man living in a good-sized city with trade links to the Mediterranean was almost as likely to see a black person as he was to see a witch. In 1596 and again in 1601, Queen Elizabeth I informed the mayors of her largest cities that she was dissatisfied about the high numbers of black people in her realm, but as the slave trade ground on, more and more blacks were brought to England. The *Gentleman's Magazine* of 1764 estimated that there were then twenty thousand black people in London; even if this was an exaggeration, the figure represented both a level of concern about the rise in the black population and the fact that it was clearly a visible presence.

We can surmise the extent of white anxiety about the black presence in England during the Middle Ages by conjecturing that, like their queen, English people feared the possible negative effects of being around so many "infidels" and worried about their "swarming" through the country. The church, taken aback by reports of alien cultures in Africa, might well have thought

---

11   Edward Langton, *Satan, a Portrait: A Study of the Character of Satan Through All the Ages* (London: Skeffington and Son, 1973), 91.
12   Russell, *Satan*, 66.

the Christian world was at risk as more and more black people came to Europe. Europeans worriedly observed that black people did not become white by virtue of living in Europe or in cold countries. This observation doubtless reflected an underlying fear of losing their hegemony in their own countries. And, though many of the blacks in Europe converted to Christianity, Christians would have remained suspicious of the former Muslims and pagans who, however real their conversion, looked just like the wicked and licentious Devil they had been reading about for centuries. Church leaders might well have wondered about the possible apocalyptic ramifications of Ham's accursed descendants making themselves at home in Europe, while common citizens may have been affected on a deeper psychological level than even they knew.

And those who may not have associated the Africans they saw with Satan might still have wondered if Africa was the real home of the "wild man" of European folklore, that mythical creature unfettered by Christian faith and the rigours of civilization. The wild man and woman had magical powers, the wild man held power over forest animals, while the wild woman was said to be knowledgeable about medicinal herbs. Their images appeared in church paintings and religious carvings, on drinking cups and on candlesticks. As future generations of Europeans were to do about blacks, medieval intellectuals and Church leaders often argued over whether the wild man was, in fact, man or beast.

The wild man, hairy and animal-like, lived in the forests and woods in a state of nature, either naked or with the barest of coverings. The stories suggested that both wild men and wild women were sexually voracious, and theologians frequently associated them with succubi and incubi, demons who sought sexual congress with mortals as they slept. Travellers who reported on the naked or half-naked African women they encountered and on the many wives of African chiefs may not have made an explicit connection between their observations and the mythology of the wild man and wild woman, but their readers could not have failed to make the association. Certainly, the alleged sexual voraciousness of both black men and women became an article of faith among white people.

Both Shakespeare and Ben Jonson linked the wild man with satyrs, mythological creatures who were companions of the Greek gods Pan and Dionysus and roamed the wild places with them. Shakespeare's *The Winter's Tale* and Jonson's *The Faerie Prince* contain scenes in which hairy men dance or leap wildly about in fairly mild versions of the original Dionysian frenzy. In fact, wild, orgiastic dancing was such an integral part of the mythology of the

Strange Encounters: Christian Captains and African Fetish Masters

Devil and the wild man that fascination with it attached itself to Africans and continued well into the 1900s. John McLeod, who went to Africa in 1803 as a surgeon aboard a slaver, on watching an African dance was unable to describe it on its own terms without imputing a resemblance to the witches' Saturnalia described by his countryman Robert Burns.

> When they meet for the purpose of dancing, it is usually by moon-light under some large tree, where individuals by turns, exhibit the most extravagant gestures; and in proportion to their ability of twisting themselves into fantastic attitudes, they are applauded with clapping of hands by the rest of the party, who formed into a circle, caper round them. The revelry of devils and witches, as witnessed by poor Tom O'Shanter [sic] in Alloway Kirk, could not have presented a more demonic scene, than such an assembly of these naked savages.[13]

Burns describes warlocks and witches dancing in his long poem "Tam o' Shanter":

> There sat auld Nick, in shape o' beast;
> A towzie tyke, black, grim, and large,
> To gie them music was his charge:
> He screw'd the pipes and gart them skirl,
> Till roof and rafters a' did dirl. –
> Coffins stood round, like open presses,
> That shaw'd the dead in their last dresses;
> And by some devilish cantraip sleight
> Each in its cauld hand held a light. –
> By which heroic *Tam* was able
> To note upon the haly table,
> A murderer's banes in gibbet airns;
> Twa span-lang, wee, unchristened bairns;
> A thief, new-cutted frae a rape,
> Wi' his last gasp his gab did gape;
> Five tomahawks, wi' blude red-rusted:
> Five scymitars, wi' murder crusted;
> A garter, which a babe had strangled:
> A knife, a father's throat had mangled.
> Whom his ain son o' life bereft,
> The grey hairs yet stack to the heft;

---

13 McLeod, *Voyage to Africa*, 97.

Wi' mair o' horrible and awfu',
Which even to name wad be unlawfu'.[14]

There are no coffins in the scene McLeod describes, no bloody weapons, no hornpipe-playing devil "in shape o' beast", but to the Scotsman it was still a demonic scene. His conclusion tells us more about him and how Africans were viewed than it does about the Africans themselves, yet the image of wildly dancing negroes was an evocative one which was to reappear frequently in stories, novels, narratives and articles all through the 1800s.

The men who ventured along the coast of Africa in the 1400s and 1500s would have been no strangers to tales of magic and witchcraft; neither would they have been unaware of the association between blackness and devilry. Their lurid reports and letters are as full of shock and horror as the reports of the inquisitors who were hunting down witches; they make it clear that the captains, like the inquisitors, saw themselves in the vanguard of a struggle against evil. To most of them, Africa – uncivilized, unknown and for the most part uncharted – was a wild landscape, home to the wild man and wild woman, and home, possibly, even to the Devil.

AFRICA IN BOOKS, LETTERS AND REPORTS

The Venetian Alvide da Cada Mosto, exploring West Africa in 1455 in the employ of Henry the Navigator, was among the first to set the tone. "The Negros are great Inchanters, using Charms in respect of every Thing; particularly serpents", he wrote. He went on to recount that a Genoese who had visited Senegal in 1454 had stayed with the king. One night, he was awakened by a strange whistling and saw his host's nephew rise and call two servants to fetch his camel. When the Genoese asked him where he was going, the man replied that he had business to attend to but would be back soon. When he came back, the Genoese asked him where he had gone, and this time the man asked him if he had not heard the hissing outside. The Genoese admitted that he had. The man then informed him that it was serpents, and that had he not "with certain Inchantments, sent them back to their own Quarters, they would have killed a great many of my cattle this Night".[15]

---

14 Robert Burns, "Tam o' Shanter: A Tale", in *Eighteenth-Century Poetry: An Annotated Anthology*, ed. David Fairer and Christine Gerrard, 3rd ed. (Chichester, UK: John Wiley and Sons, 2015), 575–76.

15 Alvide da Ca' da Mosto, "A Voyage", in *A New General Collection of Voyages and Travels:*

The Genoese expressed his surprise but the man told him that his uncle, King Budomel, was an even greater enchanter, for

> when he had a Mind to envenom his Weapons, he used to make a large circle, into which he brought, by his Spells, all the Serpents in the Neighbourhood: Then letting all go again, but that which he thought most poisonous, he killed it; and with the Blood, mixed with the Seed of a certain Tree infected his Weapons to such a Degree, that if they drew but the least Drop of Blood, the person wounded died in a Quarter of an Hour.

In expressing his belief that such a thing was possible, Mosto claimed he had seen something similar once in Italy.[16]

Many Europeans new to contact with Africa and Africans described Africans as having no religion, but they often went on to write that they did have a concept of God, however distant and detached they might have thought him. In fact, as the Europeans themselves recorded, this supreme being presided over a complex supernatural hierarchy in which intermediary spirits played the dominant role.

Captain Moore, writing about the natives of the Cape Verde Islands, thought that Africans were "for the most part . . . idolaters. Some worship the Moon; others the Devil whom they call *Katae*. When asked why they worship the Devil, they reply, because he does them Hurt, but God does not."

Anna Maria Falconbridge, wife of the British slave-ship surgeon turned abolitionist Alexander Falconbridge, related much the same thing. She notes that "the inhabitants are chiefly Pagans, though they credit the existence of a God, but consider him so good that he cannot do them any injury; they therefore pay homage to the Devil, from a belief that he is the only Supernatural Being they have to fear; and I am informed they have consecrated places in different parts of the woods, where they make annual sacrifices to him".[17] That Africans worshipped the Devil became virtually an article of faith, if one may put it that way, for Europeans.

"The inhabitant of the Kroo coast, a well-knit, muscular fellow, who refuses to be burdened with more weighty clothing than a white or striped

---

Consisting of the Most Esteemed Relations Which Have Been Hitherto Published in Any Language, Comprehending Everything Remarkable in Its Kind in Europe, Asia, Africa and America, ed. Thomas Astley (London: Thomas Astley, 1745), 572–91.

16 Ibid.

17 Anna Maria Falconbridge, *Narrative of Two Voyages to the River Sierra Leone during the Years 1791–1793* (London: L.I. Higham, 1802), 78–79.

pocket-handkerchief lightly bound around his loins, displays his nationality by the tattooed skin and black-burnt line upon his face, and his awe of Satan by the charm or talisman tied to his waist and ankle", writes F. Harrison Rankin. Of the Timmanees, he observes that they "worship the devil fervently" while offering their wives to strangers.[18] McLeod has much the same to say: "The religion of this country, [Dahomey], is paganism. They believe in two Beings, equal in power, the one doing good, the other evil; and they pray to the demon to allow them to remain unmolested by the magicians, who are constantly endeavoring to injure them."[19]

Educated Europeans of the late Middle Ages and the Renaissance would have been aware of the rise and fall of the Cathar movement which first appeared in France in the tenth century. The Cathars believed that there were two gods, a good God who ruled the spiritual world in love and peace and an evil God who ruled the physical plane. The harsh and cruel God of the Old Testament was, according to the Cathars, actually the evil God, while the loving Jesus of the New Testament was the true God whom they worshipped. Though the Cathars gave themselves the name "Good Christians", the Catholic Church was not amused by their departure from established doctrine. A Crusade launched against them in 1209 by Pope Innocent III resulted in the massacre of thousands; it was followed by the Inquisition of 1229, which eventually led to the extinction of the movement in the fourteenth century. One can well imagine how disconcerted the church must have been to hear of an entire continent apparently given over to a belief system so similar to the one they had spent so much time and money rooting out just a few centuries before.

In fact, missionaries heading out to Africa in the 1700s received instructions that made it clear they were going to the front lines of the war against Satan:

> Be sure you take no small pains to impress this deeply into their minds, giving them to understand Who and What the Devil is; that he, like a Roaring Lion, walketh about the Earth, seeking whom he may destroy and that to his Malice and Envy it is owing that so many Heathen nations and all Africa, in a Manner, remain to this day in Darkness, and in the Shadow of Death, as being ignorant of the True God and for the most part, Worshippers of Devils, or which is much the same, of Idols. . . . And as Sin in General, you may tell them, is the work of the Devil, more specifically, Idolatry, Witchcraft, Sorcery, Murder

---

18 F. Harrison Rankin, *The White Man's Grave: A Visit to Sierra Leone in 1834* (London: Richard Bentley, 1836), 1:33, 70.

19 McLeod, *Voyage to Africa*, 32.

and Lying... see that you fully and distinctly inform these Africans, that the great Design of Christ's coming into the Flesh was to destroy these works of the Devil. Nor can you be too Large on this Head of Instruction, especially in a Country where the Devil Reigns almost universally, and in some places there, even visibly and openly without Control.[20]

Europeans were firmly convinced that Africans, despite being pagans and strangers to Christianity, nevertheless worshipped the Devil with diabolical rites.

"The Bagges, Nellos, Susees, Timinees, and etc., occasionally worship and offer sacrifices to the Devil and are equally confused in their conception of the Supreme Being", of whom they will say "they never saw him and, if he lives, he be too good to hurt them", writes Joseph Corry. "The Devil, or evil spirit, which they suppose to exist also, claims their attention for the injury they supposed him capable of inflicting and is worshipped under a variety of forms."[21] Corry, an abolitionist, wrote his book to help give officials in Britain a better understanding of Africa in order to further their commercial success in the region. His book was dedicated to Viscount Castlereagh, one of His Majesty's principal secretaries of state for foreign affairs.

Indeed, "*Satakas*, or offerings to the Evil One meet the traveler at almost every step. Their variety is infinite. Conciliatory talismans protect the person; little flags flutter over the 'palaver-house' and guard many a private dwelling from the domiciliary visits of fiends. Rarities are considered acceptable to Satan, and offered to him."[22] Rankin notes that all this did not mean that Satan was adored – far from it – but the Africans were so afraid of him that they courted his approval vigorously.

John Matthews, a naval lieutenant who became a slave trader, had enlarged on this earlier:

> They make offerings indeed to their devils and genii, who they suppose are the executive ministers of the Deity. Their devils, who they imagine reign paramount upon earth, are small images of clay, often renewed and made in some resemblance of a man: these are placed at the foot of a tree and a small shed of dry leaves is constructed over them, various offerings are made to them of

---

20 Thomas Bray, "A Memorial Relating to the Conversion as Well of the Amerindian Indians, as to the African Negroes", in *Missionalia; or, A Collection of Missionary Pieces Relating to the Conversion of the Heathen* (London: W.B. Roberts, 1727), 28–29.

21 Joseph Corry, *Observations upon the Windward Coast of Africa* (London: G. and W. Nicol, 1807), 60.

22 Rankin, *White Man's Grave*, 2:267.

bits of cloth, pieces of broken cups, plates, mugs, or glass bottles, brass rings, beads, and such articles, but I never observed anything of value given to them; indeed when they want to render their devil propitious to any undertaking, they generally provide liquor; a very small libation is made to him and the rest they drink before his altar.[23]

Those who did not worship the Devil outright were said to worship snakes, which to Europeans amounted to pretty much the same thing:

> In Whydah ... they worship their Divinity under the form of a particular species of snake, called Daboa, which is not sufficiently large and terrible to man, and is otherwise tameable and inoffensive. These Daboas are taken care of in the most pious manner, and well fed on rats, mice or birds, in their Fetish houses or temples, which the people attend to pay their adoration, and where those also who are sick or lame apply for assistance.[24]

As contact with the Europeans sharpened, some of these ideas underwent an interesting evolution.

> Many of the Blacks have a notion there are two Gods: the Chief of whom, they say, is white, and call him Boffum and Jangu Man, that is Good Man. They believe him peculiarly the God of the Europeans, whom he supplies with all good Things. The other God they conceit to be black, and from the Portugueze Language call him Demonio or Diablo, being a wicked and mischievous Spirit. ... They very much dread the Devil.

Further, "the Natives of the Gold Coast say that their God is black, and their Priest affirms that he appears often at the Foot of [their] Fetish Trees, in the shape of a big, black Dog. The Whites have told them, this black Dog is called the Devil."[25]

If Christianity was the one true religion, then the various religions of the Africans were the work of the Devil. European Christians had a responsibility to challenge and destroy them, a challenge which the Inquisition had already taken up in Spain, Portugal and elsewhere. In fact, just about everything Europeans feared about the supernatural they found in Africa, offering evi-

---

23 John Matthews, *A Voyage to the River Sierra-Leone on the Coast of Africa* (London: B. White and Son, 1791), 65.
24 McLeod, *Voyage to Africa*, 32.
25 "A Description of Guinea and Benin, Including the Geography with the Natural and Civil History", in Astley, *New General Collection*, 2:520–732.

dence of what they almost uniformly described as the savagery and barbarity of the continent. Struggling to understand what they were seeing, writers offered portrayals and explanations that arose from a Christian European context, revealing their own prejudices while adding to the body of stereotypical imagery that conceived of Africans as uncivilized devil-worshippers. Idols thus became representations of a devil whom most Africans had never heard of before the advent of the Europeans, and household or community spirits or gods became associated with Satan. The continent was transformed by the pens of Europeans into a vast landscape teeming with demons and witches, sunk in sin and presided over by the Devil.

"Africa is the nursery in which magic of every species flourishes unstunted by the trampling march of intellect", writes Rankin. "Where slavery, cannibalism, and polygamy are deemed domestic virtues, witchcraft, or the exercise of a spiritual power of working ill upon a neighbour, is the darkest, though the most frequent of crimes, and when guilt is established by the appalling ordeal of the red water, it is invariably visited with a condign punishment."[26] That witchcraft was, after all, punished seems not to have surprised Europeans, despite everything they wrote about Africans being given over to devil worship. If Africans were indeed all devil worshippers, it is strange that they would seek to punish people – witches – who were colluding with the very entity they worshipped.

Interestingly, however, witchcraft was indeed punished, and in such a way as had much significance for the emerging West Indies colonies and for slave resistance. In 1791 the abolitionist Thomas Clarkson wrote that witches or those accused of witchcraft were among the criminals sold into slavery by the different slave-trading societies.

> The last source of slavery in these countries is witchcraft. If a person should have a child or relation die, whose death has been rather sudden, he may give out if he pleases and he must be attended to if he does, that such death has been occasioned by some wizard.... Having pointed out the supposed culprit, he accuses him publicly with having practiced the art of witchcraft on the deceased, and begins his accusations always by pronouncing that "the wizard has eaten up his child's or his relation's heart".[27]

---

26 Rankin, *White Man's Grave*, 330.
27 Thomas Clarkson, *Letters on the Slave Trade and the State of the Natives* (London: James Phillips, 1791), 15–16.

This information is supported by other writers. Corry, for example, writes that "the alleged crime of witchcraft, or magic, is a common means by which the chiefs increase the number of slaves".[28] Crimes "against religion, including sorcery or witchcraft, are of daily occurrence", but the other capital crimes of murder, adultery and impertinence were rare.[29] Across the Atlantic in Martinique, Père Jean-Baptiste Labat, a Dominican missionary and slave owner, was convinced that the slave ships were full of sorcerers and that most slaves knew some degree of magic, sorcery and poison.

In addition to stories of witchcraft, writers devoted several pages, if not chapters, to reports of human sacrifice and cannibalism. For example, McLeod tells a story which was related to him by a Mr Absom, who had lived in Dahomey for thirty-seven years and had served as a sort of governor for several years. According to McLeod's informant, King Adahoonza had killed 127 Badagry captives in 1785 to fill the empty spaces on the walls of his palace with their skulls:

> In order to water with their blood the graves of the king's ancestors and to supply them with servants of various descriptions in the other world, a number of human victims are yearly sacrificed in solemn form; and this carnival is the period at which these shocking rites are publicly performed. . . . Scaffolds [for the king and his guests] are erected outside the palace wall and a large space fenced in round them. . . . Into this field of blood the victims are brought in succession, with their arms pinioned and a Fetisheer, laying his hand on the devoted head, pronounces a few mystical words. The victims are then decapitated to applause and songs are sung in honour of the king. If his wars have not furnished him with enough victims, his own subjects might lose their heads which end up decorating the walls of the palace.[30]

The macabre stories rolled off the presses, fascinating horrified Europeans who were growing accustomed to the relative tameness of life after the tumultuous Middle Ages. In Africa the *danse macabre* was brought to life in ways that medieval playwrights and writers could never have imagined. The descriptions of African cultural practices conjured up Bosch-like images of a land and people that were wildly grotesque, fantastic and diabolical.

---

28   Corry, *Observations*, 74.
29   Rankin, *White Man's Grave*, 79.
30   McLeod, *Voyage to Africa*, 57.

> The King [of Dahomey] now ordered these [Whydah] Captives to be brought into Court, which being accordingly done, he chose himself a great Number out of them to be sacrificed to his Fetish or Guardian Angel; the others being kept as slave for his own use, or to be sold to the Europeans. . . . The Soldiers brought likewise some thousands of dead People's Heads into the Court, hanging on strings; as the Officers received them, they paid the Soldiers five Shilling for each. Then several People carrying them away, threw them to a Great Heap of Heads that lay near the Camp.

That was bad enough, but the next day William Snelgrave was informed "that the Sacrifices had been taken away, in the Night, by the Common People who had boiled and feasted on them as holy Food" at the instigation of the "fetisher" or local priest. Usually, according to the local interpreter, the "head of the Victim was for the King, the Blood for the Fetish, and the Body for the common People".[31]

A somewhat less grisly account (in that it did not involve cannibalism) was related to Captain William Hutton by a Mr Hutchinson, who was the British Resident at Coomassie. Hutchinson was told

> "Christian, take care and watch over your family, the angel of death has drawn his sword, and will strike on the neck of many Ashantees. When the drum is struck on Adai eve, it will be the death signal of many. Shun the king if you can; but fear not . . . " The sacrifice was in consequence of the King imagining that if he washed the bones of his mother and sisters who had died while he was on the throne, it would propitiate the fetish, and make the war [that he was currently waging] successful. . . . Those who had done any thing to displease the king were then sent for in succession and immolated as they entered, "that their blood might water the graves". The whole of the night, the King's executioners traversed the streets, and dragged everyone they found to the palace where they were put in irons.[32]

The next day was the Adai festival day and was quiet. Hutchinson reported that only animals were killed. But,

> as soon as it was dark, the human sacrifices were renewed. The victims with their hands tied behind them and in chains, preceded the bones of the deceased

---

31 William Snelgrave, "A New Account of Some Parts of Guinea and the Slave Trade in 1730", in Astley, *New General Collection*, 2:485–519.

32 William Hutton, *A Voyage to Africa: Including a Narrative of an Embassy to One of the Interior Kingdoms in the Year 1820* (London: Longman, Hurst, Rees, Orme and Brown, 1821), 331–32.

which were removed to the sacred tomb of Bantama. The procession returned about three on Monday afternoon, when the King took his seat in the marketplace with his small band, and "Death! Death! Death!" was echoed by his horns. He sat with a silver goblet of palm wine in his hand, and when they cut off any head, imitated a dancing motion in his chair, and a little before dark he finished his terrors for that day.... The sacrifice was continued till the next Adai custom, seventeen days![33]

Hutton, an employee of the Royal African Committee – what became known as the Committee of the Company of Merchants Trading to Africa – suggested giving the Ashanti king a portrait of the English king to induce him to stop the human sacrifices.

Most Europeans mention cannibalism in their accounts but few appear to have actually witnessed it first-hand, and some may have simply invented the stories they relate. For example, one particularly vivid account of a cannibalistic feast may never have happened at all. In his *Memoirs of a Slave Trader*, Theodore Canot describes being captured in a raid of a coastal town by a Chief Jen-Ken. The captives were brought back to Jen-Ken's village, where Canot reports that the most extraordinary celebrations took place:

> By degrees the warriors dropped in around their chieftain. A palaver-house immediately in front of my quarters, was the general rendezvous; and scarcely a bushman appeared without the body of some maimed and bleeding victim. The mangled but living captives were tumbled on a heap in the centre, and soon every avenue to the square was crowded with exulting savages. Rum was brought forth in abundance for the chiefs. Presently, slowly approaching from a distance, I heard the drums, horns and war-bells and in less than fifteen minutes, a procession of women, whose naked limbs were smeared with chalk and ochre, poured into the palaver house to join the beastly rites. Each of these devils was armed with a knife, and bore in her hand some cannibal trophy. Jen-Ken's wife – a corpulent wench of forty – dragged along the ground, by a single limb, the slimy corpse of an infant ripped alive from its mother's womb. As her eyes met those of her husband, the two fiends yelled forth a shout of mutual joy, while the lifeless babe was tossed in the air and caught as it descended on the point of a spear. Then came the refreshment, in the shape of rum, powder, and blood, which was quaffed by the brutes till they reeled off, with linked hands, in a wild dance around the pile of victims. As the women leaped and sang, the men applauded and encouraged.... There was a devilish spell in the

---

33 Ibid.

tragic scene that fascinated my eyes to the spot. A slow, lingering, tormenting mutilation was practiced on the living, as well as on the dead; and, in every instance, the brutality of the women exceeded that of the men. I cannot picture the hellish joy with which they passed from body to body, digging out eyes, wrenching off lips, tearing the ears, and slicing the flesh from quivering bones; while the queen of the harpies crept amid the butchery gathering the brains from each severed skull as a bonne bouche for the approaching feast!

After the last victim yielded his life, it did not require long to kindle a fire, produce the requisite utensils, and fill the air with the odour of human flesh. Yet, before the various messes were half-broiled, every mouth was tearing the dainty morsels with shouts of joy, denoting the combined satisfaction of revenge and appetite.[34]

It is a riveting account, but in an editorial footnote to Canot's book, Arnold W. Lawrence suggests that Canot probably invented the whole story, given Sir Harry Johnston's contention that cannibalism was unknown among the people he described. This book, published in 1854, was republished in 1940 by Jonathan Cape, and Lawrence, brother of the famous T.E. Lawrence (of Arabia) was the editor. He ascribes Canot's inclusion of the episode as an attempt to "suit the popular taste for horrors". But it was more than that. Canot quite deliberately uses words such as "devils" and "fiends" to evoke an association with hell and Satan in the same way that "savages" and "brutes" reminds readers of the primitivism of Africans. The monstrous unnaturalness of the scene is underlined by the description of Jen-Ken's wife, a harpy so free of the milk of human kindness that she has not only torn a babe from its mother's womb but makes sport with it before harvesting the brains of the dead. All the elements dreaded by Europeans – a wild woman, dancing savages, cannibalism – are combined to great effect in this story. Yet it is a story that was almost certainly a figment of Canot's imagination, but one that would reappear to one degree or another in much of the literature about black people, both in the Caribbean and in Africa.

Cannibalism was the ultimate taboo, yet European explorers and adventurers in Africa frequently reported wild cannibalistic orgies. In Africa, every nightmare of the Europeans was apparently given life. There you had the "severing of body parts, drinking blood, desecration of the dead, and handling, smelling, and ingesting [of] the putrefied and unclean".[35] In invoking the horrors of

---

34 Theodore Canot, *Memoirs of a Slave Trader* (London: Jonathan Cape, 1940), 251.
35 H. L. Malchow, *Gothic Images of Race in Nineteenth Century Britain* (Stanford, CA: Stanford University Press, 1996), 43.

cannibalism, the captains and explorers were able to show just how different European society was to that of the Africans. These stories of witchcraft, fetish men, human sacrifice and cannibalism allowed Europeans to assert and reaffirm their moral superiority, as well as the superiority of their civilization. Heaven and hell, angels and demons, whites and blacks – the demarcating lines drawn between them were as clear as the differences between Europe and Africa.

But most Europeans swallowed their queasiness and attended the bloody rites without trying to put a stop to them or to save the victims. Hutton, for example, had no more radical a suggestion than to present an African monarch with the gift of a painting of the English king, under the assumption that the latter's disapproving face would deter his African counterpart from the Adai custom. He knew very well that the Ashanti king would not have brooked any direct interference in his affairs and would have ended Hutton's access to the gold and slaves on which his company was building its fortunes if sterner measures were taken.

When Rankin writes that "in casting the eye down the western coast of that vast continent, whose interesting and Malthusian characteristics are slavery, polygamy, and cannibalism, it is impossible to restrain a throb of pleasure when, from time to time, the name of a European settlement breaks the long-line of barbarism", he is probably understating the case. It was probably more like a thunderous mixture of exhilaration and relief than a mere "throb".[36]

FETISHERS, MEDICINE MEN AND VAMPIRES

The writers trying to describe the fetish men and women to a European audience all took great pains to point out that these wizards were universally respected and revered, quite unlike the attitudes at home, where witches were wise not to announce themselves. According to one writer, the choicest foods were reserved for fetish men and women and they did not have to work. Instead, they supported themselves by selling fetishes, which some claimed they found hanging on fetish trees.[37] As the Europeans understood it, *fetish* was "an expression of compound meaning . . . , even the act of devotion itself; or the various charms, incantations, and buffoonery of the priests and fetish makers who abound among them".[38] The missionary Thomas Thompson, a former

---

36 Rankin, *White Man's Grave*, 35.
37 "Description of Guinea and Benin", 675.
38 Corry, *Observations*, 61.

dean of Cambridge University, observes that "[a] great part of their superstition consists in their wearing fetishes, or pieces of gold, single beads, little shells, and the teeth of some animal, which are purchased of their conjurors at an exorbitant rate, as good against poisons, witchcraft and other direful accidents".[39] Verses from the Koran written on parchment, known as *gresh* or *gris-gris*, might also be worn, in leather, silver or gold cases hung about the neck or from the waist, by those who had the most contact with Arabs. These were said to repel evil in the same way that many in Europe believed Bible verses could deflect harm.

"The most striking ornaments of a Timmanee are his feteeshes, greegrees, amulets, talismans and charms. His neck is loaded with gree-grees; he sometimes carries the hair of some dead man of good fame. A square red leather case, containing a relic of a sentence of grammaree, from the pen of the Marabout, or Foulah bookman, reposes on his breast."[40] Corry adds that "great faith is attached to their fetish, as an antidote against evil".[41] Fetishes might be worn about the person, hung over doors and in the interiors of houses, or deposited in public areas around the village. They could also be composed of feathers, clay, pieces of cloth, hair or bone.

Nicolas Villault de Bellefond, writing in the 1600s, makes his own connection when he compares the fetish men's habit of wearing small chicken bones to that of the pilgrims of Saint Michael, who wore cockleshells. Villault describes the fetish men as wearing some sort of habit made of coarse linen or serge secured with a belt or scarf into which the chicken bones were set. Otherwise they were completely naked except for leg garters, which he says were made from the fibres of their fetish tree. Some of these fetish men moved from town to town and, rather like their busker contemporaries in Europe, would perform sleight-of-hand and other tricks with the expectation that the villagers would pay them in cloth, millet or some other way.

Clarkson believed that these conjurers were responsible for keeping up the belief "that there are persons in every village capable of being [accessories] to the death of others by secret means. For the people behold these conjurers with surprize; they consider them as doing supernatural things" and consequently believe in wizardry. Though Clarkson has elsewhere pointed to witches as being among those sold into slavery, in speaking of conjurers he observes that only

---

39 Thomas Thompson, *Memoirs of an English Missionary to the Coast of Guinea* (London: Shepperson and Reynolds, 1788).
40 Rankin, *White Man's Grave*, 241.
41 Corry, *Observations*, 61.

a few were accused of witchcraft and sold into slavery. "There is not an equal inducement to accuse these as other people, most of them being crooked, lame, blind of an eye, or such as have some bodily defect, so that very little emolument is to be derived from the sale of them."[42] Conjurers were not necessarily always close to being itinerant beggars; some also came from the African nobility. "Some ladies of rank went about beating a drum with disheveled hair, and pretending to work magical cures; there was also a race of mighty conjurers, called Scingilli, who had the power of giving and withdrawing rain at pleasure."[43]

As in Europe, magic was employed for a wide range of purposes and in a variety of ways: "When they make Fetish to destroy a person who injures them, they get some Victuals and Drink exorcised by the Fetishir, and scatter them in the way where their Adversary usually passes, firmly believing this accursed Meat, if he touches it will be his Bane."[44] Even Africans who had the highest degree of contact with the Europeans continued to call on the magic of their fetishes:

> The Mulatto Women, who would pass for Christians, are extravagantly addicted to this Superstition. If one of them is married to, or kept by a European, who loves and pays her well, when he falls sick, she never fails to make rich Offerings to the Priest.... Nay there are some Europeans, who not only think well of and believe this idolatrous worship effectual, but instigate their Servants to it; and grown like-wise very fond of wearing some Trifles about their own Bodies, which were consecrated by these Priests.[45]

Thomas lamented that

> such is the delusion and obstinacy of the negroes in their own superstitious paganism that they are neither willing to be baptized themselves nor will be prevailed upon to let their children partake of that great and ineffable blessing of being lifted under the banners of the great captain of our salvation, but bring them up to be the devil's slaves, whom they worship under the disguise of their fetishes.[46]

---

42 Clarkson, *Letters*, 64.
43 Hugh Murray, *Discovery and Adventure in Africa* (London: T. Nelson and Sons, 1857), 67.
44 "Description of Guinea and Benin", 664.
45 Ibid., 658.
46 Thomas Phillips, "A Journal of a Voyage from England to Barbadoes", in *A Collection of Voyages and Travels* (London: Messrs Churchill, 1704), 173–239.

Africans not only believed in the power of fetishes to protect them and their property from harm, bring them love and aid their crops, they also "took Fetish", or swore oaths on the fetish. Thompson relates that one way of taking fetish was to pour water into a copper vessel into which the chief's string of *agrih* beads was placed. A man or woman taking the fetish might then drink the water after declaring that if they were false, it would kill them. Anyone refusing to drink was automatically judged guilty. Another kind of fetish taking recalled by Thompson was the *adom*. Those involved would drink water in large potfuls until somebody vomited; whoever vomited was declared to have right on his side. This was similar to the trial by red water reported by Corry and others, which was usually reserved for serious crimes. The accused would drink great quantities of water infused with the poisonous juice of the *gris-gris* tree. If he was guilty, the poison would kill him instantly and his family would subsequently be sold into slavery.

In the early 1700s, the French monk Godfrey Loyer claimed

> The Negros are sure to keep their Oath whenever they swear by their Fetish; more especially if they eat them. To know the Truth from any Negro, you need only mix something in a little Water, and steeping a bit of Bread, bid him eat or drink that Fetish as a sign of the Truth. If the Thing be so, he will do it freely; but if otherwise, he will not touch it, believing he should die on the Spot if he swore falsely. Their way is to rasp or grate a little of their Fetish in Water, or on any edible, and so put it in their Mouth without swallowing it. A Negro, who swears thus, meets with infinitely more Credit from his Countrymen, than those who swear on their Gospels do from their fellow Christians.[47]

The fetish oath was to figure significantly in both fictional and non-fictional accounts of Obeah decades later. For example, Edwards notes that oaths of secrecy among the Koromantyn required ingesting a mixture of grave dirt, human blood and water. The oath-taker swore that his bones should rot and his belly burst if, after swallowing the mixture, he broke his secrecy or lied. According to Edwards, this oath was often administered to wives suspected of infidelity.[48]

Another African trial by ordeal involved dipping the hand of the accused

---

47 Godfrey Loyer, "Abstract of a Voyage to Iffini on the Gold Coast in 1701", in Astley, *New General Collection*, 2:417–45.

48 Bryan Edwards, *The History, Civil and Commercial, of the British Colonies in the West Indies* (New York: Arno Press, 1972), 380.

into a "viscuous solution", then running a hot iron over it. The flesh of the guilty would burn, while that of the innocent remained unharmed. Clarkson describes a version of this:

> The man is tried [by binding him to a tree]. A red hot iron is then applied to his tongue. If it burns it, the man is pronounced guilty, if not innocent. It is said that there is an herb in this country, which if previously applied to the part to be burned, is an antidote for a moment against the effects of the fire; and it is believed that there is such an herb because some which have undergone the ordeal have been known to escape, unhurt.[49]

Again, this was a practice known to the Europeans. The Malleus Maleficarum advises against administering this particular trial to witches, because "if the hands be anointed with the juice of a certain herb they are protected from burning. Now the devil has an exact knowledge of the virtues of such herbs: therefore, although he can cause the hand of the accused to be protected from the red-hot iron by invisibly interposing some other substance, yet he can procure the same effect by the use of natural objects."[50] Women who asked to undergo this trial were considered, almost by definition, witches.

African criminals and liars could also take the "trial of the Belli":

> If a man is charged with Theft, Murder or Perjury, and the Evidence is not clear enough or that he is only suspected of this or that Crime, he is to take the trial of the Belli; a Composition made by the Belli-Mo, or Priest, with the Bark of a Tree and Herbs, which is laid on the Person's hand. If he is guilty of the Indictment, the Blacks say it will presently burn the Skin; but that, if innocent, it will do no harm.[51]

According to Loyer, Africans might also swear on parts of their body, which they believed would wither if they lied, or they might take a little sand in their mouths and demand that Anghiume or another god choke them with it if they lied.

Some Europeans were so taken aback by the fetish oath that they refused to use it even for their own purposes. When a Danish general suspected the King of Fetu's son of stealing a ring from him and accused him of it, the prince offered to swear by his fetish. Villault examined the fetish and found it to be only "a Faggot of Thorns in a Basket, which a Slave carried under his arm,

---

49 Clarkson, *Letters*, 16.
50 Kramer and Sprenger, *Malleus Maleficarum*, 234–35.
51 "Description of Guinea and Benin".

covered with a Skin. In the centre of the Faggot was a Lump of Suet and Wax, with Parrots Feathers, little Burnt Bones of Pullets and Plumes of a Bird, which was the Great Fetish of that Country, with several other Trash." A priest told him he had made the fetish as strong as possible, so that if the prince lied it would kill him within the hour. As the prince was about to take the oath, the general stopped him.[52]

The priests, with the help of the dead themselves, were also adept at finding murderers:

> Priests ask the Corpse, where, when, and by whom, he was thus deprived of Life. . . . When the Spirit, by moving the Heads of the Bearers of the Corpse, after a certain Manner, as they pretend, given them to understand, that the Sovah Mufin was the cause of it they ask him again, whether the Sorcerer is Male or female, and where he lives. This the Spirit also declares, in the same manner; and leading them to the Place where the Sorcerer abides, they seize and put him in Chains, to be examined on the Charge laid against him by the Spirit. If he persist to deny it, he is compelled to take the Kquoni, a horrid bitter Drink; and if after drinking three full Kalebashe, he vomits it up, he is absolved; whereas, if it only foams out about his Mouth, he is immediately put to Death: His Corpse is then burnt on the Spot, and the Ashes are thrown into the River, or the Sea, be he ever so great a Man.[53]

A tree bark, the kquoni was beaten in a wooden mortar and left to soak in water. It was described as a very sharp, dangerous liquor, commonly administered in the morning. Falconbridge asserts that the drink was made strong or weak by the judges, according to their belief in the suspect's guilt or their hostility towards the accused.

Corpses could also reveal in a more direct way what had happened to them. Matthews relates that when a corpse arrived at the burial site it was asked what had made him die:

> for it is a firm and universal belief among them, that no person dies without having a previous knowledge of his death, except his death be caused by witchcraft or poison, or the more powerful charms of another person over those he wears. If the corpse answers in the affirmative to any of the questions proposed, it is signified by forcibly impelling the bearers several paces forward, by a power which they say they are unable to resist – if, on the contrary, it is signified by

---

52 Ibid., 670.
53 Ibid., 541.

> a rolling motion, which they also say they cannot prevent. – If, by the sign given, a suspicion arises that the death was occasioned by poison or witchcraft, they proceed to question [the corpse as to his killer's identity] . . . and name several people . . . begin[ning] with his relations. He is then more particularly questioned whether he is certain of the person; if he is, it is requested that he will strike that hand which holds the bough. . . . Upon this the corpse immediately impels the bier forwards, and strikes the bough. In order to convince the spectators, they repeat this two or three times. The culprit is then seized, and if a witch, sold without further ceremony.[54]

Matthews adds that if the accused was poor and the deceased rich, the witch's whole family was also sold.[55] In addition to being able to identify their murderer, the African dead could also signal their disapproval of their corpse-bearers by becoming as heavy as lead and refusing to move.

The Quojas of West Africa also maintained a belief in supernatural men, the "*Sovah Mûnûfin*, that is, Poisoners and Blood-suckers. These they fancy will suck the Blood out of any Man or Beast; or, at least, corrupt it in such a Manner, as to occasion lingering and painful Diseases." The *sovah* – or, as the Europeans understood the term, the Devil –

> possesses such, who being overwhelmed with Melancholy, or grown desperate through Misfortune, withdraw themselves from the Company of other Men into the Woods and Forests: where the Sovah shews them what Herbs and Roots are to be used in their Enchantments, as also the Gestures, Words, and Grimaces proper for those wicked practices. The Blacks will seldom travel through the Woods without Company for fear of meeting them, as well as the wild Beasts; and carry with them a certain Composition, which they fancy, preserves them against the malicious Sovah, of whom they tell a thousand ridiculous Stories.[56]

Later, Captain Sutherland Rattray, writing about Ashanti vampires in the twentieth century, says that they delighted in the blood of children, travelled great distances at night and could suck the sap of various crops, causing them to wither and die. By the time he made his observations, however, it is possible that European vampire lore had affected Ashanti traditions.

---

54 Matthews, *Voyage to the River*, 123–24.
55 Ibid.
56 "Description of Guinea and Benin", 540.

Fetishers were also the medicine men of their villages:

> He who acts the Part of a Doctor is also a Fetishir or Priest, who consequently finds it no great difficulty to persuade the Relations that the Patient cannot be recovered without some Offerings made to appease the Fetish. Accordingly, they require him to consult their Divinity, what he would be pleased to have. The Priest, who, to be sure, is not negligent, where the Profit accrues to him, as soon as possible puts his cheats in Practise; after his pretended Inquiry, informs them, that they must offer a Sheep, Hog, Dog, Cat or whatever he likes best himself, which sometimes may be Gold, Cloth, Drink, and other such like good Things.[57]

But many European observers did not consider them mere con men. Villault, for example, believed that fetishers talked with the Devil, "who communicates with them, and teaches them which way to cheat the people so easily; and that which makes me say it, is this, they always mutter out some words to their Fetiches before they deliver [their charms]".[58]

Fetish men, as might be expected, played a leading role in various ceremonies. Rankin describes a performance of the "Dance of Death":

> A Mandingo greegree-man of surpassing charms, (not those of face or figure. For the most part, the most repulsive object is generally selected, but articles manufactured for the conciliation of the devil), dressed in extravagant style and graced with rough goatskins to heighten his deformity, sang a low monotonous recitative and played upon the gumbay, a simple musical instrument, whose sound is produced by striking beads strung against the sides of a dry calabash. Two Kroos approach the greegree-man.

They feint at him with their war knives, but Death keeps on beating his drum. He moves towards them with each beat of the drum. They now attack him together but he continues to advance. They are frightened and kneel before him, bowing low. He beats the drum more quickly to signify his victory, and the dance is over as quickly as it began.[59]

---

57 Ibid., 658.
58 Villault, *Coasts of Africa*, 189.
59 Rankin, *White Man's Grave*, 155–56.

CHAPTER 2

The Black Thread of Mischief Crosses the Atlantic
Egyptian *Aub* or Ashantee *Obayifo*

African slavery did not start with the Europeans. They were, in fact, relative latecomers to the trade, which was already being briskly carried out by the Arabs to the north and which saw enslaved Africans taken as far as India and China. But it was the advent of the Portuguese in the mid-1400s that presaged the establishment of an unprecedented traffic in human lives that would continue for four hundred years. Estimates differ, but perhaps as many as twenty million Africans were captured and shipped to the Americas as slaves, with at least eleven million surviving the journey. Slave dealers tore Africans from their lives, stripped them naked and burned the initials of their owners into their breasts, but they could do nothing about the things the Africans held in their hearts and minds. Africans remembered their fetish magic and bore it silently across the ocean to their new homes. It was to trouble the dreams of Englishmen and plague their waking hours for centuries.

By the late 1700s it appears that the word *Obeah* was fairly well established and well-known, though Europeans struggled to explain its origin. Most turned to Jacob Bryant's *New System; or, Analysis of Ancient Mythology*, first published in 1774–76. Bryant had attempted to tie all the religions of the world together by tracing their evolution over time. He believed that *Ob, Oph, Ops, Oub, Aub* and more were essentially different names for the serpent gods worshipped by various peoples, including the Babylonians, Egyptians and Syrians.[1] According to Bryant, serpent worship began with the Chal-

---

[1] Jacob Bryant, *A New System; or, an Analysis of Ancient Mythology*, 3 vols. (London: T.

deans and gave its name to places as well as peoples. He argues, for example, that Ethiopians ("Aithopians") got their name from Ath-Ope or Ath-Opis, their serpent god; these people then carried their religious rites with them to the Greek island of Euboea, which Bryant claims was originally known as Oub-aia, or Serpent Island. In fact, Bryant suggests that the whole of Africa was once known by the name Ophiusa. For West Indians, Bryant may have won the day in terms of explaining the origin of *Obeah* when he connected it to the serpent worship of the Greeks and Chaldeans and pointed out that the Witch of Endor was known as Oub, or Ob, which he said was interpreted as "Pythonissa". Unfortunately, the best that can be said of Bryant's questionable and, in many cases, wrong-headed theories is that they were certainly promulgated with great vigour.

The Jesuit scholar Joseph Williams later pointed out that Bryant likely got his ideas about Ob and serpent worship from Reginald Scot's *The Discoverie of Witchcraft*, which was published in 1584 and presented many of the same arguments that Bryant made relating to the association of Ob with snakes and their worship.[2] Bryant never acknowledged the debt he owed Scot, however, thus unwittingly initiating a long-held tradition in which writers on Obeah cheerfully plagiarize from each other without troubling over such small things as attribution.

Interestingly, Edward Long, author of *The History of Jamaica*, a much-quoted source on Obeah, also makes a connection between blacks and ancient Egypt. In fact, he launches into a tirade on the ancient Egyptians which borrows heavily from the opinions of Antoine Goguet, as expressed in the Frenchman's 1761 work *The Origins of Laws, Arts and Sciences and Their Progress among Nations*. According to Long,

> The Negroes seem to conform nearest in character to the Ægyptians, in whose government, says the learned Goguet, there reigned a multitude of abuses and essential defects, authorized by the laws, and by their fundamental principles. As to their customs and manners, indecency and debauchery were carried to the most extravagant height, in all their public feasts and religious ceremonies; neither was their morality pure. It offended against the first rules of rectitude and probity; they lay under the highest censure for covetousness, perfidy, and roguery. They were a people without taste, without genius or

---

Payne, P. Elmsly, B. White and J. Walter, 1774–76).

2   Joseph Williams, *Voodoos and Obeahs: Phases of West India Witchcraft* (London: George Allen and Unwin, 1933), 110.

discernment; who had only ideas of grandeur, ill understood: knavish, crafty, soft, lazy, cowardly, and servile, superstitious in excess, and extravagantly besotted with an absurd and monstrous theology.³

As bad as the ancient Egyptians were, Long considers black people to be much worse. The Egyptians "appear far superior to the Negroes who, perhaps in their turn, as far transcend them in the superlative perfection of their worst qualities. When we reflect on the nature of [blacks] and their dissimilarity to the rest of mankind, must we not conclude that they are a different species of the same genus?"⁴

At the time that both Long and Goguet were writing, of course, the Rosetta Stone had not yet been discovered. Very little was actually known about ancient Egypt, and even less about contemporary Africa. It seemed natural to Europeans to ascribe whatever they saw in the way of religion and culture in Africa to ancient Egyptian origins, since, by the evidence of their ruins, that appeared to have been the only dominant ancient civilization on the continent.

Certainly, Bryant's explanation for the etymology of *Obeah* remained the definitive one for more than a century. It was included in the 1789 *Report of the Lords of the Committee of the Council Appointed for the Consideration of All Matters Relating to Trade and Foreign Plantations*, which arguably gave it an even wider distribution than Bryant might have hoped for his dense tome. Its inclusion in the report also gave his theory a stamp of approval which made it all the more credible to writers in subsequent years. Among the writers who latched onto Bryant's explanation was Dr Benjamin Moseley, who served as Jamaica's surgeon general from 1768 and lived there until 1788. In his 1787 book *Obi; or the History of Three-Finger'd Jack*, Moseley writes that "the science of OBI is very extensive. This, OBI, or, as it is pronounced in the English West Indies, Obeah, had its origin, like many customs among Africans, from the ancient Egyptians' Obi, for the purpose of bewitching people, or consuming them by lingering illness."⁵ Moseley then goes on to repeat the story of the Witch of Endor. A few years later Moseley returned to the origin of *Obeah* in

---

3 Edward Long, *The History of Jamaica; or, A General Survey of the Antient and Modern State of That Island* (London: T. Lowndes, 1774; repr., Montreal: McGill–Queen's University Press, 2002), 354–55.
4 Ibid.
5 Benjamin Moseley, *Obi; or The History of Three-Finger'd Jack* (Newcastle: M. Angus and Son, 1787), 3.

his essay "Miscellaneous Medical Observations", adding more about the Witch of Endor for emphasis:

> When Saul wanted to raise Samuel from the dead, he said to his servants, "seek me a woman (eminent for OB) that hath a familiar spirit". His servants replied to him, "Behold, there is a woman mistress in the art of OB in Hendor . . . ." When the witch of Hen-dor came to Saul, he said to her, "Divine, I pray thee, unto me, in thy witchcraft OB, and raise him from the dead whom I shall name unto thee."[6]

About fifty years later, Richard Madden, a justice of the peace sent to Jamaica a year ahead of emancipation to monitor the slaves' transition to freedom, published *A Twelvemonth's Residence in the West Indies*, in which he quotes Bryant and offers his own insights: "Obeah is evidently a practice of Oriental origin. In my *Eastern Travels*, in speaking of the Jewish sorcerers, I have stated that the Hebrew word *shoelobh*, 'a consulter with familiar spirits,' signifies also 'python, or the spirit of divination;' obh, signifying a 'bottle' which was probably made use of in divining."[7] Writers continued to quote Bryant up to the twentieth century. One of the most recent of these was Revd Thomas Banbury, a black Jamaican rector, who wrote in 1894 that

> the word obeah or obi is said to be derived from a Hebrew term (Ob) the name of an ancient idol, and the superstitious practice itself as connected with it, to have taken its rise in Egypt, and thence spread over the whole continent of Africa. From this it is easily imagined how it reached the West Indies: – the importation of slaves from that continent. Hence we see how one evil follows in the train of another.[8]

Banbury's words were echoed by Revd J.B. Ellis, a warden of the Jamaica Church Theological College, almost ten years later. According to him, it was "very probable that Obeahism has its roots far away in the past, being a by-product of the old serpent worship prevalent in Egypt in the days of Moses".[9]

---

6 Benjamin Moseley, "Miscellaneous Medical Observations", in *On the Treatment and Management of the More Common West India Diseases (1759–1802)*, ed. J. Edward Hutson (Kingston: University of the West Indies Press, 2005), 105-6.

7 Richard Robert Madden, *A Twelvemonth's Residence in the West Indies* (London: Carey, Len and Blanchard, 1835), 2:71.

8 Thomas Banbury, *Jamaica Superstitions; or, the Obeah Book: A Complete Treatise of the Absurdities Believed in by the People of the Island* (Kingston: Mortimer C. de Souza, 1894), 6.

9 J.B. Ellis, *The Diocese of Jamaica: A Short Account of Its History, Growth and Organisation*

When Bryant published his book, Napoleon was about two decades away from invading Egypt and setting off an interest in that ancient civilization that continues today. Scholars cracked the Rosetta Stone several years after that, so much of what he wrote about the Egyptians came from Greek and other writers. Yet writer after writer unquestioningly accepted an Egyptian origin for a word used by West African slaves, it being much easier for them to believe that Obeah was derived from Egyptian culture than to accept that West Africans had a robust culture of their own. Even those who noticed that Obeah had nothing to do with serpent worship tended to suggest that this was because Obeah was just a faint shadow of the old Egyptian religion. Europeans did not recognize that their own religious and cultural background predisposed them to find an association between Obeah and serpents. For European Christians, magic and witchcraft were associated with the Devil, who was in turn identified with snakes, so a connection between Obeah and serpent worship must have seemed fully logical. The Jesuit priest Williams declared, "Obeah, as such, in its purpose and acceptance must be classified as a form of devil worship." "The Obeah man or woman . . . is the servant of the Sasabonsam or Devil who is invoked and relied upon to produce the desired effect. Consequently", he repeats, "real Obeah must be regarded as a form of Devil-worship".[10]

One of the few who had no time for the Bryant explanation was Revd James M. Phillippo, the Baptist missionary and abolitionist, who went against the grain and flatly declared that "Obeism . . . is so called from Obi, the town, city, district or province of Africa where it originated".[11] Phillippo was the exception, however, and Bryant's explanation continued to draw adherents up until the early 1900s. "Both obeah and vaudoux are variants of West African fetich", wrote C.B. in the *Manchester Guardian* of 12 March 1907, adding that it was "derived by the West Indian negroes of today from their ancestors who were conveyed across the Atlantic in slave ships to work in the Caribbean cane fields and tobacco plantations. Their root idea is the worship of the snake, the propitiation of an evil spirit that is supposed to be all-powerful in human affairs. For 'obi' is a West African word, meaning a snake."[12]

"AN EXTRAORDINARY SUPERSTITION"

(London: Society for Propagating Christian Knowledge, 1913), 219.
10   Joseph J. Williams, *Psychic Phenomena of Jamaica* (New York: Dial Press, 1934), 106–9.
11   James M. Phillippo, *Jamaica: Its Past and Present State* (London: John Snow, 1843), 247.
12   C.B., "Obeah and Vaudoux".

But all that was still very much in the future. The English public, or at least a small section of it, appears to have first been made aware of the word *Obeah* and its associated spellings in the early 1700s, through the letters of army captain Thomas Walduck to James Petiver, of the Royal Society of London for the Improvement of Natural Knowledge. According to Walduck, then stationed in Barbados, a man known as the "obia" led the religious ceremonies of Barbadian slaves and could both heal and hurt. The obia was, in fact, capable of causing "lameness, madness, loss of speech, [and] loss of the use of all their limbs". As his countrymen had done in Africa regarding the fetishers, Walduck calls Obeah a "diabolical Magic".[13]

Walduck was one of those people who are keenly interested in the world around them and he saw his stint in Barbados as an opportunity to study a country very different from his own. Though he downplayed his own intellectual abilities in contrast to the members of the Royal Society (then led by Isaac Newton), he was clearly excited about the possibilities of entering into regular communication with the prestigious organization, which included eminent men such as Edmond Halley, the astronomer and mathematician; John Arbuthnot, Physician Extraordinary to Queen Anne; and John Flamsteed, the first British Astronomer Royal. Once in Barbados, Walduck wasted little time in getting his nephew, John Searle, to offer his services to the Royal Society for their enquiries into various areas, but it appears that Petiver was the only Fellow who gave him the time of day. An apothecary, botanist and entomologist, Petiver was mostly interested in what Walduck had to say about the flora and fauna of Barbados, encouraging him to provide more information about the "pulses, Fruit and vegetable matter" of the island. Petiver gave the captain's submission "Diabolical Practises of the Negroes" little attention. (Walduck's mention of obia might, in fact, have led to the Society's criticism that he gave "too much credit to the ill-grounded reports of the Vulgar".) Petiver reported Walduck's last communication to the Royal Society in April 1716, then history loses sight of him. Walduck's letters were not published until 1948, so, beyond the circle of the Royal Society, his contribution to the general or popular understanding and awareness of Obeah in the England of his day would have been minimal.

The Barbadian connection to the Royal Society continued, however, with Revd Griffith Hughes's arrival on the island in 1736. A Welshman, Hughes was

---

13   Raymond Phineas Stearns, *Science in the British Colonies of America* (Champaign: University of Illinois Press, 1970), 352–55.

assigned to St Lucy parish at the north of the island. He stayed on the island until at least 1748, collecting much the same type of information as Walduck had on its geography, wildlife, plants and other features of scientific interest. Unlike Walduck, however, Hughes corresponded with many prominent members of English society, including Fellows of the Royal Society.

In 1748 Hughes returned to England to pursue further studies at Oxford and was himself elected a fellow of the Royal Society. Two years later he published *The Natural History of Barbados*, which became his best-known work. The ten-volume work contained extensive information on the medicinal and/or poisonous properties of the island's plants, poison antidotes, the diets of the various birds and other animals, and, of course, Obeah:

> The Negroes in general are very tenaciously addicted to the Rites, Ceremonies, and Superstitions of their own Countries, particularly in their Plays, Dances, Music, Marriages, and Burials. And even such as are born and bred up here, cannot be entirely weaned from these Customs: They stand much in Awe of such as pass for Obeah Negroes, these being a sort of Physicians and Conjurers, who can, as they believe, not only fascinate them, but cure them when they are bewitched by others.

He goes on to add that "if once a Negro believes, that he is bewitched, the Notion is so strongly riveted in his mind, that, Medicines seldom availing, he usually lingers till Death puts an end to his fears".[14]

Meanwhile, the other European powers were also taking note of certain suspicious practices. A 1742 report written for King Christian VI about life in the Danish West Indies (St Thomas and St John) related ominously that "there are strong witch-masters among these plantation slaves. They brought their witchcraft with them from Africa."[15] A year later, on 1 February 1743, Louis XV of France issued a declaration

> forbidding all slaves, of either sex, from composing or distributing remedies made up in powders, or in any other manner, or to undertake the cure of any description of disorder, with the exception of the bite of serpents, under pain of corporal punishment – even death, if the case require it. Slaves who, under

---

14 Griffith Hughes, *The Natural History of Barbados* (London, 1850; repr., New York: Arno Press, 1972), 15–16.

15 Isidor Paiewonsky, *Eyewitness Accounts of Slavery in the Danish West Indies* (New York: Fordham University Press, 1989), 124.

pretext of preparing remedies for bites of serpents, should apply them to other purposes, shall be condemned to the penalties hereby laid down.

An ordinance issued on the same day further prohibited slaves from bearing arms or knives, from stealing them and from stealing boats, canoes or piraguas.[16]

The French may not have made an explicit connection between the formulation of powders and resistance to slavery, but by the early 1800s the British were very clear on the extent of the threat posed to society by Obeah men and women. By then they had had at least two rebellions to remind them. Several missionaries had written about Obeah in their letters and reports, but it was Tacky's Rebellion of 1760 in Jamaica which made sure Obeah captured and held British attention for more than a hundred years. Tacky, a Coromantyn slave who worked as an overseer on the Frontier estate in St Mary parish, launched his rebellion just before Easter Monday with a few men, but by the next day, hundreds had joined him. Among Tacky's supporters were several Obeah men, who distributed charms to the rebels to make them invulnerable to the weapons of the militia. The Obeah men claimed that they themselves could not be killed. When the militia heard about these claims, they made a special point of capturing one and hanging him in a place for all to see, along with his bones and feathers. Many of the rebels lost heart at the sight, and Tacky himself was shot and killed not long after by a Maroon fighting with the militia. Tacky's example inspired other uprisings in the subsequent months, but they had all been put down by the end of the year. Four hundred slaves and sixty whites died in the fighting. In the aftermath, another one hundred slaves were executed and five hundred were transported to British Honduras.

The ferocity of Tacky's Rebellion and the role Obeah men had played in bolstering the confidence of the rebels shook the planters and galvanized them into action. The Jamaica Assembly wasted no time in passing legislation the same year to "remedy the evils arising from irregular assemblies of slaves . . . and for preventing the practice of obeah". The act (no. 24) identified "blood, feathers, parrots beaks, dogs' teeth, alligators' teeth, broken bottles, grave dirt, rum and eggshells" as the supplies on which Obeah practitioners depended.[17] But legislation could not ensure that this was the last that Jamaicans or West Indians would hear of Obeah. In many ways it was just the beginning, and there would be no escaping the link between Obeah and rebellion. After the

---

16 Southey, *Chronological History*, 293.
17 *Miscellaneous Papers* (London: House of Commons, 1816), 115

Hanover slave uprising in 1776, for example, a search of one prisoner's home resulted in the discovery of "egg shells tied up in plantain thrash, fowls' feet, fish bones, feathers, and sundry other matters in a basket; also a coney-skin or some such thing, stuffed in a bottle, which those who practice Obeah commonly make use of".[18]

Throughout the West Indies, the planters had previously been inclined to dismiss Obeah as harmless superstition. After Tacky's Rebellion they knew the threat it posed to their very lives, and they saw evidence of Obeah everywhere they looked. "There were few of the large estates having African slaves, which had not one or more Obeah men in the number", a planter told Hesketh Bell, a former administrator of Dominica and governor of the Leeward Islands.[19] "There is not perhaps a single West Indian estate, upon which there is not one or more Obeah men or women", agrees Mrs Carmichael, a planter's wife, adding that "the negroes know who they are, but it is very difficult for white people to find them out".[20]

The assertion that plantations were teeming with Obeah practitioners found many subscribers. "A few years since there was scarcely an estate which did not contain a priest or priestess of this deadly art", writes Revd Phillippo.[21] Thomas Atwood, a judge first in Dominica and then in the Bahamas, notes: "They have their necromancers and conjurors of both sexes, whom they call 'Obeah men and women' to whom they apply for spells and charms against sickness, to prevent their being robbed, or to find out the thief, and to punish those who do them any injury."[22]

"The fetish is the African divinity, invoked by the negroes in the practice of obeah", writes Richard Madden. "When they take an oath they say they 'take the fetish' and when they worship, they 'make fetish.' I believe the word is peculiar to the dialect of Guinea, and signifies 'a charm or incantation' as

---

18 William J. Gardner, *A History of Jamaica from Its Discovery by Christopher Columbus to the Present Time* (London: Elliot Stock, 1873), 128.

19 Hesketh J. Bell, *Obeah: Witchcraft in the West Indies* (London: Low, Marston, Searle and Rivington, 1889), 9.

20 Mrs Carmichael, *Domestic Manners and Social Conditions of the White, Coloured and Negro Population of the West Indies* (London: Whittaker, Treacher, 1833), 253. Mrs Carmichael has now been identified as a Scotswoman, Alison Charles Carmichael, wife of John Carmichael, owner of a 250-acre estate on St Vincent. She was probably in her late twenties when she arrived in the West Indies for a stay of about five years. See Karina Williamson, "Mrs Carmichael: A Scotswoman in the West Indies, 1820–1826", in *International Journal of Scottish Literature* 4 (Spring/Summer, 2008), http://www.ijsl.stir.ac.uk/issue4/williamson.htm.

21 Phillippo, *Jamaica*, 249.

22 Thomas Atwood, *The History of the Island of Dominica* (London: J. Johnson, 1791), 269.

well as a divinity", he speculates, noting, "They have a singular idea, that, if they swear falsely on the fetish, their stomachs will burst, their faces will be scratched, and their fingers will drop off; and what is still more singular, a great many of them have the same apprehension coupled with their ideas of the obligation of an oath on the Christian Scriptures." He gives the example of a girl brought to give evidence in court who, when asked if she knew what it meant to take an oath, replied, "If me swear false, my stomach would burst, my face would be scratched and my fingers drop off."[23]

If estate slaves, physically under the European sphere of influence, still subscribed to Obeah, the Maroons in their mountain fastnesses, far from white control, were considered even more under its thrall.

> Concerning the Maroons they are, in general, ignorant of our language and all of them attached to the gloomy superstitions of Africa derived from their ancestors with such enthusiastick zeal and reverential ardour as I think can only be eradicated with their lives. The Gentoos of India are not, I conceive, more sincere in their faith than the negroes of Guinea in believing the prevalence of Obi and the supernatural power of their Obeah men.[24]

Obeah, therefore, was deemed to hold sway over blacks, whatever their condition, enslaved or free.

Gardner notes that "the power [Obeah men] possess was almost unlimited. It was believed that they could cause disease or cure it, and by their mystic rites punish an enemy, or, if it was desired, win his favour. They could not only detect a thief, a murderer, or an adulterer, but by incantations, bring down the most fearful judgments upon them. They could make men impervious to bullets, or restore them to life." Also subscribing to the theory that "this dread superstition is evidently a perverted form of one far more ancient, and may probably be traced back to Egypt", he launches into a Bryant-influenced discussion on Ob, Oub and the Witch of Endor.[25]

The planters' obsession with Obeah ensured that both visitors to the islands and those back in England with an interest in the West Indies also became preoccupied with it. More and more writers interested themselves in Obeah and exactly how it worked or was worked.

---

23 Madden, *Twelvemonth's Residence*, 72–73.
24 Bryan Edwards, "An Introductory Account Containing Observations on the Disposition, Character, Manners and Habits of Life of the Maroons", in *Proceedings of the Governor and Assembly of Jamaica in Regard to the Maroon Negroes* (London: John Stockdale, 1796), 29.
25 Gardner, *History of Jamaica*, 187.

Obeah "is made of grave dirt, hair, teeth of sharks, and other animals; blood, feathers, eggshells, images in wax, the hearts of birds, liver of mice, and some potent roots, weeds, and bushes, of which Europeans are at this time ignorant, but which were known... to the ancients", writes Dr Moseley. "Certain mixtures of these ingredients are burnt, or buried very deep in the ground, or hung up a chimney; or laid under the threshold of the door of the party to suffer; with incantations, songs or curses, performed at midnight, regarding the aspects of the moon."[26] The preoccupation with graveyard dirt has already been noted, but ghosts and more particularly spirits of the ancestors had always had a role to play in Obeah. "The person who wants to do the mischief is also sent to the burying-grounds, or some secret place, where spirits are supposed to frequent, to invoke his, or her dead parents, or some dead friend, to assist in the curse", Moseley writes.[27]

Moseley made a significant contribution to fixing a fear of Obeah in the minds of the English public. His drama *Obi; or the History of Three-Finger'd Jack* will be discussed in another chapter, but it was Stephen Fuller's 1789 *Report to the Lords of the Committee of the Council Appointed for the Consideration of All Matters Relating to Trade and Foreign Plantations* that provided grist for writers' mills for the next hundred years or more. The Committee wanted to know "whether Negroes called Obeah men, or under any other denomination, practicing Witchcraft, exist in the Island of Jamaica? [and] By what arts or by what means, do these Obeah men cause the deaths, or otherwise injure those who are supposed be influenced thereby?" The reply, drafted by Mr Fuller, the British Agent for Jamaica, with the aid of Edward Long and a Mr Chisholm, begins with a reference to Bryant's discussion of Oph, linking Obeah with ancient religions. Obeah is identified with the worship of Oubaios, "an ancient oracular Deity of Africa", which now, according to the report, "denoted those Africans who in that island [Jamaica] practice witchcraft or sorcery".

Fuller's submission also includes information on the examination of a dead Obeah woman's house in 1775, which revealed that

> the whole inside of the roof (which was of thatch), and every crevice of the walls [was] stuck with the implements of her trade, consisting of rags, feathers, bones of cats, and a thousand other articles. Examining further, a large earthen pot or jar, close covered, was found concealed under her bed. It contained a prodigious quantity of round balls of earth or clay of various dimensions, large and small, whitened on the outside, and variously compounded, some with hair and rags

---

26 Moseley, *Obi*, 3.
27 Moseley, "Medical Observations", 106.

and feathers of all sorts, and strongly bound with twine; others blended with the upper section of the skulls of cats, or stuck round with cats teeth and claws, or with human or dogs teeth, and some glass beads of different colours; there were also a great many eggshells filled with a viscous or gummy substance, . . . and many little bags stuffed with a variety of articles the particulars of which cannot at this distance of time be recollected.[28]

Edwards was so struck by the report that he included the entire thing in his *History*, thus setting off a virtual avalanche of plagiarism, though he himself was careful to give proper acknowledgement for the information. Decades later, Bell plagiarized the same information (either directly from Fuller or indirectly from Edwards) but attributed it to a Roman Catholic priest; he also changed the sex so that in his version it is an Obeah *man* in whose hut the various items are found. According to Bell, the priest reported that

we found under the bed a large conarie or earthen jar containing an immense number of round balls of earth or clay of various dimensions, large and small, whitened on the outside and fearfully and wonderfully compounded. Some seemed to contain hair and rags and were strongly bound round with twine; others were made with skulls of cats, stuck round with human or dogs' teeth and glass beads, there were also a lot of egg-shells.[29]

The fact that Bell uses Fuller's words almost exactly precludes the possibility that these were two distinct Obeah workers, but Bell does include additional sensational information:

In a little tin canister I found the most valuable of the sorcerer's stock, namely, seven bones belonging to a rattlesnake's tail – these I have known to sell for five dollars each, so highly valued are they as amulets or charms – in the same box was about a yard of rope, no doubt intended to be sold for hangman's cord, which is highly prized by the negroes, the owner of a piece being supposed to be able to defy bad luck.[30]

There is nothing to doubt in his assertion that the hangman's noose was a valued charm among blacks, for it had long been considered so in Europe and the superstition could well have made its way from there to the West Indies,

---

28 Edwards, *History Civil and Commercial*, 164–75.
29 Bell, *Obeah*, 16.
30 Ibid.

though Bell fails to speculate on its origin. Rattlesnakes, however, are not to be found in the Caribbean, but the line would have reminded readers of the association between Obeah and snake worship.

Most writers over the next 150 years agree on the basic implements. The Moravian missionary J.E. Hutton notes that Surinamese Negroes "relied on fetishes and obeahs. These were found in various forms such as a common pearl, a snail's shell, and a tiger's tooth."[31] Revd Banbury explains that "Obeah is made in the simplest way possible. Anything that the obeahman can come at conveniently – pieces of broken bottles, cats' or serpents' teeth, nails and bones, pins and needles, vials, pieces of cloth, etc."[32]

Other writers also take careful note of the ingredients. For example, Madden relates that when he lived "in St Andrews . . . I found a piece of dirty rag tied up like a bag, about the size of a walnut. It contained some dried brown leaves broken into small bits, shreds of red wood rolled up, mixed with hair and some dirt."[33] William Burdett, one of those who helped popularize the legend of Three-Fingered Jack, lists "images in wax, the hearts of birds, livers of mice, and some potent roots, weeds, and bushes, of which Europeans are at this time ignorant".[34] Bessie Pullen Burry, a Fellow of the Royal Anthropological Institute and the Royal Geographic Society, contributes "bottles with turkey or cock's feathers stuck into [them]", "drops of blood" and "coffin nails".[35] Folklorist May Robinson lists several Obeah charms: a "bag containing pieces of horseshoe nails and broken bottles; a packet containing myrrh, grey human hair, bladder, assafoetida, and herb roots; and a doll's head bandaged with black cloth".[36]

A planter who examined one of the vials an Obeah man had hung up around his field to prevent thievery told Bell that he found it to contain "nothing but sea-water, with a little laundry blue in it, and . . . a dead cockroach floating on the top". Bell notes that "they nearly all contain almost exactly the same things, some may have besides the cockroach, a few rusty nails and a bit

---

31 J.E. Hutton, *A History of Moravian Missions* (London: Moravian Publication Office, 1922), 122.
32 Banbury, *Jamaica Superstitions*, 6.
33 Madden, *Twelvemonth's Residence*, 2:72.
34 William Burdett, *The Life and Exploits of Three-finger'd Jack, the Terror of Jamaica*, 5th ed. (London: A. Neil, 1802), 21.
35 Bessie Pullen-Burry, *Jamaica As It Is* (London: T. Fisher Unwin, 1903), 135.
36 May Robinson, "Obeah Worship in East and West Indies", *Folklore* 4 (1893): 207–18.

of red flannel".[37] In the early twentieth century, the American folklorist Martha Warren-Beckwith noted that "the obeah-man uses as a charm the seeds of a certain plant (unidentified) called "jiggey" which are supposed to be given him by "Death" at a dance when "Death is pleased with him".[38]

There is no reason to believe that these lists are not credible, though few writers name their sources. Certainly the accounts of Obeah trials furnish much information about the practice and about the implements used. For example, the Obeah man Andrew Marble was brought before a Jamaican court for having in his possession a bag containing "hog's teeth, broken glass, chalk, fire-coal, dog's teeth, goat's horn, shark bones, soap berries and three or four alligator scales with sundry other Obeah tools".[39]

Brother Tank in Suriname provides a description of Obeah that differs from most reports but is illustrative of the confusion felt by observers about the distinctions between Obeah, voodoo and other practices. He agrees that "when they have anything to ask of their Obeahs, that is, to make a bargain with them for the fulfilment of their wishes, they generally have recourse to some Obeah-man or woman of repute". But from here he veers off into a portrayal of Obeah that characterizes it more as a religion with its own ceremonies and rites rather than as simple witchcraft. The fact that Tank, like several other writers, lumps together the religious and spiritual customs of the slaves under the heading of Obeah, while telling in and of itself, does not, however, mean that to the transplanted Africans they were one and the same.

According to the good brother, believers with requests go to the Obeah practitioners and

> dances and conjurations are engaged in, to induce the spirit to appear. Frequently a long time passes, and nothing is seen; often, too, the spirit is perceived but he goes away again without saying anything; in which case, the dancing, drumming, and shouting are renewed with double vigour. Sometimes this goes on for many days, and the conjurations become more and more vehement, till the spirit or winti makes his appearance, being often, as they say, visible to all present, and then enters into the consulting party, who thereupon, being seized with a sort of ecstasy, pronounces what is to be done. Sometimes they are enjoined to undertake journeys of several weeks' duration, and to perform

---

37 Bell, *Obeah*, 4.
38 Martha Warren Beckwith, *Notes on Jamaican Ethnobotany* (Poughkeepsie, NY: Vassar College, 1927), 10.
39 "Trial for Practising Obeah", *The Times*, 25 August 1824, 3.

new obeahs along with persons named; sometimes to catch this or the other beast and bring it home alive; sometimes, also, to throw the most valuable articles they possess into the river, or suspend them till they rot on branches of trees, and often to give large sums to the Obeah priests, or even to forsake their families and places of abode. Whatever it be, implicit obedience is rendered, "for else", runs the oracle, "I will kill thee." It is, indeed, a bondage under the fear of death. The subject of such a possession afterwards sinks into a state of complete exhaustion on awaking from which, he knows nothing of what has passed. And though they comply most punctually with all that is prescribed, and live in constant anxiety and fear, they often find themselves disappointed in all their expectations.[40]

Most writers on the subject were quite clear that Obeah took place in secret, however, between a practitioner and his or her client, unless the aim was to provide protection during a rebellion, when it became a more public ceremony.

All observers agreed on the extent of the terror Obeah aroused in black people. While the physician and botanist Thomas Dancer acknowledges that dirt eating might be the result of grief or a "discontented mind", he speculates that "Obeah, or the terror of witchcraft", was "a much more frequent cause than any". The very secrecy of dirt-eaters was a cause for suspicion. "Nothing can extort from them a confession which shows they are either under the influence of some horrible superstition or bent on some fell purpose." Dancer suggests that "if [the dirt-eaters] appear to be under the influence of magic or superstition, the Obeah people should be searched for, and brought to punishment, and the bewitched negroes should be christened. This is the best and perhaps the only way of exorcising them."[41]

Whether by dirt eating or by other means, writers were convinced that the mortality rate from Obeah was very high: "The victims of this nefarious art, among negroes in the West Indies, are more numerous than is generally known. No humanity of the master, nor skill in medicine, can relieve a negro, labouring under the influence of OBI", writes Moseley.[42]

---

40 *Periodical Accounts Relating to the Missions of the Church of the United Brethren* (London: Brethren's Society for the Furtherance of the Gospel, 1846), 18:318.

41 Thomas Dancer, *The Medical Assistant; or Jamaica Practice of Physic: Designed Chiefly for the Use of Families and Plantations* (Kingston: Alexander Aikman, 1701), 175–78. That Dancer also recommends a change of master or overseer and a change of residence for the slave affected by dirt eating suggests that, to some extent, he was willing to consider other causes. The symptoms of dirt eating included bloating, retching, shortness of breath and listlessness. If untreated, it could result in death.

42 Moseley, "Medical Observations", 107.

"I have myself known persons who, under the fear, sickened and died, and some who even committed suicide", writes the Moravian missionary J.H. Buchner in 1854. He warns that, along with Myalism, "there is no sin against which a missionary who knows the consequences, should be more watchful to guard his people [than Obeah, or] it might prove the ruin of a congregation".[43]

Throughout the eighteenth and nineteenth centuries (and, indeed, up to the present) observers continued to report on the fear of Obeah, though most were simply recycling the information supplied by Fuller: "The Negroes in general, whether Africans or Creoles [those born in the island], revere, consult, and fear [the Obeah man or woman] . . . they no sooner find Obi set for them near the door of their house, or in the path which leads to it, than they give themselves up for lost."[44] Included in Edwards's *History Civil and Commercial*, the following passage from the Fuller report was plagiarized by Burdett in 1803 and the British traveller Robert Renny in 1807: "Sleep, appetite, and cheerfulness forsake him; his strength decays, his disturbed imagination is haunted without respite, and his features wear the gloom of a settled despondency; dirt or any other unwholesome substance, becomes his only food; he contracts a morbid habit of body, and gradually sinks into the grave."[45] Fuller's report contends that, so strong was the power of Obeah over the minds of blacks, "a very considerable portion of the annual mortality of the Negroes" could be attributed to "this fascinating mischief".[46] This assertion is repeated by almost every other fiction and non-fiction writer commenting on Obeah in the 1800s. For example, Fuller, through Edwards, was very likely the source for Pullen-Burry's sensational claim that "whole plantations have been known to be almost depopulated by this extraordinary superstition".[47]

"A little bag, with a few trumperies and harmless ingredients hung up over a door, was sufficient to break down the health and spirits of the stoutest hearted African", Madden declares. He believed that "the dread of [Obeah] is greatest amongst the Africans. Some of the Creole negroes affect to laugh at it; but when I have seen their courage put to the test when they have been menaced

---

43   J.H. Buchner, *The Moravians in Jamaica: A History of the Mission of the United Brethren's Church to the Negroes in the Island of Jamaica from the Years 1754 to 1854* (London: Longman, Brown, 1854), 138–41.
44   Edwards, *History Civil and Commercial*, 85.
45   Ibid., 86.
46   Ibid., 166–69; Burdett, *Three-Finger'd Jack*, 18–19; Robert Renny, *An History of Jamaica* (London: J. Cawthorn, 1807), 170–71.
47   Pullen-Burry, *Jamaica*, 135–36.

with obeah, or they think it has been set for them, the old superstition takes possession of their fears." Like Fuller and Long, Madden was convinced that "hundreds have died of the mere terror of being under the ban of obeah".[48] Mrs Carmichael came to pretty much the same conclusion: "Slow poison is at times secretly administered, but in by far the greater number of cases, the mind only is affected; the imagination becomes more and more alarmed, – the spirits sink – lassitude and loss of appetite ensure, and death ends the drama."[49] Obeah turns a man into a "good for nothing", Revd Banbury writes, observing that "he may kill himself, steal, commit murder, rape when under an obeah spell".[50]

Renny and Madden, like most who were generally sympathetic to black people, subscribe to the position that Obeah had begun to decline by the early 1800s. "Formerly the influence of obeah practitioners was very great over the negroes", Madden writes in 1835.[51] Renny observes, meanwhile, that the punishment of practitioners had rendered the "destructive art . . . less frequent", though it had failed to eradicate it altogether.[52] The end of the British slave trade in 1807 had seen a drastic reduction in the number of Africans being introduced into the colonies, and this was seen as one of the major reasons for Obeah's decline: "The original Obeahmen were natives of Africa, and their Jamaica-born successors never had the same power or dire influence. That is natural enough."[53] But other writers beg to differ. "The practice of Obeah is too common among negroes, and very fatal to them; I knew of an instance where fifteen people in the course of a few months, died from no other cause", writes Mrs Carmichael. So strong was people's fear of Obeah that Carmichael says it was "in vain to reason with them: "'Miss, I'm obeahed – I know I'll go dead,' is all you can obtain from them."[54]

At opposite ends of the nineteenth century, several writers repeat the words of Fuller's report from the preceding century (as found in Edwards): "The stoutest among them tremble at the very sight of the ragged bundle, the bottle or the egg shells which are stuck in the thatch or hung over the door of a hut or upon the branch of a plantain tree to deter marauders."[55] Burdett lifts the

---

48 Madden, *Twelvemonth's Residence*, 72–74.
49 Carmichael, *Domestic Manners*, 254.
50 Banbury, *Jamaica Superstitions*, 10.
51 Madden, *Twelvemonth's Residence*, 71.
52 Renny, *History of Jamaica*, 172.
53 Ellis, *Diocese of Jamaica*, 220.
54 Carmichael, *Domestic Manners*, 254.
55 Edwards, *History Civil and Commercial*, 167.

passage wholesale, while Bell, Renny and Pullen-Burry make minor amendments. For example, "the bravest among them tremble at the very sight of the ragged bundle, the egg-shells or Obeah bottle stuck in the thatch of a hut, or in the branches of a plantain-tree to deter thieves", writes Bell.[56] And in 1903 Pullen-Burry notes: "In the morning the stoutest-hearted negro gives himself up for lost when he sees the well-known, but much dreaded insignia of the Obeah man upon his door-step or under the thatch of the roof . . . sleep becomes an impossibility, his appetite fails him, his light-heartedness disappears as the every-growing fear possesses his imagination more and more and he generally dies."[57] None provide any attribution for their information, making their declarations statements of bald facts.

The argument went back and forth during the 1800s but the majority of commentators believed Obeah was still very much alive, despite the end of slavery and the efforts of the missionaries. For example, Dr John Davy reports in 1854 that in St Lucia, "as in Grenada, the people of colour and especially the negroes, are said to adhere to their African superstitions and the practice of sorcery – 'Obeah' or 'Kembois' as it is called in St Lucia".[58]

Bell's Roman Catholic priest had no doubt about it:

> This terror of witchcraft is no doubt fostered by the stories handed down to them by their fathers and mothers of what happened in slavery time, when the slaves of an estate would sometimes be decimated by the machinations of an Obeah man, or woman, who, under the name of working Obeah, would simply make away with their victims by the use of poisonous plants only known to Africans, and the effects of which, being unknown to medical science, prevented the crime from being brought home to its author.[59]

The priest himself appeared to believe in magic. According to him, he had been living in a room next to an old woman and a little girl whose room opened into his through what was the only means of entrance or exit. Neighbours told the priest that the old woman was suspected of Obeah, so one night he put a chair against the door to prevent her from leaving. The next morning, when he knocked on the door, he got no answer. When he opened the door, neither

---

56 Burdett, *Three-Finger'd Jack*, 19; Bell, *Obeah*, 9–10; Renny, *History of Jamaica*, 170.
57 Pullen-Burry, *Jamaica*, 135.
58 John Davy, *The West Indies Before and Since Emancipation* (London: W. and F.G. Cash, 1854), 280.
59 Bell, *Obeah*, 20.

the old woman nor the child was in the room and all their heavy mahogany furniture had disappeared. According to the priest, neither the girl nor the woman was seen again.[60]

Witnesses and testimonials to the continuance of Obeah around the Caribbean abounded. "The people here are very superstitious, and what is called 'Obeahism' is very common among them", wrote Magistrate Louis Dyston Powles of Bahamians in 1888.[61] As the nineteenth century drew to a close, Obeah's hold on people was still in evidence, according to many: "At the 1891 Jamaican Exhibition, a collection of Obeah 'equipment' had to be removed because the people were frightened of it." Robinson relates that a figure seized from an Obeah man and decorated with senseh fowl feathers was included in a Mr Thomas's collection at the Exhibition. The figure was displayed under the fanciful title "Amphitrite, the Living Obeah" and proved popular, but exhibition officials decided it was an "undesirable exhibit" and, after the first ten days or so, Thomas was asked to remove it. Robinson suggests that its undesirability probably related to its "malign influence", but it is also possible that its display lent a legitimacy to Obeah that officials were reluctant to countenance.[62]

English readers were told about Obeah through a variety of sources, even those that would have seemed immune to the hysteria. The 1 May 1899 issue of the *Journal of the Royal Colonial Institute*, for instance, carried an article by William Robinson, GCMG, on "Trinidad and Its Capabilities and Prominent Products", in which, after discussing the glories of asphalt, he launches into a discussion of Obeah. "Obeah", he writes,

> is a kind of fetishism introduced from Africa. These self-constituted Obeah priests, whose stock-in-trade consists of an image of wood with a clay head, glass eyes and human hair and teeth, are much dreaded by the common people on account of their assumed mystic powers. . . . There is no doubt that these impostors have a knowledge of poisonous herbs, and it is possible, if not probable, that they occasionally make use of them.

He goes on to add that it took "years to shake [blacks'] faith in it and generations to eradicate it".[63]

---

60   Ibid., 17–19.
61   Louis Diston Powles, *The Land of the Pink Pearl; or Recollections of Life in the Bahamas* (London: Sampson Low, Marston, 1888), 238.
62   Robinson, "Obeah Worship", 212.
63   William Robinson, "Trinidad and Its Capabilities and Prominent Products", *Journal*

"I heard of a respectable young woman who had been so terrified with threats of obeah by a fellow-servant that, seeing a black soldier accidentally taking his place beside her in Church, she straightway went out of her mind, and continues a maniac to this day", writes Grenville John Chester, a member of the Royal Archaeological Institute, adding that "not long since a person near Bridgetown [Barbados] found a neat little coffin placed at his door, which being opened, was discovered to contain the body of a skinned cat, a hint which filled him with the liveliest apprehensions".[64]

"'I put obeah 'pon you!' – that is the worst threat that can be made to a West Indian negro", C.B. assured readers of the *Manchester Guardian* in 1907, explaining that

> It may be done in a thousand ways. Once when I walked into the house of a planter friend of mine in Jamaica I called his attention to a rusty knife hanging by a string in the doorway. 'They are putting obeah on me again', he laughed. 'I must have offended one of the servants.' Perhaps when you go to bed you may find a queer assortment of articles on your pillow – a dried lizard, some chicken bones, a couple of sen-seh feathers from the white cock, and a little bottle of evil-smelling liquid from a neighbouring swamp. That is obeah. You may find something similar when you open your cigar box – or even – as I did once – in the pocket of a dress coat.[65]

Certainly the anonymous writer in the *Pall Mall Gazette* of 21 July 1896 had no doubt about the malevolence of Obeah:

> In Jamaica, Hayti, and other parts of the West Indies, there exists among the coloured population a singular survival of savage practices learned in Africa in the days antecedent to the enforced migration. It is commonly referred to as a form of religious worship, and one of its manifestations is undoubtedly in this direction. Obeah rites and orgies are a thing sufficiently notorious, to dwellers in Hayti, for instance – to the whites by repute (for few have been permitted to witness them), and to the blacks by participation. But Obeahism, pure and simple is a desire for revenge, and in practice affords a means of attaining it.[66]

Not all writers were as willing to believe in the magical malevolence of

---

of the Royal Colonial Institute 10, no. 5 (1899), 408.

64   Greville John Chester, *Transatlantic Sketches in the West Indies* (London: Smith, Elder and Co., 1869) 82 – 83.

65   C.B., "Obeah and Vaudoux".

66   "The Obeah Man", *Pall Mall Gazette*, 21 July 1896.

Obeah. William Pringle Livingstone, for example, discounts the idea of any mystique around Obeah men: "Obeahism runs like a black thread of mischief through the known history of the race. It is the result of two conditions, an ignorant and superstitious receptivity on the one hand, and on the other, sufficient intelligence and cunning to take advantage of this quality." Or, to make the matter plain, "the Obeahman is any negro who gauges the situation and makes it his business to work on the fears of his fellows. He claims the possession of occult authority, and professes to have the power of taking or saving life, of causing or curing disease, of bringing ruin or creating prosperity, of discovering evil-doers or vindicating the innocent."[67] The writer in the *Pall Mall Gazette* comes to the same conclusion:

> The Obeah man is always rather smarter than his companions. He is bright enough to see an easy way to provide himself with a few luxuries, and he must be able to make his comrades believe in him. The Obeah man is in no sense a priest or spiritual guide. He is a compounder of poisons, and at this he is ordinarily only too skillful. He has no temple, and pretends to no sacred rites beyond a few simple incantations which he adds for effect. He works as much as any of his companions, either on his own little place or on the neighbouring estate, and he does not often even pretend to have inherited powers from an ancestor. He picks up the trade, and in a small way makes it profitable. It is an easy matter for any ordinarily bright negro to establish a local reputation as an Obeah man. He provides himself with some of the stock belongings of an Obeah man – three white rooster heads among the first – and drops a sly hint here and there. One of his neighbours has injured him, perhaps, and the neighbour's chickens suddenly die, or his donkey falls seriously ill. A little home-made poison does it, and if he is smart there is no danger of his being caught. His companions begin to regard him with awe and to fear him. From that moment he is a recognized Obeah man.[68]

For some religious writers such as Revd Ellis, writing more than a decade after Livingstone, Obeah was not just a cynical money-making ploy; it was a supremely, if not diabolically, evil practice,

> a strange compound – a sorcery which played on and took advantage of the nerves of a nervous and superstitious people; a knowledge of the healing power of certain leaves and certain roots and of the bark of trees, together with an

---

67 William Pringle Livingstone, *Black Jamaica: A Study in Evolution* (London: Sampson, Low, Marston, 1899), 19–22.
68 "Obeah Man", *Pall Mall Gazette*.

equal knowledge of the baneful and poisonous power of other vegetable substances; a claim to possess some mysterious power, sometimes to detect, sometimes to prevent crime, sometimes to kill, sometimes to concoct a harmless and sentimental love-philtre. . . . The exercise of the art was accompanied by a ritual at once debasing and indescribable and terrifying and, as it now seems, foolish and unmeaning. Often too, it worked in secret and then it was most harmful. Anyone who wants to know what unrestrained Obeahism might have developed into should read Hesketh Pritchard's "Where Black Rules White".[69]

Wanting to give the hard-working missionaries credit for eliminating it, he ends on a triumphant note: "But the point is that in Jamaica it has been restrained."[70] As a churchman, he could hardly have come to any other conclusion.

Meanwhile, Joseph Hutton, the Moravian missionary, notes that in the Netherlands Antilles sorcerers commanded influence in several ways:

> In each of these four departments, the Sorcerer exercised his influence. By means of his intimate knowledge of poisons he not only committed himself, but also enabled others to wreak revenge; by means of his acquaintance with wintis – obtained during a hypnotic trance – he became the only spiritual guide; by means of his powers as an Obeahman he was able to manufacture gods, sold those gods in thousands at fabulous prices, and thus became a financial magnate; and by means of his knowledge of the future, he, like prophets, in many other countries, controlled the policy of the State.[71]

In 1934 Joseph Williams claimed to have observed that "men and women literally pine away from fear of obeah which they have heard is being worked against them, and frequently death has resulted when there was no indication whatever of poisoning". He goes on to say that he had "personally come in contact with such cases and have felt convinced that death was due entirely to the state of nervous fear that haunted the victims day and night, depriving them of all nourishment and repose until they actually wasted away, and died of exhaustion". He assures his readers that "the great mass of the populace, whatever their protestations to the contrary may be, live in veritable dread of some nefarious influence of the obeah-man whose enmity must be avoided at any cost".[72]

---

69 Ellis, *Diocese of Jamaica*, 219.
70 Ibid.
71 Hutton, *Moravian Missions*, 123.
72 Joseph J. Williams, *Psychic Phenomena of Jamaica* (New York: Dial Press, 1934), 105.

"UNERRING PROPHETS"

"The late Discoveries and Navigations made into the West Indies, can furnish us with abundant testimonies hereof, in which the minds of the inhabitants are both terrified and their bodies massacred by [the Devil's] visible sight, and cruel tortures; yet (which is the opinion of many learned) he cannot so perfectly represent the fashion of a man's body, but that there is some sensible deformity, by which he betrays himself", writes Alexander Roberts in his 1620 *Treatise of Witchcraft*.[73] In other words, the Devil cannot hide. It was a popular view, as Roberts suggests. Matthew Hopkins, the English Witchfinder General, also subscribed to it, pointing out that, for example, witches could be known by their dry skin, as their blood was sucked by their familiars.[74]

If Europeans believed that those who worshipped the Devil could be identified by their appearance alone, it was no great logical leap for them to declare that the Obeah man or woman could easily be distinguished from his fellow slaves. Moseley contends that the "most deformed Obian magicians are the most venerated", and that those who were handicapped in some way often became exiles from slave society, managing to survive though "becoming also hideously white in their woolly hair and skin. . . . Thus these ugly, loathsome creatures are oracles of woods, caves, and unfrequented places, and are resorted to secretly by the wretched in mind, and by the malicious for wicked purposes."[75] To give further weight to this thesis, Moseley adds that veneration of the deformed was something also noticed among the Egyptians and Chaldeans. And as the Obeah man "grew more mis-shapen, [he] generally became more subtle; . . . as if Nature disliked people being both cunning and strong". Moseley points out, however, that "poverty, ugliness, wrinkles, palsied head and trembling limbs" had been enough to raise suspicions of obi in England not very long before, and that "many old women have been tried, condemned and hanged, as perpetrators of every untoward accident in their neighbourhood".[76]

The conviction that Obeah men and women did not look like other blacks was particularly beloved of chapbook writers and novelists. "Those whose hoary heads, and a somewhat peculiarly harsh and forbidding aspect, together

---

73 Alexander Roberts, *A Treatise of Witchcraft* (1620), Project Gutenberg, http://www.gutenberg.org/files/17209/17209-h/17209-h.htm.

74 Matthew Hopkins, "Discovery of Witches" (1647), Project Gutenberg, http://www.gutenberg.org/files/14015/14015-h/14015-h.htm.

75 Moseley, *Obi*, 4.

76 Moseley, "Medical Observations", 105–7.

with some skill in plants of the medicinal and poisonous species, have qualified them for impositions on the weak and credulous, usually attract the greatest devotion and confidence", Burdett writes, paraphrasing the Fuller report as found in Edwards.[77] Bell was so taken with the description that he quotes it word for word.[78] In "The Obeah Woman", a story which appeared first in the August 1832 issue of *The Metropolitan* and then in the 12 January issue of the *Oriental Observer*, the Obeah woman was old and looked like "one of the most miserable and disgusting objects that could be imagined. Her face was shriveled up like a Norfolk biffin, her thin hair as white as snow, her eyes nearly closed with a running sore, her mouth toothless, her frame bone and skin, her hands withered and her body trembling."[79]

The popular weekly periodical *John Bull* excerpted an account of an Obeah trial in which the Obeah man, William Waite, was described as a "terrible personage". Waite was "coal black, of the ordinary size, with a few red spots on his cheeks and forehead, about 70 years of age, with four protuberances on the back of his head, which would defy Spurzheim to phrenologise, a tuft of white wool on the crown of his head, surrounded by an irregular circle of black; eyes yellow, nose extremely flat, and legs that bore the form of anchors' bows".[80] In 1856 the novelist Theodora Elizabeth Lynch assured readers that "the more terrible the appearance of the Obeah man, the more power [he] can exert over his victims. If his face be deeply furrowed with the harshest lines of age, if his beard be matted and grizzled; his gait loitering and his figure deformed; so much the better for his purpose." According to her, Obeah men also affected a "husky and croaking voice", the better to win over the credulous. The "shriveled old man is viewed as the unerring prophet; and the implicit belief in his pretended communion with demons is apparent in the horror-stricken countenances of those around him".[81]

Pullen-Burry makes the point that "the Obeah man, as I have heard him described, is generally a most forbidding looking person, craftiness and cunning being stamped on his features".[82] "There is something indescribably sin-

---

77 Burdett, *Three-finger'd Jack*, 18; Edwards, *History Civil and Commercial*, 166.
78 Bell, *Obeah*, 9.
79 "The Obeah Woman", *Oriental Observer*, 12 January 1833, 13.
80 *John Bull*, 11 November 1843, 711. Johann Spurzheim was a German physician and the leading advocate of the now discredited science of phrenology.
81 Theodora Lynch [Mrs Henry Lynch], *The Wonders of the West Indies* (London: Seeley, Jackson and Halliday, 1856), 161.
82 Pullen-Burry, *Jamaica*, 135.

ister about the appearance of an obeah-man, which is readily observed by persons who have mixed much with the negroes", writes Charles Rampini, who served as a district judge in Jamaica: "With a dirty handkerchief bound tightly round his forehead, and his small, bright, cunning eyes peering out from underneath it."[83] Besides being ugly, the Obeah man might also be mad. "The Africans, like all other people who profess the Mahometan faith, have an opinion that insanity and supernatural inspiration are frequently combined, and consequently, knaves and lunatics are commonly the persons who play the parts of sorcerers." For the most part, however, Madden dismisses Obeah workers as "generally . . . old women whose wrinkles are their chief titles to the character of wise women".[84]

However, most writers believed the higher percentage of Obeah practitioners were men. Gardner, for example, does not appear to believe that Obeah women were in the majority, writing that "women, *occasionally* practiced, in which case age and ugliness were great recommendations".[85] But leaving aside questions of gender, if a black man or woman looked different or was somehow disabled or deformed, then, according to European observers, the chances were he or she was an Obeah practitioner. "The Africans carried most of their superstitions to our colonies, and, amongst others, their reverence for those whose physical or mental peculiarities distinguished them from the multitude: and such were the persons, who, in advanced age, usually took on themselves the obeah character."[86]

It was a popular belief. According to Revd Banbury, "You may easily distinguish [the Obeah man] by his sinister look, and slouching gait. . . . [He] seldom looks any one in the face. He never goes without a *banera*, wallet or bag in which he carries his 'things'. Generally he is a dirty looking fellow with a sore foot." Banbury only grudgingly admits that "some few have been known to be decent in their appearance, and well clad".[87]

The medieval idea that one could indeed "find the mind's construction in the face" persisted for a long time. Quaker abolitionists Joseph Sturge and Thomas Harvey insist that "it is not difficult to tell, by a negro's countenance,

---

83 Charles Rampini, *Letters from Jamaica: The Land of Streams and Woods* (Edinburgh: Edmonston and Douglas, 1873), 133. Rampini first published this book anonymously, perhaps out of deference to Jamaican society.
84 Madden, *Twelvemonth's Residence*, 2:76.
85 Gardner, *History of Jamaica*, 187 (emphasis added).
86 Madden, *Twelvemonth's Residence*, 2:74–76.
87 Banbury, *Jamaica Superstitions*, 7.

whether he is in Christian communion".[88] About half a century later, a planter conceded that "in these days, an Obeah man would be hard to distinguish from other blacks, and might only be known by wearing his hair long, or some other peculiarity".[89] Robinson appears to believe that one could identify an Obeah man because "he usually has a 'wall eye', or a 'sore foot', or some deformity, and is miserably poor, to outward appearance; and his fee is small, but he does a good trade".[90] In 1907, readers of the *Manchester Guardian* were assured that "the obeah man can always be easily recognized by one who has had much to do with negroes. He has an indescribably sinister appearance. He is unwashed, ragged, often half-mad, usually diseased, and almost always has an ulcerated leg. This last, indeed, is a badge of the tribe. Often he is a very old negro who knew 'slavery days' and more than half believes in his magical pretensions." But, the author continues – and it was a very big *but* – he was also aware that "not all are of this disreputable type. I knew one – the pontiff of the cult in Jamaica – who had himself elected a member of the City Council of Kingston, and successfully defied all the efforts of the police to catch him red-handed. Another, a mulatto, was a prosperous merchant in a country town, a deacon of his church, and the chairman of the Parochial Board."[91]

In fact, the claim that observers could distinguish Obeah men by their looks continued almost into the middle of the twentieth century: "Pretenders to expertness in Obeah affect a disregard for cleanliness and hygiene, at strange variance with the Jamaican's characteristic love of bathing and neatness. If not actually disfigured, then, the Obeah man usually presents a disgusting and filthy appearance especially while actually making Obeah", Williams maintains. He asserts confidently that "in the days of slavery, the expert in Obeah was frequently distinguished by being physically or mentally defective or abnormal".[92]

A few writers mention that Obeah men carried sticks. One of the earliest references asserts that "Negroe – conjurers, or Obia-men, as they are called, carry about them a staff, which is marked with frogs and snakes. The blacks imagine that its blow, if not mortal, will at least occasion long and trouble-

---

88   Joseph Sturge and Thomas Harvey, *The West Indies in 1837* (London: Hamilton, Adams, 1838), 37.
89   Bell, *Obeah*, 9.
90   Robinson, "Obeah Worship", 211.
91   C.B., "Obeah and Vaudoux".
92   Williams, *Voodoos*, 217.

some disorders."[93] Rampini makes the same observation: "As an outward and visible sign of his power, the obeah-man sometimes carries about with him a long staff or wand, with twisted serpents, or the rude likeness of a human head carved round the handle."[94] This assertion that Obeah men and women carried around an outward and highly visible sign of their involvement in an illegal practice bears some examination, as their much-vaunted secrecy would seem to have precluded the custom.

The authors of the Fuller report appear to discount the likelihood of being able to tell an Obeah woman by how she looked: "It is very difficult for the white proprietor to distinguish the Obeah professor from any other negro on his plantation."[95] Though they paid close attention to everything else in the Fuller report, most writers ignore that particular claim.

All agree on Obeah's association with Africans direct from Africa:

> As far as we are able to decide from our own experience and information when we lived in the island and from the current testimony of all the negroes we have ever conversed with on the subject, the professors of Obi are and always were natives of Africa and none other and they have brought the science with them from thence to Jamaica where it is so universally practised that we believe there are few of the large estates possessing native Africans which have not one or more of them.[96]

This was a common theme, particularly popular among abolitionists and missionaries anxious to prove that blacks could indeed improve and advance in civilization. Buchner subscribes to that view: "The common superstition of the Negro is the belief in Obeah or sorcery; some persons, mostly old Africans were always found, who pretended to be adepts in the mysteries and who were largely paid for practicing Obeah."[97] W.J. Gardner, an English missionary who arrived in Jamaica in 1849 and published his history of that island in 1873, says as much. "The professors of this are or were almost exclusively native African", he writes, adding "where Obeah was practiced, it was more secretly than before, and creole pretenders were never supposed to have the same powers as

---

93 James Grainger, "The Sugar Cane", in Hutson, *Treatment*, 71. The explanation comes in William Wright's footnote to the article, originally published in 1764 and footnoted by Wright in 1802.
94 Rampini, *Letters*, 132.
95 Edwards, *History Civil and Commercial*, 167.
96 Ibid., 166.
97 Buchner, *Moravians*, 138.

their African predecessors".[98] Robinson notes that one class of "professional Obeah-men" was "the grossly ignorant, generally an African by birth or parentage, who firmly believes in the art he professes".[99]

This association with Africa and being African-born influenced the way in which Obeah men and women were viewed by whites and the mythology that arose around them. As we will see in future chapters, writers usually depict Obeah men and women as very dark-skinned, while blacks with whom readers are expected to sympathize are often mulattoes or brown-skinned. For example, Mary Princess, the Obeah man's victim in W.R. Trowbridge's *Gossip of the Caribbees*, is "young, tall and comely. One of her progenitors had had enough white blood in him to relieve her complexion from that of a pure blooded African, and to redeem her features from coarseness."[100]

"PROFESSORS OF OBI"

Most slaves left no record of their lives, and Obeah men and women left none at all, but we can catch real-life glimpses of them in the writings of others. One of the earliest accounts of an Obeah man comes from the work of Père Jean-Baptiste Labat, the French missionary, who arrived in the Caribbean in 1694 and left in 1706. Labat relates how, during his 1701 trip to St Thomas, the managing director of the Brandenburg Company, Monsieur van Belle, told him of an experience with an Obeah man.

According to van Belle, the Obeah man, a slave, was convicted of sorcery for having made an earthen figure speak. On his way to his execution, he passed van Belle, who told him, "You will never make your little figure speak again. They have broken it." The Obeah man responded that it made no difference to him and that he could make van Belle's walking stick speak if he wanted to. The sceptical van Belle then requested the judge to grant the Obeah man a stay of execution so he could put him to the test. The judge granted his request and van Belle handed the Obeah man his stick. The Obeah man planted it in the ground and performed some sort of ceremony before asking Van Belle what he wanted to know from the stick. Van Belle enquired about the status of his ship. The Obeah man repeated his incantations, then retreated and asked van Belle

---

98 Gardner, *History of Jamaica*, 187, 392.
99 Robinson, "Obeah Worship", 211.
100 Trowbridge, *Gossip*, 65.

to approach the stick. When he got closer, a little voice issued from the stick and gave him precise details about the ship, its captain, its whereabouts and its date of arrival. When van Belle had heard all he wanted, the Obeah man was executed. Van Belle told Labat that three days later his ship arrived in the harbour just as the stick had predicted, and everything it had said was true.[101]

Labat was a member of the Dominican order, which was responsible for most of Europe's witch hunts, so it is no surprise that he greeted these stories with less scepticism than many of his English contemporaries. Labat's *Memoirs* were published in 1722 in France, but, though an English translation was not available until 1931, most members of England's educated class were able to read and speak French and would have been aware of his writings. Indeed, the Fuller report mentions Labat and the cases of witchcraft or Obeah that he reported on.

One Obeah man who gained international fame was a Surinamese slave by the name of Quassie, who learned the medicinal purposes of the plant that now bears his name from the Amerindians. The secret of its use to reduce fevers was purchased from him "for a considerable sum" by a student of the botanist and physician Carl Linnaeus, who took it back to Europe with him in 1756. Five years later, in 1761, Carl Gustav Dahlberg, a Swedish planter, gave Linnaeus a specimen of the tree, apparently hoping it would be named after him. According to Schiebinger, he was appalled when it was named after Quassie instead.[102] Hoogbergen informs us that Quassie was born on the Guinea Coast in 1690 and was captured and transported to Suriname while still a child. There he later became a *lukuman* or *loekomen* (a sorcerer considered able to see into the future) who put his services at the disposal of the whites in detecting and capturing those who practised the *wisi*, or black magic, that so distressed Joseph Hutton. Quassie was so successful at this and so esteemed by the whites that in 1730 the Court of Policy awarded him a golden plaque inscribed "Quassie, loyal to the whites".[103]

Another account of a real-life Obeah man comes from Matthew "Monk" Lewis, an English novelist, poet and playwright who inherited two large plantations from his father and visited them in 1815–16 and again in 1817. A keen observer of his social environment as well as a man deeply interested in the

---

101   Paiewonsky, *Eyewitness Accounts*, 137.

102   Londa Schiebinger, *Plants and Empire: Colonial Prospecting in the Atlantic World* (Cambridge, MA: Harvard University Press, 2007), 213.

103   Wim S.M. Hoogbergen, *The Boni Wars in Suriname* (Leiden: Brill Academic, 1997), 37.

supernatural,[104] he gives a fairly detailed account of an Obeah man by the name of Adam, in his *Journal of a West India Proprietor*, published in 1834:

> [He] has long been the terror of my whole estate. He was accused of being an Obeah-man; and persons notorious for the practice of Obeah, and who were afterwards convicted and transported had been found concealed at his house. He was strongly suspected of having poisoned more than twelve negroes, men and women, and, having been displaced by my former trustee from being principal governor, in revenge he put poison into his water jar. Luckily, he was observed by one of the house servants [and] put in the stocks for a long time.

During his first visit, Lewis had learned that Adam had tried to poison his former attorney but had been discovered by another slave, Bessie. Adam had cursed her, saying she would "never be hearty again; and from that very time, her complaint [leprosy] had declared itself; and her poor pickaninies had all died away one after another". In reaction to Bessie's story, Lewis lets loose a bombastic tirade about God not suffering a "low, wicked fellow like Adam" to cause the death of good people or innocent children, but later he acknowledges his fear of Adam, whom he describes as "a most dangerous fellow . . . clever and plausible" and the extent of his mischief "incalculable". Lewis laments that he could not sell him, since nobody would buy him, and neither could he give him away, since nobody would accept such a "dangerous present". He even toyed with the idea of encouraging Adam to run away but realized that "the law would seize him and bring him back to me", and that he himself would be made to bear the expense of his capture and of any time Adam might be forced to spend in the workhouse as a punishment. Matters resolved themselves near the end of Lewis's first stay when Adam appeared to turn over a new leaf; he was christened on the eve of Lewis's departure from the island.[105]

It is possible that Adam converted only in order to regain the position of slave driver, which he had lost because of Bessie's accusation. At any rate, when Lewis returned to Jamaica in 1817, Adam let it be known that he had every intention of being reinstated. He is reported to have said on many different occasions that

---

104   In her introduction to the 1999 Oxford World Classics edition of Lewis's *Journal*, Judith Terry notes that in his first novel, *The Monk*, published in 1796, he "piled horror upon horror with cheerful exuberance: a sexually rapacious abbot, a cross-dressing female demon, dank dungeons, ghosts . . . murder and sorcery" all made an appearance. Matthew "Monk" Lewis, *Journal of a West India Proprietor, Kept During a Residence in the Island of Jamaica* (London: John Murray, 1834; repr., Oxford: Oxford University Press, 1999), ix.

105   Lewis, *Journal*, 137–48.

he fully expected Lewis to give him his old position back. His conversion had convinced no one that he deserved the post, so Adam resorted to his old tricks.

> Two of the cooks declared that he had severally directed them to dress Sully's food apart, and had given them powders to mix with it. The first to whom he applied refused positively; the second he treated with liquor, and when she had drunk he gave her the poison, with instructions how to use it: being a timid creature, she did not dare to object, so threw away the powder privately and pretended that it had been administered: but, finding no effect produced by it, Adam gave her a second powder, at the same time bidding her remember the liquor which she had swallowed, and which he assured her would effect her own destruction, through the force of Obeah, unless she prevented it by sacrificing his enemy in her stead. The poor creature still threw away the powder, but the strength of imagination brought upon her a serious malady, and it was not till after several weeks that she recovered from the effects of her fears. . . .
>
> However, on searching Adam's house, a musket, with a plentiful accompaniment of powder and ball was found concealed, as also a considerable quantity of materials for the practice of Obeah: the possession of either of the above articles (if the musket is without the consent of the proprietor) authorizes the magistrate to pronounce a sentence of transportation. In consequence of this discovery, Adam was immediately committed to gaol; a slave court was summoned, and today a sentence of transportation [possibly to Cuba] was pronounced after a trial of three hours.[106]

Among the items discovered in Adam's hut was a "string of beads of various sizes, shapes and colours, arranged in a form peculiar to the performance of the Obeah-man in the Myal-dance". The purpose of the beads was so well-known that Adam did not even try to deny they were used for Obeah; instead, he explained that they were not his but had belonged to another man who, Lewis says, was recently transported, presumably for the crime of Obeah. Defiant to the end, after hearing he had been found guilty, he snapped, "Well! I can't help it!" and walked "coolly" out of court. Interestingly, Lewis goes against the grain to describe Adam as "a fine-looking man, between thirty and forty, square built and of great bodily strength . . . his countenance equally expresses his intelligence and malignity". Adam was also a creole, not an African.[107]

Another of Lewis's Cornwall slaves, Edward, may or may not have been an Obeah man. Edward and another slave, Pickle, were great friends until they

---

106 Ibid., 164–68.
107 Ibid., 168.

had both decided to press their suit on the same woman. Pickle secured the woman's hand, but his amity with Edward was restored only when Edward married her sister. Some time after that, Pickle's hut was broken into and he was robbed. Pickle fell sick and, during his time in the sick-house, came to the conclusion that Edward was the thief and that he had, moreover, Obeahed him; so while he was recovering from his initial complaint, he became convinced that he would soon die.

Pickle claimed that before his sickness Edward had volunteered to set Obeah to catch the thief. Edward had "gone at midnight into the bush [and] had gathered the plant whangra, which he had boiled in an iron pot, by a fire of leaves, over which he went puff, puffie". Edward had

> said the sautee-sautee [over the pot]; and then had cut the whangra root into four pieces, three to bury at the plantation gates, and one to burn; and to each of these three pieces he gave the name of a Christian, one of which was Daniel; and Edward had said that this would help him to find his goods; but instead of that, [Pickle] had immediately felt this pain in his side, and therefore he was sure that, instead of using Obeah to find his goods, Edward had used it to kill him.

Pickle was also convinced that Edward had Obeahed his marriage, which was not, apparently, a happy one. Lewis finds this latter charge most amusing, and he gives short shrift to Pickle's accusations. The fact that Edward had helped to detect and corner an Obeah priest who was "harboured in one of my negro huts last year" (probably the same man caught in Adam's hut) indisposed Lewis to consider that Edward could be an Obeah man himself. The other slaves agreed and ridiculed poor Pickle, who returned to the sick-house, unwilling to give up his suspicions.[108]

Pickle may have been wrong, but Edward's assistance in collaring an Obeah man was hardly proof against his being one himself. His alacrity in the matter may have owed more to his desire to see off a rival than anything else; after all, Obeah was a fairly lucrative undertaking and, by the time of Monk's visits, punishable only by transportation, not death. (Several writers make the claim that the Obeah man "is a professional man that is as well paid as the lawyer or doctor and sometimes better".[109])

Lewis also mentions a runaway Negro by the name of Plato; in 1780 he led a gang of robbers who kept the parish of Westmoreland "in a perpetual state of

---

108   Ibid., 85.
109   Banbury, *Jamaica Superstitions*, 7.

alarm". According to Lewis, "Every endeavour to seize this desperado was long in vain: a large reward was put upon his head, but no negro dared approach him; for, besides his acknowledged courage, he was a professor of Obi and had threatened that whoever dare to lay a finger upon him should suffer spiritual torments, as well as be physically shot through the head."[110] Quite the opposite of the decrepit Obeah man of popular description, Plato was described as not only tall and athletic but attractive enough that several female slaves ran away to join him.

Plato was also an alcoholic, however, and that proved his downfall. A visit to a friend's hut near the Canaan estate, where he drank himself into an alcoholic stupor, resulted in his capture. He was taken to Montego Bay and sentenced to death. Ever defiant, Plato told the magistrates that his death would be revenged by a storm that would wreak havoc on the island that same year. As he was being bound to the stake, he assured his black gaoler that he had put Obeah on him and he would soon die. Lewis records that

> strangely enough, before the year was over, the most violent storm took place ever known in Jamaica; and as to the gaoler, his imagination was so forcibly struck by the threats of the dying man, that, although every care was taken of him, the power of medicine exhausted, and even a voyage to America undertaken, in hopes that a change of scene might change the course of his ideas, still, from the moment of Plato's death, he gradually pined and withered away, and finally expired before the completion of the twelvemonth.[111]

In October 1780, a hurricane destroyed the port town of Savanna La Mar before moving on to Cuba, where it resulted in more than 1,115 deaths.

A few years after Lewis's last visit, pro-slavery advocate Cynric Williams recorded the story of Cato, a runaway from the estate of a Mr Brissett in Hanover. According to Diana, the black girl who told Cynric the story, Cato was feared as an Obeah man by his fellow blacks: "The negroes imagined [that he] possessed some magic superiority by means of obeah, which protected him from wounds, and so prepared him against surprise, that he could never be taken prisoner except, indeed, it were by a white man." Whites, by virtue of their Christianity, were supposed to possess a stronger Obeah, in the same way that, as we saw in the previous chapter, some Africans concluded that the god of the whites was stronger than theirs. Given that the blacks were afraid to go

---

110 Lewis, *Journal*, 91.
111 Ibid., 61.

after Cato and no white showed an inclination to do it, the next best thing was to send a "proxy white" – that is, a baptized black.

A slave by the name of Plato was promised his freedom if he would go, but, though he possessed "great strength and courage", he was hampered "by the apprehension of Cato's obeah; to overcome which it was necessary to find some counter charm, or an equivalent obeah. This the ingenuity of his white master easily communicated to him by Christian baptism." Plato was able to track Cato and found him in the woods. Cato, realizing he was discovered, "held up the amulet suspended from his neck (a bag containing among other things bones, teeth, and hair) cried aloud 'While I wear this, Plato, no one can take me.' 'And I,' returned the other, 'have also an *ahpetti*, a charm, a better charm – I wear the white man's spell.'" Plato subdued Cato and took him in. The runaway was brought to trial and sentenced to execution. Moments before his execution on the scaffold, Cato cursed Plato and told him he would die before the moon rose again. That same night, Plato was woken by a nightmare; he relived the fight with Cato, remembered the curse, screamed out, "Cato, I remember", and died.[112]

This story is so similar to Lewis's that, even leaving aside how often slaves shared the same name and the fact that one is reported as having been burnt at the stake while the other was hung, it is very likely that Williams's Cato is, in fact, the same as Lewis's Plato. By the time of Williams's book, the events of 1780 were already more than forty years in the past, and Diana, described as a young woman, was repeating a story she had heard, not lived through. That the details were confused and, perhaps, embellished is understandable.

Theodora Lynch also weighs in on the story of Plato, including it in *The Wonders of the West Indies*:

> During the last century there was another man who rose to some celebrity as an Obeah chief. A runaway slave named Plato established himself in the heart of the Jamaican mountains, and soon had a lawless and wild banditti at his command. Robbery and murder lengthened the catalogue of their crimes. . . . Any negro who ventured to hint at the place of [Plato's] retreat . . . became tortured with dreams, and in every shadow fancied he discovered the dark presence of the evil one; he never doubted that this Obeah chief, learning by intuition the revelation he had made, set Obi for him . . . Plato threatened that

---

112   [Cynric Williams], *A Tour Through the Island of Jamaica from the Western to the Eastern End in the Year 1823* (London: Thomas Hurst, Edward Chance, 1827), 141–49.

whoever put a hand on him should not only suffer physically, but should endure spiritual torments, and that there would be the fearful precursors of insanity.[113]

Like Lewis, Lynch records that Plato drank himself into a stupor and was thus captured, put on trial and convicted of more than one murder. In the Montego Bay courthouse, Plato

> told the magistrates and it is affirmed that his skin grew supernaturally black as he spoke, that God would avenge his death by a terrible storm, which that very year would shake the island to its foundations, and cause the waters surrounding it to rush in as a destroying flood upon the land: and . . . in that very year, 1780, a fearful hurricane devastated Jamaica, and . . . the sea passing its usual boundaries, rolled in and deluged the land.

Plato also told his black executioner that he would "meet his retribution by death before the expiration of the year. The unfortunate young man became careworn and emaciated and medical skill could do nothing for the fear which was gnawing at his heart. He was sent to America in the hope that a change of air might revive him: no expense was spared, but all was in vain . . . he pined away, and, before the year was over, died." Lynch, who earlier speaks about the decrepitude of Obeah men, describes Plato as "a handsome, athletic man".[114] Though her story clearly owes much to Lewis, Lynch never cites her source.

A few other writers, such as Charles Kingsley, who visited the Caribbean in the late 1800s, also relate stories about Obeah practitioners. In one such, Kingsley tells us about Madame Phyllis in Trinidad, who "like Deborah of old, sat under her own palm-tree, and judged her little Israel – by the Devil's law instead of God's. Her murders (or supposed murders) were notorious: but no evidence could be obtained; Madame Phyllis dealt in poisons, charms, and philters; and waxed fat on her trade for many a year." Like most of her colleagues were said to do, Madame Phyllis lived in the forest. When the government conceived a plan to construct a road near her house, she made her objections known to the workmen, who immediately downed their tools in fear. The chief official, a white man, arrived onsite and was informed of her opposition. He remained obdurate and would not back down, despite all her arguments. One can imagine his suspicion when her next move was to offer him a drink.

---

113 Lynch, *Wonders*, 168–71.
114 Ibid.

According to Kingsley, "Madame, finding that the Government official considered himself Obeah-proof, tried to bribe him off, with the foolish cunning of a savage, with a present of bottled beer." He drank it in the presence of the workmen, who all expected him to either drop down dead or swell up. When nothing happened, he ordered the men back to work. Amazed that he was still alive and in good health, the workmen resumed work; they never knew that he had surreptitiously examined the bottle to make sure it had not been tampered with. After that incident, a trap was laid for Madame Phyllis and she was arrested for selling a love potion to a policeman. She went to prison upon conviction, and when her neighbours realized that her Obeah had not protected her from the law, they levelled her house to the ground. According to Kingsley, they were looking for the bones of an Obeah man who had challenged Madame Phyllis to a test of skills; he had gone to her house one night and was never seen again.[115]

A story with more macabre detail was repeated to Kingsley by Trinidad's chief of police, who heard it from a coloured stipendiary magistrate. Kingsley calls the Obeah man of this third-hand story "Martin", but says that was not his real name. Martin lived and worked on an estate owned by a relative of the stipendiary magistrate, who was a boy of seventeen when the story took place. The youth caught Martin stealing sugar and they had a confrontation which would have turned physical had Martin not slipped on the ground and hit his head. Martin suspected that the overseer, Jean Marie, had revealed the theft to the boy and became hostile to him.

Some time later, the Negroes planned a "jumby dance" and the boy persuaded Jean Marie to go with him, since he wanted to see it. The stipendiary magistrate related that at the hut "we found assembled some thirty Africans, men and women, very scantily dressed, and with necklaces of beads, shark's teeth, dried frogs, etc., hung around their necks". Martin himself was "almost naked and with his body painted to represent a skeleton". He was officiating and was also the drummer. "In the centre [of the hut] was a Fetish, somewhat of the appearance of a man, but with the head of a cock. Everything that the coarsest fancy could invent had been done to make this image horrible; and yet it appeared to be the object of special adoration to the devotees assembled." Martin began to beat the drum while singing a song in what appeared to be an African language. First, a woman danced around the Fetish. The drumbeat got

---

115   Charles Kingsley, *At Last: A Christmas in the West Indies* (London: Macmillan, 1871), 138–40.

quicker and quicker. A man joined the woman and the drumbeat quickened even more until other couples were dancing on the floor. We are told that then "the true sorcerer's Sabbath" began.

The boy watched from the sidelines while Jean Marie climbed up onto one of the hut's crossbeams and sat with one leg hanging down, almost above Martin's head. As candle after candle was being extinguished, Jean Marie let out a loud laugh. Martin reached up and grasped the overseer's foot. Jean Marie fell to the ground, convulsing; his body swelled and he died two hours later. Kingsley relates that Obeah men were suspected of carrying a drop of snake poison under a sharpened fingernail and speculated that this might have been the method by which Martin killed the overseer. Martin is described as "a tall, powerful Negro . . . a formidable opponent from his mere size and strength".[116] (As we can see from these few accounts, real-life Obeah men and women were often described in more attractive terms than their fictional counterparts.)

It was not only the English and the French who were interested in Obeah men and women and their abilities:

> Danish historians, almost without exception, seemed fascinated by tales of negro witchcraft [and] in their writings one finds an abundance of anecdotes dealing with such tales brought back to Denmark by ship captains, returning visitors and others. One of these stories concerns a slave by the name of Obediah who was going back to his hut one day when he heard wailing and the sound of a mewing cat. He investigated and saw a large black cat on the threshold of a nearby house. The cat hissed at him. Obediah apparently claimed that he felt spellbound, weakened, as if he were being pulled to the cat. Then he heard a voice and the spell was broken. Obediah staggered away. That night and for several nights, the cat appeared in his dreams. In its fierce, revolving eyes he saw the gnarled and bony fingers of an old woman beckoning him. On awaking, he had to fight the urge to obey and return to that house. Greatly frightened, he went to an Obeah man on Estate Slob who told him that the old woman in whose house he had seen the cat collected black cats. She would kill six of them at a time and boil the flesh off their bones. She then extracted their rib bones and held these up to a black mirror. The bones that were not reflected in the mirror she would dry, crush and feed to the remaining cats which developed strange powers and did her bidding.[117]

The Obeah man advised Obediah to strip seven new shoots from a tamarind

---

116 Ibid., 147–48.
117 Paiewonsky, *Eyewitness Accounts*, 142–45.

tree, go back to the old woman's house at the exact time that he had first seen the cat and say to the woman, "Maldina, Maldina, I have come to lash you." Each lashing was to be called by odd numbers but he was to make sure to lash her twenty-eight times so the spell could be broken. Obediah did as was recommended, so well that the old woman died and Obediah was convicted of her murder and deported.[118]

The Jesuit Williams provided a description in 1934 of how an Obeah man worked that probably comes as close to reality as any offered in the previous centuries. He suggests that an Obeah man making obi

> would have been [sure] of his privacy and would have squatted on the ground surrounded by his paraphernalia and this would have been the scene with little variation. Most of the ingredients to be used are concealed in a bag from which he draws them as he needs them. The special offering of his patron which must include a white fowl, two bottles of rum, and a silver offering are on the ground beside him. Before him is the inevitable empty bottle to receive the ingredients. The incantation opens with a prolonged mumbling which is supposed to be "an unknown tongue". This is accompanied by a swaying of the body. Gradually ingredients are placed in the bottle, and a little rum is poured over them. The throat of the fowl is deftly slit and drops of blood are allowed to fall first on the silver offering, and then on the contents of the bottle to which is finally added a few feathers plucked from various parts of the fowl with a last libation of rum. During all this process the obeah-man has been drawing inspiration from frequent draughts of rum, reserving a substantial portion to be consumed later when he makes a meal of the flesh of the fowl.[119]

To Williams, the Obeah man's patron was, of course, the Devil. As he puts it, "Obeah men in the 'bush' take themselves seriously and weave their spells and utter their invocations to Massa Debbil without disguise, placing their unbounded confidence in him as their chief reliance, and continuing on this phase of demonolatry that has come down in direct descent from their forebears, the servants of Sasabonsan back in Ashantiland."[120]

Williams's efforts to find out more were stymied. "Time and again I sought to draw out in conversation the professional obeah-men, but I invariably found them evasive and non-committal. As occasion offered, I closely questioned youngsters who, according to common reports, were apprenticed to

---

118   Ibid.
119   Williams, *Psychic Phenomena*, 142–45.
120   Ibid.

obeah-men as disciples to acquire the art, but they had already learned their lesson of secrecy and I could make no impression on them." Their refusal to take Williams into their confidence led him to conclude that "Obeah is secretive, malicious, and has gradually taken on a form of devil-worship".[121]

Whatever their views on Obeah, whether they thought it was in decline or growing in influence, almost all writers were agreed on its evil. Sir Henry "Harry" Johnston, a British explorer and colonial administrator, was exceptional in his mystification at the excitement with which fellow Europeans regarded Obeah.

> From the fiss-fass-fuss which is made by writers on American subjects relative to Obia and Vudu, one would think that this mixture of nonsense, of empiricism, of nauseous superstition, malignity, kindly feeling, pathetic "feeling after God", positive knowledge of genuine therapeutics, glimmering of the possible latent in the human brain was peculiar to the mental composition of the Negro. Whereas it is (or was yesterday) just as evident in the white man's religion, freemasonry, medicine, quacks and quackery, Mrs Eddys, Cagliostros, peasant witchcraft, and ex-voto offerings: it is equally sublime and not much more ridiculous.[122]

THE POISONER'S ART

From early on, botanists were particularly interested in the poisons available in the West Indies. Thomas Dancer divided the vegetable poisons into two categories: "the acrid" and "the narcotic". Under the former he lists "Dumb-cane, Manchioneal Apple, Milkwood, the Savana Flower (*Echites Suberecta*) called also the Nightshade", and under the latter "Tobacco, Thorn Apple (Datura Strama), Manihot or Bitter Cassava, Cabbage Bark, Worm grass, Opium, Hemlock".[123] His list of animal and mineral poisons includes serpents, fish, insects, arsenic, cobalt, corrosive sublimate, antimony and "Sugar of Lead".

According to him, "many other indigenous plants are suspected to be endued with poisonous qualities and to be in use among negroes, for occasioning a slow or distant death; but of this I have never seen any sufficient proof". Dancer, who wrote nothing about Obeah, comes to the conclusion that blacks usually used arsenic or ground glass to poison.[124]

---

121 Ibid., 4, 59.
122 Harry H. Johnston, *The Negro in the New World* (London: Methuen, 1910), 253.
123 Dancer, *Medical Assistant*, 311.
124 Ibid.

The "Savana Flower", *Apocynum erectum fruticosum*, was widely known to be poisonous and, despite Dancer's findings, was often identified as employed by poisoners, however. In a story Kingsley would have appreciated, the botanist Dr Henry Barham relates:

> a practitioner of physic was poisoned with this plant by his negro woman, who had so ordered it that it did not dispatch him quickly, but he was seized with violent gripings, inclining to vomit, and loss of appetite; afterwards, he had small convulsions in several parts of him, a hectic fever, and continual wasting of his flesh. Knowing that I had made it my business some years to find out the virtues of plants, especially antidotes, he sent to me for advice' upon which I sent him some nhandiroba kernels to infuse in wine, and drink frequently of, which cured him in time; but it was a considerable while before his convulsive fits left him. The whole plant is full of milk; it is always green, and no creature will meddle with it.[125]

Barham enjoyed a regular correspondence with Hans Sloane during the early 1700s, and the latter used much of Barham's information in his *Natural History of Jamaica*. Correspondingly, Barham's *Hortus Americanus*, published in 1794, after the author's death, relied heavily on Sloane's studies. Sloane includes Barham's information on the savana flower in the introduction to his own work, but it was another bit of information entirely that set off the rumour which Gardner did his best to dispel.

In his discussion of cassada (cassava), Barham writes that while

> [t]he expressed juice of the root is very sweet to the palate, but soon putrifies and breeds worms, called topuea, which are a violent poison, and which Indians too well know the use of: They dry these worms or maggots, and powder them; which powder, in a little quantity, they put under their thumb-nail, and, after they drink to those they intend to poison, they put their thumb upon the bowl, and so cunningly convey the poison; wherefore, when we see a negro with a long thumb-nail, he is to be mistrusted.[126]

Interestingly, Barham identifies the symptoms as "first, a pain and sickness of the stomach, a swelling of the whole abdomen, then violent vomiting and purging, giddiness of the head, then a coldness and shaking, dimness of sight, swoonings, and death, and all in a few hours".[127]

---

125   Henry Barham, *Hortus Americanus* (Kingston: Alexander Aikman, 1794), 168.
126   Ibid., 34.
127   Ibid.

It is probably from that one paragraph that the legend of "fingernail poison" grew to the point where it was still being mooted about a century later by such writers as Kingsley and Pullen-Burry. Several repeat the information almost verbatim. Sir Hans Sloane, the doctor and collector whose artefacts became the foundation of the British Museum, seized on the macabre report: "[Barham] says also that the Powder of the Maggots bred from the Corruption of the Juice of this Root, put under the Nail, given to drink, poisons the person taking, therefore, on such accidents, they suspect Negroes with long Nails."[128] The claim fascinated many. Lewis writes:

> one of the deadliest poisons used by the negroes (and a great variety is perfectly well known to most of them), is prepared from the root of the cassava. Its juice being expressed and allowed to ferment, a small worm is generated, the substance of which being received into the stomach is of a nature the most pernicious. A small portion of this worm is concealed under one of the thumbnails, which are suffered to grow long for this purpose; then, when the negro has contrived to persuade his intended victim to eat or drink with him, he takes an opportunity, while handing to him a dish or cup, to let the worm fall, which never fails to destroy the person who swallows it.[129]

Banbury relates the case of a man named Shelley who, according to him, was tried at Montego Bay "more than 35 years ago" and who "poisoned by means of maggots bred in the juice of the bitter cassava which is a rank poison when dried and reduced to powder". Shelley apparently plied his trade in Canaan in Trelawney and was "paid in watches, jewellery, and other valuables".[130] A few years later, Bessie Pullen-Burry notes that she has

> read in an American magazine that one of the well-known Obeah poisons is made as follows. The negro takes the juice of the cassava plant, which he squeezes on to a copper pan, and places it in the sun. The most horrible insects are the result which are dried and ground to a powder. The Obeah man or woman drops into the victim's coffee or soup a tiny particle of this powder, which produces death without leaving a trace of the drug.[131]

(She does not identify the magazine.)

---

128 Hans Sloane, *A Voyage to the Islands Madera, Barbadoes, Nieves, St Christophers, and Jamaica* (London 1725), 363.
129 Lewis, *Journal*, 153.
130 Banbury, *Jamaica Superstitions*, 9.
131 Pullen-Burry, *Jamaica*, 139.

Kingsley's stipendiary magistrate later claimed that he had observed almost all the same symptoms in Jean-Marie that Barham identifies.

Just as Europe's wild men and women were said to know much about plants, Europeans were convinced that Africans also had a special knowledge of plants, both those that healed and those that poisoned. Many were convinced that the knowledge had been granted them by the Devil. Sloane refers to Sir John Hawkins's account of a slaving raid in Cape Verde, where the islanders fought off the slavers with "envenom'd Arrows . . . there hardly escaped any . . . but died in strange sort with their mouths shut some ten Days before" expiring. Sloane also notes that the "the Indians and Negros make use of [dogwood tree] bark to take Fish, especially in deep Holes in inland Rivers". He explains that "the Bark of this Tree, stamp'd and thrown into a standing Pool where Fish are, intoxicate them for some Time, they turning their Bellies up, and coming above Water, but if they are not presently caught, they come to themselves and recover". He adds that a powder made from the soapberry did the same thing.

In fact, the New World's "wild men", the indigenous people, were said to have a deep lore of secret poisons. Sloane quotes Hawkins as describing poison arrows made with "mansaneel apples together with venomous Bats, Vipers, Adders and other Serpents".[132] Several writers list poisons which, applied by indigenous Americans to the tips of their arrows, paralysed their prey almost instantly. Among these, Madden mentions *vejuco de mavacure* and the juice of the upas tree (*Antiaris toxicaria*); the upas is native only to Africa, Australia and Asia, so he may have mixed it up with one of the varieties of curare which the indigenous peoples used for hunting and fishing. Madden also mentions *woorara* as being used by the natives of Guyana. He claims that, applied to a wound, *woorara* produces immediate death, but when taken internally, it takes longer to act.[133] (The word *curare* is derived from *wurari*, a name from Guyana's Macusi people.) Some writers speculate that the indigenous people shared all of this knowledge with the newly arrived Africans.

Legislation passed in 1749 outlawed the use of poison in Jamaica, but Obeah was not at that time either taken very seriously or identified with poisoning, so there was no mention of it. As more and more information began to circulate about Obeah, however, it became so closely associated with poisoning that many whites as well as blacks could barely sleep for fear. One of the earliest anecdotes about cases of poisoning comes from Père Labat, who writes:

---

132 Sloane, *Voyage to the Islands*, 5–6, 39, 152.
133 Madden, *Twelvemonth's Residence*, 52–53.

M St Aubin [of Martinique], the former proprietor, had lost a number of slaves who died suddenly and in great pain. Their deaths had been caused by the malice of one of his slaves, who had poisoned anyone the moment he perceived that his master was pleased with him, or had shown him any kindness. The miserable wretch sent for his master when he was dying and confessed that he had poisoned more than thirty of his comrades. He had allowed one of his fingernails to grow long, and said that when he intended to kill a man, he would scratch the stem of a plant, which grows on the Carbesterre [the eastern side of the island], till his nail became full of the sap. He would then go home and ask his victim to have a drink with him. Having poured some rum into a coüi, he would first drink some himself and then hand it to his victim, taking care, however, to soak his nail in the rum as he did so. This was sufficient to poison the drink and kill the victim in less than two hours' time. On being asked what was the remedy for this poison, he replied that it was the root of the little thorny sensitive plant which must be pounded to a paste and mixed with wine.[134]

Labat concludes his anecdote without further comment, and one cannot help but wonder if this poisoner was motivated by mere jealousy or whether he acted out of a wish to deprive the plantation owner of his best slaves. Certainly his confession can be interpreted as stemming from a gloating desire to let the owner know he had been responsible and, more than that, that he had gotten away with it. It can also be argued that by furnishing the remedy he sought to make amends, but Labat names neither the poison nor the remedy. We do not know if this is because the slave himself withheld the information. If he did withhold it, the planter would have been little wiser than before and no better prepared to respond to a similar situation in the future. (This is all assuming that everything Labat writes about this incident is true and indeed happened as he says it did, and that the deaths did not occur because of some unknown disease that swept through the estate or from something as simple as being malnourished and overworked. In that case, the alleged poisoner may have wanted nothing more than the satisfaction of terrifying the planter with a false confession.)

Interestingly, Labat never makes an association between the Carbesterre poisoner and Obeah or witchcraft, and neither does Sloane or Dancer. However, later writers never miss an opportunity to make it clear to their readers that Obeah and poison went hand in hand. In fact, successive generations of European writers repeated the story of fingernail poison as proof of the great

---

134 Jean-Baptiste Labat, *The Memoirs of Père Labat, 1693–1705*, trans. John Eaden (London: Constable, 1931), 69.

danger posed by poisoners and, concomitantly, by Obeah. Long contends that "the most sensible among [the slaves] fear the supernatural powers of the African obeah-men or pretended conjurers, often ascribing those mortal effects to magic which are only the natural operation of some poisonous juice or preparation dexterously administered by these villains".[135]

The writers of *Poems on the Abolition of the Slave Trade* paraphrase Long, writing that "the Obeah-men, however, as frequently accomplish their object by administering poison, as by working on the imaginations of their intended victims; and they have attained to so much skill in this deadly trade, that the negroe affected is seldom able to ascribe his malady to the proper cause".[136] For his part, Long's contemporary Benjamin Moseley makes the startling claim that "a negro Obi-man will administer a baleful dose from poisonous herbs, and calculate its mortal effects to an hour, day, week, month, or year". According to him, "the masters could instruct even Friar Bacon". Here Moseley demonstrates the great awe in which he held the Obeah men, for he was a great admirer of the medieval Franciscan friar whose mechanical and magical skills he thought had no equal in history.[137]

A story recounted by Labat appears to bear Moseley out. According to the French missionary, a sick slave woman was dying of an unknown illness that refused to respond to treatment. Labat suspected poison but he had no proof; then he found a medicine man in her hut one morning.

> The sick woman was lying stretched out on a mat. A little pottery figure, somewhat similar [to one he had previously smashed at another estate], was placed on a stool in the centre of the hut, and the witch-doctor was kneeling before it, apparently praying very earnestly. After a moment or two, he took half of a calabash containing fire, sprinkled it with some gum, and waved the incense over the idol. After several censings and more obeisances he asked whether the negress would be cured or not.

Labat broke in to stop the proceedings. The man was given five hundred lashes and the priest had cayenne pepper rubbed into the wounds – ostensibly to stop gangrene but also, no doubt, to add to the man's suffering. Labat smashed the

---

135 Long, *History of Jamaica*, 416.
136 James Montgomery, James Grahame and Elizabeth Benger, *Poems on the Abolition of the Slave Trade* (London: R. Bowyer, 1809), 20. Of course, at this point in the history of medicine few doctors were able to make accurate diagnoses of illnesses, and many confused symptoms with cause.
137 Moseley, "Medical Observations", 217.

idol, burnt it to ashes and threw it in a nearby river. However, the fetish figure had predicted that the woman would die in four days, and despite all Labat did and his railings against witchcraft and invoking of God, the woman died on the fourth day after the prediction.[138] The witch doctor may well have used poison to bring the fetish's prediction to fruition, but if so, he would have had to have a very fine knowledge of dosage and administration.

Thomas Atwood, a former judge in Dominica, was quite convinced that Obeah men and women had extensive knowledge of poisons.

> These people are very dangerous on any plantation, for although there is no credit to be given to the power of their pretended charms, yet, they are in general well acquainted with the quality of many poisonous herbs that grow in the West Indies, and which they often give to others who apply to them for charms to be administered to the persons upon whom they are to operate. By this means, many white people have been killed by poison under the persuasion of these Obeah men that it was to make them love their slaves by whom it was obtained.[139]

Obeah men and women were not to be feared simply because of their claim to supernatural powers; what really exercised planters and the pro-slavery lobby was the clear and present danger posed by poisoning. Poisoners were a threat to other slaves – that is, to the property of the planters – and, just as important, they were a threat to the lives of the planters themselves. As the pro-slavery lobby saw it, an end to slavery would remove effective white control over blacks and assure a resurgence of Obeah with all its attendant dangers, including poisonings on a massive scale.

The abolitionist William Wilberforce took notice of what was being said about Obeah practitioners and their reputation for poisoning but thought those claims were being exaggerated to heighten the fear of abolition. "The Jamaica planters long imputed the most injurious effects on the health and even the lives of their slaves, to the African practice of Obeah, or witchcraft", Wilberforce writes, adding that "the Agent for Jamaica declared to the privy council, in 1788, that they 'ascribed a very considerable portion of the annual mortality among the Negroes in that island to that fascinating mischief'".[140]

---

138 Everild Young and Kjeld Helweg-Larsen, *The Pirates' Priest: The Life of Père Labat in the West Indies, 1693–1705* (London: Jarrolds, 1965), 45.

139 Atwood, *Island of Dominica*, 271–72.

140 William Wilberforce, *An Appeal to the Religion, Justice and Humanity of the Inhabitants of the British Empire in Behalf of the Negro Slaves in the West Indies* (London: J. Hatchard and Son, 1823), 28–29.

He notes that Obeah men had been sentenced to death or to severe lashings and goes on to say:

> I know that of late, ashamed of being supposed to have punished witchcraft with such severity, it has been alleged that the professors of Obeah used to prepare and administer poison to the subjects of their spells: but any one who will only examine the laws of Jamaica against these practices or read the evidence of the agents, will see plainly that this was not the view that was taken of the proceedings of the Obeah-men, but that they were considered as impostors, who preyed on their ignorant countrymen by a pretended intercourse with evil spirits, or by some other Pretences to supernatural powers.[141]

Wilberforce's comments drew a swift response from slavery apologist Revd George Wilson Bridges in his *A Voice from Jamaica*, who dismisses the abolitionist's analysis of the situation and howls that "obeah and death [are] synonymous: the latter is the invariable end and object of the former".[142]

Certainly there were few who thought the reports of poisoning were exaggerated. Lewis, for example, notes:

> A person after being brought to the doors of death by a cup of coffee, only escaped a second time by his civility in giving the beverage prepared for himself to two young book-keepers, to both of whom it proved fatal. It indeed came out afterwards, that this crime was also effected by the abominable belief in Obeah: the woman who mixed the draught had no idea of its being poison; but she had received the deleterious ingredients from an Obeah man, as a "charm to make her massa good to her": by which the negroes mean: the compelling of a person to give another everything for which the other may ask him.[143]

Lewis accepts, apparently without question, the motive the woman offered, yet he notes that this was the second time the woman had attempted to poison the man and that he had been made seriously ill the first time. However innocent the woman may have been, she could not have failed to notice the effects of the first "charm" she tried. That she tried again suggests she intended to kill him and only came up with the self-serving and fawning excuse of wanting her massa to treat her better after being caught.

In *Jamaica: Its Past and Present State*, published in 1843, the Baptist mission-

---

141 Ibid.
142 George Wilson Bridges, *A Voice from Jamaica; in Reply to William Wilberforce* (London: Longman, Hurst, Rees, Orme, Brown and Green, 1823), 29.
143 Lewis, *Journal*, 83.

ary James Phillippo reported that "C–, a plantation attorney who had been a great tyrant to the slaves under his charge, was so afraid of being poisoned by some of them that he would not eat anything unless it had been prepared and cooked for him by his 'housekeeper'. . . . He, at one time, thought that his vigilance had been eluded and that he was slightly poisoned. He was wretched and his health became gradually impaired."[144]

About ten years later, Theodora Lynch had her protagonist in *The Mountain Pastor* relate the story of a dinner he had attended, where he met a Mr Walker, a wild-looking white man. "Throughout dinner I observed that he raised his plate to his nose every time it was replenished, to detect if poison had been put therein."[145] Lynch presents this as but further evidence of Walker's paranoia. He also put a sword across the foot of his bed "and a pair of loaded pistols were carefully placed under his pillow". There is nothing in the chapter that suggests an attempt to poison him or kill him was ever made, but when we learn that he was in the habit of keeping his wife locked in her room, we can extrapolate much about how he might have treated his slaves, giving them more than enough reason to want him dead. (Walker appears to have been beset by ill fortune: he lost his grand house, his eldest daughter set fire to another house, and his middle daughter died of yellow fever. An observer might well be forgiven for thinking that his household had been "Obeahed"!)

Planters in the English-speaking islands would probably also have been aware of cases of poisoning in the French, Spanish and Dutch islands. In 1826, for example, about thirty men and women were brought before a Martinique court for a conspiracy involving a group of slaves who had plotted to ruin two plantations by poisoning every living thing on them.[146]

Revd Gardner discounts most of these stories as mere fiction:

> Tales were at one time current, and are still repeated, of a knowledge and use of poisons so potent, that sufficient to destroy life could be concealed beneath the fingernail, and so be quietly dropped into a glass of rum or a cup of coffee. Other poisons were supposed to cause insanity, or a slow lingering death. The Obeah men were commonly reputed to be skilled poisoners: their ability in this respect has been greatly exaggerated. It is quite possible that some Africans, like savages of other countries, had a knowledge of vegetable poisons beyond what

---

144 Phillippo, *Jamaica*, 133. Quite often "housekeeper" was a euphemism for mistress.
145 Theodora Lynch, *The Mountain Pastor* (London: Barton, 1852), 39.
146 John Savage, "'Black Magic' and White Terror: Slave Poisoning and Colonial Society in Early 19th Century Martinique", *Journal of Social History* 40, no. 3 (2007): 635.

most are disposed to give them credit for. Yet, in nearly every case in Jamaica, the crime has been committed in the most clumsy manner; arsenic, rat poisons, or some other well-known compound being employed.[147]

Dr Madden, too, thought that the claims were wildly exaggerated. "It is evident to any medical man who reads these trials that, in the great majority of cases, the trumpery ingredients used in the practice of obeah were incapable of producing mischief, except on the imagination of the person intended to be obeahed", he writes.[148]

Gardner and Madden were lone voices crying in the wilderness. Writers continued to maintain that Obeah men and women had a superior knowledge of poison. More than twenty years after Gardner's book was published, Revd Banbury asserts that any Obeah man was "well versed in all the vegetable poisons of the island, and sometimes has them planted in his garden".[149] Evoking the myth of Medea, Banbury claims that Obeah men could "poison by the skin as well as by mouth. He is known to make a thin decoction of these poisons and soak the undergarments of people taken to him. . . . When put on by the unsuspecting owner, the poison is absorbed along with the perspiration, and engenders some direful disease in the system." The Obeah man "is up to the knowledge that vegetable poison is not so easily detected after death as mineral, and therefore prefers to do his diabolical work with that".[150]

Bell's planter sounds an ominous note: "through the knowledge possessed by some of the old negroes of numerous poisonous bushes and plants, unknown to medicine, but found in every tropical wood, it is to be feared that numerous deaths might still be traced to the agency of these Obeah men".[151] Kingsley was quite prepared to believe it:

> We shall not be surprised to find that a very important, indeed the most practically important element of Obeah is poisoning. . . . Travelers of late have told us enough – and too much for our comfort of mind – of that prevailing dread of poison as well as of magic which urges the African Negros to deeds of horrible cruelty; and the fact that these African Negros, up to the very latest importations, are the special practisers of Obeah, is notorious though the West Indies.[152]

---

147 Gardner, *History of Jamaica*, 190.
148 Madden, *Twelvemonth's Residence*, 76.
149 Banbury, *Jamaica Superstitions*, 7.
150 Ibid.
151 Bell, *Obeah*, 12.
152 Kingsley, *At Last*, 2:136–37.

He adds that "the existence of this trick of poisoning is denied, often enough. Sometimes Europeans, willing to believe the best of their fellowmen . . . simply disbelieve it because it is unpleasant to believe". On the other hand, "white West Indians will deny [stories of poisoning], and the existence of Obeah beside, simply because they believe in it a little too much, and are afraid of the Negros knowing that they believe it".[153] According to Kingsley's line of reasoning, informants who believed in Obeah could be believed, but not those who discounted it.

Bell was convinced that more murders were caused by poison than were being detected. "Owing to the defective state of the laws relating to declarations of deaths and inquests, it is to be feared that very many deaths occur from poisoning, which are set down to a cold or other simple malady", he writes. He points out: "A death need not be reported till seven days after the occurrence, and only the very strongest suspicions of foul play would induce a registrar to report the matter to the coroner, in view of an inquest; and even then, a post-mortem in the tropics, on a body exhumed after seven days, would hardly be reliable."[154]

The American folklorist Beckwith asserts that "the poisonous properties of plants are well-known in Jamaica, but the obeah man is supposed to be especially conversant with their mysteries. . . . A white woman pointed out a fern . . . which she said was used for obeah poisoning."[155] And Joseph Williams had no doubts about the danger of poisoning: "too frequently, the Obeah man makes use of this knowledge of herbals in connection with his art. In a particular case of Obeah poisoning that came under my personal notice, just as the victim was on the point of losing consciousness, the very individual who was for good reasons suspected of being the cause of the trouble, suddenly entered the sick-room unannounced and administered the antidote."[156]

Almost all the writers mention poison of one kind or another, though not all the cases are mentioned in association with Obeah. Lewis attended a slave court during the trial of Minetta, a fifteen-year-old servant girl accused of introducing corrosive sublimate into her master's brandy. She was found guilty and sentenced to execution. In another, similar case, "a neighbouring gentleman, as I hear, has now three negroes in prison (all domestics, and one of them grown grey in his service) for poisoning him with a corrosive sublimate; and

---

153 Ibid.
154 Bell, *Obeah*, 10–11.
155 Beckwith, *Jamaican Ethnobotany*, 9.
156 Williams, *Voodoos and Obeahs*, 133.

his brother was actually killed by similar means".[157] Lewis's failure to mention Obeah suggests that it was not implicated in every poisoning. In another case he mentions that an "agent who appears to be in high favour with the negroes whom he now governs, was obliged to quit an estate, from the frequent attempts to poison him".[158]

Poison or the threat of poison made whites uneasy. Even the tolerant Lewis worried about it: "Another means of destruction is to be found (as I am assured) in almost every negro-garden throughout the island: it is the arsenic-bean, neither useful for food nor ornamental in its appearance; nor can the negroes, when questioned, give any reason for affording it a place in their gardens; yet there it is always to be seen."[159] His anxiety and suspicion leap off the page.

Writer after writer expresses an anxious fascination with the subject of poisoning. "I have inquired a good deal respecting poisons of the negro doctors, and found it difficult to overcome their disinclination to enter on this subject. But if their accounts are to be trusted, there are vegetable poisons known to exist here hardly less powerful than any known to us in Europe", writes Dr Madden to Dr Webster. "The West Indies have no dearth of poisonous plants; and in former times it is very certain their nature was better known to the negroes than even their names now are to the white inhabitants."[160]

"The negro sorcerer is, at worst, only a poisoner", wrote the journalist and author Lafcadio Hearn in 1890,

> but he possesses a very curious art which long defied serious investigation, and in the beginning of the last century was attributed, even by whites, to diabolical influence. In 1721, 1723, and 1725, several negroes were burned alive at the stake as wizards in league with the devil. It was an era of comparative ignorance but even now things are done which would astonish the most skeptical and practical physician.

Hearn goes on to give the example of a labourer

> discharged from a plantation [who] vows vengeance; and the next morning the whole force of hands ... are totally disabled from work. Every man and woman on the place is unable to walk; everybody has one or both legs frightfully swollen. ... They have trodden on a "malifice". .... All that can be ascertained is that certain little prickly seeds have been scattered all over the ground, where the bare-

---

157 Ibid., 153.
158 Lewis, *Journal*, 83, 99.
159 Ibid., 153.
160 Madden, *Twelvemonth's Residence*, 52.

footed workers are in the habit of passing. Ordinarily, treading on these seeds is of no consequence; but it is evident in such a case they they must have been prepared in a special way – soaked in some poison, perhaps snake venom.[161]

Writers such as Gardner and, later, Joseph Williams, also list ground glass as a popular poison. Williams claims that powdered glass was called "obi-water" and notes that it produced "dysentery and a slow-wasting death".[162]

A bush named after the famous French poisoner Marie de Brinvilliers is cited by Kingsley as "one of those deadly poisons too common in the bush, and too well known to the Negro Obi-men and Obi-women".[163] Brinvillier's bush (*Spigelia anthelmia*), also known as wormbush, causes vomiting, giddiness, dilation of the pupils, delirium, palpitations and convulsions and can lead to death. Kingsley wondered how the name had come to be given to the bush and worked himself up into a fit of fanciful dread:

> How were the terrible properties of the plant discovered? How eager and ingenious must the human mind be about the devil's work, and what long practice ... must it have had at the said work, ever to have picked out this paltry thing among the thousand weeds in the forest as a tool for its jealousy and revenge. It may have taken ages to discover the Brinvilliers, and ages more to make its poison generally known. ... Surely this is one of the many facts which point towards some immensely ancient civilization in the Tropics, and a civilization which may have had its ugly vices, and have been destroyed thereby.[164]

Yet *Spigelia anthelmia* also has medicinal properties, and it kills only when given in high doses. Whether or not it was in fact an ingredient in the poison Madame de Brinvilliers administered to her father, brothers and others in France of the mid-1600s is not clear, as the plant is native to tropical and subtropical America.

If Kingsley and other writers are to be believed, everyone knew someone who knew someone who had been poisoned:

> It was but a few years ago that in a West Indian city an old and faithful free servant, in a family well known to me, astonished her master, on her death-bed, by a voluntary confession of more than a dozen murders. "You remember such and such a party, when every one was ill? Well, I put something in the soup."

---

161 Lafcadio Hearn, *Two Years in the French West Indies* (London: Harper and Brothers, 1890), 373.
162 Williams, *Voodoos and Obeahs*, 135.
163 Kingsley, *At Last*, 244–45.
164 Ibid., 245.

As another instance; a woman who died respectable, a Christian and a communicant, told this to her clergyman: – She had lived from youth, for many years, happily and faithfully with a white gentleman who considered her as his wife. She saw him pine away and die from slow poison, administered, she knew, by another woman whom he had wronged. But she dared not speak. She had not courage enough to be poisoned herself likewise.[165]

Writers recycled the stories of other writers, creating a crescendo of fear.

Poisoning is a much easier matter for tropical negroes than one might imagine, by reason of the many poisonous vines, plants, and roots with which the experience of generations has made them familiar. Then the manner of keeping the water of the household helps the Obeah man considerably. Every house has its big porous earthen jar, in which the drinking water is kept and through which leaves dropped into the water-jar will, in a few days, put an end to a whole family. It is not hard to have these leaves put into the water because the Obeah man knows all the servants in the house and some of them are very likely to have put themselves in his power and must do as he tells them. Whether they are in his power or not they are all very much afraid of him. When the Obeah is set for a coloured man, the mode of operation is simple. One of the most frequent complaints in the country districts is dysentery, and the Obeah man can produce all the symptoms of dysentery in a whole family without difficulty. It is done by mixing small quantities of pounded glass with their food; and, if this is continued long enough, the result is death. The symptoms are so nearly like those of dysentery, that nothing short of an autopsy will reveal the truth, and in the Jamaica mountains an autopsy is a very unusual thing so the poisoner goes unpunished. The first warning a coloured man receives is usually the finding of a little packet in his bed, or any place where he is sure to find it, containing a tooth, a bit of glass, and a few hairs. This is sometimes varied with a bottle containing parts of a toad, a spider, some rusty nails, and dirty water. The black, unless he is more than usually intelligent, gives himself up for lost when he finds these things. He knows that sickness or death will overtake himself or some of his family, or at the least that his donkey or his poultry will die. Many of the Obeah men draw the line just short of actually killing. But not one of them hesitates to inflict mental tortures upon the ignorant by pretending to catch their shadows, and by other catchy devices with which they are familiar. No man of learning has made a closer study of Obeahism than Charles Kingsley. And he says unhesitatingly that "the most practically important element of Obeah is poisoning". The Obeah man who hesitates to

---

165 Ibid., 137.

take human life with poisons does not hesitate to throw whole families into sickness, or to kill their domestic animals.[166]

As late as 1936, Bell was assuring British newspaper readers that "there is much reason to fear that many of the mysterious deaths which take place in the West Indies, and especially certain strange forms of lunacy, may be due to the effects of vegetable and other poisons, the knowledge of which was transplanted to the islands of the Caribbean Sea by the slaves who came from West Africa".[167]

However, if there was evidence that blacks had extensive knowledge of herbal cures and poisons, there was also evidence that this knowledge had some gaps. Sloane recounts that Barham told him about a case where "several Negros had been poyson'd in the year 1711". Apparently, a servant carrying rum had noticed that the container was leaking and stopped the leak with leaves of *Apocynum erectum fruticorum*. Later, several people drank the rum and were poisoned. Sloane writes that the "Negro was try'd for his Life" while the "rest recovered by the use of the Juice of the Indian Arrow Root or *Canna Indica radice alba Alexipharmaca*".[168] Sloane does not indicate whether the servant who stopped the rum from leaking had also imbibed the poisoned liquor, but there is no suggestion in his account that it was done deliberately.

Again and again we see writers offering information about Obeah that fed the fears of readers, whether the writers intended to argue that the practice was fading or continuing. Again and again, writers link the practice to the "dark traditions" of Africa, "the Dark Continent", and to an uncanny, if not supernatural, knowledge of plants which echoed or evoked the old folktales of bogeymen and wild women of the European forests and their association with the Devil. Nobody was writing in *The Times* of London about the Green Man in the 1930s and 1940s, but they *were* writing about the Obeah man. Could the London landlords who put up "No Negroes" signs in the 1960s to ward off West Indian tenants have feared that they might fall prey to the dark magic and poison about which they had been reading since they were children? They had been told nothing of Obeah's positive roles in the Caribbean. They would have known nothing about why, in the absence of proper medical care and their inability to obtain justice in the courts or to have any sense of power over their lives, black people kept faith with Obeah.

---

166   "Obeah Man", *Pall Mall Gazette*.
167   Hesketh Bell, letter to *The Times*, 27 July 1936, 8.
168   Sloane, *Voyage to the Islands*, 8–9.

CHAPTER 3

"Prophet, Priest and King of His District"
THE OBEAH MAN IN HIS SOCIETY

"BY ST PETER, BY ST PAUL, ME NO TIEF HOG"

Obeah men and women fulfilled a wide variety of roles within their society. As Edwards notes, they were resorted to "upon all occasions whether for the cure of disorders, the obtaining [of] revenge for injuries or insults, the conciliating of favours, the discovery and punishment of the thief or the adulterer, and the prediction of future events".[1] He could have added: to help lovers, protect the innocent, shield believers from the law, grant luck, administer oaths, assist one's business to prosper and endow to rebels immunity from harm or capture. Indeed, as one observer puts it, the Obeah man's "influence over the country people is unbounded. He is the prophet, priest and king of his district".[2]

Some observers make a distinction between the powers of Obeah men and those of the women who practised it. "It is the province of Obi-women to dispose of passions. They sell foul winds for inconstant mariners; dreams and phantasies for jealousy; vexation and pain in the heart, for perfidious love", Moseley proclaims.[3] In fact it was often said that women especially made use of the Obeah man to "tunn him yeye", or prevent their man from straying. The same charm could also secure a man. Revd Banbury reports that a love potion or "tempting powder" was concocted "in such an immoral, filthy and disgusting manner" that he cannot give the details, though he does offer the

---

1 Edwards, *History Civil and Commercial*, 2:166.
2 Rampini, *Letters*, 131.
3 Moseley, "Medical Observations", 107.

tantalizing hint that it involved the sacrifice of the woman's honour and virtue (likely the blood spilled when the hymen is broken).[4]

Men who wanted to know if their wives had been unfaithful could also apply to an Obeah practitioner. "Sometimes the mixture of human blood, grave dirt, and other abominations, was administered to a woman whose fidelity was questioned; and who, on taking it, was required to express a wish that her belly might rot, and other evils come upon her, if she had been unfaithful", Gardner writes, pointing out the similarity with the bitter water trial in Numbers 5.[5]

Moseley contends that while the Obeah women specialized in matters of the heart, "Obi-men are more sagacious than Obi-women in giving or taking away diseases; and in the application of poisons. It is their department to blind pigs and poultry and to lame cattle."[6] They did far more than that, however. A slave who had fallen from grace with his master might apply to the Obeah man for a charm to restore him to favour, while prisoners might feel that they needed the supernatural on their side if they were to avoid conviction. That Obeah men were "able to stop the mouths of the prosecution and his witnesses" and were capable "of influencing the Judge and jury" was a common belief. Rampini notes that sometimes the Obeah man "visits the courts of petty sessions throughout the island, if some unfortunate client of his who has got into trouble requires his aid to defend him".[7]

As with European witchcraft, Obeah often depended on sympathetic magic. "Things got from the possession of the person designed to be injured or over whom some influence or advantage is to be gained are thought most efficacious", Banbury observes. "Such materials are nicely wound up with thread, or placed in a vial, or bottle or gourd; words are muttered over it by the obeahman, which converts it into an incantation." But magic depended not just on the skill of the Obeah man or woman; its effectiveness also depended on how well the client or subscriber adhered to its rules. That person "must not stop on the way, look behind, or speak to any one, nor allow rain to wet him on the way, as this would either tend to destroy the efficacy of the 'bush' as it is sometimes called or the obeah might 'turn upon' the person carrying it, and do him material injury".[8]

---

4 Banbury, *Jamaica Superstitions*, 6–7.
5 Gardner, *History of Jamaica*, 185.
6 Moseley, "Medical Observations", 107.
7 Rampini, *Letters*, 133.
8 Banbury, *Jamaica Superstitions*, 7.

"Prophet, Priest and King of His District"

The aid of Obeah in catching or punishing thieves was indispensable and shows the important role practitioners played in the life of plantation society. As the Fuller report notes,

> When a negro is robbed of a fowl or a hog, he applies directly to the Obeah man or woman. It is then made known among his fellow blacks that Obi is set for the thief and as soon as the latter hears the dreadful news, his terrified imagination begins to work and no resource is left but in the superior skill of some more eminent Obeah man of the neighbourhood who may counteract the magical operations of the other. But if no one can be found of higher rank and ability or, if after gaining such an ally, he should still fancy himself affected, he presently falls into a decline under the incessant horror of impending calamities. The slightest painful sensation in the head, the bowels or any other part, any casual loss or hurt, confirms his apprehensions and he believes himself the devoted victim of an invisible and irresistible agency.[9]

Again, what the report has to say on this subject was plagiarized or paraphrased extensively by Renny, Pullen-Burry and others.

If one was fairly certain about the suspect but, for whatever reason, could not approach them directly, then one could employ more arcane methods. Gardner relates that "when Obi was set for a suspected thief, the magic charm was usually buried at his gate, or in some place over which he was accustomed to walk. The tale of what had been done reached his ears. He could no longer rest, for the mighty power was at work." Under the weight of his guilt, the thief pined and died.[10] Buchner had related much the same thing in 1854 but gave additional details about the precise contents of the charm. According to him, the Obeah man buried

> at the gate or in the residence of the person who was to be dealt with, a box of cloth, containing earth from a grave, feathers of a fowl, and other articles, which in their belief would produce sickness and death, or an entire change of mind. The object was frequently obtained with the credulous and superstitious. An indescribable fear came over them when they believed themselves under the influence of supernatural powers.[11]

Alternatively, the Obeah man might burn seeds of the wanga bush with pepper and salt and place the mixture on the road where the thief walked

---

9   Edwards, *History Civil and Commercial*, 2:167–68.
10 Gardner, *History of Jamaica*, 188.
11 Buchner, *Moravians*, 38.

at night. This would catch the thief by throwing the king's evil, or *cocoaba* (leprosy, also spelled *cocobay* or *cocobey*), on him and was much feared. According to Banbury, thieves would return whatever they stole if threatened with the "burning wanga".[12] Other methods of detecting thieves were a bit more dangerous:

> On the twelfth of February, a fire broke out in town near the market. . . . It was occasioned by the carelessness of a Curacao negro woman, by the name of Martina, who had fixed a light in a barrel, shut up the house and gone to her work. She acknowledged in her declaration to the judge, that she did this to find out who was the thief who had lately stole her turkeys, and she did not want to burn and harm him with this light until he brought them back to her.[13]

The Fuller report notes that "common tricks of Obi [included] hanging up feathers, bottles, egg shells, &c &c in order to intimidate negroes of a thievish disposition from plundering huts, hog styes, or provision grounds".[14] Long elaborates on this in his *History of Jamaica*:

> bits of red rag, cats teeth, parrots' feathers, egg shells, and fish bones are frequently stuck up at the doors of their houses when they go from home leaving any thing of value within; sometimes they hang them on fruit trees and place them in corn fields to deter thieves. Upon conversing with some of the Creoles upon this custom, they laughed at the supposed virtue of the charm, and said they practised it only to frighten away the salt water Negroes of whose depredations they are most apprehensive.[15]

Since Obeah men and women were believed to have the power to harm livestock, it is likely that the objects hung in fields had a dual purpose: to deter thieves as well as to deflect curses. Carmichael notes that "negroes . . . have bottles hung round and about their houses, and in their grounds, full of some sort of infusion which they prepare to prevent the Obeah from affecting them".[16]

Whites were not above using the fear of Obeah to protect their property too. Bell describes how a planter hired an Obeah man to dress his garden. The Obeah man, Mokombo, was

---

12 Banbury, *Jamaica Superstitions*, 10.
13 Johan Peter Nissen, *Reminiscences of a Forty-Six Years' Residence in the Island of St Thomas* (Philadelphia: A.H. Senseman, 1838), 141.
14 Edwards, *History Civil and Commercial*, 2:170.
15 Long, *History of Jamaica*, 2:420.
16 Carmichael, *Domestic Manners*, 254.

> a wizened-up old African, attended by a small black boy carrying a large covered basket. . . . he produced a number of small and large medicine bottles, each filled with some mysterious liquid; then taking up a position in front of a plantain, he tied one of the vials on to a bunch of fruit and then began muttering a sort of incantation in what seemed a most uncouth African lingo, accompanying his spell the while, by frequently waving his arms and constant genuflexions. He would then pass on to another row of trees and perform the same ceremony. . . . [He] next produced from his basket a tiny little black wooden coffin, apparently empty. This he placed with much ceremony in the branches of a cocoa-tree, and on the top of it put a saucer, containing a little water and a common hen's egg floating in it.[17]

When he was finished, Mokombo told the planter, "Me let go plenty cribo, Massa, and now, if any one da go and tief dem plantains, he must go swell up and bust!" According to Bell, "blacks firmly believe that when one of these sorcerers 'dresses' a garden or field, he lets go in it, by means of spells and incantations, a large number of the most ferocious criboes [large black snakes], which would infallibly destroy" a thief.[18]

While in Barbados, the antiquarian Greville Chester "heard also of an estate manager who, missing some property, buried some of the same article in the earth at night as a threat. By this disgraceful pandering to a vile superstition he recovered his property; for the thief, fearing his own speedy death and burial, restored the stolen goods to the place whence he had taken them."[19]

The phenomenon of white people using Obeah for their own purposes was remarked on in the news:

> even some of the white planters themselves do not scorn to make use of obeah, although, of course, they have no belief in it. The theft of growing crops by the negroes is one of the greatest trials of their lives. Sometimes they adorn the trees around the edge of a "banana piece" or orange grove with miniature coffins, old bones, bottles of dirty water, and other obeah; and then the negroes will not dare to enter and steal. But there is an even easier means of prevention. If you have lost a few bunches of bananas in the night, you have only to go round in the morning and say loudly, in the hearing of the negroes: "It's all right. I don't care. I've got the footprint." Before long a repentant black will fling himself on

---

17 Bell, *Obeah*, 2–4.
18 Ibid., 4–5.
19 Greville John Chester, *Transatlantic Sketches in the West Indies* (London: Smith, Elder, 1869), 82–83.

his knees before you and confess his guilt. It is part of obeah that if you find the footprint of a thief, dig up the earth in which it is impressed and fling it into the fire; the offender will waste away and die unless he confesses.[20]

Whites continued to make use of Obeah up to at least the early 1900s. "Some planters adopt Obi to ensure themselves against thieving", writes Pullen-Burry. "They take a large black bottle, fill it with some phosphorescent liquid, and place within it, the feather of a buzzard, the quill sticking uppermost. This they fasten to a tree on the outskirts of their coffee-patch or banana-field, where it can be well-observed by all who pass near. The dusky population firmly believes it to be the work of the Obeah man, [and] refrain their thieving propensities accordingly."[21] Since the Fuller report makes no mention of phosphorescent liquid in its discussion of Obeah, we can be reasonably certain that, at least in this instance, if she did not fabricate it, Pullen-Burry is reporting something she actually witnessed.

When stratagems to prevent thievery failed, methods to detect thieves were required. Vice-Admiral Edward Vernon, son of the secretary of state to William III, took time out from fighting the Spanish to relate in his *History of Jamaica*:

> when anything about a Plantation is missing, they have a solemn kind of oath, which the eldest Negro always administers, and which by them is accounted so sacred, that except they have the express Command of their Master or Overseer, they never set about it, and then they go very solemnly to work. They range themselves in that spot of Ground which is appropriated for the Negroes Burying-place, and one of them opens a Grave. He who acts the Priest, takes a little of the Earth, and puts it into every one of their Mouths; they say, that if any has been guilty, their Belly swells, and occasions their Death. I never saw any Instance of this but one; and it was certainly Fact that a Boy did swell, and acknowledge the theft when he was dying: But I am far from thinking there was any Connection between the Cause and the Effect; for a Thousand Accidents might have occasioned it, without accounting for it by that foolish ceremony.[22]

Edward Vernon never mentions Obeah by name, but his use of "the Priest" could be read as a nod to his awareness of the phenomenon. Hughes notes

---

20   C.B., "Obeah and Vaudoux", 8.
21   Pullen-Burry, *Jamaica*, 140.
22   Edward Vernon, *A New History of Jamaica: In Thirteen Letters from a Gentleman to His Friend* (London: J. Hodges, 1740), 308.

that the dirt should ideally come from the "grave of their nearest Relations, or Parents" and that "this being mingled with water, they drink it, imprecating the divine Vengeance to inflict immediate punishment upon them". He adds: "few, if any (provided they are conscious of the imputed crime) will put the proof of their Innocency upon the Experiment".[23]

As the missionaries made incursions into the slave communities and the number of their converts grew, some of these practices began to take on a uniquely West Indian character that hinged on the perceived magic of the Bible. Edward Graham, a man brought before the St Catherine slave court in Jamaica in 1824 as a witness at Andrew Marble's trial "for practising Obeah, and for having in his possession various articles notoriously used in such practices" had the following interesting exchange with a court official:

> Chairman – "Are you christened?" – "Yes."
> Chairman – "If you take the book and kiss it, and swear false, what will happen to you?" – "I will dead."
> Chairman – "And where will you then go to?" – "To Heaven."
> Chairman – "Suppose you swear false, what will happen to you?" – "Me will purge, and my belly will swell."
> Chairman – "He does not understand the nature of an oath." – "Yes, Massa; know well, belly will swell."[24]

Graham was deposed without having to take the oath but was warned that if he lied, he would suffer the same punishment as the prisoner. A footnote to the article explains that the Slave Law allowed for slaves to be punished with whatever crime the prisoner was charged with if they lied, and suggested that this was a method by which the planters sought to extract the truth from those who "were not aware of the nature of a Christian oath". The writer notes, "We doubt, however, whether this is a legitimate construction of the statute. By the rules of evidence, a witness must be sworn according to his faith, as a Mahomedan on the Koran; and therefore where a negro thinks kissing the Bible will occasion his death, if he takes a false oath, we [unclear] he might be sworn."[25]

Outside of the courts, the procedure was much simpler. Madden writes:

> To find out the person who has committed a theft, all parties present are called upon to open a Bible, 10th Chapter of Kings: they then place a key between

---

23 Hughes, *Natural History*, 15–16.
24 "Trial for Practising Obeah, St. Catherine's, Jamaica", *The Times*, 25 August 1824, 3.
25 Ibid.

the leaves, and tie it in the closed book with a slender thread; the key is held between the tips of two second fingers; the book is then struck after a portion of the 50th Psalm has been read, and if the person is present who committed the theft, the key will remain in the hands of the holder, and the book will fall to the ground. This is a singular instance of an African superstition ingrafted on Christianity.[26]

Madden appears to be unaware that the Bible-and-key ordeal was a feature of the Middle Ages and was widely practised in the Britain of his own time.

Frances Lanaghan, a British woman who lived on Antigua for several years, also reported on the trial of the Bible and key but adds more descriptive details:

> Another trial by ordeal which I believe has formerly been practised in England and has probably been taught them by the whites is thus performed. A door key is placed between the leaves of the Bible upon the 18th and 19th verses of the 50th Psalm and the book is then bound tightly round so that the key cannot fall out; care must be taken at the same time that the key is sufficiently large that, after being placed upon the verses mentioned, part of the handle or bole may be left out. Two persons, the accused and the accuser, balance the bound book by placing the first finger of the right hand under the bole of the key and make use of the following incantation as I must call it "By St Peter, by St Paul, you tief hog or whatever else it may be that is stolen." The accused answers "By St Peter, by St Paul, me no tief hog." This is repeated thrice by both parties. If the accused is guilty, the key immediately turns but if not, the charm is tried upon all who are suspected until the event takes place.[27]

The Bible-and-key ordeal was only one of many used to detect criminals.

> The Broom Ordeal is practiced by cementing two layers of light broom, with ashes mixed with water: the suspected person is then placed on a stool, and calls on God to show who is the guilty person. The slight broom wicker is then pressed round his throat: if it happens to give way, it is proof that he is innocent; but if the pressure should cause him to fall from the stool, that circumstance is an evidence of his guilt.[28]

Lanaghan reports on a similar custom in Antigua:

---

26   Madden, *Twelvemonth's Residence*, 70–71.
27   [Frances Lanaghan], *Antigua and the Antiguans* (London: Saunders and Ottley, 1844), 55–60.
28   Madden, *Twelvemonth's Residence*, 70–71.

One of these trials by ordeal is thus performed – they procure some of the leaves of the flower fence or Barbados pride called by the negroes doodle doo and lay them in a heap in some peculiar manner with a black dog, not a quadruped, but a small copper coin of about three farthings sterling current in this island a few years ago, in the middle. They do not tie this bundle together but by the manner in which it is placed they are enabled to raise it to the neck of the suspected person without its falling to pieces. . . . The accused is then to say, holding the bundle under their throat at the same time, "Doodle doo doodle doo if me tief de four dog or whatever it may be that is missing me wish me tongue may loll out of me mout." If nothing takes place the person is innocent and the charm is tried upon another until the guilty one's turn comes when immediately their tongue hangs out of their mouth against their will.[29]

Some writers suggest that Africans were more likely to believe in Obeah, while creoles only used it to safeguard their property. But the power of Obeah to intimidate thieves continued into the twentieth century, long after the last slave ship had left the coast of Guinea. "Even in my time in Jamaica, it was enough to threaten to 'burn whangra' within the hearing of some petty thief, to have the goods returned at once", Williams writes. "I understood that failure to do so would cause the body of the thief to break out into the most terrible sores, in case the threat had been carried into execution."[30] All these stories not only helped to ensure that readers considered Obeah and the belief in it pervasive among black people, but also that they thought of them as credulous thieves. It is a stereotype which lingers to this day.

Another, perhaps rarer, use of Obeah was to discover treasure:

> when an Obeahman is consulted about the recovery of buried treasure – which is not an infrequent event – he usually, after making his preparations describes the place where the treasure is, and all about it; and generally concludes by saying: There is a Duppy of such and such a description living there in charge of it, (or a big snake as the case may be) and he won't let you take the treasure unless "you give him a soul." That phrase means that the place . . . has to be sprinkled with the blood of some animal, which must be sacrificed there, together with rum or some other spirit. The meat of the animal and some of the liquor become the perquisites of the Obeahman.[31]

---

29 [Lanaghan], *Antigua*, 60.
30 Williams, *Voodoos and Obeahs*, 186.
31 "Myal Djumboh Cassecanarie", *Obeah Simplified: The True Wanga!* (Port-of-Spain: Mirror, n.d.), 8. This is undoubtedly a made-up name, but while the author takes on a satirical tone throughout, much of the information presented is at least hinted at in other sources.

> [An] owner of some 300 acres [went] treasure-hunting under the guidance of an [Obeah man] for about two years or more; with the result that he had sacrificed over twenty-five head of cattle, besides a large number of smaller animals, and a quantity of liquor; he has also sold over one hundred acres of his land at a ruinous rate to raise funds for his purpose, and he has had excavated four or five large holes, twenty-four feet deep by ten feet square, in which no treasure or anything of value has been found. Finally, he has absconded leaving behind him a duly registered deed of gift conveying the remainder of his property to the Obeahman, his chief advisor.[32]

Beyond demonstrating the strength of the faith that many people placed in Obeah men and women, the preceding story also provides some insight into the profitability of Obeah.

That Obeah men and women did not lose by magic is noted by several writers. Atwood reports that "these Obeah people are very artful in their way, and have a great ascendancy over the other negros, whom they persuade that they are able to do many miracles by means of their art; and very often get good sums of money for their imaginary charms".[33] Robinson agrees, claiming that the "professional" Obeah man "is miserably poor, to outward appearance; and his fee is small, but he does a good trade".[34] These stories about Obeah's profitability bolstered arguments about the credulity of black people; the theory ran that blacks, being superstitious and ignorant, were unusually susceptible to the confidence tricks of Obeah men and women, which in turn argued against their advancement as a race. Blacks preferred to put their trust in supernatural powers rather than in science. In an age of growing scientific exploration and knowledge, when scientists were pushing the boundaries of the known with their experiments and discoveries, the hold that Obeah had on black people appeared to be both a symptom and a cause of their backwardness. Few writers mention that there were no schools for black children during slavery, or that such schools as existed were of generally very low standard, a situation which continued during the post-emancipation period, well into the 1900s.

Similarly, black people had few ways of earning money, especially if they were physically challenged in some way, as many Obeah men and women were said to be. "The trade which these impostors carry on is extremely lucrative. A negro would not hesitate to give an Obeah man four or five dollars for a love-

---

32 Ibid., 8.
33 Atwood, *Island of Dominica*, 269.
34 Robinson, "Obeah Worship", 211.

spell, when he would grudge three shillings for a bottle of medicine, to relieve some painful sickness", according to a planter Bell spoke to. Most other informants made the same claim about the rewards of Obeah. The Roman Catholic priest told Bell that he had found "an old preserved-salmon tin ... stuffed full of five-dollar bank-notes, besides a number of handsome twenty-dollar gold pieces" in the dead Obeah man's room. In fact, as another planter explained to Bell, Obeah men and women could be distinguished from other blacks if they were in possession of "a good substantial house", which he claimed would have been built from "the money obtained from his credulous countrymen, in exchange for rubbishing simples or worthless love-spells".[35]

Without recourse to the law and the courts, blacks had very few options when it came to achieving justice. Getting their own back on those perceived to have wronged them probably made the relatively high cost of Obeah seem worth it. An Obeah man made a princely sum in one case reported to Pullen-Burry. "I had been told by a coffee-planter whose dealings with his black labourers had been somewhat acrimonious that they had 'set Ob' for him. Although the matter in dispute between him as landlord, and the negroes as tenants amounted only to a few pounds, the latter, collectively, had paid as much as £25 to an Obeah man to Obi him", she writes. The coffee-planter "had laughed at them and had pointed out to them the futility of their spells and curses, so far as he and his health and prosperity were concerned. . . . They had come to the conclusion: they could not Obi a white man."[36]

BUSH DOCTORS

Diseases common in the Caribbean during the plantation era included yellow fever, yaws, ulcers, elephantiasis, dropsy (oedema), leprosy, cholera and dysentery. Epidemics often carried off scores of people on a plantation, with whites being as susceptible to many of the afflictions as blacks, but Europeans quickly noted that Africans were able to treat maladies on their own. "When [the slaves] are sick, there are two remedies that cure them; the one an outward, the other, an inward medicine", wrote Richard Ligon as early as 1673.

> The outward medicine is a thing they call Negro-oyle, and tis made in Barbary, yellow it is as Beeswax but soft as butter. When they feel themselves ill, they

---

35 Bell, *Obeah*, 16, 9.
36 Pullen-Burry, *Jamaica*, 133.

call for some of that, and anoint their bodies, as their breasts, bellies, and side, and in two days they are perfectly well. But this does the greatest cures upon such, as have bruises or strains in their bodies. The inward medicine is taken, when they find any weakness or decay in their spirits and stomachs, and then a dram or two of kill-devil revives and comforts them much.[37]

Long reports on the use black people made of a wide variety of what he calls "medicaments", including "lime juice, cardamoms, the roots, branches, leaves, bark, and gums of trees and about thirty different herbs".[38] He points out that "the latter [are] wonderfully powerful and have subdued diseases incident to their climate which have foiled the art of European surgeons at the factories". Typically, he is careful to note, however, that "the Negroes generally apply them at random without any regard to the particular symptoms of the disease; concerning which, or the operation of their *materia medica*, they have formed no theory".[39] In other words, black people, unlike whites, used the herbs unscientifically.

Sloane and Barham, botanists and physicians both, note exactly which plants were used in what ways by blacks. "Negroes and Indians use the Root [of the lime tree, *Malus arantica*], ground with Water for Claps, and the stalk to Clean their Teeth", Sloane writes, quoting Barham. Barham also reports that "Negroes plaister over the Body with the Root [*Radix fruticosa lutea*] ground with Water to a Paste in Fevers, Agues, Colics, Headaches, etc.".[40] Some of the medicaments used by blacks in the Caribbean were known to them from Africa. Sloane records: "The seed [of the Bichy-Tree, *Ceratonia affinis*] brought in a Guinea ship from that Country was here planted by Mr Gosse in Col Bourden's Plantation beyond Guanoboa. It is called Bichy by the Coromantyn Negros, and is both eaten and used for Physick in Pains of the Belly."[41] After himself being afflicted, Barham writes: "I was cured by a negro of Hydropical, swelled and inflamed Legs after a Fever, with bathing five or six times in a Decoction of the Leaves and bark of [the Hog-Plum, *Prunus brasiliensis*], wiping and sweating on a Couch after."[42]

---

37 Richard Ligon, *A True and Exact History of the Island of Barbadoes* (London: Peter Parker, 1673), 51. "Kill-devil" and "rum-bullion" were early names for rum.
38 Long, *History of Jamaica*, 381.
39 Ibid.
40 Sloane, *Voyage to the Islands*, 2:390.
41 Ibid., 1:61.
42 Barham, *Hortus Americanus*, 387.

In fact, many Europeans were convinced that Africans and the indigenous peoples of the Americas had a vast knowledge of plant medicines and felt that more should be done to discover their secrets. "Some Physicians and Chirurgeons should be sent to the East and West Indies, and the continent of America to seek what may be found of useful Medicines among the Indians and negroes", suggests John Bellers, a Quaker and a member of the Royal Society.[43] He points out that "we have several valuable Remedies already from thence, as the Bark, Cochineal, etc. It is not to be doubted, but that there are many others yet unknown to Europe. Some Negroes in our islands will cure the Dry Gripes (one of the painful diseases) better than any other Physicians." Bellers hoped that the discovery of more medicines would particularly help Europe's poor.[44]

Unlike Barham and Bellers, Sloane was sceptical of some of the Negro cures. "A Negro-Doctor who was very famous for the Cure of Asthma's, made use of [mistletoe] gather'd off of Sweet-Wood, and Bean or Coral-Tree Tops, but altho' he sometimes cured with it, yet at other Times, he was not so fortunate." He also notes that "they pretend to cure the Pox with Ash-colour'd Saunders [powder]".[45] He relates that turtlers from Jamaica feasted on turtles in the hope of a cure for the Pox, "yet I never saw that this Method, or any other boasted of by the *Indian* or Negro Doctors of any kind, was to be depended upon, but generally deceived those who trusted in them, who were oblig'd to come into the *European* Methods if they intended to be safe".[46]

The white nurses attending to Maria Nugent, wife of the Jamaican governor at the time, were also sceptical. When Nugent was about to give birth, "the old black nurse brought a cargo of herbs, and wished to try various charms to expedite the birth of the child. . . . But the [white] maids took all her herbs from her, and made her remove all the smoking apparatus she had prepared for my benefit."[47]

No doubt there were charlatans among them. Sloane tells the story of

> one Hercules, a lusty Black Negro Overseer, and Doctor who was not only famous amongst the Blacks in his Master Colonel Fuller's plantation, but amongst

---

43   John Bellers, *An Essay Towards the Improvement of Physick, in Twelve Proposals* (London: J. Sowle, 1714), 9, 16.
44   Ibid.
45   Sloane, Voyage to the Islands, 2:92.
46   Ibid., 342.
47   Maria Nugent, *A Journal of a Voyage to, and Residence in, the Island of Jamaica, from 1801 to 1805* (London, 1839), 305–6.

the Whites in the Neighborhood, for curing several diseases, and particularly Gonorrheas. He had been three years before troubled with that Distemper, which he thought by the country Simples he had cur'd, but came to me complaining of a very great heat in making water with intolerable pain, and scalding. Looking upon the part Affected I found he had his Clap, and that Caruncles had grown up and stopt almost quite the passage of Urine... I order'd him some Mercurial Medicines; and would have try'd several other Remedies for his Cure, had I not soon after left the island. There are many such Indian and Black Doctors, who pretend, and are supposed to understand, and cure several Distempers, but by what I could see of their Practice, (which because of the great effects of the Jesuit's Bark, found out by them, I look'd into as much as I could) they do not perform what they pretend, unless in the vertues of some few Simples. Their ignorance of Anatomy, Diseases, Method, etc. renders even that knowledge of the Vertues of Herbs, not only useless, but also sometimes hurtful to those who imploy them.[48]

Sloane's view is shared by Nissen:

It is very true there are many different sorts of physical herbs which are very good and of use, and with the properties of which our physicians are unacquainted but they [black herbalists] have a bad habit of mixing these herbs with spirits and other different useless things. I do believe that many of them understand to heal a wound, or to put a sprained leg in its place again, but as for inward sickness, they should not be permitted to have anything to do with it.[49]

A few decades after Sloane and Barham, Dancer made his own contributions to the study of herbal remedies. In his index of prevailing diseases he noted that yellow thistle, euphorbia, wild cassava, castor oil and hog plum were good for bellyache, while capsicum, dumb cane, cow itch, wild cinnamon and garlic pear were used to treat palsy. "Female weaknesses" were treated with guava, pomegranate, logwood, cashew and star apple.[50] He also records that "a negro at Grenada is said to have been very successful in curing the Yaws, by placing the patient in a cask, with a pan of burning coals, and thus sweating

---

48   Sloane, *Voyage to the Islands*, 92, 115, 141, 342. A sendup of Sloane's work noted that after Hercules became his patient, Sloane's reputation "on the island outshone the black as much as the sun does the black of night"; [William King], *The Present State of Physick in the Island of CAJAMAI* (London, 1710), 2
49   Nissen, *Reminiscences*, 140.
50   Dancer, *Medical Assistant*, 371.

him twice in the day".⁵¹ Dancer drew from various sources, including Barham and Long.

Several medical men suspected that there was much they did not know about the herbal cures used by black people. For example, a Dr William Hillary in Barbados thought "the caustic juices of certain escharotic plants" was used by the slaves to cure yaws, but notes that white people were excluded from knowing how it worked.⁵² Madden, meanwhile, was thoroughly "persuaded that a variety of very valuable plants is known to the negroes, whose medicinal uses we are unacquainted with"; echoing Bellers, he adds that "any person who would undertake an account of the popular medicine of the negroes, would bring to light much information serviceable to medical science".⁵³

Madden was particularly impressed by Benjamin Cochrane, a Muslim who, he said, had begun his study of herbs in Africa before he was captured during war with another village and sold to slave dealers. Cochrane, whose African name is given as Anna Moosa or Gorah Condran, claimed to have taught himself by observing which plants sickened cattle and which plants they ate when they were sick. He told Madden that he had tried out a good many of the remedies on himself. "His skill as a negro doctor, one of the English physicians of Kingston assured me was considerable. He had lately known him called to a young lady, where with his herbs and simples he had effected a successful cure of a serious malady." Cochrane got into the habit of visiting Madden on Sundays and offered insights about "the medicinal plants and popular medicine of the country".⁵⁴

Examples abound of blacks with medicinal knowledge, including the mother of famed nurse Mary Seacole who was a noted doctress and, of course, Mary Seacole herself, and there were many others. Bessie, a leprous slave on one of Lewis's estates, informed him that she wanted to go to a black doctor by the name of Ormond, a slave on a neighbouring estate. Lewis investigated and discovered that Ormond had a good reputation in the area, so he gave Bessie permission to seek him out. He also makes reference to Nancy, the mistress of Lewis's attorney, who "can bleed and mix up medicines and . . . is of more service to the sick than all the doctors".⁵⁵ Few writers do not have similar stories to tell. Madden, for example, recounts the story of a sick white man who had been looked after

---

51 Ibid., 223.
52 Hutson, *Treatment*, 19.
53 Madden, *Twelvemonth's Residence*, 2:48.
54 Ibid., 99–100.
55 Lewis, *Journal*, 81, 84, 94.

by a "brown woman, Mary Logan", to whose skill he was "indebted . . . for his life".[56] Gardner, too, acknowledges that "some of these people [black slaves] were rather famed as doctors, and consulted even by the whites; they had some knowledge, not always lawfully used, of plants and herbs".[57]

So admired were these herbalists that sometimes their white counterparts were very willing to work with them and, perhaps, even learn from them. According to Paiewonsky, "a group of Jews and surgeons conducted a 'rehabilitation' farm on the eastern end of St Thomas to which they carried many . . . desperately sick slaves. After intensive care with the help of experienced 'bush doctors' as well as full utilization of medical knowledge available at the time, they effected a considerable number of remarkable recoveries."[58]

Reports about black people's use of medicinal herbs came from many quarters. The missionary Phillippo was struck with a fever while out riding and went to the nearest house, which happened to belong to a "family of colour". He reports that the whole neighbourhood got involved in his treatment. "Some gathered medicinal herbs; others were sent in different directions for medicinal ingredients; and while some prepared them, others applied leaves to my oppressed and burning head."[59]

In the early twentieth century, Pullen-Burry reported on the bush bath:

> This consists of equal proportions of the leaves of the following plants: ackee, sour sop, jointwood, pimento, cowfoot, elder, lime-leaf and licorice. The patient is plunged into the bath when it is very hot, and is covered with a sheet. When the steam has penetrated the skin, the patient is removed from the bath, and covered with warm blankets leaving the skin undried. A refreshing sleep is invariably the consequence, and a very perceptible fall in temperature.[60]

Years later, observers were still remarking on the effectiveness of local remedies. "Anyone who has lived for some time in Jamaica has come in contact with really marvelous 'Bush remedies'", Williams declares. "For example, a throbbing headache is quickly relieved by the application of a particular cactus which is split and bound on the forehead; and a severe fever is broken effectively by a 'bush tea' made from certain leaves and twigs known only to the old woman

---

56 Madden, *Twelvemonth's Residence*, 2:92–93.
57 Gardner, *History of Jamaica*, 99.
58 Paiewonsky, *Eyewitness Accounts*, 52.
59 Phillippo, *Jamaica*, 259.
60 Pullen-Burry, *Jamaica*, 140–41.

who gathers them and whose only explanation is 'Jes seben bush, Sah, me pick dem one one.'"[61]

Clearly, many black men and women had a reservoir of personal knowledge about herbal medicines and treatments, and whites were well aware of this. Whites were equally conscious that when this knowledge fell short, blacks sought cures and treatments from the nearest Obeah man with the best reputation. "They stand much in Awe of such as pass for Obeah Negroes, these being a sort of Physician or Conjurers, who can, as they believe, not only fascinate them, but cure them when they are bewitched by others."[62] The Obeah man "can cure all diseases; ... he can even reanimate the dead. His knowledge of simples is immense."[63]

The 1824 trial of Andrew Marble before the St Jago de la Vega slave court offers a very interesting insight, not only into Obeah but also into its role on one plantation. According to the sometimes confusing statements taken during Marble's trial, he had propositioned a woman by the name of Pamila, who refused his advances and subsequently fell sick. She refused to take the medicine prescribed her by the white doctor, as she was convinced that Marble "had done her so" and was the only one who could cure her. The single dose she took of the doctor's medicine was administered by Marble. She was sick for more than a year with what the doctor who was brought in on the case suggested might be a "dropsical condition", which he cautiously admitted "might have been produced from other than natural causes".

Pamila called for Marble constantly but at first he refused to attend to her, pointing out that he was not a doctor. The overseer commanded him to go to Pamila, but he still refused and even spent some time in the stocks over it. When he finally *did* go, Pamila's son, Edward Graham, was present. He testified that upon seeing the woman, Marble declared that "she had too many things in her skin, besides [an] iron bar, for there was toots, and glass, and nough *swate*". Marble began by stripping Pamila naked; after calling for water and rum, "he put his mouth to [her] skin, sucked it, spit out teeth, then glass". Edward said that Marble told him "there was something in the ground which did his mother so", and he removed "some pieces of glass and other things all tied up together". Marble explained to Edward that "if you take a hair out of person's head, and put it into the ground with them *swate*, it will catch the somebody the hair come from".

---

61 Williams, *Voodoos and Obeahs*, 325.
62 Hughes, *Natural History*, 15.
63 Rampini, *Letters*, 132.

On another occasion, Marble was escorted to Pamila's hut by Anthony James, on the orders of the overseer. James, described as a Christian, reported that

> the prisoner, [Marble], asked for salt, which was given him. He went out and got some limes, called for rum, which he got, threw it into rum and salt, and took out a bag from his pocket (which was produced). Prisoner opened it, and showed the witness some soap, berries, chalk, and shell; took six, threw them in water, when four swam, and two sunk. He said there was something in the old woman's skin. He took chalk, and marked the old woman's skin; put his mouth to old woman's skin, held it hard, and shook it like a dog biting, and spit out some glass and teeth, which he said came out of the old woman's skin.

At this point, James, suspicious and not wanting to be a made a fool of, asked to search Marble's mouth but said he found nothing in it. Marble went back to what he was doing and sucked out more teeth and pieces of glass bottles. After that "he took lime and rubbed all over her, then mixed the chalk and lime, and bid her drink". The woman refused, saying he must drink it first if it was good, but Marble would not and left the hut.

Despite Marble's ministrations, however, Pamila succumbed to her illness and died some two or three months after he began attending her. In his defence, he pointed out that "'he was not an Obeah man to kill, but an Obeah man to cure'". Intriguingly, the overseer admitted knowing that Marble was considered an Obeah man and did not seem troubled by it. Also intriguing is the fact, pointed out by the chairman of the proceedings, that the overseer had originally reported Pamila as dying from natural causes, not from Obeah. Perhaps the fact that Marble associated himself with "Obeah to cure" had granted him some sort of immunity, but the case certainly shows that at least a few overseers and managers were prepared to tolerate Obeah as long as it was perceived as causing no harm.[64]

Whites were often reluctant to accept claims by black patients that Obeah was responsible for their illness, but sometimes they expressed bafflement at the symptoms they witnessed for themselves. "Ann Elizabeth Smith, aged 50, Sambo, domestic servant, mother of three children; had a miscarriage between first and second, and an interval of seventeen years between second and third child. During that interval was in bad health and under the delusion that she

---

64 "Trial for Practising Obeah", 3.

was hurted (Obeahed), and is now under that delusion", writes Dr A. Stobo in the article "Spasmodic Action of the Uterus – Obeism", which appeared in the *Medical Times* of 1851. Smith complained of "intermittent fevers, . . . constipated bowels, colicy pains, singing in her ears as if surrounded by crickets, crawling pains in her abdomen, especially about the lower part of it".[65] On one occasion, Stobo observed that

> There was great jumping (if I may be allowed the expression) in the bowels; it shakes her and the bed on which she is lying. It appears to commence about the left side, a little below the umbilicus, with three or four spasmodic twitches; the uterus then appears to rise up like a ball, and, for the space of thirty seconds or so, violent contractions seem to be made in longitudinal fibres . . . the patient complains of fixed pain above the pubes.

Stobo treated her with castor oil, infusion of senna and a painkiller composed of tincture of opium and "aether sulph[uricus]".

Following the birth of a healthy girl, Smith continued to complain of pain. Stobo observed

> an undulating going on constantly from side to side; at short intervals the whole abdomen rose up into a ball, the navel forming the apex and this was constantly repeated. I observed patient always groaned when this occurred. She says she never has been able to lie on her sides since this last pregnancy. She has not slept well for the last two nights owing to an increase in the spasmodic motions. Her appetite good, bowels open, milk plentiful, the child thriving.[66]

Stobo dismissed the woman's claim that she was Obeahed as a delusion, but his use of the word Obeism in the article's title suggests some conflict on his part, due, no doubt, to his inability to offer a diagnosis with which he could be comfortable.

During his 1836 visit to the West Indies, Dr William Lloyd related an anecdote that he, too, appeared unable to explain. According to him, "an intelligent 'quadroon', a book-keeper on the estate . . . says that the Obi man called at his house, and asked him to change some silver; he offered what change he had; Obi said it would not do, and went away muttering vengeance". That night,

---

65 A. Stobo, "Spasmodic Action of the Uterus – Obeism", *Medical Times*, n.s. 3 (5 July–27 December 1851): 306.
66 Ibid.

the bookkeeper had frightful dreams about Obi, and a severe pain seized his head and limbs; he went to Obi, and asked him what he had done, and told him he would be punished: a boy afterwards called at his house, and told him he must look at his legs; there were things to come out, though they had no sores at the time; after examining them, the boy produced a basin with odd things in it, shells, bits of pipe, charcoal, insects, and feather, which things he said he had extracted. The bottle and its contents I saw, and the man showed me his legs; on one of them, there are three irritable ulcers, and two in the other; the sufferer is reduced so much, as to make his recovery doubtful. The Obi man is imprisoned waiting the event. The bookkeeper's present state is one of actual disease; and of that kind, and to that degree, which would seem to be impossible to be produced solely by a terrified imagination: if not, it was a curious coincidence that disease should establish itself at the precise juncture, when Obi said he should be "Obeahed".[67]

Thus Obeah could both cure sickness and cause it.

A negro who is taken ill inquires of the Obeah man the cause of his sickness whether it will prove mortal or not and within what time he shall die or recover. The oracle generally ascribes the distemper to the malice of some particular person by name and advises to set Obi for that person but if no hopes are given of recovery, immediate despair takes place which no medicine can remove and death is the certain consequence.[68]

The despair could affect not only the victims but also their family members, and not even Christian conversion guaranteed immunity. Brother J.R. Holland offers an interesting story which demonstrates the spiritual conflicts faced by converts:

Quite lately I discovered in that neighbourhood a painful instance of the influence still held over some minds by obeahism or witchcraft. A young married woman in connection with our congregation had been afflicted with disease of a dropsical nature and, to my regret and mortification, I was unable to prevail upon her husband to employ a medical man though he evidently had it in his power to do so. At last his wife died without any proper means having been used to arrest her disease. On occasion of my visit to his wife, I had sufficient evidence to convince me that the husband was not devoid of sensibility or af-

---

67 William Lloyd, *Letters from the West Indies During a Visit in the Autumn of 1836 and the Spring of 1837* (London: Darton and Harvey, 1838), 167–68.
68 Edwards, *History Civil and Commercial*, 168.

fection and, while I could not account for his neglect in one particular, it never entered into my mind that it was owing to any superstitious belief. When too late to counteract it I learnt that his relatives had persuaded him "not to throw away his money" – the woman was "obeahed" and no medicine could do her any good. Among other places, Lititz was named as the probable scene of the obeah man's spell and, the time, the Sabbath day when she went to church. All this was carefully concealed from me and a few hints that came to my ears by a circuitous route first induced me to put plain and pointed questions to one of the neighbours, a communicant, who, with evident timidity, disclosed what he had heard.[69]

As Christian converts, it is possible that this couple may also have disdained assistance from the local Obeah man or woman but saw no contradiction between their Christian beliefs and their belief in the inevitability of the Obeah curse.

Drawing objects out of their patients was a common practice, as described by Hughes:

> A Negro Woman, who was troubled with Rheumatic Pains, was persuaded by one of these Obeah Doctors, that she was bewitched, and that these pains were owing to several Pieces of Glass, rusty Nails, and Splinters of sharp Stones, that were lodged in different Parts of Her Body; adding, that it was in his Power, if paid for it, to cure her, by extracting these from her through her navel. Upon payment of the stipulated Premium, he produced his Magical Apparatus, being two Earthen Basons, a Handful of different Kinds of Leaves, and a piece of Soap. In one of these Basons he made a strong lather, in the other he put the bruised Herbs; then clapping with one Hand to the navel, and pouring the Suds by degrees upon them, he stroked the parts most affected with the other Hand, always ending toward the navel: In a short time after, thrusting his Finger and Thumb into the Cataplasms of Herbs, he produced several Pieces of broken Glass, Nails and Splinters of Stones.[70]

Greed undid the Obeah man, who

> unluckily demanded a farther reward than what was stipulated; but as the woman's husband was one of those very few, who had no faith in such pretended cures, being accidentally knowing in some of their secrets, instead of an

---

69   *Periodical Accounts* 18 (1846): 302.
70   Hughes, *Natural History*, 15.

additional reward, he made him, by threats, refund the money he had already received, bidding him, if he was a conjurer, find out by his art some Means of getting it again restored to him.[71]

Hughes omits to tell us if the woman was indeed cured or suffered a relapse upon the return of the money.

While the above events do not appear to have involved any particular ceremony, Phillippo describes a dance which ended in a similar extraction of strange material:

> The master of ceremonies, who was usually denominated Doctor, by violent and excessive dancing, as well as by the use of poisonous drugs, deprived his victims of sensibility, and apparently of life; and when, by the use of medicinal herbs, he had restored them to their former condition, pretended that he had done so by extracting pieces of glass bottles, snakes, and other Obeah ingredients and reptiles from their skin.

He relates that "seldom, however, did the constitution of the patient recover from the effects of the experiment".[72]

Atwood observed much the same thing in Dominica but describes it with less detail. We see certain differences between Andrew Marble's *modus operandi* and that of the practitioners familiar to Atwood. For example, Marble simply went about his work without offering oral incantations, though he did appear to rely heavily on the use of divination. In Atwood's account,

> Every preliminary being settled between the patient and the operator, the latter begins his work with mumbling over a few strange words, and having everything ready, the patient so placed in a dark room, that he cannot discover the cheat, he pinches and pulls him till the other cries out with the pain; after which, the conjuror produces sticks, knives, pieces of glass, and even whole bottles, which he persuades the other that he actually took out of the place he complained of; and then rubbing it over with grease and soot, or some such thing, the simple patient believes himself to be perfectly cured.[73]

Gardner was quite aware of the trick: "sometimes by a little clumsy jugglery the Obeah practitioner appeared to extract all sorts of rubbish, or even living

---

71 Ibid.
72 Phillippo, *Jamaica*, 248–49.
73 Atwood, *Island of Dominica*, 270–71.

things such as frogs and lizards, from the body of the sufferer. The arms, the legs, the head, or the stomach of the patient was manipulated upon, and presently the cause, or one of the causes of the painful symptoms, fell out upon the floor!"[74]

Certainly, it would seem that where bush medicine failed to work, other measures were called upon. William Waite, the Obeah man discussed in the previous chapter, did his best for one patient but was rewarded only with arrest and, upon conviction, thirty-eight days' hard labour. In his defence, he had explained in court:

> dem say me obeah man, but, massa, me no sabe obeah at all; all me do me will say; Shaw been sick long time; bad sick, and as ebberybody call me obeah man, dem say must call me, an me go, and me bin carry some lilly piece glass and bone with me, and when me go, and dem teaze me, me say well me will pull dem ting wha make him sick, an me had de glass and de bone in my mouth, and me put me mout to him belly so suck, suck, long time, den me say me pull out dem ting so show dem; when me done, Shaw say him feel more dere, an as me hab no more dat time, me say him too training, me will come narra time, ... massa, if dem fool, me can't help; massa, if me do wrong, me sorry.[75]

But if there was a belief that they could pull things out, then there was also a conviction that they could insert things as well, a phenomenon that was surely easier to accomplish. The witch masters "can put into people a lump of twisted hair, cut-off nails, or sharp thin pieces of rusted iron and in a short time their victim dies".[76] Atwood also reports that Obeah men and women persuaded their clients that they were "possessed by the devil, as a punishment for some hidden crime; but if not well paid for it, besides promising to submit to every direction of the Obeah master, he will not undertake the cure". He adds that "many instances have been known in the West Indies, of negros who have been persuaded by these Obeah people, that they were possessed in this manner, till they have killed themselves in despair".[77]

Most of the cases reported on concern Obeah men, but some women also had formidable reputations as Obeah practitioners. For example, according to Paiewonsky, in the Danish West Indies, Mongo Maud was credited with

---

74   Gardner, *History of Jamaica*, 129.
75   *John Bull*, 11 November 1843, 711.
76   Paiewonsky, *Eyewitness Accounts*, 124.
77   Atwood, *Island of Dominica*, 270–71.

raising the dead. A herbalist originally from West Africa, she was usually called not to attend the sick

> but to preserve the dead, an art for which she had also achieved notoriety. The wife of a prominent planter had died after a long and serious illness. The death had occurred in her husband's absence. He was due back on the plantation in a matter of days. The family was anxious to postpone the funeral until his arrival. Mongo Maud was sent for by messengers on horseback. When [she] arrived . . . , she brought with her several sacks full of dried leaves, twigs, and the cut bark of special trees. Enlisting the services of several muscular field laborers, she mixed her ingredients together then had them pounded in large mortars until they attained the consistency of a coarse powder. All of this was done in a matter of two or three hours. Then Mongo Maud laid down the law. If her work was to be effective, it was vital that she be left alone with the corpse. She wanted no one prying into her techniques. She guaranteed that when the husband arrived, the body of his wife would be in excellent condition.[78]

Her work was so effective that when the husband came back, he actually found his wife alive. It was suggested that she had fallen into a cataleptic trance from which Mongo Maud had woken her during the application of the preservative.

Decades later, Lafcadio Hearn devoted a couple of paragraphs to Martiniquan shop owner Manm-Robert, who was "skilled in the knowledge and use of medicinal herbs, which she gathers herself upon the *mornes*. But for these services she never accepts any remuneration. She is a sort of Mother of the poor in her immediate vicinity." She not only helped to heal, "if anybody is afraid of being bewitched (*quimboisé*) Manm-Robert can furnish him or her with something that will keep the bewitchment away".[79] Though their knowledge of herbs might have been extensive, at times the Obeah man or woman offered nothing more than a charm. Hearn relates that "Manm Robert brings me something queer, something hard tied up in a tiny piece of black cloth, with a string attached to hang it round my neck. I must wear it, she says. . . . It is to keep me from catching the *verette* [smallpox]! And what is inside it? Three grains of corn with a bit of camphor."[80]

Healing and herbalism were the more benign aspects of Obeah, but as we have seen, even in discussing them, writers often expressed their observations in ways that contributed to racial theories, by emphasizing the simple gullibil-

---

78 Paiewonsky, *Eyewitness Accounts*, 129–30.
79 Hearn, *Two Years*, 202–3.
80 Ibid., 223.

ity of blacks or their superstitious nature. Many readers would also not have missed the unspoken message that, being primitive creatures, blacks were closer to nature and thus knew its secrets.

CATCHING SHADOWS AND PULLING OBEAH:

THE RISE OF MYALISM

Most historians now make distinguish between Obeah men and women and myalists, but in the eighteenth and nineteenth centuries, when writers first took notice of myalism, it was seen as a facet of Obeah. In his *History of Jamaica,* Long writes that it was the Obeah men who actually initiated myalism.

> not long since some of these execrable wretches in Jamaica introduced what they called the myal dance and established a kind of society into which they invited all they could. The lure hung out was that every Negroe initiated into the myal society would be invulnerable by the white men and, although they might in appearance be slain, the obeah man could at his pleasure restore the body to life. The method by which this trick was carried on was by a cold infusion of the herb branched colalue; which, after the agitation of dancing, threw the party into a profound sleep. In this state he continued to all appearance lifeless, no pulse, nor motion of the heart being perceptible, till on being rubbed with another infusion as yet unknown to the Whites the effects of the colalue gradually went off, the body resumed its motions and the party on whom the experiment had been tried awoke as from a trance entirely ignorant of any thing that had passed since he left off dancing.[81]

In his footnote to the above account, Long informs us that

> the myal gentry make the infusion [of the branched calalu, *Xanthosoma hastifolium*] with rum. In regard to the other infusion which puts an end to its operation we can only conjecture. It is possible that, by frequent trials, the Negroes have found pretty accurately the length of time which the sleep may last and so take care to proportion the dose. Besides it has lately been discovered that vegetable acids such as lime juice, vinegar, etc. are antidotes to the effect of opium, and all vegetable poisons taken internally: their external application has not been tried but might answer the same purpose especially towards the decline of the sleepy fit and I think it is that these Negroes use them to revive their myal men.[82]

---

81 Long, *History of Jamaica*, 416–17.
82 Ibid.

The Fuller report also makes no distinctions, explaining that Obeah "is . . . the general term to denote those Africans who . . . practice witchcraft or sorcery comprehending also the class of what are called Myal men".[83] Phillippo agrees that "Myalism, as well as Fetishism, [are] constituent parts of Obeism",[84] and Madden also comes to the same conclusion: "There are two descriptions of obeah; one that is practiced by means of incantations; the other by the administering of medicated potions – in former times, it is said of poisons, and these practitioners were called myal men."[85]

Intriguingly, Martha Warren Beckwith claims an identification of myal with John Canoe (or junkanoo), the masquerade festival:

> A group of avowedly myal songs from the Cockpit county of St Elizabeth neighboring the Maroon settlement of Accompong; in their similarity to and in some cases their identity with the John Canoe songs from Lacovia and Prospect prove the contention that in this section of Jamaica the John Canoe mask and dance is associated with the invocation of spirits of the dead. . . . [Her informants] James White and William Forbes were, in 1924, when this material was collected, old song leaders of the Cockpit country with a reputation for knowledge of herb medicines and of songs to raise the dead. [They told her that] the Lacovia group [of John Canoe dancers] was led by an oldish man named Ewan. He wore neither mask nor wig. . . . His cap, which stood fully four feet high, was two storied, with four pillared porticoes at right angles to each other roofed with a long peak like a fool's cap topped with a tuft of feathers. . . . Ewan was a notorious myal man in Lacovia, that is a man who held communication with the spirits of the dead. He was believed to be able to summon the spirits of the dead to work mischief upon an enemy. . . . Mary Campbell, [Ewan's] leading singing girl at that time, told me that he always took the cap out into the grave-yard on the night before it was to be brought out upon the road, and performed the songs and dances there among the dead. . . . When I told Gracie this, the old woman who acted as sexton to the church, she said "I believe that the dead come out and play with it, and they cast their shadow upon it", and she went on to explain that for this reason Ewan was able to use the cap to work obeah, or witchcraft.[86]

More generally, however,

---

83 Edwards, *History Civil and Commercial*, 2:91.
84 Phillippo, *Jamaica*, 248.
85 Madden, *Twelvemonth's Residence*, 2:68.
86 Beckwith, *Jamaican Ethnobotany*, 10–11.

the Myal-man is . . . summoned to the sick person's yard, the drum played, and a company of dancers formed and songs sung invoking the spirt of the dance, in order "to bring the spirit to tend the sickness". When the company is worked up to the proper pitch of excitement, the Myal-man or an associate claims possession by the spirits, in which condition it is revealed to him what herbs to use for a cure or what sorcery to employ to overcome the obeah which has been "laid" for the patient. If the patient eventually dies, it can be claimed that he has not followed the prescription exactly or that his enemy's obeah has too strong a power over him for the remedies to prove effectual.[87]

Perhaps to a degree that did not occur with Obeah practitioners, myalists were said to be in touch with spirits. Revd Abraham J. Emerick notes that it was "persons who are favoured with communications with spirits [who] are called 'mial' people. They are said to be 'fo-eye', that is four eyed, by which is meant that they can see spirits and converse with them. Both sexes make pretensions to this power; hence you have mial men and mial women."[88] Emerick claims that with the aid of these spirits, Myal men and Myal women could "kill or injure anyone. . . . The mial man harms by depriving persons of their shadows, or setting deaths upon them."[89] The malevolence of myalists was disputed, however, with some writers believing that they were fairly benign and working to undo the evils of Obeah. Williams, for example, claims that in his own experience it was the Obeah man who set deaths or shadows on people and the myal man who released them.[90] Gardner is of a similar view, pointing out that "of late years, Myalism has generally been regarded as an art by which that of the Obeah man could be counteracted".[91]

Many writers reported on the myalists' identification with the powers of good. According to the Moravian missionary Buchner, "the Myalmen . . . were accounted good and holy. They pretended to be able to make Obeahism of no effect; that they could discover and destroy it; and maintained that they were sent by God to purge the world from all wickedness; and that they had received power to procure rest for the wandering spirits, or shadows as they were called."[92] Phillippo understood that Myalism was supposed "to

---

87 Ibid., 49–50.
88 Quoted in Williams, *Voodoos and Obeahs*, 155.
89 Ibid.
90 Ibid., 154.
91 Gardner, *History of Jamaica*, 191.
92 Buchner, *Moravians*, 138–39.

counteract the effect of Obeism", but, he argues, it "was often much more demoralizing and fatal in its results".[93] In fact, some myal men "laid claim to an immediate intercourse with God; and divine revelations".[94] Revd Banbury notes that while "an obeahman can always 'pull' as well as 'put,' cure as well as kill", Myalists claimed to be "angel men [who] believed [the] world was coming to an end, Christ was coming and God had sent them to pull all the obeahs and catch the shadows that were spellbound at the cotton trees". They took their appointed role so seriously that some even "went into the churches on Sundays and interrupted divine service by pulling out persons whom they suspected dealt in obeah, or who were so reported to them".[95]

How they accomplished their work was a source of fascination.

> This true story is about a man who is a duppy catcher and a doctor who works by a spirit. He is capable of giving medicines to cure all manner of diseases. . . . In order to see the so-called duppy on the patients when they are approaching, he ties long pieces of white calico all about his yard to let the duppy appear upon them as the image of a magic lantern upon the screen. He is always heard saying "Wet up the calico, Lord." . . . He believes that there is obeah in many people, especially in women. To eradicate this obeah, he performs what he calls the "balm" when he beats the patient with wet calico and rams his abdomen with clenched fists.[96]

The invocation of the Christian god by the myalists certainly indicates that some level of syncretism had occurred between Obeah and Christianity.

Those myalists who caused their clients to enter a sleep so deep they were considered dead were regarded as highly suspect. Gardner believed that trickery was involved but could not identify the narcotic used.

> A mixture was given in rum, of a character which presently induced sleep so profound, as, by the uninitiated and alarmed, to be mistaken for death. After this had been administered to someone chosen for the purpose, the Myal dance began, and presently the victim staggered and fell, to all appearances dead. Mystic charms were then used: the body was rubbed with some infusion; and in process of time, the narcotic having lost its power, the subject of the experiment rose up as one restored to life, a fact for which the Obeah man claimed all the merit. The plant said to be used was the branched calalue, or solanum

---

93 Phillippo, *Jamaica*, 248.
94 Buchner, *Moravians*, 139.
95 Williams, *Voodoos and Obeahs*, 155.
96 "Folklore of the Negroes", *Folklore: A Quarterly Review* 15 (1904): 87–94.

... [but] if it was the Solanum, it can only be the cold infusion which has the narcotic power, and which is stated to belong to the European variety; for when it is boiled it is harmless.[97]

Like all things connected with Obeah, myal dances fascinated writers and were, as we will see in future chapters, to provide inspiration for many novelists, poets and short-story writers looking to include sensational accounts of imagined savagery in their writing. Indeed, Lewis's account below is remarkable for its restraint, given its author's earlier forays into Gothic fiction. Note that he uses the terms *Obeah-man* and *Myal-man* interchangeably. According to him, "The Obeah ceremonies always commenced with what is called by the negroes the 'Myal dance.' This is intended to remove any doubt of the Chief Obeah-man's supernatural powers; and, in the course of it, he undertakes to show his art by killing one of the persons present, whom he pitches upon for that purpose." He then

> sprinkles various powders over the devoted victim, blows upon him, and dances round him, obliges him to drink a liquor prepared for the occasion; and, finally, the sorcerer and his assistants seize him and whirls him rapidly round and round till the man loses his sense and falls on the ground, to all appearances and the belief of the spectators, a perfect corpse. The Chief Myal-man then utters loud shrieks, rushes out of the house with wild and frantic gestures, and conceals himself in some neighbouring wood. At the end of two or three hours he returns with a large bundle of herbs, from some of which he squeezes the juice into the mouth of the dead person; with others he anoints his eyes and stains the tips of his fingers; accompanying the ceremony with a great variety of grotesque actions, and chanting all the while something between a song and a howl, while the assistants, hand-in-hand dance slowly around them in a circle, stamping the ground loudly with their feet to keep time with his chant. A considerable time elapses . . . but at length the corpse gradually recovers animation, rises from the ground perfectly recovered and the Myal dance concludes.
>
> After this proof of power, those who wish to be revenged upon their enemies apply to the sorcerer for some of the same powder which produced apparent death upon their companion; and as they never employ the means used for his recovery, of course, the power once administered never fails to be lastingly fatal. It must be superfluous to mention that the Myal-men on these occasions substitutes a poison for a narcotic.[98]

---

97 Gardner, *History of Jamaica*, 191, 199.
98 Lewis, *Journal*, 166–67.

Buchner, the Moravian missionary, discusses a myal revival in much more lurid terms, as a way of illustrating the "satanic" forces against which missionaries had to contend: "In the year 1842, African superstition and fanaticism made a strong effort to gain once more the ascendancy over the minds of many; especially in the northern parts of the island . . . the infatuation was so great, and the temptation so strong, that a satanic agency, an effort of the prince of darkness to keep the captives in his chains, could not be mistaken."[99] He goes on to explain that in 1842, "several Negroes on an estate near Montego Bay gave themselves out to be Myalmen, and began to practice the heathenish rites openly and boldly". Myalism caught on, spreading through the parishes of St James, Westmoreland and Trelawny.

> Hundreds and thousands laid claim to the same distinction or followed them. . . . As soon as the darkness of evening set in, they assembled in crowds in open pastures, most frequently under large cotton trees, which they worshipped and counted holy; after sacrificing some fowls, the leader began an ex tempore song, in a wild strain, which was answered in chorus; the dance followed, grew wilder and wilder, until they were in a state of excitement bordering on madness. . . . At times, Obeah was to be discovered [by the myal men], or a "shadow" was to be caught; a little coffin being prepared, in which it was to be inclosed and buried.

The outbreak was so worrying to the government that several hundred special constables were sworn in to assist in arresting myalists. "As many as a hundred at once" were jailed for weeks at a time.[100]

Despite their reputation as the antidote to Obeah, myalists were said to specialize in "duppy catching", which Phillippo claims entailed causing "the death of victims by pretending to catch their shadows, or holding them spellbound, as within a magic circle. By the slave law it was punishable by death."[101] "Shadow catching is invariably done in the night", declares Emerick, who arrived in Jamaica in 1895 and went on to write what is perhaps the definitive book on contemporary myal practice.

---

99 Buchner, *Moravians*, 156.
100 Ibid. According to Gardner, one Myal man, a Dr Taylor, "drew great crowds after him in Manchester and Clarendon". He was "accidentally killed" in prison. Gardner, *History of Jamaica*, 461.
101 Phillippo, *Jamaica*, 247.

The person suspected of having lost his shadow is taken to the cotton-tree, where his shadow is . . . spellbound, or to which it was nailed. The mial men and mial women are accompanied by a large concourse of people. The victim is dressed all in white, with a white handkerchief about his head. Eggs and fowls are taken together with cooked food to the cotton tree. . . . The cotton tree is pelted with eggs, and the necks of fowls are wrung off and the bodies are cast at it. This is done to propitiate the deaths or duppies that had their shadows enthralled at the tree. The singing and dancing proceed more vigorously as the shadow begins to make signs of leaving the tree. A white basin of water to receive it is held up. After they have sung and danced to their heart's content, they suddenly catch up the person and run home with him, affirming that this shadow is caught and covered up in the basin. When the patient has reached his home, a wet cloth is applied to his head and his shadow is said to be restored to him.[102]

Cotton trees were often associated with Obeah, so it stands to reason that they would also be important in myal rites. Gardner reports that African Obeah practitioners celebrated "mysterious rites . . . under the shadow of the gigantic cotton trees". Decades later, Joseph Williams quotes Emerick as stating that "[the cotton] tree was held in veneration and it is hard to get Negroes to cut it down because they are afraid that if they did so the deaths which took up their abode at its roots would injure them". Emerick was also of the conviction that, during slavery, the trees themselves had been worshipped and sacrifices were often laid at their roots. James Anthony Froude reports that "the ceiba is the sacred tree of the negro, the temple of Jumbi, the proper home of Obeah. To cut one down is impious. No black in his right mind would wound even the bark. A Jamaican police officer told me that if a ceiba had to be removed, the men who used the axe were well dosed with rum to give them courage to defy the devil."[103]

The image of half-naked black people dancing under a cotton tree captured the imagination of fiction and non-fiction writers alike. Gardner, for example, describes how "they were accustomed to meet together after nightfall, generally beneath the shadow of a cotton-tree. Fowls were sacrificed, and wild songs sung, in the chorus of which the multitude joined. Dancing then began, becoming more and more weirdlike in character, until one and another fell exhausted to the ground, when their incoherent utterances were listened to

---

102   Quoted in Williams, *Voodoos and Obeahs*, 155.
103   Gardner, *History of Jamaica*, 392; Williams, *Voodoos and Obeahs*, 155; James Anthony Froude, *The English in the West Indies; or, The Bow of Ulysses* (London: Longmans, Green, 1888), 69.

as divine revelation." He notes with some pride that "very few members of churches were implicated in these proceedings".[104]

If myalists were "good" sorcerers, then it stands to reason that their appearance would not be as malevolent as that of Obeah practitioners, or so at least one observer claims. May Robinson notes that the myalist was "often of strikingly good physique, respectable appearance, and always decently dressed. He does more in the 'duppy-catching' line, and does not accept a small fee; ... his motives for adopting the calling being ... the facilities it affords him for gratifying his animal passions, debauchery being the principal feature of this ceremonial."[105] She then titillates the imagination of readers by noting: "of that ceremonial little is really known, and the orgies on grand occasions are said to be beyond description, and any white man venturing to intrude on them would do so at the peril of his life". What Robinson claims to know is that "a night is fixed for the operation, rum is provided, perhaps a white cock is killed (one of the breed known as 'senseh'), feasting, drinking, and drumming with occasional intervals of manipulation of the body, continue all night, and, if successful, the duppy is caught enclosed in a bottle, taken away and buried". According to her, "'duppy-catching' finds a great many votaries. A child suffers from epileptic fits, a woman is barren, or a man has an incurable ulcer; the duppy-catcher is consulted, and they are told so and so 'has set a duppy' on them, which he for a consideration, undertakes to catch."[106]

Banbury provides some examples of Obeah pulling songs.

> Lord have mercy, oh!
> Christ have mercy, oh!
> Obeah pain hot, oh!
> Lord, we come fe pull he, oh
> A no we put he, oh
> And we come fe pull he, oh

Another song went

> Dandy obeah day a, oh
> Me wi pull he, oh
> A any way him run, oh
> Me wi pull he, oh.[107]

---

104 Gardner, *History of Jamaica*, 461.
105 Robinson, "Obeah Worship", 211.
106 Ibid.
107 Banbury, *Jamaica Superstitions*, 21–22.

According to Banbury, pulling Obeah had a cost of four shillings, while pulling shadows or ghosts required the payment of six shillings.[108]

Phillippo was among those who were suspicious of everything connected with myalism and ascribed dark designs even to what might have been interpreted as beneficial actions:

> The Myal-men, having most of them been employed in attendance on the sick in the hospitals of estates, and thereby acquired some knowledge of medicine, have, since the abolition of slavery, set up as medical men; and in order to increase their influence, and consequently their gains, have called to their aid the mysteries of this abominable superstition; in many cases accomplishing their purpose by violence as well as by terror.[109]

On one occasion, he "saw a negro suffering from a gum-boil, who persisted in affirming that the Myal Doctor had extracted a snake from the affected part".[110]

Myalists or duppy catchers, like Obeah men and women, continued their trade into the twentieth century, as observed by the American folklorist and ethnographer Martha Warren Beckwith, who notes:

> Every Myal-man, Obeah-doctor, or revivalist "Shepherd" is accompanied by a "Mammy" or "Shepherdess" (not his wife) whose general knowledge of herbs aids her in prescribing locally in simple cases. For more serious illness, a gathering is held at the home of the sick person or at the doctor's yard where under the influence of rhythmic dance and song the spirits are persuaded to yield the secret of the patient's malady and the cure to be employed.[111]

While some differentiate between what myalists did and what Obeah practitioners did, others make it clear that whether worked for good or for evil, Obeah was still Obeah.

The *Daily Gleaner* of 28 September 1926 quotes Grace Garrison as saying, "I don't work obeah, but I can pull obeah." Two years before, George Neil, on trial as an accessory to murder, declared on the other hand, "it is not me who kill the woman. I don't work that sort of obeah. The sort of obeah that

---

108 Ibid.
109 Phillippo, *Jamaica*, 249.
110 Ibid., 263.
111 Beckwith, *Jamaican Ethnobotany*, 9.

I work is to drive away spirits or cure sickness."[112] Officialdom itself made no distinction. "The Rules and regulations for the Jamaica Constabulary of 1867 required constables to 'arrest every person pretending to be a dealer in obeah or myalism'."[113]

Myalists seized the imagination of writers back in England. William George Hamley, scion of the famous Hamleys toy store family, notes in his 1862 novel, *Captain Clutterbuck's Champagne*, that

> there was another class of impostors calling themselves Myallmen, who asserted that they had the power of reanimating dead bodies, and who sometimes exercised their art to the astonishment and terror of many witnesses. Either the seeming dead were in collusion with the Myallmen, or the latter knew how to induce a temporary coma by means of drugs, or by a mesmeric process. It appears that great perplexity was once caused by the execution, for some capital offence of a magician, who, up to the last, assured his friends and admirers that death had no power over him. Hanged in their sight he undoubtedly was; but whether the evidence of their senses was strong enough to overpower belief in the supernatural, it is not so easy to determine.[114]

Sorcerers able to raise people from the dead, wild dances under great cotton trees, unknown poisons whose effects mimicked death – all these and more proved heady inspiration for English novelists and other writers. Again and again, stories that included one or more of these plot devices occurred and recurred in British writing, contributing to stereotyped views of blacks that underpinned the racism of the day. But, perhaps more than anything else, it was the association of Obeah with rebellion that ignited the fear and loathing with which writers viewed it.

---

112 Diana Paton, "Obeah Acts: Producing and Policing the Boundaries of Religion in the Caribbean", *Small Axe* 28 (2009): 2–18.
113 Williams, *Voodoos and Obeahs*, 102.
114 William George Hamley, *Captain Clutterbuck's Champagne: A West Indian Reminiscence* (London: William Blackwood and Sons, 1862), 156–57.

CHAPTER 4

Challenging Order and Inspiring Resistance

RUM, GUNPOWDER AND BLOOD: A REVOLUTIONARY BREW

The planters soon recognized that obeah was associated with rebellion. Their experiences during the early 1700s with Nanny, a Maroon leader who established a settlement of free slaves at Nanny Town in Portland, had alerted them that those said to have Obeah powers were held in high regard. A note made in Jamaica's Assembly papers for 1733 records the citation of one William Cuffee for "having killed Nanny, the rebels' old obeah woman".[1] In his 1950 travel book *The Traveller's Tree: A Journey Through the Caribbean Islands*, Patrick Leigh Fermor relates his discovery of an old book containing a note on "the notorious Nanny . . . [who] was possessed of supernatural powers, and spirited away the best and finest of the slaves from the outlying estates. She never went into battle armed like the rest, but received the bullets of the enemy that were aimed at her and returned them with fatal effect in a manner of which decency forbids a nearer description."[2]

The Maroons continued to maintain a belief in Nanny's magical powers long after she died. Colonel C.L.G. Harris of the Moore Town Maroons told folklorist Laura Tanna that "many people ascribe magical powers to Nanny. I [do] so and I think every Maroon who has a right to call himself or herself so, believes so." According to him, "Nanny at one time in her career decided to defeat a whole British battalion single-handedly and so she placed her pot in a particular spot, [on a narrow] pathway [where] the English could march only in

---

1   Wikipedia, "Nanny of the Maroons", http://en.wikipedia.org/wiki/Nanny_of_the
_Maroons.
2   Patrick Leigh Fermor, *The Traveller's Tree: A Journey Through the Caribbean Islands* (1950; repr., London: John Murray, 1965), 374.

125

single file and so when the British came, each man peeped into the pot because it was boiling, boiling, but no fire was underneath it." Each man who looked into the pot fell down and rolled off the cliff; the "army was completely decimated and then Nanny stopped the last one before he could look in", showed him what had happened to the others and sent him back to tell his commander of their defeat. Harris added that "it was this great Nanny who, after the signing of the Treaty, caught the bullets. Of course, so many people know the method that she used and she caught them and returned them whence they came." Tanna records that Harris gestured like a woman lifting her skirts when speaking about how Nanny caught the bullets.[3] (Legend has it that she caught them in her bottom.)

How much the planters knew about Nanny's reputed supernatural skills is open to speculation. It is quite probable that they attributed her success in battle to the guerrilla tactics employed by the Maroons, and to the difficulty of fighting over terrain as challenging as Jamaica's Blue Mountains and, to the west, the Cockpit Country, wooded and pitted as it was. Her reputation for Obeah was something which they would have scoffed at and dismissed as laughable. Europe's witches had led no uprisings and had been involved in no wars. Any participation in war by people with assumed supernatural powers had died out with the Celts, so the planters had little understanding of the psychological power that Obeah practitioners wielded over adherents. Their ignorance of the threat posed by Obeah baffled later commentators who, with the unacknowledged benefit of hindsight, thought it should have been as clear as day. "Planters were entirely blind to the presence of witchcraft among the slaves, and completely unsuspicious of the element of devil-worship that was becoming accentuated. . . . If, at times, the Planters did hear stories of existent obeah, [they] regarded it with amused toleration as foolish superstition and nothing more, and failed absolutely to associate with it the increasing menace of subservient fear that was effectively supplemented by secret poisonings", writes Williams about conditions in Jamaica during the early 1700s.[4]

But in 1760, Tacky's Rebellion erupted, as we have learned, robbing the whites of their indulgent complacency and erasing their amusement. That year, Coromantyns throughout the island, many of whom were concentrated in the parish of St Mary, rose up, determined to end their slavery and create their

---

3 Laura Tanna, *Jamaican Folk Tales and Oral Histories* (Kingston: Institute of Jamaica, 1984), 20.
4 Williams, *Psychic Phenomena*, 75.

own communities. Obeah men played key roles in the rebellion, administering the fetish oath, offering a balm to make the rebels invulnerable, and doubtless doctoring whatever hurts may have occurred despite the balm. Long gives us an account of one Obeah man's capture:

> In St Mary's parish a check was fortunately given at one estate by surprizing a famous obeiah man or priest much respected among his countrymen. He was an old Coromantin who, with others of his profession, had been a chief in counseling and instigating the credulous herd to whom these priests administered a powder which, being rubbed on their bodies, was to make them invulnerable: they persuaded them into a belief that Tacky their generalissimo in the woods could not possibly be hurt by the white men for that he caught all the bullets fired at him in his hand and hurled them back with destruction to his foes. This old impostor was caught whilst he was tricked up with all his feathers, teeth, and other implements of magic and, in this attire, suffered military execution by hanging: many of his disciples when they found that he was so easily put to death notwithstanding all the boasted feats of his powder and incantations soon altered their opinion of him and determined not to join their countrymen in a cause which hitherto had been unattended with success. But the fame of general Tacky and the notion of his invulnerability still prevailed.[5]

The Fuller report provides much the same information but mentions the administration of the fetish oath as being among the Obeah man's duties:

> In the year 1760 when a very formidable insurrection of the Koromantyn or Gold Coast negroes broke out in the parish of St Mary and spread through almost every other district of the island, an old Koromantyn negro, the chief instigator and oracle of the insurgents in that parish who had administered the fetish or solemn oath to the conspirators and furnished them with a magical preparation which was to render them invulnerable, was fortunately apprehended convicted and hung up with all his feathers and trumperies about him and his execution struck the insurgents with a general panic from which they never afterwards recovered. The examinations which were taken at that period opened the eyes of the public to the very dangerous tendency of the Obeah practices and [gave] birth to the law which was then enacted for suppression and punishment.[6]

---

5   Long, *History of Jamaica*, 450–51.
6   Edwards, *History Civil and Commercial*, 170–71.

The report claimd that Tacky's rebels "surrounded the overseer's house, at Ballard's Valley, in which eight or ten white people were in bed. All these they put to death in the most savage manner, and drank their blood mixed with rum".[7] No explanation or source is given for this account.

The authors of the Fuller report were so determined to drive home the point about the involvement of Obeah men that they include a statement from a planter which, for the most part, goes over ground covered elsewhere in the report:

> In the year 1760 the influence of the professors of the Obeah art was such as to induce a great many of the negro slaves in Jamaica to engage in the rebellion which happened in that year and which gave rise to the law which was then made against the practice of Obi. Assurance was given to these deluded people that they were to become invulnerable and, in order to render them so, the Obeah men furnished them with a powder with which they were to rub themselves. In the first engagement with the rebels, nine of them were killed and many prisoners taken; amongst the latter was one very intelligent fellow who offered to disclose many important matters on the condition that his life should be spared which was promised. He then related the active part which the negroes known among them by the name of Obeah men had taken in propagating the insurrection; one of whom was thereupon apprehended, tried for rebellious conspiracy, convicted and sentenced to death (this was the Koromantyn Obeah man alluded to in our first paper). At the place of execution he bid defiance to the executioner telling him that it was not in the power of the white people to kill him. And the negro spectators were greatly perplexed when they saw him expire. Upon other Obeah men who were apprehended at that time various experiments were made with electrical machines and magic lanterns but with very little effect except on one who, after receiving some very severe shocks, acknowledged that his master's Obi exceeded his own. The gentleman from whom we have this account remembers having sat twice on trials of Obeah men who were both convicted of selling their Obeah preparations which had occasioned the death of the parties to whom they had been administered notwithstanding which the lenity of their judges prevailed so far that they were only punished with transportation.[8]

According to the Fuller report, the Maroons captured Tacky, shot and killed him, and then decapitated him in order to preserve his head as a trophy. Not content with that, they also "roasted and actually devoured [his] heart

---

7   Ibid., 374–75. Burdett later repeats the information in its entirety without attribution.
8   Ibid., 174–75.

and entrails".⁹ Fuller does not say so, but if the Maroons did indeed engage in this type of cannibalism, it was probably for their own superstitious reasons; they may have hoped to physically internalize Tacky's courage and strength.

The story of Tacky's Rebellion and the role played in it by Obeah practitioners resonated through the centuries. The 1760 conspiracy "extended throughout the island, and, aided by the mysterious terrors of Obeah, was hatched with the greatest secrecy", writes Gardner in 1873, adding that the rebels

> were greatly stimulated by their confidence in the powers of Obeah men; a powder was distributed by these impostors which was said to make its possessor invulnerable. Tacky, it was asserted, could even catch the bullets of the soldiers, and throw them back among them. At last, an Obeah man was captured, dressed up in all the grotesque costume of his craft, and hung in a public place. His death did something to convince the negroes of the falseness of his pretensions.¹⁰

Now that Tacky's Rebellion had brought Obeah out into the open and demonstrated its power, the planters saw Obeah everywhere they looked. "In 1760, an obeah instigator to rebellion was put to death. During the twenty years subsequent to this period, a great many negroes were hanged for obeah crimes", writes Madden.¹¹ But the brutal suppression of Tacky's Rebellion and of Obeah brought the planters little respite from the threat of insurrections.

> It was well known, that many of the Coromantins, who had been in arms whilst their cause appeared promising, had now withdrawn themselves from the rebellious ranks and returned to their work, affecting great abhorrence at the outrageous conduct of their countrymen; and it was expected that, in St Mary, these people who had taken their inviolable oath, the Fetishe, were now only waiting for a favourable opportunity to recommence their sanguinary attempts. And so it eventually happened. In July, 1765, they held their midnight meetings; with horrid ceremonies they renewed their oaths, and fixed on the ensuing Christmas for the opening of an extended insurrection. But the impatience of some of them disconcerted the plans of all: it fortunately led to a premature attempt to murder the white settlers on Whitehall estate, and to the eventual suppression of this formidable band; not, however, without the loss of many a valuable life and the expenditure of a vast treasure, which the colony could ill afford.¹²

---

9 Edwards, "Introductory Account", 38.
10 Gardner, *History of Jamaica*, 132–33.
11 Madden, *Twelvemonth's Residence*, 2:74.
12 George Wilson Bridges, *The Annals of Jamaica* (London: John Murray, 1827), 501–2.

Finding that violent suppression had done little to quench either the thirst for freedom or the belief in Obeah's ability to aid rebels, some members of Jamaica's House of Assembly came up with an interesting proposal. Since most, if not all, the rebellions originated with Coromantins, it was proposed "that a bill should be brought in for laying an additional duty upon the Fantin, Akim, and Ashantee negroes, and all others, commonly called Coromantins, that should be imported and sold in the island". This met with little support, however, because "the Coromantin negro was endowed with the useful qualifications of superior strength", and planters did not want to lose their labour. Bridges claims that

> the public tranquillity was sacrificed to this visionary conceit, and the salutary measure was unfortunately neglected. Another rebellion was the expected and speedy consequence; and nineteen white persons fell a sacrifice, in the short space of one hour, to the knives of a few merciless Coromantins, in the parish of Westmoreland. In various other points, conspiracies were daily developed; insubordination and alarm reigned universally; the gaols were crowded with dangerous criminals and the harassed planters were provoked, by the continual murders of their dearest relations, to the infliction of those heavy, and in some cases, sanguinary punishments, which have been foully charged against their innocent descendants.[13]

In 1843 Phillippo describes "the circumstances attending the Fetish oath, which was a pledge of inviolable secrecy, and usually administered previously to insurrections or individual murders was terrible. Blood was drawn from each individual of the party present; this was mixed with grave-dirt and gunpowder in a bowl, and was partaken of by each individual in the secret as a ratification of his sincerity."[14] Decades later, in 1873, Gardner furnishes the following unsourced details of a 1765 conspiracy: "Into a quantity of rum, with which some gunpowder and dirt taken from a grave had been mingled, blood was put, drawn in succession from the arm of each confederate. With certain horrid ceremonies this cup was drunk from by each person and then came the council, at which the participants evidently decided to rise at Christmas."[15] Gardner notes that a premature uprising on 23 November on the Whitehall estate was quickly quashed, leading to the collapse of the planned rebellion.

---

13 Ibid.
14 Phillippo, *Jamaica*, 249.
15 Gardner, *History of Jamaica*, 141.

As the 1800s ground on, more and more rebellions began to be attributed to the slaves' growing expectation of freedom. Lewis's account of an 1816 plot takes on an excited tone:

> A plan has just been discovered in the adjoining parish of St Elizabeth's, for giving themselves a grand fete by murdering all the whites in the islands. The focus of this meditated insurrection was on Martin's Penn, the property of Lord Balcarras.... Above a thousand persons were engaged in the plot, three hundred of whom had been regularly sworn to assist in it with all the usual accompanying ceremonies of drinking human blood, eating earth from graves, [and so on].[16]

He gives some information about the upcoming trial of the captured rebels and notes that "above two hundred and fifty had been sworn in regularly, all of them Africans; not a Creole was among them". Sometime later, Lewis relates that the rebel captain had broken out of prison but was found "concealed in the hut of a notorious Obeah-man".[17] The perception that rebels often found refuge in the homes of Obeah men had already given rise to Moseley's observation that "in their banishment, [the huts of Obeah men] often become the receptacles of robbers and fugitive negroes".

Accounts of rebellions and planned rebellions now consistently included reports on the participation of Obeah men and women. In 1824, for example, the *Jamaica Courant* detailed a trial of nine Negroes at Buff Bay for a conspiracy to revolt and murder the white inhabitants. According to the paper, Louis Celeste Lecesne, a Haitian agitator, had supplied weapons to a slave by the name of Henry Oliver and others. Henry had assumed the title of king and drilled his followers nightly with sticks and wooden swords. A fortnight before Christmas "they assembled in the presence of an Obeah-man, who cut Henry's finger and mixed the blood with rum, which they drank as a charm to make them brave for the battle against the whites". The rebels were supposed to rise the night after Christmas and take over the Balcarras plantation first before proceeding on to "a general massacre". No arms were actually found but Henry was sentenced to hang along with two other men, and the rest were transported for life.[18] On 22 March 1824, the *Morning Chronicle* of London carried a story about the same Balcarras rebellion, with more details about the Obeah man, who was known as "Obeah Jack":

---

16 Lewis, *Journal*, 120–21.
17 Ibid.
18 *Jamaica Courant*, 21 March 1824.

We have received by the packet, Jamaican Papers to the 11th ult., the island remained at that date in an agitated state from the detection of the late conspiracy, which is said to have been more extensive than was first imagined. At any rate, several more executions of the unhappy negroes have taken place. The plot is now ascribed to the introduction into the island of some black men from St Domingo; but it is likely that we shall speedily receive more correct particulars of it, as the principal conspirator, Jack, a celebrated Obeah (a compound of fortune-teller, thief, and dealer in the "black art"), has been apprehended; and the Paper of 9 February states "We are happy to find the chief conspirator, Jack, the Obeah has made a full confession of the whole conspiracy, and which has been sent to the Governor."[19]

Several British papers, including the *Bristol Mercury* and the *Newcastle Courant*, carried the story with varying degrees of comprehensiveness, and we learn that a mistrial was declared. Obeah Jack's second trial began on 7 April. *John Bull* of 14 June 1824 reported that Jack was put on trial "for pretending to supernatural powers, and for practising obeah". According to witnesses, Jack "mixed the swear with rum, blood and gunpowder" and gave it to each of the conspirators to ingest, though he himself, as "the obeah", did not take any. Additionally, Jack was said to have had a "coffin, about one foot long, with white men's hair in it, which he intended to bury on the King's road the day of the battle, that when the white people passed they would break their necks". He also "broke some bush and rubbed all their faces with it, and said 'this will make you strong against the white people'". Jack had ordered that all the white people be killed first, starting with the overseer and bookkeeper at Balcarres. He was found guilty and was valued at eighty pounds, which was to be paid in compensation to his owner upon his execution.[20]

The oath administered during Samuel Sharpe's 1831 Christmas Rebellion was apparently quite unlike Jack's or Tacky's. "The negro Sharp, who was one of the chief planners of the later rebellion . . . confessed the form of oath administered to the negroes . . . at a house on Retrievo Estate. A bible was brought and put on the table. The person to be sworn got up and said 'If ever I witness any thing against my brother and sister concerning this matter, may hell be my portion.'"[21] Sharpe was both creole and a Baptist minister, characteristics that, as many writers often point out, often precluded indulgence in Obeah.

---

19 *Morning Chronicle*, 22 March 1824.
20 *John Bull*, 14 June 1824, 197.
21 Madden, *Twelvemonth's Residence*, 2:73.

Of course, Jamaica was not the only island on which rebellions occurred, and neither was it the only one in which Obeah practices were employed by the rebels. The 3 April 1824 issue of the *Liverpool Mercury* contained a story that first appeared in a Jamaican paper concerning a rebellion in Trinidad.

> The Jamaica Courant of the 2nd ult., contains an account of an intended conspiracy in Trinidad. It appears from this that the negroes intended to rise on All Saints Day and murder the whites. They had previously been in the practice of dancing at night, and on one occasion, had toward morning, killed a cock, and strewed the blood upon their drums, and etc. going through certain mystical signs; a day or two after, one or two of the negroes gave information of the plot. Many of the white and free inhabitants flocked in alarm to the town.... There are twenty-three of the ring-leaders committed to gaol for trial.[22]

As we have seen with Nanny, some Obeah men and women went further than simply offering protection to rebels. Some led those rebellions themselves, and others acted as instigators by laying the blame for illnesses not on other slaves but on the planters.

The association of Obeah with rebellion continued past emancipation and well into the nineteenth century. In 1865 Governor John Eyre's high-handed administration of Jamaica resulted in what would become known as the Morant Bay Rebellion, during which more than four hundred blacks lost their lives. "Some of the rebels, it was stated, were Obeahmen, dealers in magic and secret arts, and on that account alone worthy of death", wrote the Baptist missionary Edward Dean Underhill about the Morant Bay uprising.[23] In Britain, the news that Obeah men had indeed been involved in this latest rebellion did not surprise people such as George Augustus Sala, a journalist and writer of the "Echoes of the Week" column for the *Illustrated London News*. About a month after the events in Morant Bay, he wrote the following:

> At the bottom of this horrible black business in Jamaica, with its worse than Sepoy-like atrocities, and its utter indefensibility – for provocation to revolt was wholly wanting – there may lurk, unsuspected save by a very few, a predisposing cause, an element of savagery and fanaticism, as powerful for evil in its way as the "Deen, Deen!" or faith-cry of the Mahometans, and the vegetarian superstitions of the Hindoos. What, then, is this mysterious predisposing cause,

---

22 *Liverpool Mercury*, 3 April 1824.
23 Edward Dean Underhill, *The Tragedy of Morant Bay: A Narrative of the Disturbances in the Island of Jamaica in 1865* (London: Alexander and Shepheard, 1895), 111.

> this element of evil? . . . It is "Vaudouism". I do not even know whether I am spelling the word correctly. The infernal mysteries of the "Vaudou" is far above the niceties of grammar. But what is Vaudouism? It may be best described as "Obeah" disguised under a veil of fictitious civilization. The Parliamentary blue-books on the abolition of slavery between 1812 and 1838 will tell you all about Obeah; how, in certain cases, the maleficent deity was propitiated by hanging a negro woman up to a tree by her thumbs, and beating her to death with tamarind brushes; and how, in others, the sacrificial rites were not complete without libations from the skull of a new-born baby filled with rum and blood. These are no gobemouch stories. You will find them all duly set down in the bulky records of trials for Obeahism presented, by the Sovereign's command, to both Houses of Parliament. With the end of slavery, the overt practice of Obeah disappeared from the British West India colonies. The negroes ceased to be banded together in large bodies; they became more or less isolated squatters, or loafers about the cities, where it was difficult and dangerous to practice the horrid incantations of the sect. The old slave women who had been the chief possessors of its mysteries, faded away. But as Obeah died out, Vaudouism crept in. Some say it was imported from Hayti, and that Faustin Souloque was a noted Vaudou; others that it came from Louisiana.[24]

Sala, a founder of the Savage Club, which included luminaries such as Sir Henry Irving, Wilkie Collins and James McNeill Whistler, recounted stories of voodoo in New Orleans, Haiti and French Algiers, claiming to have personally witnessed it in the last country.[25] He believed, however, that the version of voodoo observed in Algiers by the "sable devotees" was of a somewhat less bloodthirsty form than the one in the Americas.

> Depend on it, the Vaudou has something to do with the uprising of the blacks in Jamaica. Its most perilous feature is, that no white man can tell with precision what Vaudouism really is. A Vaudou may appear a perfectly peaceable black man. He may send his children to Sunday-school, and be himself an attendant at a Methodist chapel; but every now and then the cloven foot of the real Vaudou peeps out. Then it means always the same thing. Rum and gunpowder in a cocoanut-shell to begin with; next human blood in a calabash; then outrage, plunder, "chopping de bucra up fine" – anything you choose to mention. Perhaps you may think it philosophical to laugh at Vaudouism, and

---

24 G.B. Sala, "The Outbreak in Jamaica: 'Vaudouism'", *Belfast Newsletter*, 22 November 1865.
25 In the late 1800s, a Masonic lodge associated with the club was consecrated with the support of the then Prince of Wales. Both the lodge and the club still exist but are no longer formally connected.

to hold that the subscriber has been filling you with tales full of sound and fury, signifying nothing. Laugh on; but your humble servant can remember when, less than nine years since, everybody was laughing at some wild stories told about certain lotus flowers and "chupatties" which were being mysteriously circulated among the natives in our Indian Empire.[26]

As a contributor to the *Daily Telegraph* who wrote for Charles Dickens's various publications and who also had articles published in William Makepeace Thackeray's *Cornhill*, Sala was particularly well-connected and influential. His observations would have influenced many.

LAW AND THE OBEAH MAN

As we have seen, West Indian planters considered Obeah something of a joke until Tacky's Rebellion in Jamaica. Spurred to action in its aftermath, the Jamaica House of Assembly passed draconian legislation banning the practice. The *Act to Remedy the Evils Arising from Irregular Assemblies of Slaves* stipulated:

> Whereas on many Estates and Plantations in this Island there are Slaves of Both Sexes commonly known by the name of obeah-men and obeah-women by whose influence over the minds of their fellow Slaves through an Established opinion of their being endued with Strange Preternatural Faculties, many and great Dangers have arisen Destructive of the Peace and Welfare of this Island; In order to prevent for the future such Rebellions or Rebellious Conspiracies and in order to prevent the many Mischiefs that may hereafter arise from the Wicked Art of Negroes going under the Apellation of obeah-men and women pretending to have Communication with the Devil and other Evil Spirits whereby the weak and Superstitious are deluded into a Belief of their having full Power to Exempt them whilst under their Protection from any Evils that might otherwise happen, be it therefore enacted that any Negro or other Slave who shall pretend to any supernatural power, and be detected in making use of any blood, Feathers, Parrots Beaks, Dogs Teeth, Alligators Teeth, broken bottles, Grave Dirt, Rum, Egg-shells or any other Materials relative to the practise of Obeah or Witchcraft in order to delude and impose on the minds of others, shall upon conviction thereof, before two magistrates and three Freeholders, suffer Death or Transportation.[27]

---

26   Sala, "Outbreak in Jamaica".
27   Williams, *Psychic Phenomena*, 78.

The fact that the 1760 act also extended to free people is not very remarkable, but "white persons present at such meetings" were also liable to be arrested, suggesting, at the very least, a suspicion on the part of the planter elite that certain whites were colluding with black rebels.[28] This suspicion received its full expression in the fictional *Hamel, the Obeah Man*, discussed in chapter 8.

Most of the English colonies in the West Indies quickly enacted their own similar legislation and the colonies of the other European powers also had comparable laws. For example, the governor of the Danish West Indies, Philip Gardelin, had issued a prohibition on witchcraft and poisoning in 1733. Jamaica's 1760 act and the legislation modelled on it in the other English colonies codified in law the association the first Europeans in Africa had made between Africans and devil worship.

Interestingly, the last execution of a witch in England had taken place in 1684, and in 1735 the Witchcraft Act made both prosecutions and executions for witchcraft illegal in the Kingdom of Great Britain. Instead, persons claiming or pretending to supernatural powers were charged as frauds. Essentially the British act sought to eradicate people's belief in witchcraft and substitute for it a healthy dose of scepticism. But planters in the West Indies were terrified of poisoning and they were terrified of their slaves. Tacky's Rebellion had revealed how Obeah could bring their darkest, bloodiest nightmares to life. Obeah could no longer be considered a joke, and neither was the Obeah man a harmless con artist, a danger only to the deluded and the superstitious. Tacky's Rebellion ended the jocularity and replaced it with fear. For the next century and a half, Obeah men and women symbolized integration of the planters' twin terrors, murder and poison. The Obeah practitioner – deformed, hideous, possibly insane – became the bogeyman lurking in the shadows of the plantation world whose dominance over his fellow Africans needed to be broken.

The tough law found favour among the pro-slavery lobby:

> The slave code was now remodeled, its provisions amended and its powers enlarged. The punishment of offenders was rendered more effectual, the inveigling of negroes prevented, and the practices of obeah and midnight assemblies were by every means suppressed. Free negroes were obliged to register their names in the books of their respective parishes, to carry a probationary ticket and to wear a distinguishing badge. The number of African slaves poured into the island within the period of these last ten years amounted to no less than 71,115. . . . So overwhelming and so dangerous to the peace of the colony was the influx of

---

28   *The Laws of Jamaica* (St Jago de la Vega: Alexander Aikman and Son, 1816), 6:513–14.

barbarians forced upon Jamaica by British merchants and English laws during these years of disturbance and destruction and so great the proportion of Coromantins who in their native land were bred to war and habituated to blood, that the extinction of the disproportionate planters was seriously apprehended. In 1764 the importation amounted to 10,223 and from January 1765 to July 1766 it increased to 16,760. Twenty-seven thousand savages, some of them cannibals, many of them condemned malefactors in a country where the measure of crime was unbounded and a still greater proportion of them captive warriors burning for revenge, thus turned loose upon a handful of Europeans dispersed over a wooded island abounding with almost impenetrable fastnesses, would have quickly made that island their own had not undaunted bravery and unshaken patriotism led its warriors and inspired its legislators.[29]

(This theme of white fortitude and courage against savage hordes recurred again and again in the writings of the period and was to find particular favour with Victorian-era authors of swashbuckling adventures set in Britain's various imperial outposts.)

The new law allowed "two justices and three freeholders [to] have the power to inflict capital punishment on slaves convicted of the practice of obeah, or found in arms; while every encouragement was given to the Maroons and others who should destroy or capture deserters". According to Bridges, these measures brought some success, for "peace soon prevailed" and "no internal commotion of any serious magnitude disturbed the colony during the succeeding twenty years, nor indeed until the breaking out of the fatal Maroon rebellion in the year 1795".[30]

The planters set about enforcing the law with gusto, but it is unclear that the results were anything but ambiguous. Renny points out that "severe examples have frequently been made of the practitioners of this destructive art, which, though they have rendered it less frequent, have by no means totally destroyed it".[31] Decades later, Carmichael notes that "the practice of Obeah is death, by the laws of St Vincent but, there is no possibility of conviction".[32]

The 1760 act was followed by other legislation. For example, legislation in 1809 provided for "slaves pretending to supernatural power" to be sentenced to death; "slaves preparing or giving poison, though death does not ensue,

---

29 Bridges, *Annals of Jamaica*, 499–500.
30 Ibid., 500.
31 Renny, *History of Jamaica*, 172.
32 Carmichael, *Domestic Manners*, 254.

to suffer death"; and "punishment on slaves having any poisonous drugs, pounded glass and etc. in their possession".[33] Southey also relates that slaves found "at any meeting formed for administering unlawful oaths by drinking human blood mixed with rum, grave dirt or otherwise . . . shall suffer death, or transportation for life, as the court shall direct".

The tough laws had the support of the planters, most of whom sat in the House of Assembly of their respective islands, and the death sentence was certainly carried out on several Obeah men and women. *The Observer* of 5 April 1812 reported that "two slaves of the ages of 52 and 64 were hanged at Kingston in January for practising Obeah".[34] But whatever comfort the laws may have given some people, Moseley and others dismissed them as unequal to the task almost as soon as they were passed. "Laws have been made in the West Indies to punish Obian practice with death; but they have been impotent and nugatory", Moseley points out. "Laws constructed in the West Indies, can never suppress the effects of ideas, the origin of which is in the centre of Africa."[35]

More than a hundred years after Jamaica's 1760 act, laws against Obeah were still on the books of the English-speaking Caribbean islands. An examination of the 1904 *Obeah Act* of the Virgin Islands (British) reveals as much about the fears of those who passed it as it does about those at whom it was directed.[36] The act starts out by providing a definition of the term "instrument of obeah", which is said to "mean anything ordinarily used in the practice of obeah or intended to be so used in such practice, and anything used or intended to be used by a person and pretended by such person to be possessed of any occult or supernatural power".[37] The act also specifies that Obeah means "obeah as ordinarily understood and practised, and included witchcraft and working or pretending to work by spells or by professed occult or supernatural power".

Section 5 of the act provides a maximum prison term of six months, with

---

33   Southey, *Chronological History*, 471.
34   *The Observer*, 5 April 1812.
35   Moseley, "Medical Observations", 107.
36   This act, which was adopted by the Leeward Islands legislature and applied to all the presidencies which made up the colony, was based on a much earlier one and would have been similar to legislation found in the other, larger English-speaking islands. In the Virgin Islands it went through several revisions until it was abrogated and incorporated in the Criminal Code of the same year in 1997.
37   *The Revised Laws of the Virgin Islands*, 1:525. The section relating to the publication of Obeah pamphlets was probably inspired by events in Jamaica, where booklets detailing the exploits of Obeah practitioners such as John Nugent, George Elleth and Old Mother "Firerush" Austin had made their popular appearance in the early 1890s, only to be banned in 1898.

or without hard labour, for "any person who pretends or professes to tell fortunes, or uses any subtle craft, means or device, by palmistry or otherwise, or pretends to cure injuries or diseases or to intimidate or affect any purpose by means of any charm, incantation or other pretended supernatural practice".[38] The Obeah practitioner himself could, on summary conviction, receive a prison term of twelve months, also with or without hard labour. In the event that the magistrate decided to commit him or her to trial, a conviction could then result in a maximum prison sentence of five years, also with or without hard labour, which at that time might have meant working on roads or cutting stone.

An 1845 Jamaica law had criminalized those who sought the services of Obeah practitioners, and the 1904 Virgin Islands law contains a similar provision. Under section 7, "Whosoever, for the purpose of effecting any object, or of bringing about any event, by the use of occult means or any supernatural power or knowledge, consults any person practicing obeah shall be liable to a fine not exceeding two hundred and forty dollars or to be imprisoned for any period not exceeding twelve months." Furthermore, police officers and members of the local constabulary did not require warrants to arrest "any person practicing obeah, or reasonably suspected to be practicing obeah".

Even after the Obeah practitioner had served her sentence at His Majesty's Pleasure, she could still find herself under police supervision for a period of up to two years. Additionally, composing, writing, printing, selling, distributing, publishing or circulating any pamphlet or printed or written matter calculated to promote the superstition of obeah was also against the law and was punishable by a fine of as much as $240 or six months' imprisonment.[39]

A similar act was passed in the Leeward Islands at the same time. Three years later, officials deemed it a resounding success. *The Times* of 24 October 1907 carried an excerpt from the colony's annual report:

> it is very pleasing to be able to record that the Act has been a marked success, and that the degrading and dangerous crime of practising obeah has received a check from which it is never likely to recover . . . "obeah", "voodoo", or "juju" is, in the West Indies, the survival of the whole body of primitive beliefs and customs of fetichistic African tribes. Its great danger is the power which a belief in its practices places in the hands of some degraded but sharp-witted scamp, who, with no belief in it himself, terrorizes over the community he visits or resides in.

---

38   Ibid., 527.
39   Ibid., 530.

The Act referred to makes the possession of any "instrument of obeah" a proof of the crime of practising obeah unless the contrary be proved, and provides for the whipping of males and for police supervision. Whipping is never ordered for a first offence. The police were encouraged to take energetic action under the new law, and several obeah men quickly discovered that the Leeward Islands were no longer a fitting place for abode. The obeahman now finds it a difficult and dangerous thing to keep his stock-in-trade by him, and deprived of his paraphernalia of human skulls, cocks' heads, bones, and filthy messes, his fame has vanished. When, as in the case of a well-known obeahman ordinarily resident in Montserrat, but whose operations extended over the colony, a flogging is added to some wholesome detention, ridicule of his practices takes the place of the dread which they formerly inspired. Up to the last the peasants believed, in the case referred to, that the threatened degradation of a flogging would be warded off by some magic influence. It is probable that obeah, in this colony at any rate, is responsible for very few cases of poisoning. It would not appear that any knowledge of African bush poisons survives in these islands, and any attempts to use the ordinary poisons that would be within his reach are too dangerous for the average obeahman. Though it is, perhaps, too much to hope that the ignorant portion of a race that has only been in its new environment some four or five generations will completely lose yet awhile the beliefs that its African ancestors held for, perhaps, thousands of years, yet the spread of education and repressive measures of the kind here referred to have worked a marvelous change for the better in a very short space of time.[40]

Less than thirty years later, Hesketh Bell, in a 1936 letter to *The Times*, was not quite so admiring. Citing the same *Obeah Act, 1904*, he concluded that it had "failed in its object as we find that in 1932 the Obeah Act was amended and that a term of imprisonment up to five years was made the penalty for 'practising obeah'". According to Bell, in presenting his support for the amendment, the attorney general had "claimed it was needed in order to combat the increase of superstition in the islands".[41] Islands that have repealed their Obeah legislation include Barbados, Trinidad and Tobago, Anguilla, and St Lucia.[42]

---

40 "The Obeah in the Leeward Islands", *The Times*, 24 October 1907, 11.
41 Bell, letter to *The Times*, 27 July 1936.
42 Paton, "Obeah Acts", 5.

OBEAH TRIALS AND SENTENCING

The anti-slavery lobby was not generally supportive of harsh sentences for Obeah. Wilberforce notes that "the idea of rooting out any form of pagan superstition by severity of punishment, especially in wholly uninstructed minds, like that of extirpating Christianity by the fire and the faggot, has long been exploded among the well-informed; and it has even been established that the devilish engine of persecution recoils back on its employers, and disseminates the very principles it would suppress".[43]

Eventually the Obeah laws were amended to remove the threat of execution. Offenders could either be imprisoned or transported to other colonies. The softening of the law was greeted with approval in many quarters. Madden, referring to a case related by Sir Walter Scott in which a crazy old woman was burnt for witchcraft in Scotland, reveals his conviction that "hundreds of poor negroes [who] have been executed in Jamaica for witchcraft [were] equally weak in intellect".[44] According to him,

> though judicial barbarities were practiced in Jamaica within the last forty years, which have been unknown to Europe for upwards of a century, and executions for witchcraft and obeah, and torturing practices . . . been had recourse to . . . within the last thirty years in Great Britain the mob has endeavoured to revive the savagery of the law, and have taken into their own hands the punishment of the crime of witchcraft.

Besides, of course, the saving of lives, Madden believed that the softer laws had the salutary side effect of reducing belief in Obeah. "When humanity came to the aid of legislative wisdom, and softened down some of the most prominent barbarities of former enactments – that, especially respecting obeah – the practice was deprived of the principal source of the reverence it exacted, when the exposure of its absurdities was divested of the cruelties which made a merit, in former times, of persisting in them."[45] Madden clearly thought that the Obeah men and women who were hung or whipped were considered martyrs by fellow blacks, who were all the more convinced that there must be something to Obeah if the whites were so frightened of it that it warranted death. "So long as these poor bodies were hanged or flagellated for the exercise

---

43 Wilberforce, *Appeal*, 29.
44 Madden, *Twelvemonth's Residence*, 74.
45 Ibid.

of their African sorcery, obeah flourished – like some other things, which the more they are persecuted, the more they prosper."[46]

However, Madden's view was not shared by Gardner: "It appears also, from records of slave trials [that] those found guilty of Obeah practices rarely suffered the extreme penalty of the law. Two cases are on record where actual poisoning was proved, and yet the culprits were only transported (deported). This unaccountable lenity had the tendency of making negroes believe more implicitly the assertion that 'Buckra could not kill Obeah man'."[47] Certainly, many of the cases on record appear to bear Gardner out with regard to the sentences handed out to Obeah men and women. Prosecutions may have increased but the planters appear to have been somewhat restrained in their application of the death penalty, usually reserving it for those who had participated in uprisings.

Madden provides his readers with the outlines of a few cases from the criminal record book of the parish of St Andrew in the years following the passage of the 1760 act, which bear out this observation. In 1773 a woman named Sarah was tried "for having in her possession cats' teeth, cats' claws, cats' jaws, hair, beads, knotted cords, and other materials, relative to the practice of obeah, to delude and impose on the minds of the negroes". Sarah was found guilty and sentenced to transportation, as was a man by the name of Solomon who was convicted in 1776 of "having materials in his possession for the practise of obeah". A year later, Tony was tried "for practising obeah, or witchcraft, on a slave named Fortune, by means of which said slave became dangerously ill"; Tony was cleared of the charge. In 1782 Neptune was charged "for making use of rum, hair, chalk, stones and other materials, relative to the practise of obeah, or witchcraft"; he was found guilty and sentenced to transportation.[48]

Lewis recalls that "not about ten months ago, my agent was informed that a negro of very suspicious manners and appearance was harboured by some of my people on the mountain lands". The agent detained the man and discovered that he was holding

> a bag containing a great variety of strange materials for incantations; such as thunder-stones, cat's ears, the feet of various animals, human hair, fish bones, the teeth of alligators, etc. He was conveyed to Montego Bay; and no sooner was it understood that this old African was in prison; than depositions were

---

46 Ibid., 75–76.
47 Gardner, *History of Jamaica*, 190.
48 Madden, *Twelvemonth's Residence*, 69.

poured in from all quarters from negroes who deposed to having seen him exercise his magical arts, and in particular to his having sold such and such slaves medicines and charms to deliver them from their enemies; being in plain English nothing else than rank poisons. He was convicted of Obeah ... and sentenced to be transported.[49]

As in the case of Andrew Marble, monies were awarded to slave owners to compensate them for the loss of their transported slaves. The maximum available was one hundred pounds in the currency of the island.[50]

The English media took a keen interest both in reports of poisoning and in Obeah. On 30 August 1817, London's *Morning Chronicle* reported that "at a slave court in Jamaica, in June, Harriet belonging to Dr E Melhado, was found guilty of an attempt to poison her owner's family by mixing verdigris with ground coffee. Her sentence of death was commuted to transportation for life. Several Negroes had been convicted of Obeah practices."[51] The 5 December 1818 edition of *The Times* of London notes that "by a recent Act of the House of Assembly (Barbados), an endeavour has been made towards more effectively suppressing the practice of obeah. Our readers are aware, that by this name is designated a kind of necromantic power, which is mostly exercised by the Negroes for the attainment of the worst purposes."[52] In the same way that writers of the time often borrowed from each other's books, almost all the newspapers were in the habit of repeating each other's stories; for example, Edinburgh's *Caledonian Mercury* of 14 December 1818 offers the very same news that *Times* readers had already read.[53]

Readers of the 28 January 1822 issue of the *Glasgow Herald* were treated to an extract from the *St Jago (Jamaica) Gazette* which contained information on some recent trials.

> A Special Slave Court was held at the Court-House at Buff Bay in St George's on Saturday the 17th ult. when the following trials took place: – Kingston, a negro man belong to Cedar Valley plantation, in the said parts, charged with pretending to possess Supernatural power and practising Obeah – acquitted. John, a negro man, belonging to G.H. Gillespie, charged with pretending to possess

---

49 Lewis, *Journal*, 95.
50 United Kingdom, *British Parliamentary Papers*, 21 November 1826–2 July 1827, vol. 25, *State Papers Relating to the Slave Population in the West Indies* [...], 221.
51 *Morning Chronicle*, 30 August 1817.
52 Williams, *Psychic Phenomena*, 87.
53 *Caledonian Mercury*, 14 December 1818.

supernatural power, and being found in the possession of materials notoriously used in the practice of Obeah, found guilty of having pretended to supernatural power, and, sentenced to one month's hard labour in the Workhouse, to receive thirty-nine lashes on going in, and the like number on being discharged.[54]

The number of cases brought to court continued, and it was plain that, whatever the attitude of some whites, many blacks continued to take Obeah seriously and sought out practitioners for a variety of purposes, such as to uncover thieves, to redress wrongs and to get or keep a lover, among other things. For example, Madden relates that "a negro was tried some years ago in Spanish Town, for practising obeah under the following circumstances: Dr — being about to get married, a person of colour, who up to this period had been his housekeeper, had recourse to the obeah man, to break the Doctor's attachment to his betrothed lady". (Madden is being somewhat coy; it is more than likely that the housekeeper was the doctor's live-in lover.) The doctor became suspicious of the housekeeper and followed her to a house where "on his entrance he found the customary obeah dance going on, both repeating incantations, the necessary part of the ceremony, ablutions, and the administering of a potion having taken place".[55] The Obeah man was brought to trial and condemned to life in the workhouse, where, Madden notes, he died some years later.

An illness that had no other perceivable cause was often attributed to Obeah, sometimes to the detriment of the Obeah man or woman. In a letter dated 8 September 1834, Madden also writes about

> An obeah man [who] was lately committed to the Spanish Town prison for practising on the life of a negro child. It appeared in evidence that he went to a negro hut and asked for some fire to light his pipe; that he was seen to put some bush (herb) into the pipe, and then placing himself to windward of the child, commenced smoking, so that the fumes were directed by the wind towards the child. Immediately after he went away, the child was taken alarmingly ill: the father pursued the man suspected of obeahing, and brought him back. He was accused of being an obeah man, of having "injured the child" and being threatened with violence if he did not take off the obeah, he consented to do so, and accordingly performed certain ceremonies for that purpose: the child improved and he was suffered to depart. The improvement, however, was only temporary: he was again sent for, and with a similar result.

---

54   *Glasgow Herald*, 28 January 1822.
55   Madden, *Twelvemonth's Residence*, 68.

> ... He confessed that he was a practiser of obeah; that he did it not for gain or vengeance, but solely because the devil put in into his head to do bad. He had learned the use of the bush from an old negro man on — estate where the master had been poisoned by an old man. It was a small plant which grew in the mountains, but he did not know the name of it. He said it did him no hurt to smoke this plant; but whoever breathed the smoke was injured by it: he had no spite against the father or mother of the child, no wish to injure them. He saw the child, and he could not resist the instigation of the devil to obeah it; but he hoped he would never do it any more: he would pray to God to put it out of his head to do it. Such was the singular statement made to the attorney-general by the prisoner; and the attorney informed me, made with an appearance of frankness and truth which gave a favourable impression of its veracity.
>
> My opinion in this case was, that, notwithstanding the confession of the man, and the evidence against him, the plant was innoxious in the way it was administered.⁵⁶

Madden adds, "On further inquiry into this case, I discovered that the threat of the torture of thumb-screwing had been had recourse to by the father of the child and other negroes before the confession was made." Madden asks himself

> why should an innocent man persist in a confession of guilt extorted from him in a moment of terror, when he is no longer subject to its tyranny? To this I answer – The impression of a great terror is not so easily effaced, even by the removal of the cause that inspired it; the importance of the means in self-defence adopted for its dissipation becomes an exaggerated sentiment, which dupes the enfeebled mind, and actually converts a deceit into a delusion.

Essentially, the man confessed to Obeah in order to escape torture and then convinced himself that he had, in fact, Obeahed the boy.

In another case related by Madden,

> a negro was brought before me ... charged with obeahing the only child of a negro woman, after having caused the death of three others of her children. The mother gave her evidence in a state of great excitement; several of her female neighbours confirmed it, and it amounted to this – that the prisoner's wife had no children, and was jealous of the complainant on this account; that she had persuaded her husband to obeah [the] children one after the other, till they had all died, and had now put obeah on herself, in order to prevent her from having any more.

---

56   Ibid., 65–69.

Madden and his fellow magistrate tried to persuade the woman that Obeah was not to blame for the death of her children, "but it was only when I called on the man to declare, that even if he had the power to put obeah on her, which was impossible, he would never do it, that she appeared at all satisfied, or the friends who accompanied her". Madden notes, "In this instance the man bore an excellent character, and there was no earthly ground for the charge: nevertheless, in former years he might have been hanged on such a charge, for an obeah man."[57]

Charles Rampini, a judge, was interested enough in the subject that he dug up several old cases. "I have before me the records of the slave courts held for the parish of Portland between the years 1805 and 1816", he writes. "They are full of cases of Obeah. One woman attempts to murder her master by putting arsenic into his noyeau; another by mixing pounded glass with his coffee; a third is charged with practising upon the credulity of his fellow-slaves by pretending to cure another of a sore in his leg, and 'taking from thence sundry trifles, – a hawk's toe, a bit of wire, and a piece of flesh'." He then launches into an in-depth account of two of the trials, which provide a fascinating insight into obeah practice and the way in which it was viewed by blacks and whites.

> On 22d February 1831, William Jones was tried and sentenced to death "for conspiring and contriving to destroy William Ogilvie, overseer of Fairy Hill estate in the parish of Portland". The notes of the evidence taken at the trial state: - "This prosecution arises out of the confession of Thomas Lindsay, who was shot to death "pursuant to the sentence of a court-martial, on the 31st day of January 1832. The part of the confession which inculpates William Jones is as follows : — 'About three weeks before Christmas, me and David Anderson, and William Rainey, and Alexander Simpson being together, the devil took hold of us, tell us we must destroy the overseer; and he agreed to go to a man named William Jones, belonging to Providence Mountain, an obeah-man, to give us something to kill the busha, so that his horse may throw him down and break his neck in a hole. Jones said as this was a great thing he could not do it for less than a doubloon, and we had only five shillings to give him. But we agree to carry him a barrow (a hog) with five dollars, and a three-gallon jug of rum, and three dollars in cash. He then gave us something and told us to give it to the waiting-boy to throw it in the water, and that would kill him. The waiting-boy, James Oliver, did throw it into the water, but it did the busha no harm, and the waiting-boy said the obeah-man was only laughing

---

57 Ibid., 69.

at us. We then went to the obeah-man, and he said the waiting-boy could not have put the things into the water. And then he came himself one day . . . '" "Here", says the report, "follows an account of obeah tricks practised". It then goes on: – "David Anderson, sworn. He [witness] was run away three months before Christmas in consequence of the overseer flogging him for stealing some rum from his brother Henry Simpson and putting water in the place of it. He and four others went to William Jones. William Rainey explained the cause of their coming – that he carried one macaroni, and four bitts, and a jug of rum, and that Alexander Simpson carried a pig. The obeah-man (the prisoner) asked for a doubloon. He gave them something in a nancy bag, pounded up, which James Oliver put into the busha's drink, but it did not do him. That they then fetched the obeah-man down to the estate, where he gave them something to put in the step of the door – all to kill the busha. The prisoner had a cutacoo. They gave him a two-dollar piece, beside the money they had before given."

In the second trial, conducted on

13th April of the same year William Fisher was tried and convicted for pretending to supernatural power. Edward Francis, slave to Fairfield, being "sworn and admonished", said: – "On Wednesday, about the first week in May of last year, I was at my father-in-law's house. This was shortly after Mr Speed came as overseer to the estate." Tom, alias Richard Mein, Richard Passley, the driver of Fairfield, prisoner, and others, came in. Fisher called for a fowl's egg, which he put into a basin. Tom Crowder sat beside him. Fisher threw rum over the egg, and set it on fire, and when the egg was boiled in the rum he broke it, gave it to Tom to suck, who declined. Fisher, after sucking the egg, rubbed part of the shell in his hand until it was mashed. He then put it with some stuff which he said was cinnamon into a phial. It was a thing which he said would turn anybody's mind. He then gave it to me, and said it was to be given to driver Richard, who would give it to the horse-stable-boy, to put under the horse's tail, when the horse would throw the busha, Mr Speed, down and break his neck. I was obliged to go back to Fairfield to fetch the money before he gave me the phial. . . . Fisher likewise gave me some of the egg-shell, and [told me] to rub it up and strew it about the yard – that if the stuff in the phial did not make the horse throw the busha, this would. Robert Mein [slave] to Cold Harbour, had a bad leg. Fisher pricked the place, and black blood came. Fisher then sucked the part and spit out two beads. At another time, when I ran away, I met Fisher in the pass, and he took me up to his mountain and gave me a bush to chew, and said if I went home without it I should get fum fum, as the busha was swearing after me very much. I gave him four bits for it. When I went home busha did fum me, and I then went back to Fisher to get the money from him. He said,

> 'No, there is a different way to manage the busha,' which was to kill him. On the Wednesday night before mentioned, Fisher gave Solomon Passley a little bit of stick, which he told him to chew and spit it all about the pass, and this would kill busha. The whole estate said they would go to somebody to kill the busha. . . . We all employed Fisher [to do it].'"

Witness after witness confirmed that Fisher was indeed an Obeah man and that he had been paid to kill the overseer: "'Alexander Hartley to Fairfield, sworn – saith that he knows Fisher. He is a Mungola man. He is a bush man – an obeah man. Heard when runaway, and living in a cave, that money had been thrown up for the purpose of killing Mr Speed.'"[58]

We do not know if Fisher was sentenced to death but it is likely, as passions ran high in Obeah cases where practitioners were accused of conniving in the murder of a white man or woman. They ran even higher for those involved in uprisings. Gardner quotes the report of the royal commission that looked into the Morant Bay Rebellion of 1865, in which it is noted that

> a reputed Obeah-man was tried by court-martial and convicted. One of the favourite assertions of these people has been that "Buckra can't hurt them". Colonel Hobbs directed him to be placed on a hill-side, about 400 yards from the firing party. The bullets caused almost instantaneous death, and it is stated that the effect on the minds of the prisoners was so great, that the colonel felt at liberty to release a considerable number then in his camp, many of whom were heard to say they never would believe in Obeah again.[59]

The actual report gives much more detail:

> The execution of Arthur Wellington after trial took place on the 21st of October at Monklands. He belonged to Somerset one of the settlements of the valley and had the reputation among the people around Somerset of being an Obeah man. . . . Poison was said to have been found in Wellington's house at Somerset. The house and the works of Monklands are in the bottom of the valley and the hills on each side stand apart about half a mile. Colonel Hobbs has stated that he hoped by means of the example of Arthur Wellington's death to disabuse the other prisoners and the people in the valley of the folly of their belief in the powers of the Obeah man. In order that his execution might be seen by all who were watching upon the hills as well as by the prisoners, he caused Wellington

---

58 Rampini, *Letters*, 135–39.
59 Gardner, *History of Jamaica*, 483.

to be taken half way up the hill on one side of Monklands. This was done and at a spot about 400 yards from the Barbacue occupied by the firing party, the prisoner was stationed and shot. He was there visible from the surrounding heights. The effect of the volley which was fired was very soon fatal nor does any cruelty appear to have attended his death. A constable, without any authority for the act, severed the head from the body prior to interment and both head and body were afterwards buried in a trench at the bottom of the hill.

A heavy flood from the hill side during the night seems to have washed away the remains out of the grave and carried it down the stream. It is stated that the head was subsequently placed on a pole but it does not appear this was done by or with the knowledge of any persons in authority. The circumstances of this execution and the accidental effect of the flood were adduced as proofs of intentional cruelty and barbarity but the suggested object of an example and the facts when explained relating to the head have in our investigations disposed of this charge. The effect produced by the example given in this execution upon the other prisoners is stated to have been very good and many were heard to say that they never would believe in Obeah again.[60]

Like everything connected with the Morant Bay Rebellion, Wellington's execcution received extensive coverage in the British papers, including *The Times*.[61] But he was not the only Obeah man to lose his life in the rebellion, if contemporary accounts are to be believed. A "special correspondent" in Spanish Town, Jamaica, reported to the *Daily News* of 7 April 1866 that Colonel Fyfe, who commanded the Maroons and was also a member of the Legislative Council and the stipendiary magistrate for St David, had acknowledged that the Maroons had summarily shot two black men "without any authority but their own".[62]

Fyfe defended the Maroons, noting that "these two men were both Obeah men, [and] one of them had passed eighteen months in the penitentiary". The colonel had apparently declared himself confident that "while martial law was in force none deserved [execution] more than these men". The article notes that, according to Fyfe's account (which was confirmed by other witnesses), "an Obeah man is a poisoner, and through the instrumentality of this class of persons, hundreds of deaths are occasioned in Jamaica". Fyfe realized that sceptics about this claim abounded and trotted out the hoary old stories contained in the Fuller report:

---

60 United Kingdom, *British Parliamentary Papers*, 1866, vol. 31, *Report of the Jamaica Royal Commission*, 504–5.
61 "The Outbreak in Jamaica", *The Times*, 3 March 1866, 9.
62 *Daily News*, 17 March 1866, 2.

there is in Jamaica no law requiring the production of a medical certificate as to the cause of death before a body can be buried; and as not one person in fifty is seen by a doctor, there is but little check upon poisoning. But it is not by poison alone that the Obeah man, according to Colonel Fyfe and others, destroys his victims. The negroes entertain so much fear of these persons, that, as the colonel said, they can kill any black whom they choose. "If a negro fancies that he is being Obeahed, he is like a bird under the eye of a snake, and dies to a certainty." Death in this case is partly due to fright, but the operation of terror is frequently accelerated by the administration of poison. The Maroons have a great terror of these people; and it was to this that Colonel Fyfe attributed their shooting the two already mentioned without reference to him.[63]

Despite all this, Obeah did not die and its practitioners continued to be prosecuted. In 1887, for example, Alexander Ellis was caught with a wooden "Obeah figure decorated with 'senseh' fowls' feathers", which, according to May Robinson, "was regarded as a particularly powerful and evil Obeah".[64] Ellis was arrested in Morant Bay and brought before the acting stipendiary magistrate, N.S. Haughton. Upon conviction, he was sentenced to fifteen days' imprisonment. Robinson notes that the figure was taken to England by a Royal Navy commander, a Mr Hastings, who sent it back to Jamaica for the 1891 Jamaica Exhibition. Protests condemning its inclusion in the Exhibition, as a validation of Obeah, led to its removal; it was returned to England, where, Robinson reports, it "no longer exerts its malign influences". She does not indicate how it originally came to be in Hastings' possession, nor does she pass comment on the irony of prosecuting one (black) man for possession of an item which was then handed off to another (white) man with no legal repercussions. While it was illegal for blacks to own Obeah items, the same was clearly not true for whites.[65]

Local constables and officers in the rest of the West Indies, would probably have had something similar to the *Sub-Officers' Guide of Jamaica*, a helpful booklet published in 1908 which identified the implements of Obeah for officers who might not have known what they were. The guide lists "grave dirt, pieces of chalk, packs of cards, small mirrors, or bits of large ones, beaks, feet, and bones of fowls or other birds, teeth of dogs and alligators, glass marbles, human hair, sticks of sulphur, camphor, myrrh, asafetida, frankincense, curi-

---

63   Ibid.
64   Robinson, "Obeah Worship", 212.
65   Ibid.

ous shells, china dolls, wooden images, [and] curiously shaped sticks" as being among the implements used by Obeah men and women.[66]

In 1910 Harry Johnston observed that "the negro police of Jamaica are now (no doubt by order) very much – and very rightly – 'down' on those who practice Obeah", but not everybody was so supportive of the police's role in suppressing the practice. A correspondent to the *Daily Gleaner* the year before had "complained that the police dealt too harshly with men and women whose utmost crime was little worse than that of some of the new, ostensibly religious sects in Jamaica – the obtaining money under false pretences. Severe floggings (it is alleged) 'until the blood runs from the wounds' are inflicted on so-called Obia men who have merely attempted to tell fortunes by palmistry or crystal-gazing".[67] Robinson takes comfort from the flurry of legislative activity: "The powers [of the 1845 act were] increased so the fangs of the Obeah-man have been drawn and cases of murder are rare."[68]

The law and the justice system were everything Obeah was not; they symbolized order, white authority and its power. Many felt or hoped that the law would succeed where the Cross had patently failed. Charles Kinsgley, who had thrown his support behind Eyre's draconian imposition of martial law in Jamaica, was convinced that "nothing but the strong arm of English law can put down the sorcerer", though he grimly acknowledges that it would happen only "seldom enough, owing to the poor folks' dread of giving evidence".[69] But even when the "sorcerers" were imprisoned, it proved hard to keep some of them behind bars. The following tale from Cynric Williams is entertaining enough to be given in its entirety.

One morning Cynric was out for a ride with his host when they

> overtook a tall strapping negro so like in figure to one of my friend's slaves that he saluted him with "how d'ye, Cudjoe? Which way are you going?" But, before he could get an answer, looking in the man's face he perceived his mistake and asked again, "What's your name? Whom do you belong to? Where are you going? This is no pass." – The man replied "Me belong to massa, me watchman, me going to mountain." My friend inquired again sharply, "What massa? What mountain?" "You massa, for you mountain, me no your neegar Cuffie." "Well," says my friend, "this is a curious piece of effrontery. I think I ought to know all my own negroes. You must be a runaway, my man, and

---

66   Williams, *Psychic Phenomena*, 102.
67   Johnston, *Negro in the New World*, 253.
68   Robinson, "Obeah Worship", 210.
69   Kingsley, *At Last*, 2:199.

about no good here, so turn about and walk with me to the works." The negro found himself in a scrape and looked about to see how he could escape but we headed him and manoeuvred with our horses to keep him in the road till he came to the negro houses, where he jumped over a penguin fence that protected the gardens from the road, hoping, no doubt, to hide himself among them before we could get round by the gate. But my friend was too active for him, and, giving his horse rein and spur, cleared the fence like an old hunter. It was negro dinner-time, and the driver and his gang were at home. Of course, Cuffie was instantly secured, and led to the overseer's house, where an examination immediately took place. Partly by his own confession and partly by the recollection of a white man present, we discovered that he belonged to a neighbouring estate, and my friend was going to send him there in custody, with a note to his overseer, according to the usual practice in such cases among neighbours, when a sharp lad, a book-keeper, said to my friend, "I wish, sir, you would let me search his cutacoo; I have a strange fancy he has something there he ought not to have." It is impossible to convey to the reader, by description, an idea of the look which the culprit gave the young man, when he observed, in answer to his suggestion, "Warra debbil cun poor negar hab in him cutacoo but lilly bit nyamnyam?" However, permission was given to search. The young man, in an instant, leaped down off the steps, grappled with Cuffie, who made stout resistance, and at last succeeded in wresting the cutacoo from his grasp. The contents were immediately displayed on the steps of the overseer's house. There was an old snuff-box, several phials, some filled with liquids and some with powders, one with pounded glass; some dried herbs, teeth, beads, hair, and other trash; in short, the whole farrago of an Obeah man. The old Scotch carpenter's attention was attracted by the snuff-box, and he had taken out of it a pinch of the contents, which he was conveying to his nose, when the young lad jumped up in great agitation, with, "What are you doing? don't you know it's poison?" and with a smart rap on the knuckles kindly baulked the carpenter's gratification. We were all easily convinced of the uses to which these articles were intended to be applied, and the confusion of the man himself, at this discovery, confirmed our opinion of his guilt. My friend, on further inquiry, found that this fellow had been for some time frequenting his negro houses, and therefore in some degree accounted for sundry abortions among his women, and some other fatal occurrences among his negroes, which had previously much distressed him. He could not, however, by any direct proof, bring home to this man any interference in the calamities which he deplored, and therefore pursued his former resolution of sending him to the estate to which he said he belonged. The messenger and the culprit soon returned with a note from the overseer, stating that it was true Cuffie had formerly belonged to that estate, but having been convicted of Obeah, he had been sentenced to transportation.

He was consequently sent to gaol, where the keeper instantly recognized him, and wrote to tell my friend that, in pursuance of his sentence, he had been sold to a Mr H— for transportation. It appeared, however, that the delinquent had found means to pay Mr H— a few more pounds than he had given for him, and Mr H—, thinking it a good opportunity of turning an honest penny, had pocketed the fellow's money, and turned him loose again on the public.[70]

As we have seen, sorcery paid well, and Cuffie had earned enough to secure his freedom. Hearn's story of a prison escape in Martinique has more of the magical about it. Apparently, a quimboiseur caught stealing cattle confessed, but informed the magistrate that he would not remain in prison. "They put him in irons, but on the following morning the irons were found lying on the floor of the cell, and the prisoner was gone. He was never seen in Martinique again."[71]

The ability to evade the law would have been much sought after by the criminal element. Accused persons often desired an Obeah charm to obtain a verdict of not guilty or to, in one way or the other, bring the prosecutor's case against them to naught. In a Montserrat case related by Kingsley, the Obeah man became his own customer after trying to do his best for someone else:

> The "pièce de résistance" of the day was to be the examination and probable committal of the Obeah-man of those parts. That worthy, not being satisfied with the official conduct of our host, the warden [a Mr Mitchell], had advised himself to bribe, with certain dollars, a Coolie servant of [the warden's] to "put Obeah upon [the Warden]"; and had, with that intent, entrusted to him a Charm to be buried at his door, consisting, as usual, of a bottle containing toad, spider, rusty nails, dirty water, and other terrible jumbiferous articles. In addition to which attempt on the life and fortunes of the warden, [the Obeah man] was said to have promised the Coolie forty dollars if he would do the business thoroughly for him. Now the Coolie well understood what doing the business thoroughly for an Obeah-man involved; namely, the putting [of] Brinvilliers or other bush-poison into his food; or at least administering to him sundry doses of ground glass, in hopes of producing that "dysentery of the country" which proceeds in the West Indies, I am sorry to say, now and then, from other causes than that of climate.[72]

Instead, the servant took the bottle to the warden, who had the Obeah man arrested.

---

70 Williams, *Tour Through the Island*, 342–46.
71 Hearn, *Two Years*, 154–55.
72 Kingsley, *At Last*, 132–34.

A sort of petition, or testimonial, had been sent up to the Governor, composed apparently by the hapless wizard himself . . . and signed by a dozen or more of the coloured inhabitants: setting forth how he was known by all to be far too virtuous a personage to dabble in that unlawful practice of Obeah, of which both he and his friends testified the deepest abhorrence. . . . those who read [the testimonial] said that it was not worth the paper it was written on. Most probably, every one of these poor fellows [who had signed it] had either employed the Obeah-man themselves to avert thieves or evil eye from a particularly fine fruit-tree, by hanging up thereon a somewhat similar bottle. . . . It was said again, that if asked by an Obeah-man to swear to his good character, they could not well refuse, under penalty of finding some fine morning a white cock's head – sign of all supernatural plagues – in their garden path, the beak pointing to their door; or an Obeah bottle under their door-step; and either Brinvilliers in their pottage, or such an expectation of it, and of plague and ruin to them and all their worldly belongings, in their foolish souls, as would be likely enough to kill them, in a few months, from simple mortal fear.[73]

CHRISTIANITY: THE WHITE MAN'S OBI

In the early years of the plantation era, the missionaries of the Church of England or the "established Church" ignored the slaves. In fact, some churchmen thought Africans beyond the reach of Christianity, too far gone in savagery and superstition, and they were reluctant to waste their labours on them. Additionally, the planters distrusted the influence that Christianity might have on the slaves. As the novelist Theodora Lynch notes, "it was considered dangerous to instruct a slave in the precepts of Christianity; and no one spoke to the poor man of the Balm in Gilead".[74] The planters were well aware that to acknowledge that blacks too could become Christians, just like whites, was to admit their basic humanity and put them on a more equal footing with whites. The logical conclusion of this kind of thinking would be the ensuing recognition that it was wrong and immoral to enslave people who differed little from you in matters beyond those of race. The planters focused instead on the savagery, stupidity and childishness of blacks and denied the possibility of their having the capacity to become Christians.

Long derided the abolitionists and missionaries who thought blacks would

---

73 Ibid.
74 Lynch, *Wonders*, 171.

even be interested in Christianity. "Some good persons have expressed their wishes that the plantation Negroes might be all converted to the Christian faith", he writes, adding

> The planters would be the last to oppose such a scheme if it were thought practicable; well knowing, that their becoming true Christians would work no change of property and might possibly amend their manners. But few if any of the African natives will listen to any proposition tending to deprive them of their favourite superstitions and sensual delights. . . . The laws of Jamaica require the planters to do their utmost for converting their Negroes and causing them to be baptized so soon as they can be put into a fit capacity of sentiment to admit of it. But their general inappetency to become converts, together with their barbarous stupidity, and ignorance of the English language, which render them incapable of reasoning upon what is said to them, would foil the most zealous endeavours. Besides the planters are averse to exert a constraint over their minds which might wear the appearance of religious tyranny. They do not think the cause of Christianity at all honoured by adding involuntary proselytes; they hold it rather for a shameful hypocrisy and insult to the true worship. But any of their Negroes having made request to be baptized I never knew, nor heard, of a planter's having refused compliance with it.[75]

Long points out that the Anglican priest Griffith Hughes, author of *The Natural History of the Island of Barbados*, is of the same opinion. "'To bring them,' says he, 'in general, to the knowledge of the Christian religion is undoubtedly a great and good design, in the intention laudable, and in speculation easy; yet, I believe, for reasons too tedious to be mentioned that the difficulties attending it are and I am afraid ever will be insurmountable.'"[76]

Where Long and others blame the slaves themselves for their lack of genuine conversion, many blame the plantation system, which allowed the enslaved no time for religious instruction:

> The Negroes cannot attend on their service on a Sunday; and when I left Jamaica no regulations had been made, or I believe thought of, for allowing them time in the week. These Missionaries are expected to visit several estates every week for the purpose of preaching to the slaves if they can obtain leave of the proprietor or person acting in his place to do so. But this they very seldom get; on some estates not at all, on others once or twice in the year; so that their presence in the island can be of little importance. I have heard it, indeed, repeatedly

---

75 Long, *History of Jamaica*, 428–29.
76 Ibid.

declared that the Curates Act was intended for England, not for Jamaica; and this really appears to me to be viewing the subject in its true light; for it must have been known, before it was passed, that the planters would not allow the slaves any opportunity for attending on their new instructors, and that, consequently, such a law could have no tendency to improve their condition. In a thousand instances the clergy are rather to be pitied than blamed; and I have not the least doubt that many a curate most deeply laments that ever he crossed the Atlantic.[77]

Whatever the laws encouraging the baptism of slaves may have been like in Long's time, they appear to have been vastly different decades later, when legislation restricting who could preach entered the books. In 1803, in an article about the mulatto Baptist preacher Moses Baker, the editors of the *Evangelical Magazine* expressed their concern

that an Act of Assembly has been passed in Jamaica, which subjects all persons "not qualified according to the laws" in that island and who shall "presume to preach and teach in any meeting or assembly of negroes, or people of colour", to be "deemed and taken to be rogues and vagabonds": and accordingly, such are liable to be apprehended and committed to the common gaol: and upon conviction before three magistrates, may be committed to the workhouse, where they were to serve one month's hard labour which was to be increased to six months if they were arrested again for the same offense.[78]

Baker had arrived in Jamaica with his wife in 1783 and found work instructing Mr Wynn's slaves in "religious and moral principles" on the Stretch and Set estate (later renamed Adelphi). Baptized by his fellow American preacher George Lisle, a black man, Baker became one of the first Baptist preachers on the island. He is credited with galvanizing an interest in the island among members of the English Baptist Missionary Society, which sent out its first missionary, Revd John Rowe, in 1814. Aggrieved by the new law, Baker sent copies of letters commending the work he was doing among the slaves to an acquaintance in England. In a letter dated 30 August 1802, the addressee is told: "This will be presented by Mr Baker, whom I send in consequence of your request. You will find he will soon eradicate all obeah from your estate, which is one of the many

---

77 [Zachary Macaulay], *Negro Slavery; or, a View of Some of the More Prominent Features of That State of Society* (London: Hatchard and Son, 1823), 46.
78 "An Account of Moses Baker, a Mulatto Baptist Preacher Near Martha Brea in Jamaica", *Evangelical Magazine*, September 1803, 365–71.

good consequences I have found from his attendance at F——." Neither the writer nor the addressee is named, in order to maintain their privacy and also, one suspects, to prevent them from drawing the ire of the more hostile planters.

Baker decried the passage of the law, which he appears to have taken as a personal affront:

> From this [law] we can expect nothing but a great falling away of the weaker Christians. The poor destitute flock is left to go astray without a shepherd . . . we cry and crave to God, night and day, for his great mercy and assistance. We trust God will put it in your power to send us assistance, for the Lord Jesus Christ's sake, and for the sake of so many poor souls that will be totally lost for the want of your assistance.[79]

To support his argument, he relates the situation with the slaves when he was first employed by Wynn and was greeted with some suspicion:

> I continued going among them for two weeks when one of the leading men took me out, and said "Sir, what I have heard you say is very good; but the way our people are in, they cannot follow it." I asked him, what way they were in? He said, "If you will go with me, I will let you see." Accordingly, he took me to his own house first: there I found bottles, horns and other things, I know not what. Some of them buried. All these were employed in their way of witchcraft. When I saw this, I said to him, "Old man, these are the works of the Devil; the very things that God has sent me among you to root out and destroy": which I actually did wherever I found them. He said, "The things which you find here, you will find the like in every house; for this is the way we all live"; and believed there was no other way.[80]

Baker persisted in his preaching and slowly gained more converts. "Now when some of them became convinced of their evil ways, they told me, that he who had the most money among them did the best; and even confessed, that some of them now on the estate, had killed others by this wicked means."[81]

The Jamaica House of Assembly was less impressed and followed up with another law aimed at curtailing the activities of the missionaries, issuing. On 15 June 1807, the House issued "An ordinance for preventing the profanation of religious rites and false worshipping of God, under the pretence of

---

79 Ibid.
80 Ibid.
81 Ibid.

preaching and teaching, by illiterate, ignorant, and ill-disposed persons, and of the mischiefs consequent thereupon".

> whereas nothing can tend more to bring true devotion, and the practice of real religion into disrepute, than the pretended preaching, teaching, and expounding the word of God . . . by uneducated, illiterate, and ignorant persons and false enthusiasts, – and whereas the practice of such pretended preaching, teaching . . . to large numbers of persons of colour and negroes, both of free condition and slaves . . . hath increased to an alarming degree; and, during such pretended preaching, teaching . . . divers indecent and unseemly noises, gesticulations, and behaviour, often are used and take place . . . to the disrepute of religion itself; and also to the great detriment of slaves [who are kept from their master's business] and, in some cases, the minds of the slaves have been so operated on . . . as to become actually deranged.[82]

Violators could face a fine of up to one hundred pounds or be sentenced to the workhouse for six months or up to thirty-nine lashes. Further, preachers could not preach before six in the morning or later than sunset. Persons who allowed prayer meetings to take place on their property or on property they occupied could also find themselves before the court. If white, they faced a one hundred-pound fine and up to three months in jail; if black, one hundred pounds or up to three months in the workhouse. If the violator was a slave, he or she faced confinement and hard labour for up to six weeks.[83]

At least in part, if not wholly, this act was aimed at preachers like Baker and Lisle, though neither was illiterate or uneducated. Baker was once arrested for allegedly preaching against slavery. He was placed in the stocks and the Baptist meeting house was fired into.[84] Lisle was also imprisoned for a short period for preaching sedition. Of these years, Phillippo writes that "the press was also enlisted in the same unhallowed cause, and poured out torrents of blasphemy from day to day; whilst the whole community, regarding religion as hostile to their interests as it was opposed to their propensities, opposition to its introduction by missionaries was to be expected".[85]

Various eminent persons weighed in on the controversy. "Surely then it

---

82 *The New Annual Register, or General Repository of History, Politics, and Literature for the Year 1807* (London: John Stockdale, 1808), 289.
83 Ibid., 289–90.
84 John Clark, Walter Dendy, and James M. Phillippo, *The Voice of Jubilee: A Narrative of the Baptist Mission, Jamaica* (London: John Snow, 1865), 34.
85 Phillippo, *Jamaica*, 126.

might have been expected, that, if from no other motive, yet that for the purpose of rooting a pagan superstition out of the minds of the slaves, the aid of Christians would have been called in, as the safest species of knowledge?" asks Wilberforce. He adds, "It was strange if the Jamaica gentlemen were ignorant of the indubitable fact, that Christianity never failed to chase away these vain terrors of darkness and paganism. No sooner did a Negro become a Christian, than the Obeah-man despaired of bringing him into subjection."[86]

"I can scarcely imagine, that there is any one, who would hesitate for a moment in the choice between Christianity as taught by missionaries whose dogmas may be the least generally approved, and those gloomy, and hateful superstitions which place the life and soul of the negroe in the hands of the pagan Obeah-man", writes Sir George Henry Rose, an absentee plantation owner himself and the member of Parliament for Christchurch.[87]

Always when the question of the Christianization and civilizing of blacks came up, so also did Obeah. The ability of black people to gain entry into European civilization stood or fell with the degree of their attachment to the magical practices and beliefs of their ancestors. Even those well disposed towards blacks conceded that great difficulties existed. "The slaves, mostly Africans, were at that time, much attached to their heathenish religion, which is of the lowest kind, the worship of the Fetish; any object that may be chosen for religious worship, and accounted holy . . . by far the great part adhered to their heathenish practices, such as the sacrifice of fowls, and other offerings at the grave of departed friends and many such customs", Buchner notes. "Their faith in witchcraft or Obeah was at that time very strong, and this and similar customs were much practiced. Those who were baptized and became communicants, found unspeakable comfort in the simple belief that they were now the property of the Lord Jesus, and that witchcraft had lost its power over them."[88]

Conversions were indeed often temporary, however. Labat, for example, reports converting the slave of one of his parishioners, a man whose clairvoyance was vouched for by his owner. The man could find lost articles and predict the future, "as much as the devil was able to foresee and tell him about". He was

---

86   Wilberforce, *Appeal*, 29.
87   George Henry Rose, *A Letter on the Means and Importance of Converting the Slaves in the West Indies to Christianity* (London: John Murray, 1823), 21. Though the *Oxford Dictionary of National Biography* does not mention that he was a slave owner, Rose inherited a small estate in Antigua, presumably through his mother, the daughter of a planter on that island; *Methodist Magazine* 6 (1823): 354.
88   Buchner, *Moravians*, 30–31.

baptized after promising to "renounce all pacts and understandings that he could have made with the Powers of Darkness". But a few months later the man went back to Labat, requesting the return of a little bag and a terracotta figurine that the priest had confiscated from him at his baptism. He said that their confiscation had made him poor, as he could no longer earn his living from them. At that, Labat flew into a temper. He had the bag burnt and smashed the figurine into smithereens after the man claimed it gave him the answers to all his questions. He also destroyed the pot containing the spool of thread used to find lost items. The man was later sold off the island by his frightened owner.[89]

Writer after writer express their belief that superstition was practically innate in blacks, that, having come from a heathen continent, they were and forever would be heathens, despite their apparent conversions. Born savage and barbarous, they would remain savage and barbarous, and the stronger their belief in Obeah, the more uncivilized they were judged. For many whites, the superstition of blacks could no more be eradicated than could the blackness of their skins. Atwood typically declares that

> negroes are in general much addicted to witchcraft and idolatry, both of which seem to be inherent in them, so that though many of them profess the Christian Religion, especially that of the Roman Catholicks, and some of them pay great attention thereto, yet, in all matters which concern themselves, they have recourse to their superstitious confidence in the power of the dead, of the sun and moon; nay, even, of sticks, stones and earth from graves hung in bottles in their gardens.[90]

Since Africans' superstition was innate or "inherent", many whites, particularly those who considered blacks a substantially inferior race, argued that conversions could neither be genuine nor long-lasting. Long, for example, dismisses the idea of a truly Christian slave:

> I have known some Creole slaves desire to be baptized; but they had no other motive than to be protected from the witchcraft of obeiah men or pretended sorcerers which affords a plain proof of the influence which superstition holds over their minds. But the mere ceremony of baptism would no more make Christians of the Negroes in the just sense of the word than a sound drubbing would convert an illiterate faggot maker into a regular physician.[91]

---

89 Young and Helweg-Larsen, *Pirates' Priest*, 42.
90 Atwood, *Island of Dominica*, 268.
91 Long, *History of Jamaica*, 428.

Long's view had a lot of support, even among those who supported the abolition of slavery. "Chastity is utterly out of the question amongst the whole tribe and both men and women are found to vindicate as innocent practices that which it is scarcely allowable to name amongst Christians", wrote Revd Thomas Cooper, who went to Jamaica in 1817 and stayed three years.

> This is followed by low cunning and contempt of truth, a determined resolution to thieve and the greatest aversion to every species of labour. Gratitude, fidelity, activity, and courage make no part of the character of the West India slave and yet thousands and tens of thousands have been received into the congregation of Christ's flock. . . . I have been present more than once at the christening of two or three hundred of them. . . . Need I add that the whole is a solemn mockery. . . . The poor creatures get a new name with which they are mightily pleased and some of them are said to fancy themselves out of the reach of Obeah or witchcraft.[92]

Given his character sketch of blacks, some might find it surprising that Cooper was actually an advocate for the gradual abolition of slavery and a vigorous supporter of the rights of black people "as human beings and British subjects".[93]

Buchner gives short shrift to any criticism of Moravian conversions: "The Brethren never administered baptism as a mere formal rite; they made it conditionally dependent on an earnest desire to know the Saviour; and a real willingness, from love to him, to make a public confession of faith."[94] Whether that was true or not, some slaves saw Christian conversion as nothing more than an alternative way of gaining the support of supernatural powers, not all were completely convinced that it was the best or most powerful way. Dallas notes that it was "the weaker ones, whether Maroons or others, [who] dreaded the arts of Obeah even after baptism", but, he adds, "the greatest dupes to [Obeah] were the most ignorant; and it was a generally received opinion, that the charm of Obeah could have no power over any negro who had been baptized".[95]

For many slaves, the Obeah of baptism trumped African Obeah, as the story of Plato has shown. Missionaries, abolitionists and others who were

---

92 [Macaulay], *Negro Slavery*, 45–46.
93 Thomas Cooper, *Correspondence between George Hibbert Esq. and the Rev. T. Cooper, Relative to the Condition of the Negro Slaves in Jamaica, Extracted from the Morning Chronicle* [. . .] (London, 1824), http://www.recoveredhistories.org/pamphlet1.php?catid=131.
94 Buchner, *Moravians*, 74.
95 Robert Charles Dallas, *The History of the Maroons* (London: T.N. Longman and O. Rees, 1803), 1:92.

generally well disposed to blacks and anxious to refute any claims that they were beyond civilization or redemption clung fervently to their belief in Christianity's transformative powers. Obeah, as the most potent symbol of African Otherness, was their primary target. "[Obeah] has for some time been losing ground, and will probably disappear entirely, as soon as Christianity shall have been generally established throughout our West Indian colonies", writes the abolitionist author of *Poems Chiefly on the Superstition of Obeah*, noting that it was "confidently believed by the Negroes that Baptism is a certain preservative against the effects of Obeah".[96]

Ironically, the struggle for the souls of black men and women became a battle between "white Obeah" and "black Obeah". Which was stronger? Kingsley, for example, notes that "Obeah men in the West Indies are said to hold of the Catholic priests – that 'Buccra padre's Obeah was too strong for his Obeah'".[97] Indeed, according to Pullen-Burry, "so ingrained in them is this belief in the spell of their wizards . . . that they look upon the 'passon' as the white Obeah man".[98]

Some black people did not think this applied to the priests of every faith, but only to those of the Catholic Church. The Jesuit Williams explains that "there is a conviction among [Obeah men and women] that the priest can exercise a more powerful influence than any obeah-man. This belief is expressed by the aphorism: 'French obi, him strongest'." Williams attributes this to the fact that "the first priest to become known throughout the Jamaica bush was a Frenchman, and the Catholic Church in consequence came to be known familiarly as the French Church", so "French obi" meant that "the Catholic Church exercises the strongest obeah". The priest was said to have the "power of the candle"; he could frighten people by saying he would light a candle on them (a belief that persists in some quarters today).[99]

There was also a significant coterie which believed that the Catholic religion itself, with its rituals, effigies and incense, encouraged a belief in superstition. "Negroes are the aptest subjects in the universe to be kept in subordination and discipline by the awful ceremonies, the indulgencies, injunctions, mummery, and legerdemain of the Romish church and its ministers", Long writes, contrasting Catholicism with Anglicanism, which he notes was founded on the "princi-

---

96   *Poems*, 20.
97   Kingsley, *At Last*, 2:142.
98   Pullen-Burry, *Jamaica*, 133.
99   Williams, *Voodoos and Obeahs*, 107.

ples of reason".[100] Sir Henry Rose expresses concern about the "slight varnish of Popery over a gangrenous mass of heathenism" affecting the slaves on his Antiguan estate.[101] Years later, Froude notes that in Dominica, "Obeah is not forgotten; and along with the Catholic religion goes an active belief in magic and witchcraft".[102] Froude and others had forgotten about all those planters and their supporters who preferred that their slaves continue in paganism.

Cynric Williams spoke to many who shared their views liberally. For example, he reports that one planter voiced the opinion that the "religious progress [of the blacks] does not seem to improve their morality. Their superstition is overcome, and the mental restraints against thieving and roguery are overcome with it." According to the same planter, "formerly, people minded the puntees, hung up in the trees and grounds as charms to keep off thieves, but since there was so much *preachy preachy*, the lazy fellows did nothing but tief".[103] This was a rather backhanded way of acknowledging the good that Obeah did in society, but Williams comes close to accusing the missionaries themselves of working a type of Obeah, by using language that would have reminded readers of the accusations traditionally made against Obeah men and women. Some blacks were driven mad, while others killed themselves "brooding over the terrors with which the preachers have inspired them", Williams says, making the same charge that Walduck and almost every other commentator had made about Obeah.[104] Henry Nelson Coleridge (nephew of the famous Samuel Taylor Coleridge) writes that the Methodists' "dominion over these poor people is as absolute as was ever that of Jesuits over Jesuits".[105] If Anglicans hated the Roman Catholic Church and all it stood for, with its ceremonies and elaborate hierarchy, they reserved a particular distrust of the Society of Jesus, or the Jesuits, as they were commonly known. And to some Anglicans – Coleridge clearly among them – Methodists were as bad as the worst of Catholics.

Coleridge avers that the Methodist conversion of blacks rested mostly on their intimidation by the missionaries. "The fear of being turned out of their class operates like the dread of losing the caste in Hindostan and the negroes know that this formidable power rests entirely with their ministers."[106] The Methodists

---

100 Long, *History of Jamaica*, 430.
101 *Methodist Magazine* 6 (1823): 354.
102 Froude, *English in the West Indies*, 152.
103 Williams, *Tour Through the Island*, 18–19.
104 Ibid., 37.
105 Henry Nelson Coleridge, *Six Months in the West Indies* (London: Thomas Tegg, 1841), 171.
106 Ibid.

were "cunning, intriguing, meddling, fanatical, hypocritical, canting knaves, cajoling the poor negroes . . . of all their little savings and every species of property they can amass, under the pretence of saving them from the Devil and everlasting damnation", a slave owner told Cynric Williams.[107] "And the fears of all are lest these [the slaves] should be seduced by the example of others, of runaway, of the maroons, and *more than all*, by the incantations (if I may so call them) of the missionaries."[108] This is a hugely damning indictment, but its exaggeration alone testifies to the inroads that the Methodist missionaries – almost all of whom were abolitionists – were making among the slave population.

It was even more important to undermine Methodist influence back in Britain, where Methodists had followed their leader, John Wesley, in a boycott of sugar that cut into the planters' profits. Methodists had to be made into villains, and Williams does his best to paint the worst possible picture of them. In one instance, he recounts an incident in which he claims that a slave, Isaac, was brought before his owner on charges of stealing a lamb. Isaac revealed that he had stolen it in order to make a partial payment on a Bible he had gotten from a Mr Macauly, a Methodist missionary who had asked for provisions in payment. "Those who send you bibles should send them *gratis*, and not make a trade of their books to get negroes into mischief", snarled the proprietor, ordering a whipping for Isaac.[109]

The well-meaning Methodists, staunch in their support for abolition, were a favourite target. "The Methodists will pardon the freedom I take in expressing my suspicions that the evil, which they have done upon the long run both at home and abroad, is but scantily counterpoised by a certain sobriety of exterior which they have inflicted on their sect", writes Coleridge. "Do not [the gentlemen of Jamaica and Antigua] repent their encouragement [of the missionaries]; do they not fear the power of the Methodists? They will not deny it", he declares, arguing that the Anglican Church should never have left the door open for the Methodists and other sects to make progress in educating and cavilling the Negroes.

> The planters in the West Indies profess to be apprehensive of insurrection; nevertheless they admit sectarians of one denomination or another into their estates. The negroes are a very curious and observant race, and after they have learnt that there is a God, the next thing they learn is, that their master does not

---

107 Williams, *Tour Through the Island*, 37.
108 Ibid., 89.
109 Ibid., 12.

worship him in the same manner with themselves. They believe their worship is true, and therefore they must think their master's false.[110]

At least one group of Methodists cracked under the pressure. At a meeting held in Kingston, Jamaica, on 6 September 1824, the Wesleyan missionaries "observed with deep regret the numerous misrepresentations and calumnies which have been circulated concerning their principles and motives". They enumerated each of the main charges against them:

> That they believe Slavery to be incompatible with the Christian Religion; That their doctrines are calculated to produce insubordination among the Slaves; That they are secretly attempting to put in operation means to effect the Emancipation of the Slaves; That they are connected and correspond with the Members of the African Institution; That they are the most decided although disguised enemies of the West Indian Colonies; And are enriching themselves by extorting money from the Slaves.[111]

They went on to try to exonerate themselves by issuing a statement, declaring:

> their decided belief that Christianity does not interfere with the civil condition of Slaves. . . . In answer to the Second Charge they reply that it is what no man living can or ever could prove respecting the doctrines taught by any Member of this Meeting. . . . The Third Charge they most peremptorily deny . . . and moreover believe that if the design of the Emancipatists was carried into effect it would be a general calamity injurious to the Slaves, unjust to the Proprietors, ruinous to the Colonies, deleterious to Christianity, and tending to the effusion of human blood. . . . As to the Fourth Charge, the Members of this Meeting most solemnly declare that they have not the least connection with the African Institution. . . . They therefore feel themselves most unjustly treated by the suspicions expressed.[112]

The missionaries concluded by directing that those proceedings and resolutions should be circulated as widely as possible on the island, with copies going to the leading officials, such as the Duke of Manchester, governor-in-chief, and Sir John Keane, commander-in-chief.

---

110   Coleridge, *Six Months*, 170, 172. Coleridge did not have a problem with the Moravians, however, describing them as "a good and innoxious class of people."
111   Alexander Barclay, *A Practical View of the Present State of Slavery in the West Indies* (London: Smith, Elder, 1826), 449.
112   Ibid., 451.

The meeting and the missionaries' effort to explain themselves drew wide attention in Great Britain, with several papers publishing accounts of what had transpired. Aghast at what they saw as something of an insurgence, the Wesleyan Society in London called an emergency meeting of its committee on 5 January 1825. The committee members sharply disavowed the resolutions of their Jamaican colleagues and made it clear that

> if it was intended as a declaration that the system of Slavery . . . is not inconsistent with Christianity, the Committee and the Wesleyan Body . . . hold no such opinion; but while they feel that all change in such a System ought to emanate solely from the Legislature, they hold it to be the duty of every Christian Government to bring the practice of Slavery to an end as soon as it can be done prudently, safely, and with a just consideration of the interests of all parties concerned; and that the degradation of men merely on account of their colour, and the holding of human beings in interminable bondage, are wholly inconsistent with Christianity.[113]

The Committee further notes, with "great grief", the attack made on the "excellent and benevolent men" of the abolitionist cause and distances itself from those views, which it notes were clearly "written under evident ignorance".[114]

While Coleridge's *Six Months in the West Indies* appeared in 1826 and Cynric Williams's book in 1827, both men were in the region in the early 1820s, when feeling against the missionaries was particularly strong and when the rumours the Methodists listed were fairly widespread. Both Williams and Coleridge were ardent supporters of slavery, of course. "Slavery was not only suffered but authorized by Divinity, and practiced by the Jews", Williams points out, arguing that "the Saints", as he called the Methodists, were misleading people.[115] And even if it were not so, the slaves themselves had no quarrel with slavery, according to Coleridge. "The slaves are so well aware of the comforts which they enjoy under a master's purveyance that they not unfrequently forego freedom rather than be deprived of them. . . . Many negroes in Barbados, Grenada and Antigua have refused freedom when offered to them", he writes, with all the authority lent him by his six months in the region.[116]

Cynric Williams prefaces his book by declaring that "the wealth of the

---

113 Ibid., 452.
114 Ibid., 453–56.
115 Williams, *Tour Through the Island*, 71.
116 Coleridge, *Six Months*, 10.

rich, in the colonies, is *slaves*, secured to them in the first place by the laws of England; and that to tamper with the feelings of these slaves must produce alarm, consternation, and hatred in the minds of their owners, mingled with no small portion of indignation at what they consider ignorance and presumption on the part of the Reformers". He claims to have met a mulatto whose slaves had run away, and who, he says, declared that "if he lost them entirely in consequence of the insurrection, he and twenty or thirty more in similar circumstances would take refuge in the woods, and would make war on every preacher and missionary, until not one should remain alive in the Island". Fighting words indeed, but probably an accurate representation of how at least some planters felt. The anti-slavery society in Britain might be out of their reach and some of its members too eminent to attack or even threaten, but the evangelical missionaries were both closer at hand and less exalted.

Williams claims that the animus felt by the planters towards the missionaries was shared by black people. It was all well and good for him to show that the planters despised the Methodists, but if he could show that blacks themselves, on whose behalf the Methodists were lobbying, also hated them, he could undermine their credibility and sow seeds of discord within Methodism itself. Towards this end he announces that he met several blacks who made fun of Methodists (black people were often stereotyped as ungrateful, so he would have good reason to hope that his claims would be believed). One, a slave girl, derided a missionary "who was always pretending to preach God Almighty and yet was the wickedest villain in all Jamaica". Williams is careful to emphasize that he has used "her words" exactly. Later he describes meeting another black woman who sings

> Hi! de Buckra, hi!
> You sabby wha for he da cross de sea,
> Wid him long white face and him twinkling yeye;
> He lub, make lub, as he preach to we,
> He fall on his knees, but he pray for me,
> Hi! de Buckra, hi!
>
> Hi! de Buckra, hi!
> Massa W—f—e da come ober de sea,
> Wid him roguish heart and him tender look;
> And while he palaver and preach him book,
> At the negro girl he'll winkie him yeye.
> Hi! de Buckra, hi!

Williams says the woman claimed the song was composed by a slave who "preach like the missionaries, for fun, and tell how dey make love to black and brown girls".[117] According to him, the slave composer had gone to England and had been educated as a Methodist missionary but decided to remain a slave.[118] Williams fails to offer the man's name.

In the song and in an anecdote about the missionary "Macauly", Williams lampoons the famous abolitionists Wilberforce and Macaulay, themes he would return to in his novel *Hamel, the Obeah Man*. His antagonism towards the missionaries and the anti-slavery lobby had the strange effect of transforming him into a supporter of Obeah. Williams tells the story of a slave by the name of Swipes who tried to poison a preacher in Montego Bay. In his defence, Swipes said that since the preacher was always talking about laying down his burden and quitting this mortal life, he decided to help him "to heaven and the glory for which he was so anxious".[119] Swipes was put on trial but escaped into the woods, where he called himself Saint John and started holding church services. For the wine, he substituted rum, and for bread, roasted plantains. According to Williams, a crucifix with an effigy of "Saint Wilberforce" presided over the ceremonies. He says that Saint John was held in check only by an Obeah man who prevented him from taking the property of the credulous.

> This fanatical rascal has really great power over the minds of the negroes, which is, however, moderated by the efforts of an Obeah man, his declared rival, or he would urge them into the most abominable excesses. . . . His rapacity almost equals that of the priesthood of old, but his Obeah rival still retains an influence over even his followers, – an influence under which they were born, – and, by his spells, his charms, and his fetishes, guards the property of his less enterprising and more peaceful neighbours.
>
> As the practice of Obeah is illegal, and the persuasion of Saint Swipes in fashion, the latter affects to defy the wizard, and threatens to give him up to the law, forgetting that he lies at the mercy of his adversary, and may in turn be called to account for poisoning the methodist.[120]

One senses that in relating these stories, fictional or not, embroidered or not, Williams is flexing the storytelling muscles he would employ in *Hamel*.

Interestingly, Buchner tells the story of a former slave, George Lewis, who

---

117 Williams, *Tour Through the Island*, 93, 297.
118 Ibid., 297.
119 Ibid., 38–41.
120 Ibid.

had been baptized as a Baptist in Virginia but who affiliated himself with the Moravians on his return to Jamaica in the early 1800s and later struck out on his own. Lewis was disliked by the planters for his influence over the slaves and was once nearly arrested for holding night meetings. He was also accused of dishonesty, though we do not learn what form this took. Buchner writes of him that "it was difficult to say whether Lewis was really a worthy character", but he acknowledges that the man did do some good. "For instance; on several estates in the parish of Manchester, the people worshipped a cotton tree, had an idol in every house, and lived in the greatest enmity, frequently poisoning one another: by his persuasion, they forsook their idol worship, and sought Christian instruction." Yet Lewis himself was accused of combining his "religious notions with a great deal of superstition". In time he broke away from the Moravians and retired to a distant part of Manchester, where he practised what the slaves called "the Negroes' home religion".[121] The similarities between what Buchner relates about him and Williams's description of Swipes are striking.

In their defence of slavery, most planters were at great pains to point out what they saw as the yawning gap between Europeans and Africans. The European was civilized, a Christian; the African was a savage. All acknowledged that Christianity was, in and of itself, a good thing, but most were just as persuaded that Africans were not amenable to either civilization or Christianization – which, to them, were one and the same. Just as some whites believe today that blacks, by virtue of being black, cannot be British or participate in "Britishness", so many in the 1700s and 1800s believed black people were incapable of and uninterested in becoming true Christians. Buchner himself admits that while the slaves were commanded to attend religious meetings on the estate owned by the missionaries, "no more than four or five would go".[122]

"The Christian is not only the best system of religion calculated [to eradicate superstition and promote happiness] . . . but by leading the mind to the knowledge of truth and immortality, contributes more than any other to amend the heart, and exalt the human character", trumpets Bryan Edwards. Yet "the conversion of savage men from a life of barbarity to the knowledge and practice of Christianity, is a work of much greater difficulty than many pious and excellent persons in Great Britain seem fondly to imagine", he argues, pointing out how attached the Maroons in particular were to their "gloomy

---

121 Buchner, *Moravians*, 49.
122 Ibid., 21–22.

African superstitions".[123] Edwards, with his pointed reference to the "pious and excellent", is taking a swipe at the anti-slavery lobby and the evangelicals who were its leading members and made up its base. As the anti-slavery movement began to gain momentum near the end of the eighteenth century, the conflict between, on the one hand, the missionaries of certain religious denominations such as the Methodists, Baptists and Moravians and, on the other, the planters and their supporters, became ever more hostile.

> I have observed, that the society [for the abolition of the slave trade] professed to have nothing more in view than to obtain an act of the legislature for prohibiting the further introduction of African slaves into the British colonies . . . the leading members . . . and even the society itself (acting as such) [used] every possible endeavour to inflame the public of great Britain against the planters, [and] distributed at a prodigious expence throughout the colonies, tracts and pamphlets without number, the direct tendency of which was to render the white inhabitants odious and contemptible in the eyes of their own slaves and excite in the latter such ideas of their natural rights and equality of condition, as should lead them to a general struggle for freedom through rebellion and bloodshed.[124]

The threat of rebellion was the nightmare of all planters, a terror that was forever uppermost in their minds.

Edwards acquits Wilberforce, one of the leaders of the Society for Effecting the Abolition of the Slave Trade, of blame and places it squarely at the feet of Revd Percival Stockdale, who had written a letter to another abolitionist, Granville Sharpe, in which he prayed for an insurrection. Edwards was particularly outraged by Stockdale's question "Should they even deliberately inflict the most exquisite tortures on those tyrants would they not be excusable?" Referring to the Haitian revolution, Edwards thunders that he has

> not the smallest doubt that the negroes on every plantation in the West Indies, were taught to believe that their masters were generally considered in the mother country, as a set of odious and abominable miscreants, whom it was laudable to massacre! The Society in the Old Jewry had made no scruple to avow this doctrine in its fullest extent, by causing pamphlets to be distributed among such of the negroes as could read, and medals among such as could not, to apprize them of the wretchedness of their situation.[125]

---

123   Edwards, "Introductory Account", 27.
124   Bryan Edwards, *An Historical Survey of the Island of Saint Domingo* (London: John Stockdale, 1801), 109.
125   Edwards, "Introductory Account", 1.

He indignantly mentions Samuel Johnson, who "often in the presence of his negro servant would raise a toast to 'a speedy rebellion of the negroes in Jamaica, and success to them'".[126]

The Anglican priest Revd Bridges may also have Stockdale in mind when, in response to Wilberforce, he furiously writes:

> In your 28th page you speak of the African practice of witchcraft called Obeah and, referring to the laws which make the dreadful effects of that superstition punishable by death, you call it folly to attempt rooting out pagan superstition by severity of punishment. Are you then so ignorant, Sir, of the manners and customs of the people whose cause you profess to advocate as not to know that obeah and death are synonymous: that the latter is the invariable end and object of the former and that this imported African superstition is widely different from the harmless tales of witches and broomsticks which once frightened you in the arms of your nursery maid. Your feelings have probably been shocked, by stories of burning old women for bewitching pigs, and swimming them for assuming the shape of an hare, but are you now to be told that obeah is a superstition dreadfully different from these fantasies; that it is, in fact, the practice of occult poisons by which thousands have suffered in these islands and which though gradually giving way beneath the spreading influence of Christianity, must nevertheless, in every proved case, be punished by human laws as severe as those which attach to the convicted murderer in every land. But here your false philanthropy calls out against the authority of Scripture itself merely because the murderer is an African and the murdered perhaps a slave master![127]

Bridges's *A Voice from Jamaica in Reply to William Wilberforce* was of course published in the same year that Louis Celeste Lecesne and John Escoffery, two Haitian anti-slavery activists, were deported from Jamaica for allegedly funnelling arms to Henry Oliver and his rebels and engaging in treasonous activities. Bridges later accuses them of being "impatient to sheathe their daggers in the breasts of [Jamaica's] white inhabitants", a libel which drew a lawsuit against his publisher and resulted in the withdrawal of volume two of *The Annals of Jamaica* and its subsequent amendment and republication without the offending sentence. Interestingly, sometime after the publication of *A Voice from Jamaica*, Bridges received a grant of seven hundred pounds from the Jamaica House of

---

126 Edwards, *Historical Survey*, 110. Johnson was known as something of a provocateur and a contrarian, however, and much would not have been made of this remark had the issue not become so sensitive and had the planters not known just how precarious their position was.

127 Bridges, *Voice from Jamaica*, 28–29.

Assembly, ostensibly to help with the raising of his son but quite probably in gratitude for his advocacy on behalf of the interests of the planters who made up the Assembly.

If planters and the pro-slavery lobby were going to make the argument that Obeah in particular and the superstition of blacks in general pointed to a need for the continuation of slavery, and that white rule was the only means by which the savagery of blacks could be suppressed, then the abolitionists had to make the case that Obeah was neither as potent a force as feared nor unamenable to the influence of Christianity. James Stephens, Wilberforce's brother-in-law and architect of the *Slave Trade Act* of 1807, which abolished the British slave trade, subscribed to the former opinion:

> Obeah also is a practice which has, by laws of Jamaica and Dominica, all of a modern date, been constituted a capital offence; and many negroes have of late years been executed for it in the former island, though in many of our other islands it has never been considered as worthy of having a place in the copious and comprehensive catalogues of crimes furnished by their penal slave laws. Obeah, and poison, are deserving of a particular consideration because they were once seriously alleged by the agent of Jamaica, and other colonists, as great causes of the dreadful mortality which prevails among the slaves in our islands. The subjects also are curious in their nature; and I was prepared to offer much authoritative information upon them, tending to prove that they are for the most part the grounds only of fanciful, though fatal imputations on the unfortunate slaves; but being anxious to contract as much as possible the bounds of this work, I will omit the discussion of these subjects here, and print it, if at all, in an appendix.[128]

Stephens does not actually return to the subject, but this did not prevent the pro-slavery Alexander Barclay from calling him out on "his prejudices":

> Another part of the slave law which Mr Stephens disapproves of, is the punishment of obeah with death; but he has not assigned his reasons thinking that "it has been, for the most part, the ground of a fanciful though fatal imputation on the poor slaves". The deaths which obeah-men occasioned by working on the imaginations of their superstitious countrymen, and by poison, certainly were not "fanciful", whatever their pretended supernatural powers might be.
>
> I was present, some years ago, at the trial of a notorious obeah-man, driver

---

128   James Stephens, *The Slavery of the British West India Colonies Delineated* (London: Joseph Butterworth and Son, 1824), 1:305.

on an estate in the parish of St David, who, by the overwhelming influence he had acquired over the minds of his deluded victims, and the more potent means he had at command to accomplish his ends, had done great injury among the slaves on the property before it was discovered. One of the witnesses, a negro belonging to the same estate, was asked – "Do you know the prisoner to be an obeah-man? *Ees, massa, shadow catcher, true*. What do you mean by a shadow-catcher? *Him ha coffin* (a little coffin produced,) *him set for catch dem shadow*. What shadow do you mean? *When him set obeah for summary* (somebody), *him catch dem shadow and dem go dead*"; and too surely they were soon dead, when he pretended to have caught their shadows, by whatever means it was effected. Two other causes, besides the law, have contributed to make this now a crime of much less frequent occurrence, – the influence of Christianity and the end put by the abolition [of the slave trade] to the importation of more African superstition. In a few years it will most likely be extinct; meantime, it is quite in consistency with Mr Stephen's course towards the colonists, at one time to accuse them of leaving their slaves in ignorance and barbarism, and at another, to charge, as an act of severe oppression, a law which is calculated to put an end to the most fatal and destructive of their superstitions.[129]

Barclay's rebuttal, billed as "the most complete and interesting volume of reference that has ever been published on this momentous question", received glowing accolades from the *Congregational Magazine*, the *Courier* and the *Glasgow Free Press*, among others.

"In order to prove that the condition of a West India Negro labourer is that of a happy and contented person, we would fearlessly go into court with this one single volume", gushed the pro-slavery *Spectator*.

> We regard Mr Barclay, on internal evidence, as an extremely fair writer. He spent half a life in Jamaica and possesses perfect familiarity and intimate acquaintance with the minutest details of a West India life. To reject the testimony of such a man is to reject the means of knowledge. We are very certain that no impartial person can take up the work without giving the author credit for extreme fairness as well as abundant intelligence.[130]

In fact, both planters and missionaries considered Africans savage and superstitious, given to devil-worship, bestial. "Up to the year 1800, when other missionaries joined the Brethren, and their united efforts gradually began to

---

129 Barclay, *Practical View*, 190–91.
130 "Works in the Press or Recently Published by Smith, Elder, and Co., Cornhill, London", *The Spectator*, n.d.

make an impression . . . the Negroes were like the beasts of the field."[131] The difference was that the missionaries found in them new opportunities to bring souls to the Lord, an objective of little interest to the planters as they saw little profit in it for themselves. Of course, the missionaries also needed to justify the expenditures of the various missionary societies which sent them out and contributed to their maintenance on the different islands. The more savage they painted the Africans, the more support they could ask for. Buchner was certainly very conscious of his obligations, dedicating his book to the "Honoured and much beloved Brethren and Friends in Jesus; you have hitherto cheerfully and liberally answered the appeals made to you on behalf of the extensive Missions of the Brethren's Church. You have enabled a small body of Christians who desire and devote all their energies to the preaching of the gospel, to send out a considerable number of labourers into the vineyard of the Lord."[132]

Various articles appeared in such publications as the *Scottish Missionary and Philanthropic Register*, the *Missionary Magazine and Chronicle* and the *Missionary Register*, either proclaiming that the missionaries had put an end to Obeah or describing how they were on their way to eradicating it. The *Baptist Magazine* of 1 June 1828, for instance, carried an article from a missionary in which he reports the death of an old man: "One very old man, who had the name of being an Obeah man, (one who practiced the kind of reputed witchcraft so called,) before he joined our church, died the other day. The last time I saw him, I said, 'Well, old man, do you obeah anybody now?' 'No,' said he, 'since Jesus Christ obeah me . . . me neber dirty me hands in such a ting.'"[133]

Brother Tank in Suriname, speaking about the free or "bush negros", praises

> the Negro woman, Affiba, [who] deserves more special mention, as being the first fruits of this Negro tribe. She formerly lived in the village of Tintje, where our brother Frank Bona told her of the Saviour, and read to her out of the New Testament. It was there, that I visited her a year ago, and was greatly pleased with her childlike faith and Christian cheerfulness. She has six children, and when the youngest lay ill, and to all appearance dying, she turned to the Lord, and received strength publicly to devote herself and her child to the crucified Saviour and utterly to renounce all her obeahs and idols; and to every one's astonishment the child recovered from that hour. Another woman, named Cato, has also renounced her idols, – no easy matter for a heathen,– and declared

---

131 Buchner, *Moravians*, 9.
132 Buchner, n.p.
133 *Baptist Magazine*, 1 June 1828, 289.

her wish to come to church, because her chief god, a serpent, could not save her brother, who was bitten by a venomous serpent, and died immediately; she is now learning to read . . . that she may be able to edify herself with God's word.[134]

Tank then launches into the description of Obeah that appeared in chapter 2 and rounds off his statements by saying that his

> authorities for these statements are various members of our Bambey congregation, Job, who was formerly an Obeah priest, his brother, John Arabi, and honest Thomas, who tell, how, in former times, they harassed themselves to death to do all that their Obeahs enjoined upon them, and yet found themselves cheated. Thus Thomas and one of his wives did task-work to their false gods to save the lives of their seven children, one after the other, and every time with fresh and more severe requirements. At length, when, on the death of their seventh child, they became acquainted with the Gospel of Christ at Bambey, they plucked up courage to shake off the chains of Satan and are now happy children of the light and worthy members of the congregation.[135]

Some of the articles on Obeah decried its pervasiveness and made the point that more missionaries were needed in order to end the "heathen" practice. The authors pointed out that more missionaries meant more conversions, which for some writers meant more docile Christian slaves. "Ignorant themselves of the nature of true religion, the slaveholder who prevented their Negroes from attending the means of grace [meetings] were blind to their own interests", writes Buchner. According to him, the planters felt that "the only thing that prevented [the slave] from violence, bloodshed and murder, was fear; fear of the whip and the gallows". The issue clearly perplexed him, even at a distance of several decades. The value of a converted slave "is so plain and self-evident to every enlightened mind, that nothing but ignorance and the natural enmity of the heart to God, can explain the fact why they planters were so violent in their opposition to the introduction of Christianity among their people".[136] The superstitious and unconverted slave might rebel, the thinking went, but not the Christian convert.

> The whites were in continual apprehension of a rising among the Negroes, and not without good reason, for in spite of all they could do there were repeated

---

134 *Periodical Accounts* 18 (1846): 317.
135 Ibid.
136 Buchner, *Moravians*, 71–72.

outbreaks of a rebellious spirit. How different is it, when, by the reception of the gospel, faith in the Saviour fills the heart of a slave! It makes him a new man ... resistance and rebellion are unlawful to him, his conscience and religious convictions condemn them; his master may, therefore, safely discard all fear of violence and murder by the converted Christian slave. To gain his freedom, he will not use means which scripture does not sanction.[137]

In 1816 a debate in the House of Lords revealed that the Church of England had only two missionaries in the West Indies, one in Antigua and the other in Nevis. As the 1800s progressed, however, more and more missionaries of all Christian sects arrived in the region. Phillippo indicates the presence of fifty-two Church of England ministers and four Presbyterian, sixteen Wesleyan Methodist and sixteen Baptist missionaries in Jamaica in 1831. After emancipation in 1834, the numbers rose dramatically. According to Phillippo, there were seventy-four Church of England ministers and thirteen Presbyterian, twenty-nine Wesleyan and twenty-seven Baptist missionaries in Jamaica in 1843.

Despite their rising numbers, the missionaries' acceptance among the planters continued to be uneven. After Jamaica's 1831 Christmas Rebellion, "our missionaries were likewise suspected, and openly accused by the planters and the House of Assembly, of having occasioned discontent and insurrection". Buchner denied that any Negroes under Baptist instruction were among the rebels, but the Baptist missionary Brother Pfeiffer was arrested for colluding with them. Invoking the spectre of the white man's Obi, a witness testified that Pfeiffer had told the rebels he had "now armed you with the word of God, no bullet can hurt you". Others more prosaically accused him of telling them that they would soon be free and should not return to work in the New Year.[138]

In the immediate aftermath of the Christmas Rebellion (also known as the Baptist War), the Colonial Church Union was formed on 27 January 1832. Its members declared themselves committed to destroying all dissenting chapels and driving the missionaries from the island. Several chapels belonging to the Baptists, the Moravians and the Methodists were destroyed over the next few weeks, for example, by the St James militia and the St Ann's regiment. Instead of suppressing abolitionist-minded missionaries, however, the reign of terror spurred men such as the Baptists William Knibb and Thomas Burchell to return to England and rally support for emancipation and for the work of the missionary societies.[139]

---

137 Ibid., 72.
138 Ibid., 85.
139 Clark, *Voice of Jubilee*, 61.

CHAPTER 5

Obeah, Race and Racism

"DARK AND SAVAGE PASSIONS"

Throughout the eighteenth and nineteenth centuries, the public discussion about Obeah raged alongside fierce arguments relating to the supposed nature of blacks and, initially, their fitness for slavery, then later, once their emancipation was achieved, their claims to civilization. Racist harangues that imputed all manner of negative attributes to black people were common.

"In general, [blacks] are void of genius, and seem almost incapable of making any progress in civility or science", writes Edward Long in 1774.

> They have no plan or system of morality among them. Their barbarity to their children debases their nature even below that of brutes. They have no moral sensations; no taste but for women; gormandizing and drinking to excess; no wish but to be idle. Their children, from their tenderest years, are suffered to deliver themselves up to all that nature suggests to them. Their houses are miserable cabins. They conceive no pleasure from the most beautiful parts of their country, preferring the more fertile. Their roads, as they call them, are mere sheep-paths, twice as long as they need be, and almost impassable. Their country in most parts is one continued wilderness, beset with briars and thorns. They use neither carriages, nor beasts of burthen. They are represented by all authors as the vilest of the human kind, to which they have little more pretension of resemblance than what arises from their exterior form.
>
> In so vast a continent as that of Afric, and in so great a variety of climates and provinces, we might expect to find a proportionable diversity among the inhabitants, in regard to their qualifications of body and mind; strength, agility, industry, and dexterity, on the one hand; ingenuity, learning, arts, and sciences on the other. But, on the contrary, a general uniformity runs through all these

various regions of people; so that, if any difference be found, it is only in degrees of the same qualities; and, what is more strange, those of the worst kind.[1]

In short, black people were inferior beings and, as such, not deserving of freedom.

The Long family had been connected with Jamaica since 1663, when Admiral William Penn and General Robert Venables seized the island from the Spanish. Samuel Long, Edward's great-grandfather, was a member of that expedition and served as secretary to Oliver Cromwell's commissioners. He subsequently became chief justice and Speaker of Jamaica's House of Assembly and sat on the council. Edward's father, also named Samuel, owned the Lucky Valley sugar plantation in Clarendon and was also a member of the council. In 1757, when Edward was twenty-three, his father died. Edward left England for Jamaica to run his father's plantation and became private secretary to the lieutenant-governor of Jamaica, Sir Henry Moore, who married Edward's eldest sister in 1765, thus joining two of Jamaica's wealthiest and most prominent families. Through Edward's own 1758 marriage to Mary Ballard Beckford, daughter of Thomas Beckford and widow of John Palmer, he added more than forty thousand acres to his already considerable property. Those who owned the most slaves and land had the most to lose by emancipation. Edward Long was not just railing against ruination of the plantation economy; he was also railing against a vision of his own ruination and that of his family and class.

Certainly, if Long was trying to attract new English settlers to Jamaica, as some have asserted, he would not have wanted them frightened off by the possibility that the great riches acquired by early settlers would be out of their reach. The wealth of the planters was built on the system of free labour. Remove the free labour and the plantation economy would collapse or, at the very least, it would not be as wildly profitable as before.

"Servitude, restricted to a particular class of person, was tolerated both by the Romans and Athenians", Long argues. "Yet no people were ever more jealous of their own liberty; nor did they find their own enjoyment of it at all incompatible with the exclusive obligation to labour imposed on others

---

1 Long, *History of Jamaica*, 353. According to him, not only were blacks inferior and thus fit for little more than enslavement, ending slavery would eviscerate the plantation economy and destroy Britain's economy too, given its dependence on colonial trade. Under the pseudonym "A Planter", he elaborates on this point in his *Candid Reflections upon the Judgement Lately Awarded by the Court of the King's Bench in Westminster Hall on What Is Commonly Called the Negroe Cause* (London: T. Lowndes, 1772).

within a certain limit." Here he is responding to the protests of abolitionists who demanded to know how England, a nation that prided itself on the liberty of its citizens, could countenance slavery in its colonies. But Long is quick to point out that "what I have said does not imply that a system of servitude ought to be introduced into any free country: but only means to show that it may be permitted with least disadvantage . . . where it happens to be inevitably necessary".[2]

Bryan Edwards fully agrees:

> If Aristotle's definition be admitted, that those who are born with strong bodily, and weak mental powers, are born to serve; and on the contrary, that whenever the mind predominates over the body, it confer natural freedom on its possessor; and if it can be made to appear that the bodies of the negroes are naturally adapted to labour, but that their mental faculties are weak, it clearly follows that nature designed them for slaves.[3]

While still a young man, Edwards had left England to live with his maternal uncle, Zachary Bayly, in Jamaica. Bayly was a wealthy planter who owned approximately fifteen hundred enslaved people on his various estates in the parishes of Trelawny, St Mary and St George. He had also represented different parishes in the House of Assembly and was a member of the island's Privy Council. On his death he left five estates to Edwards who, at twenty-two, was elected to the House of Assembly as the representative for the parish of St George. Edwards lived in Jamaica for about twenty-five years before returning to Britain in 1792. He moved to Southampton but, after failing in his electoral bid for Chichester, he went on to represent the Cornish borough of Grampound, which was said to be notoriously corrupt. In Parliament, he defended the slave trade and the interests of the West Indian planters. Though he supported amelioration, he was no abolitionist, declaring that "the general treatment of the negroes in the British West Indies is mild and indulgent; that instances of cruelty are not only rare, but almost universally reprobated when discovered; and that they are severely punished whenever they can be legally proved".[4]

In fact, some planters and their pro-slavery supporters thought the slaves should be grateful that they had been enslaved by whites and not by other blacks back in Africa. "The slave trade, therefore, being lucrative and of im-

---

2   Long, *History of Jamaica*, 5.
3   Edwards, *History Civil and Commercial*, 429.
4   Ibid., 424.

memorial existence, must in the interim, pursue its present course, as a fatality attached to the condition of the African, and as a polluted alliance, which the dictates of policy and humanity impose.... While this invidious exigency obstructs the immediate manumission of the slave, it does not the less accelerate it in uniformity thereto", writes Joseph Corry in a letter to Viscount Howich, the former principal secretary of state for foreign affairs in 1807.[5] Corry makes the argument that the slave trade was natural and Britain's involvement in it was good not just for Britain but for the Africans themselves. He argued that the hasty end of the slave trade meant that "the unhappy African is now abandoned to his fate; and we have surrendered him into the hands of other nations less acquainted with his character and situation.... Instead of now being the object of matured and wise regulation, the captive is exposed to the rapacity of our enemies, who will derive great advantages from our abandonment of the trade."[6] According to Corry's way of thinking, Britain's civilizing standards, as well as the humane way in which it treated its slaves, elevated both the slave trade and slavery itself.

"This much may be said [in slavery's] favour, that the wretched victims who were slaves in Africa, are, by being sold to the whites, removed to a situation far more desirable, even in its worst state, than that of the most fortunate slaves in their native country", writes Edwards. Those who made this argument could invariably produce a slave who shared that exact sentiment. For example, Edwards relates that a sick slave said to his owner, "Massa, since me come to white man's country, me lub (love) life too much."[7]

After all, many Africans were primitive cannibals. "The Eboes are in reality more savage than any nation of the Gold Coast", Edwards argues. "For many of these tribes, especially the Moco tribe, have been accustomed to the horrid practice of feeding on human flesh." Really, Edwards finds little to admire about black people. It is "without foundation" to think Negroes are peculiarly adapted to science or music, he argues, because blacks prefer "a loud and long-continued noise to the finest harmony". Further, "it may be doubted that [the Negro] has any conception of that tender attachment to one object which, in civilized life, sentiment increases, and delicacy refines", he says, discussing love. Instead, blacks are "promiscuous".[8]

---

5   Corry, *Observations*, 126.
6   Ibid., 74–75.
7   Edwards, *History Civil and Commercial*, 377, 404.
8   Ibid., 382–89.

Corry claims to have offered to take a slave back to Africa and received this reply: "I, massa, me like that very well, me like much to look my country; but suppose, massa, they make me slave, me no see my massa again; all the same to me where I be slave, but me like my massa best, and I no look my country with you."⁹ In fact, several planters couched their opposition to abolition in terms of their supposed care and compassion for the welfare of the enslaved. "It must be obvious to the most careless observer . . . that many, very many, of the slaves are totally unfit to have the entire disposal of their own time; they must be kept in a state of pupilage, under constant, though human restraint", Cynric Williams claims a planter told him. "The better informed have no wish [for emancipation]; it is only the unruly, idle, and profligate, and the puritanical hypocrites that make any clamour about it", the planter argued.¹⁰

Williams, who declares in his preface that he has written his book to "enable the reader to form a pretty correct idea of these habits and manners [in the West Indies] of all ranks, from the rich slave owner to his slave", was, of course, more concerned with presenting a defence of slavery than with writing any objective account. He continues:

> The public, or a portion of it, will have an opportunity of learning that negro slaves are not worked and flogged alternately at the option and caprice of their masters, as many good Christians imagine, which have signed petitions for emancipating them; that they have their pastimes as well as toils, their pleasures as well as pains; and that they smile as often, and laugh as heartily, as the labouring people of this or any other equally happy country.

After seeing slave children being fed cow hide with yams, cocos, ochros and other vegetables, Williams expresses the pious wish that "my poor neighbours in Hampshire might always be assured of such a meal once a day; however, I consoled myself with the reflection that they are not slaves; I wish it would console them for their empty bellies".¹¹

Writing more than a hundred years after Edwards, Froude asserts that slaves in Africa "would otherwise have been killed; and since the slave trade has been abolished are again killed in the celebrated 'customs'". Accordingly, he draws the happy conclusion that "in many instances, perhaps in most, [the

---

9   Corry, *Observations*, 114.
10 Williams, *Tour Through the Island*, iv–v.
11 Ibid., 15.

slave trade] was innocent and even beneficial. Nature has made us unequal, and Acts of Parliament cannot make us equal".[12]

The theme of black inferiority continued long past slavery. "The negro has never counted for much in the world", goes the first line of Livingstone's *Black Jamaica: A Study in Evolution*. "Mind, as well as body, was dark and enslaved. . . . They were absolutely devoid of a consciousness of moral responsibility. A rude assortment of ideas regarding supreme Good and Evil influences floated in vague confusions upon the surface of their understanding, but their conduct was dominated solely by the evil influences, of which Obi or Obeah was the chief." Given the general backwardness of blacks, Livingstone believes that "the duty of the white race is unmistakable. It is to uplift and mould into a responsible and progressive people the black humanity lying about its feet."[13] A Scotsman and editor of Jamaica's *Gleaner*, he writes in his preface that "the following work is the outcome of ten years' careful study of the social and economic circumstances of Jamaica. It is sent out with the three-fold object of revealing to the world the negro as he really is and the potentialities of his nature; of throwing some light on what is called the West India question, now so much discussed and so strangely misapprehended."[14]

Given the dichotomy these writers perceive between the races, the existence of mixed-race people arouses interesting reactions. Hearn finds them exotic and attractive. "Compare [Martiniquans] with the population of black Barbadoes, where the apish grossness of African coast types has been perpetuated, unchanged, and the contrast may well astonish", he writes.[15] For Livingstone, the question of the people he calls "coloureds" is an interesting one: "They are a compound of both; the intelligence of the one meets and amalgamates with the animalism of the other, producing a strange nature, the good in which is perpetually reaching forward to higher things, and the evil, like an unseen hand, perpetually dragging it back to savagery."[16]

Intelligence, bravery and goodness were associated with whiteness; stupidity, cowardliness and evil with blackness. The race among the European powers to carve up Africa and to rule much of the rest of the world necessitated equating blackness with inferiority, which required – nay, demanded – white rule. "At the present day, the generality of negroes (leaving out of account

---

12 Froude, *English in the West Indies*, 235.
13 Livingstone, *Black Jamaica*, 19, 292.
14 Ibid., preface [n.p.].
15 Hearn, *Two Years*, 103.
16 Livingstone, *Black Jamaica*, 7.

exceptional individuals) are inferior in mental development and capacity to the peoples of Europe", writes Sir Harry Johnston in the preface to his *The Negro in the New World*. "As to the future of the black man in America or in Africa, it depends largely on himself", he declares. "For many thousand years he has been a relatively idle creature as compared to the industrious European or Asiatic; who when not in slavery to each other were the slaves of ambition, or art and science, of gluttony, of lust, and of religion."[17]

RACE, RACISM AND RELIGION

"Christian missionaries did not come to Jamaica to abolish slavery", writes Revd D.J. East in his introduction to *The Voice of Jubilee*. "Their vocation was infinitely higher and holier. They came because . . . [the slave was] in the darkness of ignorance, and superstition, and sin – because he was without God, and without hope in the world. . . . They came that they might shed the light of faith upon [the slave's] benighted soul."[18] "But", he goes on to note, "the gospel is the everlasting foe of every kind of bondage . . . the gospel, in its wonder-working power, having first of all provoked slavery to hostility and to arms, fought out the battle, until slavery was no more – until the fell monster, with its whips, and chains, and manacles . . . was buried, never, never, never to rise again!"

Jamaicans have to remain vigilant, however, East warns. "What if the Bible, the word of God, instead of being bowed to and obeyed as an infallible authority and guide, should be forsaken for the cunning fables of the Obeah man, or for the wild orgies of wandering bands of (so-called) Revivalists?" he asks. "This would be to abuse your past mercies and your present privileges – this would be base ingratitude indeed" for their emancipation and social progress.[19]

With their parent societies and, indeed, many in Great Britain watching them intently, it was important for the missionaries to claim victory over the "forces of darkness", and they did so frequently.

> Forty years ago, the masses of the people were sunk in the grossest abominations of African superstition; to the great majority of them there were no Bibles, no Sabbath, no schools, and some of the professed ministers of religion were

---

17 Johnston, *Negro in the New World*, xi.
18 Clark, Dendy and Phillippo, *Voice of Jubilee*, 10–11.
19 Ibid., 24.

among the most profligate and abandoned of the community. How changed the state of things now! We have superstition, and ignorance, and irreligion enough still, but, blessed be God! we have no longer a heathen community.... But now the Christian Sabbath is an institution everywhere acknowledged.... Places of Christian worship occupy not only our towns, but lift up their heads in almost every mountain village and district... and every Christian denomination has a goodly band of faithful, hard-working, godly ministers... we bless God Jamaica is not what it once was – a slave-cursed sink of abominations.[20]

Men like Long and others who defended slavery had told the missionaries and abolitionists that they were wasting their time, that they had embarked on a fool's mission, that blacks could no more become true Christians than they could turn white. They were backward, savage, their very superstition an indication of how stupid and barbaric they were. These were the stereotypes that Underhill and other missionaries were trying to dispel by their assertions that education and Christianity had indeed won the day and that Obeah, the symbol of all that was wrong with blacks, had been eradicated.

Attacked and vilified by the sugar lobby and the defenders of slavery, the missionaries had taken the blame for the rebellions and uprisings that occurred in the decades prior to emancipation. Now, after emancipation, they wanted credit for the perceived advancement of the blacks: "We are unable within our allotted limits, even to attempt to render justice to missionary efforts in Jamaica", write the Quakers Joseph Sturge and Thomas Harvey. "A few years ago, the negroes were heathen and benighted; now they are to a great extent enlightened and Christian."[21] Phillippo, too, joins in the self-congratulation: "As a further proof of the progress which the negroes have made in civilization ... it may be remarked that the spell of Obeism and its kindred abominations is broken, and the enchantment dissolved."[22] Buchner agrees, noting that "when we compare their present moral and religious state with what it was formerly, we see that there has been a wonderful, an astonishing change".[23]

It had been a long, torturous process. Gardner pointed out that, years before, when "he had obtained a parcel of Obeah trash [and made] a promise of money to any lad in a large school who would step over it, [he] failed to secure more than one volunteer", but superstitious fear was no longer as strong as it

---

20 Ibid., 8.
21 Sturge and Harvey, *West Indies*, 351.
22 Phillippo, *Jamaica*, 263.
23 Buchner, *Moravians*, 9.

once had been. By way of example, he notes that several women, "suffused with religious feeling" during the Great Revival of 1861, had not been afraid to touch an Obeah man's items.[24] Understandably proud of the gains Christianity had made among the people, Gardner ignored the probability that the women felt themselves only temporarily immune to Obeah, through their sense of being "suffused" with the greater "white Obeah". Certainly, in the half-century following emancipation, church records throughout the region show that great gains in conversions were often followed by almost equally great expulsions.

Supporters of the missionaries and of emancipation joined in the general congratulations, however. "The influence of the terror of obeah over the negroes some twenty or thirty years ago, was almost incredible", Madden observes; "even at the present time it is greatly dreaded by the least instructed of the negroes. In this, as in many other matters, the exertions of the missionaries have been evidently beneficial to the negroes: obeah no longer has the power of producing mischief to the extent it formerly did."[25] These sentiments were echoed by others. "During the period of slavery, many were the victims of Obeism; many of dirt eating, which are now never heard of", Davy writes. "The superstition of the one has passed away, with the temptations to practice it; and the disposition to the other has ceased under a better diet, better treatment, and the cheerful solaces of life."[26]

Buchner agreed but knew the battle was far from over: "The practices of Obeah and Myalism, formerly so common, became less and less frequent though to this day they are still followed, and have not lost their power and influence over the minds of those who take part in them. Again and again, we have to use all our authority and influences against these devices of the wicked one." Discussing the myal revival of 1842 in Jamaica, Buchner notes that "the revival of heathenism proved a trial and temptation to our converts . . . they were invited to return [to their old superstitions] as a dog to his vomit, and a sow to her wallowings in the mire . . . some wavered . . . but this did not last long, they soon recovered from their surprise, and actively opposed this wickedness". [27] But the revival lasted at least six months and posed a significant challenge to the authority of both the missionaries and the colonial government.

---

24 Gardner, *History of Jamaica*, 188.
25 Madden, *Twelvemonth's Residence*, 71–72.
26 Davy, *West Indies*, 102.
27 Buchner, *Moravians*, 140–41.

What the missionaries clearly found most disconcerting was how easily the myalists were able to syncretize Christian rites and dogma with traditional African practices, thus creating new customs that attracted the followers of both:

> The more effectually to delude the multitude, the priests of this deadly art [myal], now that religion has become general, have incorporated with it a religious phraseology, together with some of the religious observances of the most popular denominations, and thus have in some instances succeeded in imposing on the credulity and fears of many of whom better things had been expected. These circumstances [the myal revival] have aroused the energies of the missionaries to an exposure of the system; as also the civil authorities to the punishment of the offenders when convicted of a violation of the law; so that in a very short period it may be hoped but few vestiges of the superstition will remain.[28]

Phillippo's figures from Jamaica show that in 1837 the number of people excluded almost doubled from 7 per cent in 1836 to 13 per cent in the following year. It dipped to 9 per cent in 1838 but rose to 12 per cent in 1839, while 1842 showed the highest jump in the figures: a whopping 29 per cent.[29] People could be excluded for a range of misdeeds, including concubinage or living together without benefit of matrimony, attending races or dances, stealing, fighting, myalism and, of course, practising Obeah or for seeking it out.

If enslavement and superstition had debased blacks, then, according to abolitionist missionaries, emancipation and Christianization had improved them: "The low, stupid, and cunning slave has become a man, feeling the responsibility he is under as a subject and a christian; his outward deportment and actions bear testimony to his altered position. Jamaica has become a christian country: supplied with the means of grace, the gospel has exercised its civilizing and elevating power, and will, it is hoped, continue to do so."[30]

In Antigua, Sturge and Harvey were told by a "gentleman of great intelligence, and long resident here, . . . that the people have improved much in dress and general appearance since Emancipation. The very features of the Negroes have altered within his memory, in consequence, as he believes, of their elevation by education and religious instruction. Their countenances express much more intelligence, and much less of the malignant passions." But, their

---

28 Phillippo, *Jamaica*, 263.
29 Ibid., 297.
30 Buchner, 165.

informant lamented, "a belief in Obeah, and other superstitions, is not quite worn out, even among the members of churches". This last observation was borne out when the writers were taken by a Moravian missionary to meet a planter who had once owned two hundred slaves but now had only a hundred labourers. He took them to the village where they met a "young woman [who] was sitting on the ground, with a very young child in her lap, who had an obi necklace of horse-hair, because its neck was 'limber', as she expressed it. The minister [Brother John Morrish] took off the necklace, and spoke to her very appropriately on her sinful habits of superstition."[31]

During the past twenty years, "that cunning, craft, and suspicion – those dark passions and savage dispositions before described as characteristic of the negro, if ever possessed in the degree in which they are attributed to them, – are now giving place to a noble, manly, and independent, yet patient and submissive spirit", writes Phillippo, determined to give the missionaries credit for the transformation. He admits, however, that "superstition itself in its most disgusting forms prevailed among them to a very great extent. Dark and magical rites, numberless incantations, and barbarous customs, were continually practiced. The principal of these were Obeism, Myalism and Fetishism."[32]

"Thirty, or even twenty years ago, there was no garden, and scarcely a fruit-tree to be seen, where the Fetish or Obeah was not exhibited, to deter thieves by superstitious fears from their depredations", writes Buchner, claiming that by 1853 these had "entirely disappeared".[33] There were then thirteen Moravian stations in Jamaica, principally in Manchester, St Elizabeth, Westmoreland and St James.

"Superstition is on the wane among our negroes; they seem to confess that whatever *appetis* (spells) their magicians could once effect, these have long since failed before superior Christian incantations", writes Rampini. "The Obeah man with his cutacoo – whose mystic contents usually comprise an old snuff box, human hair, dried grass and other trash – cannot protect himself when discovered, nor gather a poor pittance from his old devotees."[34] A planter sounded a more cautionary note: "although receiving every discouragement at the hands of the white planters and clergymen, the negroes clung desperately

---

31 Sturge and Harvey, 29.
32 Phillippo, *Jamaica*, 247, 253.
33 Buchner, *Moravians*, 157.
34 Rampini, *Letters*, 148.

to their deeply-rooted notions and, no doubt, many years must still elapse before the last traces of Obeah and Wanga disappear from these islands", the man told Hesketh Bell.[35]

Meanwhile, Trowbridge's account of one battle with the influence of Obeah illustrates not just the difficulties Europeans faced but also their determination to eradicate it, a determination which ultimately proved futile. According to him, a Mrs Togson, the English wife of a Moravian missionary, required a housemaid, but blacks did not want to work at her estate, claiming that a woman by the name of Mary Princess had been bewitched there. Mary Princess, a widow, had been sought after by two men, a coachman and the chief boiler of a neighbouring plantation. She chose the former, to the outrage of the latter, who threatened her with an Obeah spell and called upon the services of an Obeah man. Sometime later, a "dried-up, evil-faced old man who was known by everyone to be an obi-man, one thoroughly initiated, too, in all the secrets of the fetich", showed up at Mary's door. "The sight of his hideous, ragged old man ... made her shudder, as she remembered the current belief in him and the boiler-man's threat. Though obi worship was under a ban, yet the negroes often secretly had recourse to the obi-men for medicines and charms to use against an enemy. Because the old fetich was only mentioned in whispers did not reason that the evil was stamped out."

The Obeah man told her to "beware of the parrot-feathers buried under the steps of the chapel. There is a charm in them to work you harm." The warning has the expected result: "A mental paralysis settled upon Mary Princess. In that moment the Established Church and all its promises were forgotten, and the fatal fear of the obeah sank into her very soul, – a haunting, benumbing fear that never left her; a fear that made day intolerable and night a hideous dream; an utterly baseless and senseless fear, but innate, hereditary, and nigh ineradicable." Mary lost all interest in the coachman, in her work and in life and retreated to her cottage to contemplate her impending death.

When this backstory was revealed to Mrs Togson, Trowbridge relates that she set to with a will and brought Mary back to live on the estate, keeping her with her at all times, and even went so far as to find the Obeah man and remonstrate with him. She threatened to have him arrested if he came back, and he disappeared from the area. It was a triumph for white obi. The blacks said to each other, "White missy bewitch he." Mary was adopted into the household

---

35 Bell, *Obeah*, 8.

and regained her spirits and looks. Mrs Togson boasted of her coup but was cautioned about overconfidence by her white friends.

Having overcome that little hiccup, Mary and the coachman set a date for their wedding, but one night, when she was at the window, the Obeah man appeared before her. "There he was with the same red light in the malevolent eyes, and the same bent, hideous form."

"A curse upon you!" he cried. "Under the silk-cotton tree yonder lies buried a curse to blight you. You have deserted the worship of your race, and the she-devil you live with has no more any power to save you! Remember the curse, the withering, never-dying curse of the obeah!"

Mary tried to struggle against her fear, but was there any use? "It was the old taint in the blood showing again." She rushed to her room to get her Bible, but on her bed was a "tiny coffin with skull and cross-bones on the lid, and in big letters underneath were the words 'Here lies Mary Princess'". The Obeah man's face appeared at the window again, "his sinister face with the magnetic, malicious eyes". Mary fled the house "a raving maniac".

Mrs. Togson had lost and the blacks stole away from Canaan and its chapel. "The obi-man was never seen in St. John's again, but Mary Princess in the strait-jacket, chained to a gloomy cell at the Asylum, is his legacy to his race. ... The old fetich is moribund, but in death-travail it has given birth to a coarse, ignorant, and groundless superstition, which is blocking the car of progress of the West Indian."[36]

Clearly, then, many had good reason to be sceptical about the true extent of the changes and about the success of the missionaries. "Very few, indeed, I believe of the native Africans, derive their fortitude from the influence of the Christian religion. They die with the eager desire of joining their Fetish divinities, of spiritually revisiting their native land, and even of feasting and rejoicing with their fathers and brothers in Africa", writes Madden.[37]

Henry Breen, author of *St Lucia: Historical, Statistical and Descriptive*, published in 1844, claims in an 1851 issue of *Notes and Queries* that Obeah – or *kembois*, as it was known in St Lucia – is "still extensively practiced in the West Indies", but adds that there is "no reason to suppose that it is rapidly gaining ground".[38] However, an article in *The Satirist; or, The Censor of the Times* carries a brief mention of a "serious affair" on the Lennox estate in Jamaica:

---

36 Trowbridge, *Gossip*, 63–71.
37 Madden, *Twelvemonth's Residence*, 1:106.
38 *Notes and Queries* 80 (1851): 351.

> It seems that an Obeah-man (we had thought from the boasted reports put forth by the Baptists, that Paganism, and particularly Obeah, had ceased to exist) who pretends to the power of drawing gold, silver and other metals from the arms and legs of his dupes, had created great disturbances on the property, and that the officers of the parish proceeded to a house at 12 o'clock at night, where they found him practising his art, surrounded by a guard of eight armed men, and a band of music. There were about four-hundred negroes in attendance, all, of course, Obeah *worshippers*.

Someone in the crowd fired on the lone white officer, who "would undoubtedly have been murdered" had he not been able to mount his horse and escape. The two "coloured" constables were told that it was the "white livered rascal" they wanted. Later the shooter was arrested, but the paper reports that "all the negroes were armed" and that the "parish was in a state of open rebellion", with many of the people threatening to withhold their rent payments. A "company of black troops" was called on to quell the disturbance.[39] Though the rebellion did not last very long, it clearly demonstrated that Obeah still had the power to inspire resistance and create the disorder that colonial authorities so feared.

The Siloah district of Jamaica was without a missionary between 1842, when Revd H.L. Dixon left, and 1844, when Revd F. Redford arrived, a fact the latter blamed for members' falling back into old habits. Under the heading "Effect of the Suspension of Missionary Labour at This Station" Redford provides an illustrative example of what can happen in the absence of a missionary: "On becoming more intimately acquainted with [the] people, Mr Redford was grieved to find, what indeed might naturally be expected, that they had in some degree fallen from their former Christian profession." On this subject he writes on 10 July 1845:

> To show to what a state of moral degradation the people would have sunk had they remained destitute of religious instruction, I will mention a fact which occurred only the week before my arrival. Two Obeah men came to this district, from the north side of the island, to practice their sinful and absurd rites; and I regret to add they had many followers. On one occasion they met in great numbers around a large silk cotton tree, when the Obeah men told the people, very gravely, that they had lost their shadows; but that if they would each give them fourpence, they would ascend the tree, and fetch them down. Many paid the money; when one of the Obeah men went to the top of the tree, muttered some

---

39 "West Indies", *Satirist; or, the Censor of the Times*, 1 September 1839, 280.

unintelligible words, and then came down with his hands closed, and told the people that he had got their shadows again, but would not let them out of his hands unless they gave him more money. This is an instance of credulity and superstition which almost exceeds belief, and gives us cause to fear that the people in other abandoned stations of the society may be following similar delusions.[40]

Some observers saw in the emancipation of blacks and their political ascendancy reason for worry. "With the political dispossession of the whites, certain dark powers, previously concealed or repressed, have obtained formidable development. The old enemy of Pere Labat, the wizard (the *quimboiseur*), already wields more authority than the priest, exercises more terror than the magistrate, commands more confidence than the physician", writes Hearn.[41]

Black men and women left alone without the civilizing influence of whites returned to barbarity – that was the message of many writers, even those who did not go as far as James Anthony Froude. Visiting the Caribbean in the late 1800s, Froude spent some time in Haiti, apparently in constant fear of being killed and eaten. "Behind the immorality, behind the religiosity, there lies active and alive the horrible revival of the West African superstitions; the serpent worship, and the child sacrifice, and the cannibalism. There is no room to doubt it", he informs his readers. "A missionary assured me that an instance of it occurred only a year ago within his own personal knowledge." Indeed, the former British chargé d'affaires in Haiti, Sir Spenser St John, had recorded his own sensationalist accounts of cannibalism just four years before, in the 1884 book *Hayti; or, the Black Republic*. Froude notes that, according to St John, "The African Obeah, the worship of serpents and trees and stones, after smouldering in all the West Indies in the form of witchcraft and poisoning, had broken out in Hayti in all its old hideousness. Children were sacrificed as in the old days of Moloch and were devoured . . . salted limbs being preserved and sold for the benefit of those who were unable to attend the full solemnities."

Froude claims that he went to Haiti "intending to judge for himself", but while he saw no evidence of cannibalism, others were quick to assure him that it was true. And why should it not be true? Froude asks, since no less a personage that St John has avowed it. "That a man in the position of a British resident should have ventured on a statement which, if untrue, would be ruinous to himself, appeared in a high degree improbable. . . . All the enquiries which I had been able to make, from American and other officers who had been in

---

40   *Church of England Magazine* 20 (1845): 451.
41   Hearn, *Two Years*, 180.

Hayti, confirmed Sir S. St John's story." Froude was never able to say he had witnessed it himself, but that did not stop him from believing it with all the conviction of his racist heart. Neither did it stop him from making references to cannibalism throughout his book. In fact, he repeats himself on the subject quite often: "But in the heart of them has revived the old idolatry of the Gold Coast, and in the villages of the interior, where they are out of sight and can follow their instincts, they sacrifice children in the serpent's honour after the manner of their forefathers."[42] Again and again he pounds at his theme:

> They are docile, good-tempered, excellent and faithful servants when they are kindly treated; but their notions of right and wrong are scarcely even elementary; their education, such as it may be, is but skin deep, and the old Africa superstitions lie undisturbed at the bottom of their souls. Give them independence, and in a few generations they will peel off such civilization as they have learnt as easily and as willingly as their coats and trousers.[43]

Neither did Froude think highly of the missionaries. "A religion, at any rate, which will keep the West Indian blacks from falling back into devil worship is still to seek", he writes, pointing out that "in spite of the priests, child murder and cannibalism have reappeared in Hayti". He admits, however, that "without them things might have been worse than they are, and the preservation of white authority and influence in any form at all may be better than none".[44]

The fear that many planters expressed during slavery still existed, and Froude pounced on it. A Grenadian planter assured him that "if left entirely to themselves, they would in a generation or two relapse into savages; there were but two alternatives before not Grenada only, but all the English West Indies – either an English administration pure and simple . . . , or a falling eventually into a state like that of Hayti, where they eat the babies, and no white man can own a yard of land".[45] Fourteen years after Froude, Pullen-Burry was still in thrall to the legend of Haitian cannibalism. "The black under British rule is not an unworthy subject of the Empire; but left to himself, and to the workings of his own sweet will, he might perhaps revert to a state of savagery", she writes, citing Haiti, where she was convinced that people ate children.[46] C.B.

---

42 Froude, *English in the West Indies*, III, 126, 183.
43 Ibid., 287.
44 Ibid., 236.
45 Ibid., 56, 344.
46 Pullen-Burry, *Jamaica*, 225.

assures his readers that the order of the red vaudoux "sacrifices black goats, and afterwards, when the worshippers are frenzied, 'the goat without horns' – a drugged child. There is only too much proof of this terrible fact in the court records and official reports of Hayti. It is equally certain that cannibalism sometimes crowns the sacrifice."[47]

The reports of Obeah's demise continued to conflict with reports of its continuation.

> The Baptist Minister, James Gardiner, drove me recently to an estate six miles in the country, to see a member of his congregation, who had been "Obeahed" by an Obi man; that is, an administration of African witchcraft, and it has such influence on the negroes, that death has been known to follow: on this account, the laws are very severe against the operators who are imprisoned and tried for their lives

writes Dr William Lloyd, who visited the region from late 1836 to spring 1837.[48] Even Gardner admits that as

> late as 1861, during the revival, as it was termed, a party of young women, in a state of religious excitement, went to the house of a reputed Obeah man, residing in one of the suburbs of Kingston, and brought him with all the implements of his art to the parade. His box contained not only nearly all the abominations mentioned, but several lizard and snake-skins. There was also a bell, said to be used to summon a sort of familiar spirit, and a pack of cards. In the midst of all, sad to say, was a number of class tickets, indicating that he had been a member of a religious body for a great number of years.[49]

How that last would have made Cynric Williams laugh! Gardner also admits that "many who had ceased to fear Obeah themselves continued to hang up a bundle of feathers, teeth, etc. in a conspicuous part of their provision grounds, as an effectual guard against the depredations of thieves". One can almost hear him sigh as he writes "superstition is among the last of all evils corrected by Gospel teaching".[50]

Near the turn of the century, Hearn was awed by the tenacity of Obeah. "Astonishing is the persistence with which the African has clung to these beliefs and practices, so zealously warred upon by the Church and so merci-

---

47 C.B., "Obeah and Vaudoux", 8.
48 Lloyd, *Letters*, 166.
49 Gardner, *History of Jamaica*, 188.
50 Ibid., 188, 392.

lessly punished by the courts for centuries", he marvels. "And how singular sometimes is the irony of Time! All the wonderful work the Dominican [Père Labat] accomplished has been forgotten by the people; while all the witchcraft that he warred against survive and flourish openly; and his very name is seldom uttered but in connection with superstitions, has been, in fact, preserved among the blacks by the power of superstition alone."[51]

But while Obeah might have been openly practised, the planters brooked no disrespect to Christianity or its symbols. Though they themselves may have been quick to smash Obeah figurines to pieces and to burn to ash the huts of Obeah practitioners, any move by blacks to treat the planters' religion with similar contempt was dealt with harshly. A planter told Hearn of a Negro who was sentenced to life with hard labour for destroying an image of the Virgin. When Hearn remarked on the severity of the sentence, the planter replied, "Severe, yes . . . relying as we have always done to some extent upon religious influence as a factor in the maintenance of social order, the negro's act seemed a dangerous example."[52] Hearn adds that the African "still goes to mass, and sends his children to the priest; but he goes more often to the *quimboiseur* and the 'magnetisé'. He finds use for both beliefs, but gives large preference to the savage one. . . . And should it come to pass that Martinique be ever totally abandoned by its white population . . . the fate of the ecclesiastical fabric so toilsomely reared by the monastic orders is not difficult to surmise."[53]

What was true in Martinique was certainly true in the English-speaking islands. The commissioner of Crown lands in Montserrat assured Kingsley: "The Africans all belong nominally to some denomination of Christianity: but their lives are more influenced by their belief in Obeah. While the precepts of religion are little regarded, they stand in mortal dread of those who practice this mischievous imposture." Kingsley also learned that "the chief centre of this detestable system is St Vincent, where – so I was told by one who knows the island well – some sort of secret College, or School of the Prophets Diabolic, exists. Its emissaries spread over the islands, fattening themselves at the expense of their dupes, and exercising no small political authority, which has been ere now, and may be again, dangerous to society." A Nonconformist missionary also informed him that Obeah was on the increase in Jamaica.[54]

---

51 East, in Clark, Dendy and Phillippo, *Voice of Jubilee*, 10–11, 24.
52 Hearn, *Two Years*, 174, 178, 181.
53 Ibid., 181.
54 Kingsley, *At Last*, 2:75, 140.

Certainly, blacks continued to hedge their bets. The United Brethren missionary J. Bartels describes:

> A man who was ill of the prevailing fever in the autumn, and was excluded on account of an adulterous connection which he kept up, was very seriously warned to turn from his wickedness, and look ... to the Lord Jesus. Confessing his sin, he expressed sorrow and repentance, and promised that, if the Lord should restore him to health, he would not repeat his transgression. While I was paying him frequent visits, however, and supplying him with medicine, I found out that he had placed himself in the hands of an obeah-man, a native of Antigua, who had informed him that a man, with whom he had been fighting a short time before, had brought this disease on him. Coming apparently casually into the house, the obeah-man inquired if any one was ill, at the same time warning the patient of his danger. Pretending to speak to the spirits, he ordered them to be quiet, while he went through his work, and thereupon proceeded to perform with quicksilver some mysterious-looking rites. He then measured a certain distance from the door with a stick, listened with his ear to the ground, and then ordered them to dig there. To the amazement of those present, a doll was found buried, which had to be burnt. Many visits were paid by the obeah-man, and baths administered, for which whole bottles of scent were used. What fee the patient had to pay could not be ascertained with certainty, probably about £4.[55]

The missionary notes drily that, "on recovery, the man renewed his sinful connection".[56]

"Notwithstanding the edifying spectacle of the whole population, dressed out in their best, filling the churches every Sunday, it is to be feared that a great deal of this outward show of piety and religion is but very superficial, and the church-going and communion is rather practised as a sign of respectability than for the moral benefit they expect to gain thereby", Bell suggests.[57] And the wife of a pastor informed Pullen-Burry that "generally the loudest singer in the church was invariably the Obeah man or women in the district".[58]

The imagery that associated blacks with the Devil continued. When his ship arrived in Kingston, Rampini was startled when "in one moment, like the sudden apparition of a troupe of demons in a pantomime, the ship was full of

---

55 *Periodical Accounts* 30 (1876): 415.
56 Ibid.
57 Bell, *Obeah*, 42.
58 Pullen-Burry, *Jamaica*, 225.

negroes".[59] Meanwhile, Revd Banbury assures readers that the Obeah man "is the agent incarnate of Satan: The Simon Magus of these good gospel days".[60]

But, for the most part, the missionaries did not participate in the strident racism of Edward Long and Bryan Edwards. Their racism was of a gentler, paternalistic sort. Davy quotes an anonymous writer in St Lucia who notes that the natural disposition of blacks "renders them peculiarly susceptible of religious impressions, and that they are mild, docile and strong in their attachments, and acted upon without difficulty by superior intelligence". Davy concurs with this assessment, pointing out that the truth of it "is borne out by all we know of the character of these people; and of the little hold that the superstitious Obeah practices alluded to, such as those of Obeah, have had over their minds, where they have been met by sound instruction".[61]

Writing in the early 1900s, the English folklorist Walter Jekyll describes Obeah as "the dark blot upon this fair island of Jamaica. In every district there is an Obeah man, or Bush-doctor, as he is often called, from his supposed knowledge of herb simples. He is by no means the innocent person which this latter designation would seem to imply."[62] Clearly, rumours of Obeah's demise had been greatly exaggerated. In 1881 "superstition was still prevalent, but it was now being affected by the spread of knowledge", Livingstone assures his readers, seemingly unaware that he is but the latest in a long line to make that declaration. "The negro is very sensitive to the ridicule of the white, and he was beginning to feel himself morally named, and to be ashamed. Obeahism was less openly acknowledged and practiced, and larger numbers of obeahmen were being brought to punishment. The influence of Christianity was freely mingling with and modifying the old beliefs, and emotional revivalism was succeeding rites of a darker nature."[63]

Trowbridge, bemused, notes that

> unlike most savage superstitions, which quickly fade under the scorching light of civilization, [Obeah] has a remarkable power of endurance. For years its "doctors", or obi-men exerted a baleful influence over the blacks in the West Indies, whither it was undoubtedly brought from the Slave Coast. Now, hap-

---

59   Rampini, *Letters*, 13.
60   Banbury, *Jamaica Superstitions*, 7.
61   Davy, *West Indies*, 280.
62   Walter Jekyll, *Jamaican Song and Story: Annancy Stories, Digging Sings, Ring Tunes, and Dancing Tunes* (London: Folk-Lore Society, 1907), 241.
63   Livingstone, *Black Jamaica*, 110.

pily, in the English colonies at least, it is under the ban of the law, and the active and public profession of it is dead. Obeah to-day is only a superstition; but until education shall have completely civilized the black race it will live in a more or less powerful, secret, and evil way.[64]

"'Thou shalt worship the Lord thy God, and Him only shalt thou serve.' When this truth is realised it leads logically to the 'Get thee behind me, Satan', which West Indian negroes have learnt to say to the Obeahman", reports Revd Ellis.[65] Displaying a complete misunderstanding of Obeah, he notes that "it must be remembered that the teaching of Christian missionaries both before and after emancipation was sufficient to prevent Obeahism from becoming a Religion or a Creed, like Vaudouism". Ellis graciously allows that "naturally, all Christian Churches have taken strong action against this evil, when and where it has been found to be indulged in, and this not merely by teaching and personal influence but by the exercise of ecclesiastical discipline". He explains: "The Church of England (Canon XXXVIII), expressly directs that 'all persons who in any way participate in the practice of Obeah shall, on the facts coming to the knowledge of the clergyman of the Church attended by them, be expelled from the Holy Communion and public notice thereof given in Church'."[66] In case this might give the impression that the Church still considered Obeah a significant threat, Ellis adds that this regulation "was passed forty years ago in the earlier days of Disestablishment, when Obeah was a much more prevalent practice than it is today". In any case, he writes, "any misguided Church member who lapses into a temporary dallying with Obeah has the grace and the shame to abstain from approaching the Lord's Table and practically excommunicates himself". He does acknowledge that the war is not completely won, however. "So in Jamaica Christian teaching, education, the gradual growth of civilisation in various forms are combining to what is hoped will be a speedy end to a foolish and degrading superstition. I refer of course to the harmful aspects of the old Obeahism as it was imported from Africa."[67]

The intertwining of racial theory with Obeah was demonstrated again at the Church of England's Synod of 1888. At a previous conference, Canon Isaac Taylor had made some derogatory comments about missionary activity in Jamaica and had apparently alleged that "the negroes of Jamaica are lapsing into

---

64 Trowbridge, *Gossip*, 63.
65 Ellis, *Diocese of Jamaica*, 220.
66 Ibid., 222.
67 Ibid., 222–23.

Obeahism". Nothing could be further from the truth, declared the Lord Archbishop of the West Indies, Enos Nuttall. "I think there is abundant evidence to show, not that [they] are lapsing into Obeahism, but that, as a body, they are developing [those qualities] which go to make up an intelligent, industrious, progressive Christian community", Bishop Nuttal told the Synod.[68]

If blacks were not yet the ladies and gentlemen the missionaries wanted them to become, Obeah could take a lot of the blame. "Obeahism is a superstition at once simple, foolish, and terrible, still vigorous, but in former times as powerful an agent as slavery itself in keeping the nature debased", writes Livingstone. He points to the lack of marital commitment among blacks and links it with Obeah. "It was this unconscious sensuality which proved the greatest obstacle to the development of their character. Scarcely less powerful and evil was their superstition and its correlatives – obeah-craft, poisoning and mental paralysis. These two tendencies were part and parcel of that side of their nature which the missionaries believe it their first duty to reach and mould" by instilling "chastity, self-respect, and independence of mind" instead.[69]

Others thought that Obeah was too widespread and that the focus on eradicating it among the "lower classes" was doomed to failure until the "higher-ups" themselves dropped the practice. An article in Georgetown's *Royal Gazette* argues that

> it is useless to look to the lowest class in the country to rebel and throw off the Obeah yoke as long as their superiors in position and general advantages are content to remain in bondage, and Ministers and others who are bent on eradicating the evil should direct their crusade, in the first place, not against the lowest grade of society, but against a higher class which provides the Churches of the Colony with the great bulk of their members. When this class has been brought to see Obeah in its true light, then it will be easier to prevail on those at the bottom of the ladder to laugh at the threats of the Obeahman; but until then the Ministers' efforts will be almost in vain.[70]

"The establishment of free dispensaries . . . and the spread of education . . . would more quickly put the obeah-man out of practice in Jamaica than all the devices of fines and imprisonment which have succeeded the even more severe

---

68 Ibid., 224.
69 Livingstone, *Black Jamaica*, 20, 47.
70 H.V.P. Bronkhurst, *The Colony of British Guiana and Its Labouring Populations* (London: T. Woolmer, 1888), 383.

hangings and deportations confessedly so inefficacious in stamping out obeah practice in Edwards's day", Beckwith observes with the cool detachment of the science-minded.[71]

Williams, writing in the early 1930s, was certainly convinced of Obeah's prevalence. "Today there is a tendency in Jamaica to shut the eyes to the true nefarious influence of the cult on the entire Negro population of the island, and to regard this practice of the black art as an exuberance of superstition and nothing more." But, he warns:

> Once the obeah-man has created what I might call a diabolic atmosphere in a district; when his communications with the Devil has given his Satanic Majesty some standing in the spiritual life of the community, and the cooperation of the clients of the obeah-man has firmly established a practice which is nothing less than demonolatry, we need not be surprised if the Power of Evil begins to manifest material phenomena, perhaps of the poltergeist type, seeking to weaken church control and so gradually to augment the tendency to evil throughout the district.[72]

Yet, despite Obeah's persistence, many writers continued to assure readers that it was indeed dying out.

---

71 Beckwith, *Jamaican Ethnobotany*, 10.
72 Williams, *Psychic Phenomena*, 106, 258.

CHAPTER 6

The Early Literary Response

"CAUSELESS FEARS" OR "SACRED HORRORS"

In the early 1800s, several plays, poems and works of fiction featuring Obeah began to appear in Britain. Arising as they did out of a society coming to grips with the ethical dimensions of slavery, as well as with the development of race theories that posited whites as superior and blacks inferior, these works reveal much about the conflicts and tensions underlying attitudes towards race.

The earliest poem or literary work to reference Obeah was "The Sugar Cane", by James Grainger, MD. Grainger, who studied medicine at Edinburgh University, departed London for the West Indies in 1759, but not before establishing his reputation as a poet and friend of eminences such as Samuel Johnson and Tobias Smollett (he later fell out with Smollett, with whom he conducted a famously public feud). Grainger's medical practice never really took off and he relied on his poems and translations of Roman writers to help pay the bills. In 1759 he agreed to accompany John Bourryau, a former pupil, to St Kitts, where the latter was heir to property. However, a shipboard romance led Grainger into marriage with a Miss Burt, daughter of a Nevisian planter who had once served as that island's governor. Grainger set up his medical practice on Nevis and also managed an estate owned by his wife's uncle.

"The Sugar Cane" was published in 1764, two years before Grainger's death and is described as "a Virgil-like West Indian georgic depicting the culture of sugar".

> Nor pine the blacks, alone, with real ills
> That baffle oft the wisest rules of art:
> They likewise feel imaginary woes;
> Woes no less deadly. Luckless he who owns

The slave; who thinks himself bewitch'd; and whom,
In wrath, a conjurer's snake-mar'd staff hath struck!
They mope, love silence, every friend avoid;
They only pine, all aliment reject;
Or insufficient for nutrient's take:
Their features droop; a sickly yellowish hue
Their skin deforms; their strength and beauty fly.
Then comes the feverish fiend, with fiery eyes,
Fatal attendants! If some subtle slave
(such, Obia-men are stil'd) do not engage
To save the wretch by antidote or spell.

In magic spells, in Obia, all the sons
Of Sable Afric trust: Ye sacred Nine!
(For ye each hidden preparation know)
Transpierce the gloom, which ignorance and fraud
Have render'd awful; tell the laughing world
Of what these wonder-working charms are made.

Fern root cut small, and tied with many a knot;
Old teeth extracted from a white man's skull;
A lizard's skeleton; a serpent's head:
These, mixed with salt and water from the spring,
Are in a phial pour'd; over these the leach
Mutters strange jargon, and wild circles forms

Of this possest, each negroe deems himself
Secure from poison; for to poison they
Are infamously prone; and arm'd with this
Their sable country daemons they defy
Who fearful haunt them at the mid-night hour
To work them mischief! This, diseases, fly;
Diseases follow: such is its wondrous power!
This o'er the threshold of their cottage hung
No thieves break in: or, if they dare to steal,
Their feet in blotches, which admit no cure
Burst loathsome out: but should its owner filch,
As slaves were ever of the pilfering kind,
This from detection screens; so conjurers swear.

In his footnotes to the poem, Grainger avers that Obeah men carry staffs marked with frogs, snakes and other animals and declares that black people, even if they do not believe they will die from a blow, are, however, convinced that "long and troublesome disorders will ensue". He admits that "a belief in magic is inseparable from human nature" but notes that

> those nations are most addicted thereto, among whom learning, and, of course, philosophy have least obtained. As in all other countries, so in Guinea, the conjurers, as they have more understanding, so are they generally more wicked than the common herd of their deluded countrymen; and as the negroe-magicians can do mischief, so they can also do good on a plantation, provided they are kept by the white people in proper subordination.

This epic poem recounts what happens on a plantation and describes the cycles of cane cultivation, but it also discusses ameliorating the treatment of slaves, their medical afflictions, and the different qualities or characteristics of the various tribes and provides advice for planters on choosing the best, most productive slaves. Much of the same information appears in his *Essay on the More Common West India Diseases*, which he published later that year.[1]

About three decades later, Tacky's Rebellion inspired a poem, "The Negro Incantation", which first appeared in the *Monthly Magazine* of July 1797 and in later editions of the *Poetical Register*. It was prefaced by an "Argument":

> In the year 1760, a very formidable insurrection of the Jamaica Negroes took place. – This was instigated by the professors of a species of incantation known among the blacks by the name of Obi. . . . The account of the above mentioned circumstances, contained in Edwards's History of the West Indies, gave birth to the following Ode:

> Hail! ye sacred horrors hail!
> Which brooding o'er this lonely vale,
> Swell the heart, impearl the eye,
> And raise the rapt soul to the sky.
> Hail! spirits of the swarthy dead,
> Who, flitting thro' the dreary shade,
> To rouse your sons to vengeance fell,
> Nightly raise the troublous yell!

---

1 James Grainger, "The Sugar Cane", in *On the Treatment and Management of the More Common West India Diseases, 1759–1802*, ed. E. Hutson (Kingston: University of the West Indies Press, 2005), 71n8, 143–46.

Hail! Minister of Ill, whose iron pow'r
Pervades resistless earth, and sea, and air,
Shed all thy influence on this solemn hour,
When we with magic rites the white man's doom prepare.

Thus Congo spake, "what time the moon,
"Riding in her highest noon!"
Now beam'd upon the sable crowd,
Now vanish'd in the thickening cloud.
'Twas silence all – with frantic look,
His spells the hoary wizard took:
Bending o'er the quiv'ring flame,
Convulsion shook his giant frame.
Close and more close the shuddering captives throng,
With breath repress'd, and straining eye, they wait –
When midst the plantains burst the awful song,
The words of mystic might, that seal their tyrants' fate.

Haste! the magic shreds prepare –
Thus the white man's corse we tear.
Lo! feathers from the raven's plume,
That croaks our proud Oppressor's doom.
Now to aid the potent spell,
Crush we next the brittle shell –
Fearful omen to the foe,
Look! the blanched bones we throw.
From mouldering graves we stole this hallow'd earth,
Which, mix'd with blood, winds up the mystic charm;
Wide yawns the grave for all of northern birth,
And soon shall smoke with blood each sable warrior's arm.

Hark! the pealing thunders roll,
Grateful to the troubled soul.
See! the gleamy lightnings play,
To point you to your destin'd prey.
Hence! with silent foot and slow,
And sudden strike the deadly blow:
Your foes, the palmy shade beneath,
Lie lock'd in sleep – their sleep is death!
Go! let the memory of the smarting thong
Outplead the pity that would prompt to save:

Go! let the Oppressor's contumelious wrong,
Twice nerve the hero's arm, and make the coward brave.²

Though the *Oxford Dictionary of National Biography* makes no mention of it in the entry dedicated to Revd William Shepherd, Unitarian minister and staunch abolitionist, he is very likely the W. Shepherd to whom the poem is ascribed. He would have been twenty-nine when it was published and, though not a member of the Society for the Abolition of the Slave Trade, he was a friend of radical abolitionists such as William Rathbone, founder of the Liverpool Committee for the Abolition of the Slave Trade, and the anti-slavery campaigners and poets William Roscoe and Edward Rushton. Shepherd had a particularly warm relationship with Rushton and wrote the latter's biography. The poem employs the imagery of the avenging slave rather than that of the supplicant and is illustrative of the rhetoric used by the radical abolitionists who so enraged Edwards and Bridges.³ (It may be worth mentioning here that, as rich as the planters were, they were never quite accepted in London society and were both envied and derided for their free spending, lavish habits and licentious ways.)

Written by James Powell, *Furibond; or, Harlequin Negro: A Grand Comic Pantomime* was first performed at the Drury Lane Theatre on 28 December 1807. This early creative work, though it never mentions Obeah by name, does have a powerful sorcerer as its lead character. The play is initially set in Jamaica, where the enchanter, Furibond, lives in a castle. Furibond is obsessed with obtaining the hand of Columbine, Sir Peevish Antique's daughter, who in turn is in love with one of her father's slaves. Sir Peevish, the owner of a coffee plantation, informs Furibond that he can marry his daughter but duplicitously sets sail for England with her before the enchanter can arrive at his house. Furibond is enraged to find them gone and draws a circle on the floor with his wand, calling forth his familiar, Maligno. Furibond tells him that he wishes to follow Columbine, and familiar and magician sink through the floor together.

In the slave quarters, meanwhile, the slave driver chastises the slave Columbine loves. When the slave expresses his resentment at his treatment, he is seized by other slaves, who are about to bind him to a tree when a large

---

2 William Shepherd, "The Negro Incantation", in *The Poetical Register, and Repository of Fugitive Poetry, for 1803* (London: F. and C. Rivington, 1805), 413–15.

3 Edwards, in his own poem, "Stanzas Occasioned by the Death of Alico, an African Slave, Condemned for Rebellion in Jamaica", portrays a man bidding his wife goodbye but remaining defiant even as the flames lick at his feet.

serpent emerges from its roots. The serpent terrifies the slaves, who try to kill it, but Columbine's lover prevents them. After the other slaves leave the scene, the serpent dissolves and becomes the fairy Benigna. The slave "complains of his black complexion" to the fairy, who asks him if he is "weary of [his] sable hue". She offers him the choice of being Narcissus (beautiful but stupid), a powerful tyrant or Harlequin, comforting the grieving. The slave chooses to be Harlequin and is transformed. The fairy then gives him a magic sword that will make him wealthy and repel illnesses.

The stage directions require "Harlequin [to] supplicate the Fairy for the emancipation of his fellow-slaves, who appear in chains, driven on by the slave-driver".

"Poor Afric's children sigh for liberty", the fairy responds, but, "Alas, that task was not reserved for me".

In more stage directions, "a figure of Britannia, with her lion, descends from the skies. The Genius of Britain and attendants enter." At the sight of them, the chains fall from the slaves, who kneel in gratitude and homage before departing "in great glee". The slave driver is swallowed by a dark cavern that opens to receive him.

> See, Britannia's Genius from the skies
> Listening to the Negro's cries,
> She heard the toil-bled father's shrieks,
> While tears roll'd down their sable cheeks
> Saw mothers from their children torn,
> Beneath the whip to waste and mourn.
> The lash she heard, she saw the wound
> And human gore pollute the ground;
> . . . .
> Her voice broke forth in words of fire
> England shall stamp the blest decree
> That gives the Negro *Liberty*.

Britannia, Genius and the rest disappear as the fairy waves her wand and Harlequin is transported to England: "Hither come and taste delight / this is the land in which all are free / This the home of Liberty." She and Harlequin disappear from the stage and Furibond and Maligno arrive, Furibond having been transformed into a "first-rate Buck", or overdressed dandy. Various adventures ensue in which Furibond and Sir Peevish try to separate Harlequin and Columbine and chase after them throughout the city. Near the end, Furibond and Sir Peevish abduct Columbine, who is borne away to Furibond's "dreadful abode" full of noxious reptiles. The fairy saves her, makes both Furibond and Maligno disappear, then takes Columbine to her own jewel-encrusted palace and reunites her with Harlequin.[4]

The pantomime clearly draws on traditions of European magic and accounts of Obeah, embodying both in the image of the serpent that emerges from the tree to save Columbine's lover and later turns into Benigna. Powell doubtless knew of the stories of serpent worship emerging out of Africa, of the connections some writers had made between Obeah and a reverence for snakes, and of the etymological associations made by Europeans between the word *Obeah* and snakes. He would similarly be aware of the horror with which whites had greeted stories of Obeah. In choosing to make the serpent of his play a benevolent creature, Powell may be seeking to underscore his recognition of the validity of alternative forms of religion. And while the pantomime may offer a liberal or progressive view of the prospect of miscegenation, the slaves are depicted as acted upon. They "sigh for liberty" but take no direct action to secure it for themselves; it is left to the benevolence of Britannia's Genius to grant them their freedom, which must have been at least vaguely reassuring to an audience not completely oblivious to sensational headlines about slave plots and uprisings.

Critics did not greet Furibond with universal praise. It in fact appears to have been something of a critical disappointment, though it ran for twenty-eight performances. The *National Register*'s critic complained about the "exceedingly defective machinery" and did not find the plot "deserving of commendation". He did allow, however, that Mr Hartland was a "graceful Harlequin" and that "Miss Sharp is assuredly the best dancer who has for some years represented the Columbine".[5] The *Monthly Mirror* also noted that "the machinery frequently failed in the working" but was good-natured enough to say that "the pantomime, though not a good one, must, from certain intrinsic merit in its scenery and acting, run a number of nights", despite the cries of "Off, Off".[6] For its part, *La Belle Assemblée* lamented

> we cannot speak of this Pantomime with any degree of praise; its great error is, that the little action which it contains is too somber. The latter part presented

---

4 James Powell, *Furibond; or, Harlequin Negro: A Grand Comic Pantomime* (London: J. Scales, 1807).
5 *National Register*, 5 January 1807, 14.
6 *Monthly Mirror* 3 (1808), 46.

us with a scene of Undertakers, and the anticks of a dead body. For this only, if for nothing else, this Pantomime should have been hissed from the stage. To say the least of it, it was grossly indecorous, – a most barbarous inelegance.⁷

Furibond was written and produced the year that Britain ended the slave trade, and the author clearly supports that initiative and is also supportive of full emancipation. The pantomime has a strong anti-slavery message but is not able to escape certain of the stereotypes under which blacks laboured, such as the alleged desire of black men for white women, a theme that shows up again and again in works of fiction and non-fiction. No critic alluded to this aspect of the pantomime, but it is more than likely that the audience did not greet the idea of a black slave making love to a white woman with joy, however far from blackness the slave may have travelled and however sympathetic they themselves may have been to the abolitionist cause. (Interestingly, the slave is able to acquire not whiteness but a state of being both black and white, which is the costume of Harlequin.) The writer clearly wants to introduce the concept of black superstition and magic; hence the character of Furibond, but this enchanter is plainly modelled according to European tropes. There is nothing particularly Obeah-like about him, though educated viewers would have known about Obeah and would have made the implicit connection in their minds.

Two years later, in 1809, the poets and abolitionists James Montgomery, James Grahame and Elizabeth Benger published *Poems on the Abolition of the Slave Trade*, with several references to Obeah. In the advertisement at the beginning of the book, the publisher says loftily, "it originated in his own earnest ... solicitude to see a late illustrious act of the British Legislature (which exalts the character of his age and country) popularly commemorated by a tribute of national genius". Montgomery's poem depicts an idyllic African village where

> Behold, at closing day,
> The negro-village swarms abroad to play;
> He treads the dance through all its rapturous sounds
> to the wild music of barbarian sounds;
> . . . .
> He feasts on tales of witchcraft, that give birth
> To breathless wonder, or ecstatic mirth;
> . . . .

---

7   *La Belle Assemblée, or Bell's Court and Fashionable Magazine*, 1 January 1808, 42.

Till Christian cruisers anchor'd on his strand
. . . .
The Negro's joys, the Negro's virtues fled;[8]

Interestingly, Montgomery imputes no negative connotations to witchcraft as experienced in Africa. Rather, witchcraft on that continent inspires innocent wonder, not dread. When the action of the poem takes place in the West Indies, however, this light-hearted innocence is not maintained and references to the supernatural turn darker. In another stanza, he refers to a planter as "the bloated vampire of a living man . . . whose torpid pulse no social feelings move".

"– Tremble, Britannia! while thine islands tell / Th' appalling mysteries of Obi's spell." Then the God of vengeance

> makes his fierce displeasure known;
> At his command the pestilence abhorr'd
> Spares the poor slave, and smites the haughty lord.
> . . . .
> And thou, poor Negro! Scorn'd of all mankind;
> Thou dumb and impotent, and deaf and blind;
> Thou dead in spirit! Toil-degraded slave
> . . . .
> He wakes to life, he springs to liberty.
> No more to Daemon-Gods, in hideous forms,
> He pray'd for earthquakes, pestilence, and storms,
> In secret agony devour'd the earth,
> And, while he spared his mother, cursed his birth:
> To heaven the Christian Negro sent his sighs
> . . . .
> Yet while he wept, rejoic'd that he was born
> No longer burning with unholy fires,
> He wallow'd in the dust of base desires;
> Ennobling virtue fix'd his hopes above,
> Enlarged his heart and sanctified his love;
> With humble steps the paths of peace he trod,
> A happy pilgrim, for he walk'd with God.[9]

---

8 James Montgomery, in Montgomery, Grahame and Benger, *Poems on the Abolition*, 24.
9 Ibid., 25–37.

In his footnote to "Obi's spell", Montgomery recommends Dallas's *History of the Maroons* and Moseley's *Treatise on Sugar*. Originally from Cornwall, Montgomery's parents, who were Moravian missionaries, spent some time in the West Indies, where they both died, but it appears unlikely that he ever visited the region. As a newspaper editor he was jailed twice for criticizing the government, but he was a staunch abolitionist and social reformer. He also composed hundreds of hymns, some of which are still in use.

Writers had only a few non-fiction texts on Obeah and the Caribbean to turn to, but, like Montgomery, turn to them they did, time and time again, whether they were composing books, poems or plays or writing non-fiction works. Books written decades earlier or in previous centuries were accepted as the gospel truth and the information they contained was repeatedly regurgitated for the consumption of new generations of readers and writers. The Fuller report was a perennial favourite, consulted by many. The author of the *Poems Chiefly on the Superstition of Obeah*, which appeared in 1816, got most of his or her information from it, perhaps via Bryan Edwards. Quoting the report, the poet informs readers that "Obi is now become in Jamaica the general term to denote those Africans who in that island practice witchcraft or sorcery".

In the first poem, a woman is struck by Obeah.

> Some withering grief hath stricken her
> For never yet was known
> A cheek so wan, an eye so dead
> A form so woe-begone.[10]

Friends and children try to comfort her, but she calls for a coffin and a winding sheet for her corpse. She begs them to dig her grave and tells them of the fire burning her bones and the fever in her blood:

> I know not who – I know not why –
> Nor what my crime, nor whence his wrath
> But he hath poison laid for me
> He hath set Obeah in my path
> And I the accursed death shall die
> . . . .
> It works in every part
> In every bone and nerve and vein

---

10 *Poems*, 21–30.

> And in my flesh, and in my brain
> And fastens on my heart.

The poet assumes a pitying tone and asks, as if speaking to an irrational child,

> And wilt thou thus, O Mary! die
> By causeless fears to death betray'd
> By self-begotten witchery
> Consum'd, by woes thyself hast made?
> Nay, there is home and comfort yet
> . . . .
> Religious hope shall make the fear
> Of superstition disappear.

A priest comes to the village and invites all who wish to be "baptiz'd to Christianity". Mary goes,

> And came to sprinkle her wan face
> With the regenerate dews of grace
> Invoking, in an accent high
> The undivided Trinity.

Mary is now overjoyed and feels herself saved from the Obeah.

> She runs, bounds, dances and leaps
> Swift to her cottage she has sped
> Has kiss'd her children o'er and o'er
> Fondled her dog, embrac'd her bed
> Embrac'd them, kiss'd them all once more.

Later on, by her cottage door, she "sate in peace",

> A tear in silence wet her cheek
> T'was that a heart intensely blest
> Can find no voice wherewith to speak.
> "O Mary! Sin brings on a curse
> Than poison or than Obeah worse."

The poet ends by calling her "Christian Mary" and urging her to shun sin and avoid an "enduring hell".[11]

---

[11] Ibid.

A second, longer poem follows that takes a much darker turn. In the opening stanza, Mira says to proud mother Eliza,

> This summer eve, a busier broom
> Shall brush those infants from your door,
> And cleaner sweep your childless home

No reason is given for the curse, and Eliza apparently believes herself immune to Obeah.

> Eliza laugh'd with scornful pride,
> . . . .
> the Priest but yester Sabbath came,
> And bless'd us in the holy name,
> And we are Christians now,

Eliza triumphantly informs the malevolent Mira.

> You plighted hands with fiends of hell
> And vow'd the devil's vow
> It makes us mirth to hear you ban;
> We fear not now the Obeah man
> She spake with a religious sense
> And holy faith in providence
> And yet her heart misgave her.[12]

Eliza quite naturally worries about her children, but as the days pass without incident she begins to think Mira has forgotten her enmity. The poet presents an idyllic picture of the life of slave children:

> The dawn returns, the glorious sun
> Out the rejoicing children run
> . . . .
> And happy in their thoughtless cheer
> The mother loses half her fear
> And half forgets her sorrow
> . . . .
> And safe from harm, and free from woe
> The children sleep and rise

---

12 Ibid., 37–57.

> ....
> Oh, yes, she hath forgot,
> the mother thinks.

In the second part of the poem, a storm has started up while Mira is in her hut.

> She had to do a desperate deed
> A deed of death; and there was need
> To throw all natural fears behind
> To brace the sinews of her mind
> And arm her for the work of blood
> With unrepenting fortitude
> ....
> Mira summon'd up her force
> And girt her for her midnight course.

The stanza brings to mind the famous villainesses Lady Macbeth and Medea. Mira makes her way in the night "thro woods . . . scal'd the mountain's breast . . . [crosses] a foaming cataract . . . plunges onward [till she arrives] within a glen . . . [where] the Obeah-Man had dug his cave".

"Devil in soul, in body man! / As friends they meet, as friends embrace." They go into the cavern together.

> What then was passing heav'n knows best
> But some have said, and many guess'd
> That fire was kindled, cauldron boil'd
> And both intensely strove and toil'd
> By root, and drug, and charm, and spell
> To get the mastery of hell.

In the final part of the poem, Eliza's children sicken.

> No spot breaks out upon the skin
> No secret ulcer spreads within
> No heat inflames the boiling vein
> Or darts in torment to the brain
> With imperceptible decay
> The tainted victims pine away
> ....

> The clouded eye, the sunken cheek
> A fearful, fatal change betray
>
> Slowly, surely works the curse
> From bad to bad, from worse to worse.

It is a long illness. "Time goes heavily by / To them, who, dying, cannot die." But at last, one by one, the three children die and

> As Christians were they plac'd in earth
> Without the rites and frantic joys
> Of African original.

Later, when Eliza visits the graves, she hears

> As for the coffin in the ground:
> "And cleanly as you swept your floor
> At summer eve, a busier broom
> Hath brush'd your infants from your door
> And cleaner swept your children home."[13]

In this second poem, the writer more closely observes the conventions of Gothic literature, and the poem is an early example of what is now termed "Caribbean Gothic". As interesting as these poems are, the fact that only two copies are known to exist is the more remarkable given that the one at the British Library once belonged to William Wordsworth. Wordsworth was, of course, a good friend of Samuel Taylor Coleridge, in whose poem "The Three Graves" two women are cursed by another and daily sink further into a weary melancholy, described in terms very similar to the one affecting Mary in the first poem. One of the women in "The Three Graves" is also named Mary. Her friend, Ellen, experiences what Coleridge calls a "haunting in the brain" and grows thin. Eventually Mary, her husband, Edward, and Ellen die – a trio of deaths that mirrors the deaths of Eliza's three children in the second of the *Poems Chiefly on the Superstition of Obeah*. It is intriguing to speculate whether the poems might have been written by Coleridge, or even Wordsworth himself.

In another instance of cross-fertilization, Joseph Williams provides an excerpt from a poem by a Jamaican which is itself contained in Revd Abraham J. Emerick's book.

---

13   Ibid.

> Crouched in a cave I saw thee and thy beard
> White against black, gleamed out; and thy gaunt hand
> Mixed lizard skins, rum, parrots' tongues and sand
> Found where the sinking tombstone disappeared
> Sleek galli-wasps looked on thee; grimly peered
> Blood-christened John Crow with a hissed demand
> Who art thou? Then like ghouls to a dim Land
> Fled for they saw thee working and they feared.[14]

The author of the poem in Emerick's book is unknown, but compare its Gothic atmosphere with the gaunt Obeah man in his cave, its enumeration of Obeah materials and reference to John Crow, the Jamaican vulture, to Robert Browning's contemptuous dismissal in his *Inn Album*, where the narrator likens himself to a "witless negro" fooled by an Obeah man. Of course, by 1875, the time of Browning's poem, the English public had been hearing about Obeah for almost one hundred years.

> Well, I have been spellbound, deluded
> Like the witless Negro by the Obeah-man
> Who bids him wither: so his eye grows dim,
> His arm slack, arrow misses aim and spear
> Goes wandering wide, – and all the Woe because
> He proved untrue to Fetish, who, he finds
> Was just a feather-phantom![15]

Interestingly, Browning's grandfather was a slave-owner who owned a plantation on Nevis. Browning's father had gone to work in the West Indies but quickly returned to England, disturbed by what he had seen of slavery. By the time The *Inn Album* was published, slavery was long over and Obeah no longer seemed quite as fearsome in an age when the British were using the rewards of the Industrial Revolution, made possible by the previous wealth of sugar, to extend the boundaries of empire. As more and more fiction writers began using Obeah in their plots, the childish naivety of Obeah adherents became the main theme, closely followed by a patronizing amusement. Familiarity with Obeah had bred contempt now that the threat of slave uprisings was over and the frequency of rebellions had decreased.

---

14   Williams, *Psychic Phenomena*, 97.
15   Robert Browning, *The Complete Poetic and Dramatic Works* (Boston: Houghton Mifflin, 1895), 773–802.

Tom Cringle's Log, by Michael Scott, would probably have made it onto the bestseller list had there been one in the 1800s. In the prefatory notice to the book, the publisher declares that "no series of papers which has appeared in *Blackwood's Magazine* ever enjoyed more general or continued popularity". The notice goes on to remind readers that the papers "were characterized by the *Quarterly Review* as the most brilliant series . . . of the time; and by Coleridge in his 'Table Talk' as 'most excellent.' When reprinted in two volumes, an unusually large edition was almost immediately disposed of; on the Continent they have been generally read and admired; and in Germany more than once translated."[16]

Judging from the reaction of Scott's fellow writers over the next hundred years, his publisher did not lie. Literary luminaries from Froude to Kingsley to Algernon Aspinall all reference the book, declaring it a "West Indian classic". Froude refers to *Tom Cringle* at least eight times, while Kingsley calls it a "delectable" book. Aspinall was so taken with it that, as late as 1937, he published a travel piece in *The Times* in which he called *Tom Cringle's Log* "a classic that must be read by a traveller to the West Indies who wants to obtain the real West Indian flavour or atmosphere of long ago and today".[17] Certainly this one book influenced several generations of Britons and helped shape their perception of the West Indies and of black West Indians in particular, long in advance of the arrival of MV *Empire Windrush*.

Scott arrived in Jamaica when he was seventeen years old and learned how to be an estate manager from George William Hamilton, the nephew of a Glaswegian friend of his father. Scott spent about fifteen years in Jamaica, returning to Scotland in 1816 and staying to get married a year later, but returning to Jamaica in 1817. He left Jamaica for the final time in 1822 and began publishing anonymous stories based on his experiences in 1829, in *Blackwood's Magazine*. The stories became wildly successful and the series continued until 1833, to be followed a year later by the publication of a volume of the stories. Scott's identity as the author was not revealed until after his death.

In the book, Tom Cringle is a sailor who spends time in Jamaica and Cuba and has various adventures while fighting pirates and the Spaniards. Alongside all the swashbuckling are some vignettes about the life of black people. For example, Tom and his companions are in a piazza in Kingston when a Negro funeral passes by. "It is a practice for the bearers when they come near

---

16 [Michael Scott], *Tom Cringle's Log* (Edinburgh: William Blackwood and Sons, 1862), vi.
17 *The Times*, 26 October 1937, 36.

the house of any one against whom the deceased was supposed to have had a grudge, to pretend that the coffin will not pass by . . . and when they came opposite to where we stood, they began to wheel round and round and to stagger under their load." The ones that accost Tom have something other than a grudge on their minds, however.

"Oh, massa, dollar for drink. . . . Bediacho say him won't pass less you pay it." They begin to spin more violently with the casket but crash into a herd of oncoming cattle, which jolts the casket so that the corpse falls out. They quickly catch it up and bundle it back in and the procession goes on its way once more.

In another section, a slave wonders if Tom is an Obeah man after Tom exclaims, "Shade of Homer", which is taken to mean that Tom has identified the person who broke a candle shade: "For true, dat leetle man-of-war buccra must be Obeah man; how de debil him come to sabe dat it was stable boy Homer who broke de candle shade on massa right hand", Jupiter says. Tellingly, Tom never gives an explanation of Obeah, depending on his readers to already know all about it. He watches black people singing at a wake.

> I say, broder, you can't go yet
> Wen de morning star rise, den we put you in a hole
> Den you go to Africa, you see Fetish there
> You shall nyam goat dere, wid all your family
> Buccra can't come there, say dam rascal why you no work
> Buccra can't catch Duppy, no, no.[18]

Scott's racism is typical. A black child is called a "little, dingy brute"; an older slave a "baboon"; and phrases such as "sable fiend" and "black savage" are common in the text. Tom never expresses any anti-slavery sentiments; his comment that his "well-meaning anti-slavery friends" should see a group of happy slaves suggests that Scott thought the energies of the abolitionists misplaced: "'And these are slaves,' thought I, 'and this is West Indian bondage! Oh, that some of my well-meaning anti-slavery friends were here, to judge from the evidence of their own sense.'"[19] In fact, in this "classic" which was read and admired by successive generations of Britons, *Tom's* black characters are not only happy but also ugly, childish, superstitious and given to drink.

The depictions of Obeah men and of superstitious Negroes in these poems and stories and in the novels that will be examined in future chapters were

---

18   [Scott], *Tom Cringle*, 125.
19   Ibid., 135.

made as white British society was developing and acting on theories of race which in turn prompted debates with itself, first over slavery and emancipation and then over colonization. The writers and poets who produced these depictions often did so in the service of their own positions. In a supreme irony, Obeah men and women, acting outside the confines of plantation society, and the black people who sought them out in an effort to sway their fate in some way, became stock characters – not actors demonstrating agency but the acted upon. To the abolitionists, the superstitious Negroes were like children who simply required the light of Christian civilization to advance, while for the pro-slavery lobby, Obeah was the bogey that cast menacing shadows over the plantations.

"CREDULOUS DUPES"

The fascination Obeah held for the British is clear not just from the creative outpourings but also from the pre-eminence of the subject in the popular media, in newspapers and the monthly magazines whose popularity grew in the 1800s even as literacy itself became more widespread.

"Ees, massa, shadow-catcher, true." That snippet of courtroom dialogue quoted in Alexander Barclay's *A Practical View of the Present State of Slavery* from the trial of an Obeah man was repeated in the *London Magazine* (1827), the *London Literary Gazette*, the *Mirror of Literature* (1828), the *Museum of Foreign Literature* (1828), the *American Masonic Record* (1828) and *Notes and Queries* (1851), not to mention several books. *John Bull* magazine, reporting on the case of William Waite, noted that Obeah was a "gross superstition" and harrumphed over the "prevalence of such practices, and the hold which Obeahism still possess of the minds of the negro population, notwithstanding the pains bestowed in educating and civilizing them".[20] Another paper assured readers that "the Obeah fanaticism still continues in the parishes on the north side of the island and the exertions of the planters are in consequence almost paralysed, through the scarcity of labour".[21]

T.H. of Mincing Lane was still unclear and wanted some clarification from the readers of the 25 January 1851 issue of *Notes and Queries*: "Can any of your readers give me some information about *obeism*? I am anxious to know whether

---

20 *John Bull*, 11 November 1843, 711.
21 *Freeman's Journal and Daily Commercial Advertiser*, 12 December 1842, n.p.

it is in itself a religion, or merely a rite practised in some religion in Africa, and imported thence to the West Indies (where, I am told, it is rapidly gaining ground again)." He also wanted to know whether "the *obeist* obtains the immense power he is said to possess over his brother negroes by any acquired art, or simply by working upon the more superstitious minds of his companions. Any information, however, on the subject will be acceptable".[22] A reply from M. appeared, in the 22 February issue of the paper:

> in the early part of this century [Obeah] was very common among the slave-population in the West Indies, especially in the more remote estates – of course of African origin – not as either a "religion" or a "rite" but rather as a superstition; a power claimed by its professors, and assented to by the patients, of causing good or evil to, or averting it from them; which was of course always for a "consideration" of some sort, to the profit, whether honorary, pecuniary, or other, of the dispenser. . . . It seems, however, hardly likely that Obeism should now be "rapidly gaining ground again" there, from the greater spread of Christianity and diffusion of enlightenment and information in general since the slave-emancipation; as also from the absence of its feeding that formerly accompanied every fresh importation from the coast: as, like mists before the mounting sun, all such impostures must fade away before common sense, truth, and facts, whenever these are allowed their free influence. The conclusion, then, would rather be that Obeism is on the decline; only more apparent, when now seen, than formerly, from its attracting greater notice.[23]

Another responder weighed in with a plethora of sources:

> T.H. will find, in the authorities given below, that it is not only a rite, but a religion, or rather superstition, viz. Serpent-worship. Modern Universal History, fol. vol. vi. p. 600; 8vo. vol. xvi. p. 411.; which is indebted for its information to the works of De Marchais, Barbot, Atkyns, and Bosman: the last of which may be in Pinkerton's Collection, vol. xvi., and a review of it in Acta Eruditor., Lips. 1705, p. 265., under the form of an "Essay on Guinea". In Astley's Collection of Voyages, there is an account compiled from every authority then known, and a very interesting description of the rites and ceremonies connected with this superstition. According to same authors, the influence of the Obeist does not depend on the exercise of any art or natural magic, but on the apprehensions of evil infused into his victim's mind. See Lewis's Journal of a Residence among

---

22 *Notes and Queries*, ser. 1, 3 (January–June 1851): 59–60.
23 Ibid., 149–50.

the Negroes in the West Indies. . . . The name of the sacred serpent, which in the ancient language of Canaan was variously pronounced, was derived from "ob" (inflare), perhaps from his peculiarity of inflation when irritated. See Bryant's Analysis, vol. i.; Deane's, Worship of the Serpent, p. 80. From a notion of the mysterious inflation produced by the presence of the divine spirit, those who had the spirit of Ob, or Python, received the names of Ob, or Pythia; according to the not unusual custom for the priest or priestess of any god to take the name of the deity they served. See Selden De Dis Syris, Synt. 1. c. 2. It is a curious coincidence, that as the Witch of Endor is called "Oub", and the African sorceress "Obi", from the serpent-deity Oub, so the old English name of a witch, "hag", bears apparent relationship to the word hak, the ancient British name of a species of snake.[24]

This was signed "T.J."

D.P.W. wrote that he was

for a short time in the island of Jamaica, and from what I could learn there of Obeahism, the power seemed to be obtained by the Obeah-man or woman, by working upon the fears of their fellow-negroes, who are notoriously superstitious. The principal charm seemed to be, a collection of feathers, coffin furniture, and one or two other things which I have forgotten. A small bundle of this, hung over the victim's door, or placed in his path, is supposed to have the power of bringing ill luck to the unfortunate individual. And if any accident, or loss, or sickness should happen to him about the time, it is immediately imputed to the dreadful influence of Obeah! But I have heard of cases where the unfortunate victim has gradually wasted away, and died under this powerful spell, which, I have been informed by old residents in the island, is to be attributed to a more natural cause, namely, the influence of poison. The Obeah-man causes a quantity of ground glass to be mixed with the food of the person who has incurred his displeasure; and the result is said to be a slow but sure wasting and death![25]

Finally, readers of *Notes and Queries* heard from Henry H. Breen, whose letter from St Lucia took longer to arrive, coming as it did from across the ocean, and appeared in the May 1851 issue. According to Breen,

Obeism is not itself a religion, except in the sense in which Burke says that "superstition is the religion of feeble minds". It is a belief, real or pretended, in

---

24 Ibid., 309–10.
25 Ibid., 150.

the efficacy of certain spells and incantations, and is to the uneducated negro what sorcery was to our unenlightened forefathers. This superstition is known in St Lucia by the name Kembois. It is still extensively practised in the West Indies, but there is no reason to suppose that it is rapidly gaining ground.[26]

Further mentions of Obeah came in 1865 when a writer to *Notes and Queries* noted that, in India, a man dressed in a cloak of feathers and wearing the mask of a bird frightened the people, relating that "amongst the African negroes of the West Indies, a similar figure causes the like agitation and in this latter case, I have been led to suppose that there may be some connection between it and the feathers, which invariably enter into the composition of an Obeah ball, such as is placed near the person whose life is being practised on".[27]

Obeah came up repeatedly, and readers were much more likely to hear that blacks continued to believe in it than the opposite. One newspaper noted, for example, that

> Numbers of very well-meaning people here, remembering for how long Jamaica has been emancipated, and perhaps, having a lively recollection of the expenses of "missions", will be surprised to learn that the rites of Obeah still flourish, and that the fetish man – whose conjurations remove death and whose travelling pack is stocked with poisons, drugs, dried animal remains, and all the rest of the fetisher's stock of deadly rubbish – is still a man of power.[28]

The *Morning Chronicle* struck an ominous note when it declared:

> The crime of Obeah has become so common that it requires the utmost vigilance to detect it when committed. It is a species of sorcery which the credulous and weak-minded negroes hold in great awe; and no wonder, as it is associated in all cases with the admixture of deleterious compounds with food; and others by infusions of juice expressed from poisonous plants that grow wild in the woods of the island, and are well known to the willing adepts in the art.[29]

The *Daily News* reprinted an item from the *Demerara Royal Gazette* which suggested that, at least in that colony, Obeah was on the decline: "On Saturday morning one of those misguided beings called 'Obeah-men' was publicly

---

26   Ibid., 376.
27   *Notes and Queries*, ser. 3, 7 (January–June 1865): 404.
28   "Topics of the Week", *Penny Illustrated Paper*, 7 April 1866, n.p.
29   *Morning Chronicle*, 1 May 1856.

whipped in front of the Stabroek Market. The flogging system seems to have led to some good result, as convictions for practising obeahism are comparatively rare."[30]

The interest in Obeah continued, however, and in the July 1899 edition of *Notes and Queries*, James Platt suggested

> the origin of this well-known West Indian term is not precisely defined in any of our existing dictionaries. We find such statements as "probably of African origin" (Webster and Chambers); "said to be of African origin" (The Century); "said to have been introduced from Africa" (Worcester). The following quotation from Revd Hugh Goldie's Dictionary of the Efik Language (of Old Calabar), Glasgow, 1874, p. 300, appears to set the matter at rest, and should interest etymologists and students of folklore; "Ubio, a thing, or mixture of things, put in the ground, as a charm, to cause sickness or death. The obeah of the West Indies".

As Joseph Williams pointed out, the *Oxford Dictionary* took notice and used Goldie's definition in its next edition.[31]

By this time, of course, *obeah* had already been in the national lexicon for more than a hundred years and was a byword for superstition and magic. For example, *The Times* of 27 September 1836 refers in its editorial to "the political Obeah" of what it termed the "titled and estated slaves" of Ireland.[32] Public fascination with Obeah continued well into the twentieth century with *The Times* of 28 December 1949 advertising "An Adventure with Obeah", a talk by A.S. Ryan on the BBC Home Service, the enduring interest fuelled by travelogues and works of fiction, which in turn all relied heavily on books published in previous centuries. [33]

---

30   *Daily News*, 4 October 1862.
31   Williams, *Psychic Phenomena*, 45.
32   *The Times*, 27 September 1936, 4.
33   *The Times*, 28 December 1949, 3.

CHAPTER 7

The Case of Three-Finger'd Jack

"THE TERROR OF JAMAICA"

Sometime around 1780, a slave ran away from a plantation in the south-eastern part of Jamaica and became a legend in Britain, celebrated in books and on the stage well into the following century. According to sensational reports, he was known as Bristol on the plantation, but in freedom he called himself Three-Finger'd Jack. In many particulars, however, Jack was so similar to Lewis's Plato and Cynric Williams's Cato that he is probably one and the same, but the embellishment of his legend under the name of Jack proved far more attractive to other writers.

The *Supplement to the Royal Gazette* of 29 July–5 August 1780 carried what may be the first mention of him in the written record. "A gang of run-away Negroes of above 40 men and 18 women have formed a settlement in the recesses of Four Mile Wood in St David's; are become very formidable to that neighbourhood, and have rendered travelling, especially to Mulattoes and Negroes, very dangerous." The article then explains that the gang has already killed a mulatto and stolen livestock, as well as linen. "They are chiefly Congos and declare that they will kill every Mulatto and Creole Negro they can catch. BRISTOL, alias *Three-fingered Jack*, is their Captain, and Caesar, who belongs to Rozel Estate, is their next officer." Oddly, the *Supplement* goes on to point out that "the banditti may soon become dangerous to the Public" if nothing is done about them. Since they had already killed a mulatto and threatened others, as well as blacks, it should have been clear that they were already dangerous, but perhaps the *Gazette* meant that they might soon attack whites. The newspaper suggests sending out the Maroons against them or forming some sort of band to arrest them.[1]

---

1 Supplement to the *Royal Gazette* 67 (29 July–5 August 1780): 458.

That creoles and free blacks or mulattoes, as well as whites, were often targeted by rebels is frequently noted by writers. As Hearn observes, "the educated mulatto class [of the French islands] may affect to despise [the *quimboiseur*] but he is preparing their overthrow in the dark". Hearn had already noted that it was "among the country people, [that] the dangerous forces of revolution exist, [where] Christian feeling is almost stifled by ghastly beliefs of African origin; the images and crucifixes still command respect, but this respect is inspired by a feeling purely fetichistic".[2]

Lloyd's Evening Post of 11 October 1780 carried the additional information that the slave killed by Jack's gang had belonged to Duncan Munro of Montrose. As was to be expected, this news was also covered by several other metropolitan papers, including the *St James' Chronicle* of the following day. About four months later, the *Royal Gazette* announced the offer of a reward of three thousand pounds and freedom for any slave who captured or killed Jack. This had the desired effect: a couple of months later, the paper reported Jack's death at the hands of the Maroon John Reeder and some other men.

The story was taken up almost two decades later, in 1799, by Dr Benjamin Moseley in his *Treatise on Sugar*, where it is included in the section on Obeah. Throughout his account, Moseley's admiration for Jack is clearly evident. In the 1800 chapbook, printed by M. Angus and Son of Newcastle, there is even a claim that Jack was "as much the terror of Jamaica, in 1780, as ever Robin Hood or Turpin were to part of the inhabitants of this country", an assertion that firmly established him among the pantheon of admired British outlaws. This association with Robin Hood and Dick Turpin does not appear in Moseley's *Treatise* or other, later editions; it is possible that Angus added his own creative touch to Moseley's work, at least with regard to that line.[3] But to Moseley, Jack was not only an outlaw, he was also an Obeah man. What is more, the doctor claims to have seen his Obeah bag, which he says was brought to him by the Maroons who killed Jack:

> His Obi consisted of the end of a goat's horn, filled with a compound of grave dirt, ashes, the blood of a black cat, and human fat; all mixed into a kind of paste. A black cat's foot, a dried toad, a pig's tail, a slip of virginal parchment of kid's skin, with characters marked in blood on it, were also in his Obian bag. These, with a keen sabre, and two guns, . . . were all his Obi;

---

2   Hearn, *Two Years*, 180–81.
3   Benjamin Moseley, *Obi; or, the History of Three-Finger'd Jack* (Newcastle: M. Angus and Son, 1800).

with which he defied capture for two years.[4] Reading over the list, one cannot help but wonder how Moseley knew the paste consisted of a black cat's blood and not, say, a white rabbit's. Or, for that matter, how he knew that human fat was one of the ingredients. No other account has ever included human fat in its list of obi materials, and the detail about the black cat seems more in keeping with European witchcraft conventions than African or West Indian traditions. Moseley also claims that, contrary to the tales of accomplices, Jack was completely alone. "He robbed alone; fought all his battles alone."

According to Moseley, in the woods near his stronghold on Mount Lebanus, Jack crossed the foreheads of some runaway Negroes "with some of the magic in his horn, and they could not betray him", but he trusted nobody and kept to himself. "By his magic, he was not only the dread of the negroes, but there were many white people who believed he was possessed of some supernatural power." Moseley relates that Jack became so ubiquitous in the area that he was even blamed for marital woes, but that Governor John Dalling was not amused. In a proclamation issued on 12 December 1780, Dalling offered the reward for Jack's capture mentioned above. In Moseley's version of events, two blacks from Scots Hall, Maroon Town, Quashee and Sam, take up the challenge, but not before Quashee gets himself christened under the name of James Reeder.

After searching for three weeks, Reeder and Sam finally come upon Jack roasting plantains over a fire at the mouth of a cave. "Jack's looks were fierce and terrible. He told them he would kill them." Reeder replies that Jack's Obi "had no power to hurt him; for he was now christened and his name was no longer Quashee". According to Moseley, this was not the first encounter between the men, as Reeder was the one responsible for the loss of Jack's two fingers several years before. Jack had almost killed him and the others with him in that skirmish, but Reeder escaped. Moseley believes that Jack should have beaten both Reeder and Sam, "but Jack was cowed; for he had prophesied that white Obi would get the better of him; and from experience he knew the charm would lose none of its strength in the hands of Reeder". The three men fight. A boy with Reeder and Sam shoots Jack in the belly, but he manages to fight on until Sam knocks Jack down with a rock and they "beat out his brains with stones".[5]

---

4   Moseley, *A Treatise on Sugar; with Miscellaneous Medical Observations* (London: John Nicholls, 1799), 197.
5   Ibid., 205.

The men cut off Jack's head and three-fingered hand and take them in triumph to Morant Bay, where they put their trophies in a pail of rum to preserve them. "Followed by a vast concourse of negroes, now no longer afraid of Jack's Obi, they carried them to Kingston and Spanish Town; and claimed the rewards of the King's proclamation and the House of Assembly." In another edition of his story, Moseley gives the date of Jack's murder as 27 January 1781.

Moseley studied medicine in London and Paris and sailed to Jamaica in 1768 after completing his training. He became a surgeon-apothecary and also held the post of surgeon general for the island, staying on in Jamaica for eighteen years and publishing works on dysentery and coffee while there. His *Treatise on Sugar* was not published until 1799, fifteen years after his return to Great Britain in 1784. Though he obtained the prestigious post of physician to the Royal Hospital at Chelsea, Moseley is probably best remembered in medical circles for his vehement objections to vaccination. He claimed that vaccination, then an innovative procedure in Great Britain, resulted in insanity and *facies bovilla* (a cowlike facial appearance), among other things.[6] He also warned that vaccination might result in droves of British Pasiphaes invading the fields, seeking sex with bulls. His fantastic claims are suggestive of a somewhat cavalier attitude to facts, which raises an interesting speculation: did Moseley conflate what was known of Plato/Cato with the story of Bristol/Three-Fingered Jack to create a myth aimed at appealing to the British reading public?

Nowhere in the official accounts reported on in Jamaica's *Gazette* is anything ever said about Bristol or Jack being an Obeah man or of his having any sort of concourse with Obeah. Yet Moseley claims that Jack's supernatural powers were as widely known and dreaded by black people as were those of Plato/Cato. Neither is anything said about Reeder – whose name is given as John in the *Gazette*, not James – submitting to baptism in order to beat Jack's Obeah with "white obi". We remember, however, that the Plato of Cynric Williams's story was induced to pursue Cato after being baptized as a specific antidote to Cato's Obeah powers. Whether conscious plagiarism and embellishment of an existing story or not, Moseley's creation acted as a spark, lighting a literary fire that continued to burn throughout the next century.

The next version of Jack's story – *Obi; or, The History of Three-fingered Jack,*

---

6 Deborah Brunton, "Moseley, Benjamin (1742–1819)", *Oxford Dictionary of National Biography*, ed. Lawrence Goldman (Oxford: Oxford University Press), http://www.oxforddnb.com/view/article/19387.

in a Series of Letters from a Resident in Jamaica to His Friend in England – was written by William Earle and appeared later in the same year as Moseley's offering. Today, little is known about William Earle, who had something of a minor literary reputation in his heyday, having published at least one play, a book about Welsh legends, and several novels. His early success did not last; almost three decades after the publication of *Obi*, it appears that Earle fell on hard times and was incarcerated in Fleet Prison, where debtors and bankrupts often ended up.

It is safe to say that Earle sympathized with the abolitionist cause. The frontispiece to *Obi* contains an excerpt from Robert Southey's "Sonnet III":

> Oh! ye who at your ease
> Sip the blood sweetened beverage! thoughts like these
> Haply ye scorn: I thank thee, gracious God!
> That I do feel upon my cheek the glow
> Of indignation, when beneath the rod
> A sable brother writhes in silent woe.

Below this excerpt are lines from Erasmus Darwin: "Hear him! ye Senates! hear this truth sublime. HE WHO ALLOWS OPPRESSION SHARES THE CRIME."

Earle's story is written in the form of a series of letters from the fictional George Stanford to Charles, a friend in England, and clearly owes much to Moseley's account, which he heavily embroiders. Earle is concerned with immediately conveying to his English audience the excitement generated in Jamaica by Jack's depredations:

> I shall put off answering [your letter], until I have eased myself of my insufferable burthen, by dispatching Jack, his three fingers, and his Obi, and all that belongs to him; for, positively, I can think of nothing else. And so it is with every body in the Island; go wherever I will the name of Jack is perpetually buzzed in my ears. . . . Nay, there is not a thing called Jack, whether a smoke-jack, a boot jack, or any other jack, but acts as a spell upon my senses and sets me on the fret at the bare mention of it.

All the whites, except Stanford, are afraid of Jack.[7]

Earle establishes Stanford's sympathetic abolitionist credentials quickly: "Jack is a noble fellow, and in spite of every cruel hard hearted planter, I shall

---

7 William Earle, *Obi; or, The History of Three-fingered Jack* (London: Isaiah Thomas, 1800), 3

repeat the same to the last hour of my life. 'Jack is a Negro,' say they. 'Jack is a MAN,' say I. 'He is a slave.' 'MAN cannot be a slave to MAN.'" This exchange continues in that vein, with the narrator pointing out that stealing slaves from their homes is worse than the actions of highwaymen, yet the latter are hung while the slave traders openly prosper in society. The fact of the slave trade's legality makes it no more honourable than prostitution, Stanford argues. Such, he says, "is the daily altercation" he has with Jamaican planters.

Earle then gives Jack a backstory that provides him with a beautiful mother, Amri, the slave of a Mr Mornton of Maroons Town. "Torn from the arms of ... her family" in Africa, she "vowed to curse the European race for ever; and had a son, in whose breast she never failed to nurture the baneful passion of revenge". Evoking Lady Macbeth's murderous tutelage of her husband, Amri teaches Jack to "despise his groaning companions ... meanly submitting to the christian whip", and Jack grows up "to imagine himself the destroyer of all Europe".

"He was of the most manly growth, nearly seven feet in height, and amazingly robust; ... his limbs were well shapen and athletic ... [he could] perform the office of any two negroes within the plantation ... his nose was not like the generality of blacks, squat and flat, but rather aquiline, and his skin remarkably clear."[8] Without an official description to contradict his claims, and unable to overcome his own prejudices, Earle casts his African hero in the mould of a European, with European facial features that were presumably more acceptable to readers than those of, say, a broad-nosed pygmy. Indeed, Earle designates him as "every thing in soul and person requisite for the hero".

Jack is twenty-two years old when his mother decides the time has come for him to wreak his revenge, and she tells him the story of her life. Amri was a Feloop from the Gambia who lived with her husband, Makro, near the house of her father, Feruarue. One day, a terrible storm wrecked a ship within sight of Amri, who realized that two survivors, a man and a young boy, were clinging to the wreckage. She hastened to the shore, pulled them out and offered them brandy, taking pity on them though they were European and foes to her people. Though Captain Harrop sickened, Amri's care restored him, and the two recovered and were offered food by their hosts. Captain Harrop attempted to convert them to Christianity, apparently teaching them about the Creator by pointing out the beauty of the land around them, which conceivably they

---

8   Ibid., 12–16

had never noticed before Harrop's arrival (this was a fond belief of many Europeans – that Africans, sunk in barbarity, were ignorant of beauty or had no sense of aesthetics).

Over a period of two months, as Harrop convalesced, he disarmed their defences, but one day they heard him telling the young boy, William: "Have I not enlightened them, fertilized their minds, told them of the duties of this life, and how to enjoy society? What were they, when first we set foot on their shore? savages, dwelling with savages." Here Harrop was voicing the claims made by slavery's defenders, who argued that their enslavement benefited Africans.

Makro and Amri understood that Harrop was planning to leave them but did not grasp his plans for them. Thinking kindly of him, Amri gave Harrop a "Saphie", which a footnote explains was an "amulet or charm; a scrap of paper written on by a Mahomedan Priest, [which] is enclosed in a horn, and sold at a high price to the natives . . . a pagan native believe[s] in the virtues of the Saphie, though they deny the religion". On the day of Harrop's departure, they saw a long slave coffle passing, and Amri tells Jack, "Such [were] the scenes we daily witness in Africa, such is the christianity of the Europeans who profess humanity."

Makro and Amri did not guess Harrop's true nature until they went to tell him goodbye. They were then seized and taken aboard the slave ship that had come for him. Harrop told Makro that he was taking him away from Africa to civilization, but Makro responded, "Man was His noblest work, and I am a man . . . I never can own a superior but my Creator." Makro went on a hunger strike and Harrop ordered him to be given five hundred lashes. Defiant to the end, Makro managed to get hold of a pistol and shoot Harrop before dying from his wounds. The pregnant Amri, however, arrived alive in Jamaica and was sold off. Jack was born a few months later.

Amri tells Jack that during his childhood there were several insurrections but that they failed because of the absence of a leader. After one such rebellion, some captured rebels led the militia to the hideout of an Obeah man, who was arrested, tried and convicted. He was sentenced to execution and every slave was brought to witness his death. When the "Obi-man" was brought out, Amri recognized her father, Feruarue, and threw herself into his arms. The execution was stopped and Mr Mornton offered to allow Feruarue and Amri their freedom if Feruarue would only tell him how he had "by some hidden means, spirited up the negroes to a rebellion" and how he had managed to kill "in the most cruel manner" those slaves loyal to their masters. Feruarue had already been tortured on the rack and the soles of his feet and his armpits burnt in order to extract his secrets, but he had held fast. In his footnotes to this section, Earle quotes extensively from the Fuller report on Obeah and on the "experiments" that were carried out on "Obia men" captured during Tacky's Rebellion.[9]

Amri begged her father to tell the planters what they wanted to know, but he refused and told her how he had offered the slave traders six of his own slaves if they would free her, but instead he was enslaved along with the people he had brought to the ship to ransom her. Like Amri, he too had sworn revenge and for that purpose had dedicated himself to the study of Obeah. "I acknowledge I spirited up the slaves to rebellion; I acknowledge I struck terror to the hearts of many that refused their aid, but how I effected this remains with me, and with me shall expire", Feruarue told his daughter. Mornton asked him again for his answer. "What shall I confess?" Feruare responded. "That I have made the pallid Europeans tremble at my power." He was dragged away from Amri and "covered over with the farrago of his weak and impotent charms". Again he was exhorted to confess, but Feruarue remained defiant. He was strung up and a fire lit at his feet. In his last words, Feruarue bade Amri to rejoice, because he was going back to his country.

His death hardened Amri's resolve to take revenge through Jack, and she has now decided that the time has come; she has learned that Harrop, who survived being shot by Makro, is to marry Mornton's daughter. Amri takes Jack to the cave of the Obeah man Bashra, who lives alone, away from other people, near Mount Lebanus. Bashra is "wrinkled and deformed. . . . Snails drew their slimy train upon his shrivelled feet, and lizards and vipers filled the air of his hut with foul uncleanliness." Bashra, the stereotypical Obeah man, is impressed by Jack's "noble appearance". He "prepared an Obi for him, of more than common qualities, a purpose preparation, that should stand by him in time of need, and the arms of his foe should fall defenceless from their grasp; in short, the charm possessed such rare virtues, that it was to answer every wish of its possessor". Amri is pleased and slings the "Obi horn" around her son's neck. A footnote to this section quotes Moseley on the implements used in Obeah.[10]

The next day Jack is working in the fields when a white man approaches and initiates a conversation with him. The man talks about the savagery of Africa

---

9   Ibid., 54–63.
10 Ibid., 73–74.

and notes that he brought a woman, "a wild untutored being . . . to happier climes . . . where the virtues born in our bosom are more refined than in the savage bowels of Africa". Jack responds with Amri and Makro's story, denouncing Europeans and speaking of the vengeance he will have for his father. The white man pales but, before he can say anything, the overseer comes up and addresses him as Captain Harrop. Jack reels with shock but quickly recovers and assaults him. The overseer attempts to draw Jack back, but Jack kills him before the other slaves can seize and restrain him. Captain Harrop is led away. Jack then exhorts his fellow slaves to join him in rebellion. They applaud his speech, and his friend Mahali vows to throw off slavery's yoke, but the troops arrive and everyone runs away. Jack, in contempt, shouts that he despises them more than their enemies, for they are cowards and traitors. Again, Earle is unable to rise above the convention by which blacks are stereotyped as cowardly. Jack, he has already made clear, is an exception in both looks and character.

The soldiers arrest Jack and put him in confinement. When Amri goes to consult Bashra, he is taken aback at this turn of events but assures her that the "Obi is good Obi" and that she has nothing to fear. Jack is put on trial, convicted, and sentenced to be hung, drawn and quartered as an example to other blacks, but he remains confident that Obeah will preserve him. On the fourth day, he escapes by removing the grille from his window and jumping to the ground far below. He kills the two guards and makes his way to Mornton's estate, where he heads to Amri's hut to let her know of his escape. She greets him joyfully and they make their way to the Great House, where Harrop is staying, but before Jack can kill him, Harrop faints at his feet. Jack swings him up over his shoulders and bears him away to Mount Lebanus, leaving Amri behind.

The next day, Amri is questioned about Harrop's disappearance and Jack's escape, but she denies knowing anything of those events. Meanwhile, Jack has made his home in a cave on Mount Lebanus, where he secures Harrop before going to visit Bashra. A gang of robbers is with Bashra and they offer to follow Jack, but he spurns their assistance. While he is there, Mahali arrives, wounded but full of admiration for Jack, whom he calls "avenger of our nation". Jack embraces him as a brother and leaves him to Bashra's care.

The governor offers a reward for Jack's capture, but blacks "feared to venture against Jack, who possessed so powerful an Obi". Then Quashee, "a brave black of Scotshall, Maroonstown", is returning home past Amri's hut when he hears her in conversation with Jack. Quashee follows Jack and sees him disappear up Mount Lebanus. The next day, Quashee rallies the townsmen to go after Jack, but he hears them coming, there is a fight and Quashee slices off two of Jack's fingers; then he loses his own weapon and flees along with the others.

Traps are set for Jack but he evades them. Then, one night, men wait outside Amri's hut for Jack's appearance. They fire at him but miss. This adds to his reputation; it is said of him that one might as well attempt to wound a shadow. "Not one of the negroes but trembled at the name of Threefingered Jack, and many of the Europeans believed in the fancied virtues of his Obi." Earle reports that when Jack goes to visit Bashra, he meets the gang of robbers. "Bashra filled Jack's horn with his Obi; and gave him an ointment, with which he rubbed the brows of his countrymen that they might not betray him!"

Sometime later, Jack comes across a widow walking through the woods; he escorts her home and gives her a purse filled with gold before showing her his three-fingered hand. She screams and faints, but when she comes to, they part on good terms, in the best tradition of heroic outlaws. Jack is full of worry, however, because the woman has informed him that his mother will be executed the following day for harbouring Jack and not revealing his whereabouts. Mahali volunteers to effect Amri's escape. He snatches her from the flames and bears her back to Mount Lebanus, but not without sustaining several injuries from the shots fired at him. Amri dies from her injuries, closely followed by Mahali. Jack's heart turns and he becomes cruel, killing innocents and sparing only black men. The governor now issues a proclamation promising a reward of three hundred pounds for whoever apprehends Jack. The House of Assembly offers a further reward of freedom to any slave responsible for Jack's arrest. Reeder and the others decide to hunt Jack down, and his end comes quickly.

Earle copies Moseley's ending virtually word for word:

> His looks were fierce, wild and terrible; up he started from the ground, and said he would kill them. But Reeder told him that his Obi had no power over him, for that he was christened, and no longer Quashee, but James Reeder. Jack started back in dismay; he was cowed; for he had prophesied that White Obi should overcome him, and he knew the charm, in Reeder's hands, would lose none of its virtue or power.[11]

The boy among them shoots Jack in the stomach, Sam knocks him down and, as in Moseley's story, they cut off his head and his hand and put their grisly relics in a pail of rum, setting off for Kingston and Spanish Town for their reward. Harrop starves to death in Jack's cave before being discovered.

---

11 Ibid., 167–68.

Coincidentally, Earle shared his name with William Earle, a prominent Liverpool merchant and slave trader whose son, also named William, followed him into the family business. Given the story of Amri and Makro's betrayal as well as that of Feruarue, Amri's father, it is intriguing to note that the Liverpool William once wrote a letter to a friendly African chieftain apologizing for the abduction his two sons and promising their return. Such cases were not altogether rare, however.[12]

The other main contributor to the legend of Three-Fingered Jack in Britain was William Burdett, who was also quick off the mark and got out his version in 1800: *Life and Exploits of Mansong, Commonly Called Three-finger'd Jack, the Terror of Jamaica in the Years 1780 and 1781. With a Particular Account of the Obi; Being the Only True one of that celebrated and fascinating Mischief, so prevalent in the West Indies. On Which Is Founded, The popular pantomimical Drama of Obi; or, Three-Finger'd Jack, Performed at the Theatre-Royal, Haymarket; An accurate Description of which is also added.* This was followed by several other editions in quick succession, resulting in at least ten editions within five years.

A classified advertisement in the 25 October 1800 issue of London's *Morning Herald* announced: "Just published, price 1s. (embellished with a beautiful plate and stitched in coloured Patent Paper) the third edition of *The Life and Exploits of Mansong, commonly called Three-Fingered Jack, the terror of Jamaica* . . . printed and published by A. Neil, Charlton Street . . . sold also by all other booksellers."[13] In fact, the author notes in the front of the fifth edition that the

> rapid sale which the former editions of this little work experience has stimulated us to render the present [edition] still more acceptable to the public. We have, therefore, in addition to our own knowledge, (acquired by many years residence in Jamaica) had recourse to the best authorities on the subject; and have made several emendations, additions, &c. so that the purchasers of this edition may rely on being in possession of a correct narrative of facts.[14]

Of course, this would not only have appealed to new readers but would also have attracted past purchasers eager for the new material.

Like Moseley and Earle, Burdett casts Jack in a heroic mould, not least by distancing him from other blacks in appearance, despite his being African-

---

12 Summary of William Earle Collection. National Archives, UK, http://discovery.national archives.gov.uk/details/r/e4024133-f616-4db7-b45b-d5b0d0ead32c.
13 *Morning Herald*, 25 October 1800.
14 Burdett, *Three-finger'd Jack*, 2.

born: "This daring marauder, whose real name was MANSONG, and who, for a considerable time, kept all *Jamaica* in awe, was of a bold and martial appearance; he was above the common stature, and his limbs well shapen and athletic; his face was rather long; his eyes keen and penetrating; his nose was not like the generality of blacks, squat and flat, but rather aquiline; and his skin remarkably clear."

Burdett's description of Jack owes as much to Earle as to Moseley, but the story is substantially different from their versions. Burdett's Jack/Mansong is African-born, the son of Onowauhee, who lived in an area called Simbing, in the African interior.

Onowauhee is the proud owner of a large herd of cattle but suffers from the predations of the Moors of the adjoining country, who often raid his herd. When Jack/Mansong grows older, he takes it upon himself to protect his father's cattle but is wounded during a raid and thought dead. His father, upon seeing the apparently lifeless body, dies of grief. His "unenlightened people" place Onowauhee's body in a mosque, hoping that he will be restored to life, but on the fourth day they finally buried him.[15]

When Jack/Mansong recovers from his wounds, he persuades the young men of the village to join him in offering their services to the king of Kaarta, who is fighting against the king of Bambarra. With Jack/Mansong's aid and that of his men, the Kaartans defeat their enemy in several battles, and at last the Bambarrans sue for peace. The king of Kaarta sends Mansong and some other men to the main Bambarra town to negotiate the peace treaty, but after three days they are imprisoned and sold to slave traders. The king of Kaarta offers four hundred slaves in exchange for the release of Mansong and his men, but they are sold on the banks of the Gambia to an English slave dealer and put on board ship.

According to Burdett, Jack/Mansong was sold to a Mr K. of Port Royal, "on whose plantation the slaves were treated with more severity than any other in the island". Burdett claims to have been transacting business with the overseer at Mr K's. plantation while Mansong was receiving "a dozen lashes with a cart-whip, for staying FIVE MINUTES at dinner after the bell had called the slaves to work" (emphasis Burdett's). Burdett explains that Mansong, having lost his African name, is now called Jack. Jack spends eighteen months in Jamaica before deciding to take revenge. He seeks out Amalkir, the Obeah man, who conforms in looks to traditional expectations:

---

15 Ibid., 5–10.

> Amalkir . . . dwelt in a loathsome cave, far removed from the enquiring eye of the suspicious whites, in the blue Mountains; he was old and shrivelled; a disorder had contracted all his nerves, and he could scarcely crawl. – His cave was the dwelling-place or refuge of robbers; he encouraged them in their depradations, and gave them OBI, that they might fearless rush where danger stood. This obi was supposed to make them invulnerable to the attacks of the white men, and they placed implicit belief in its virtues.[16]

Burdett then declares that he will "present our readers with an authentic account of this practice, so prevalent in the British West Indies, and its fatal effects, corroborated by the authorities of Mr Bryan Edwards, author of the History of the West Indies, Doctor Moseley, &c. &c.". This is followed by a long but unattributed excerpt from the Fuller report, which includes Bryant's imaginative etymology of Obeah.

When we return to the action of the story, Jack seeks out Amalkir "with reverential awe" and Amalkir engages to "set all the slaves of every plantation in the island in wild commotion". Jack's fellow slaves are "excited to rebellion by the Obeah-man" and begin stockpiling weapons and ammunition, which they hide in the mountains. The tenth of February 1780 is set aside as the date for the insurrection, and the leaders meet the night before in Amalkir's cave to discuss their plans. The next day the signal gun is fired and the rebellion gets underway, with Jack leading them in "scenes of carnage". They set a town on fire and the Maroons are sent against them. The rebels flee before the Maroons and Jack escapes to Amalkir's cave, where the Obeah man hangs an obi horn around his neck. Burdett then references Moseley's account of its contents, with attribution.

Jack becomes a solitary outlaw when the governor issues a proclamation offering a pardon to all rebels who then return to their plantations. One day, he encounters Quashee, a former friend, and demands that he hand over the provisions he is carrying. Quashee refuses and Jack draws his cutlass. Quashee shoots off Jack's two fingers with his pistol but is sorely wounded himself. Until the introduction of the character of Captain Orford, in the next few pages Burdett gives more or less the same information about the following sequence of events as Moseley.

In Burdett's version, Captain Orford is a member of the English garrison who soon falls in love with Rosa Chapman, daughter of a planter in Maroon's

---

16 Ibid., 17–18.

Town. Orford sallies out into the mountains with Tuckey, his servant boy, and is injured by Jack. Sometime later, Jack has another encounter with Orford; they fight and Jack subdues him and takes the unconscious soldier back to his cave, where he is kept prisoner. Rosa sickens on hearing the news, but on her recovery she takes to the hills to look for her lover. The governor then issues the proclamation relating to Jack's capture, which is quoted by Burdett along with the addition from the House of Assembly.

Rosa finds Jack's cave: "she beheld, with tortured eye, the frightful cave, which was hung around with the skeletons of turtles, aligators, and other reptiles".[17] Jack takes her prisoner, but later she manages to escape with Orford. Burdett's retelling of Jack's final fight with Reeder and Sam does not differ greatly from that of Moseley and Earle, so there is no need to recount it here.

For the most part, the numerous versions of Jack's story that appeared throughout the 1800s in Britain – around twenty chapbooks and various printed editions of both the pantomime and the melodrama based on it – followed either Earle's or Burdett's version of Moseley's story, to a greater or lesser degree as the author was inclined. "Carried in the packs of the pedlars, or Chapmen, to every village, and to every home",[18] chapbooks such as the ones on Obi Jack enjoyed a fairly wide readership. They were cheap and their subject matter often focused on tales of crime and punishment, but in the 1800s several religious organizations attempted to introduce worthier topics, and it is possible that they were responsible for at least a few of the editions of Jack's story.

Some chapbooks added details here and there that were not found in any of the baseline texts. For example, *The History and Adventures of Jack Mansong, the Famous Negro Robber and Terror of Jamaica*, published by William Walker, a Yorkshire printer, follows Burdett's plot but gives Jack a love story of his own.[19] In that edition, Jack falls in love with the king of Kaarta's daughter, Zaldwna, whom he is to wed after the peace treaty is concluded. Of course, his untimely

---

17 Ibid., 48.
18 John Ashton, *Chapbooks of the Eighteenth Century* (London: Chatto and Windus, 1882), n.p.
19 *The History and Adventures of Jack Mansong, the Famous Negro Robber and Terror of Jamaica* (Otley: William Walker, n.d.), 8–9. Walker was the publisher of the *Wharfedale and Airedale Observer* and printed numerous chapbooks on a range of subjects. Though Otley is only a small Yorkshire market town, it is no coincidence that this chapbook was printed there, as Otley pioneered the printing machine industry which became the largest single employer in the area during the early 1900s.

abduction and enslavement preclude that happy occasion. Later, however, it is the memory of his lost Zaldwna that inspires Jack to mercy when he discovers Rosa in his cave.

Clearly, all the writers exercise extensive creative licence with the basic storyline, but the one constant through all the stories is the dominant influence of Obeah and Jack's reliance on it. In Moseley's version, Jack himself is the Obeah man and carries the Obeah bag full of the materials that for many writers were emblematic of the profession. In Burdett and Earle, however, the bag is the charm. Jack is no longer the Obeah man but seeks the help of one, and it is from him (or her) that Jack obtains the charm.

In making Jack an Obeah man, Moseley creates a conflict for his readers; they might want to sympathize with Jack – a wronged hero whom anyone could admire for his strength and courage – but they have been reading of the horrors of Obeah and the terrible appearance of its practitioners for decades. Moseley's Jack is neither decrepit nor deformed and does not, therefore, meet conventional expectations of the appearance of Obeah practitioners. Moseley himself alludes to the fact that sufferers of yaws, whose skin and hair became "hideously white" and whose limbs and bodies were "twisted and turned, by the force of this distemper, into shocking grotesque figures", were often taught the "black arts" and became Obeah men and women. Moseley believed that the "ugly, loathsome creatures" who "became oracles of woods, and unfrequented places"[20] originally learned their magical skills from others who presumably were also deformed and decrepit. This was the conventional belief of the time: that there was indeed an art to finding the mind's construction in the face and that evil stamped itself on one's features and form. Writers such as Edwards and Long had already convinced readers that Obeah practitioners were distinguished by their ill-favoured looks. Jack, with his Europeanized features, could not be both a hero and an Obeah man.

Burdett and Earle correct this mistake on Moseley's part by creating the characters of Amalkir and Bashra, respectively, and attaching to them the repulsive appearance traditionally associated with Obeah practitioners. "The obi was a system of witchcraft, religiously believed in by all the negroes. No wonder then that the heroic soul of Jack became a prey to this weakness", writes the author of one chapbook based on Burdett's version. Jack "confidently hoped that the possession of an obi would at once render him feared by his

---

20 Moseley, *Treatise on Sugar*, 189.

fellow slaves, and secure his vengeance on the Europeans. He therefore sought the most eminent professor of the art. . . . This obi was supposed to make [the robbers] invulnerable to the attacks of white men, and they placed implicit belief in its virtues."[21]

More than a century after Jack's death, Gardner reports that Jack was "well-known, not only in the nursery tales of Jamaica, but in melodramatic literature as Three-fingered Jack. His great haunt was in St David's, among the hills near the Falls, nine miles to the windward of Kingston. He was the Turpin of the Windward Road."[22] Jack's legend, fictional though it may be, continued to exercise the imaginations and minds of the British for years. In 1889, for example, Robert Brown, who perhaps read too many chapbooks, writes:

> Those who have read the extraordinary career of Obi Jack, once a kidnapped slave from Africa, in Jamaica, in the latter part of the last century, if they knew anything of "Spiritualism", could be under no doubt as to his having been possessed by a demon – the very same obi, which prevails among the African tribes, and is applied by them to their magicians, not only suggesting but proving its original with the Hebrew word Ohv, a soothsaying demon![23]

"WE LUV YOU. MASSA. SAVE US FROM THREE FINGER'D JACK"

Obi; or, Three-Finger'd Jack! A Serio Pantomime, in Two Acts was performed on 2 July 1800 at the Little Theatre, Haymarket. Written by John Fawcett, himself a comic actor, the pantomime is based on Moseley's and Earle's versions of the story. It employs the romance between Captain Orford and Rosa as well as featuring characters familiar to readers, such as Quashee, Sam and Tuckey. Fawcett clearly felt that women needed to have a greater role, however, so the wives of Quashee and Sam are given small pieces and it is to an Obeah woman that Jack applies for his "Obi".[24]

The pantomime was eagerly anticipated. The *Morning Post and Gazetteer of London* predicted: "The forthcoming piece at the Hay-market will attract all

---

21 *History and Adventures*, 4.
22 Gardner, *History of Jamaica*, 145.
23 Robert Brown, *Demonology and Witchcraft* (London: John F. Shaw, 1889), 33.
24 John Fawcett, *Obi; or, Three-Finger'd Jack! A Serio-Pantomime in Two Acts* (London: T. Woodfall, 1800), n.p.

the world of fashionable curiosity. The story is reported to be of three fingered Jack... a sublime personage, a Jamaican Robin Hood! A hero, however, unlike Robin, who went a robbing always by himself!"[25] Charles Kemble, fresh from what the *Oxford Dictionary of National Biography* calls the "runaway success" of Pizarro at Drury Lane,[26] played Jack (the role was later taken on by Richard John Smith). The "Obi woman" was played by a Mr Abbott; the character is unnamed but wears a "tawdry dress of rags, rude head dress and drapery, ... [and an] Obi horn". Jack's costume, on the other hand, consists of a "dingy white or fawn coloured dress.... A small pouch or wallet hangs from his belt – across shoulders a sling to which is suspended the obi horn – large earrings, chip sugar loaf hat, looped at side with two or three straggling feathers."

Act I, scene I, opens with the wives of Quashee and Sam singing a duet:

> The white man come, and bring his gold
> The Slatee meet him in the bay;
> And Oh! Poor negro then be sold,
> From home poor Negro sail away.
>
> O, it be very sad, to see
> Poor negro child and father part!
> But if White man kind massa be
> He heal the wound in Negro's heart.

The Chorus then sings:

> Good massa we find
> Sing tingering, sing terry,
> When Buckra be kind,
> Then negro heart merry.

The women reply:

> We love massa, he be good;
> No lay stick on negro back:
> Much Kous-Kous he give for food,
> And save us from Three Finger'd Jack.

---

25 *Morning Post*, 30 June 1800.
26 John Russell Stephens, "Kemble, Charles (1775–1854)." *Oxford Dictionary of National Biography*, ed. Lawrence Goldman (Oxford: Oxford University Press, 2008). http://www.oxforddnb.com/view/article/15316.

The overseer addresses them as "black ladies and gentlemen" and announces that since it is Rosa's birthday they are being given a holiday. Orford arrives on the scene and makes eyes at Rosa. He is attacked by Jack the next day, on a walk into the countryside. The slaves panic but Quashee and Sam determine to hunt Jack. The slaves and the overseer sing:

> Swear by the silver crescent of the night,
> Beneath whose beams the negro breathes his pray'r;
> Swear by your fathers slaughtered in the fight,
> By your dear native land and children swear;
>
> Swear to pursue this traitor and annoy him;
> This Jack who daily works your harms,
> With Obi and his magic charms –
> Swear, swear, you will destroy him.

And the slaves respond:

> Kolli, kolli, kolli, we swear all –
> We kill, when he come near us;
> But no swear loud for when we bawl,
> Three-finger Jack, he hear us.

Another version of this song, printed in *The Overtures, Songs, Choruses and Appropriate Music in the Grand Pantomimical Drama Called Obi*, has the overseer singing, "children, swear by your dear native Land and children swear, swear to pursue this traitor".[27]

The stage directions for scene 3, which takes place inside the obi-woman's cave, specify that she is "dressed grotesquely". Her cave is "covered with feathers, rags, bones, teeth, catskins, broken glass, parrots' beaks, &c. &c.". At the start of this scene, six robbers enter the cave and each gives the obi-woman a present. She promises to give them obi in return. They have just finished this little ceremony when Jack crashes into the cave, startling the robbers, who prostrate themselves before him. The obi-woman greets him with joy. Jack has Orford's sash, epaulettes and other belongings, which he presents to the woman. She pins obi charms on the sash and gives it back to him, along with

---

27 Sam Arnold, *The Overtures, Songs, Choruses and Appropriate Music in the Grand Pantomimical Drama Call'd OBI or Three Finger'd Jack as performed at the Theatre Royal, Haymarket* (London: John Longman, Clements, 1800), 28.

a full obi horn. "Jack then crosses all the Robbers' foreheads to prevent them betraying him." A noise outside frightens everyone and Jack leaves, ending the scene.

Jack abducts Orford in scene 4, terrifying the slaves, and in scene 5 an "officer of government" appears, bearing a placard which reads "Reward for killing Three-finger'd Jack! One hundred Guineas, and Freedom to any Slave who brings in the Head of Three-finger'd Jack." Quashee resolves to go after him. The stage direction has Quashee going on his knees and making "signs of a wish to be christened. Planter promises it shall be performed. Quashee rises in great glee." The actors exit the stage but the proclamation is left behind. "At length Quashee and Sam come and look at it on opposite sides – seem as if animated by the same feeling – point particularly to the word Freedom then to their wives and children. They each take up a little Black Child and kiss it very affectionately, and swear to perform the great task."

At the Negro ball which follows, Quashee and Sam vow to destroy Jack and kneel before a clergyman who "blesses them alternately". Both men are then given weapons. Before they leave, Quashee sings a duet with his wife, who is understandably concerned about his safety. "No go to battle – big Death come in fighting", she laments but Quashee responds, "Me laugh at Obi charm, Quashee strong-hearted." Sam's wife sings:

> Jack he did good Captain wound;
> Shoot him shoulder, hurt him back.
> If by Quashee Jack be found,
> Then good-bye Three finger'd Jack.

Quashee's wife joins in:

> Jack have charm in obi bag;
> Tom cat foot, pig tail, duck beak;
> Quashee tear the charm to rag,
> Make Three-finger Jack to squeak.

In act 2, Rosa disguises herself and joins Quashee, Sam and Tuckey in their expedition against Jack. As they are out in the mountains, a storm comes up and Rosa becomes separated from the others. Tuckey, who returns to find her, shows her the mouth of a cave where she can take shelter and await their return. Rosa is exploring the cave when Jack finds her and takes her prisoner, thinking that she is a boy. He drinks rum and water, gets a little drunk, and demands that she sing to him. Rosa sings "A Lady in Fair Seville City" and Jack soon falls asleep like the old guardian in the song. Rosa is about to make her escape when she hears a groan and, on investigating, discovers Orford. Jack wakes up but Rosa pretends to be asleep. Jack ties her hands, knots the end of the rope around his hand and falls back asleep. Rosa manages to free herself and frees Orford from his padlocked cell. They make their escape, though Jack wakes and tries to stop them.

Scene 6 sees the fight between Jack and the men hunting him. Quashee crosses his forehead and tells Jack of his christening. "Jack is daunted and lets his gun fall." He tries to run but is cornered and "they fly at each other with all their might" until Jack is shot by Tuckey and severely wounded. Quashee and Sam then make short work of him.

In the next scene, the Obeah woman and two robbers who have come to tell her of Jack's defeat are captured by Orford, Quashee, Sam and Tuckey. Tuckey is the character who makes much of the play happen; he reports Orford's abduction, shows Rosa to the cave where she finds Orford, and shoots Jack and wounds him, making it easier for Quashee and Sam to fall upon him. It is Tuckey again who, at the end, shows Orford the Obeah woman's cave. The contrast between Jack and Tuckey is pronounced: Tuckey is a faithful slave, while Jack has shown his disloyalty by running away. The play gives Jack no backstory, so we are not told why he has run away.

The play offers an idyllic portrayal of plantation life; we are shown a benevolent master; happy, singing slaves; touching family scenes. By contrast, Jack's life – the life of a rebel – is portrayed as a rude one; the cave in which he sleeps is filthy, his fellow robbers live a hunted life, and his friend the Obeah woman is "grotesque".

The last scene, scene 7, consists of a grand procession with the slaves, Orford, Rosa and everybody singing:

> Wander now, to and fro,
> Cross the wide Savannah,
> Now no fright Negro know,
> Beat big drum, wave fine flag,
> Bring good news to Kingston town, O.
> O no fear Jack's Obi bag,
> Quashee knock him own, O.
> . . . .
> O through dale and over hill

> The Negro now may go
> For charm he broke, and Jack he kill
> Twas Quashee give the blow.

The overseer then sings, "Here we see villainy brought by law to short duration / And may all traitors fall by British proclamation." The chorus responds: "Then let us sing God save the King! / Wander now to and fro, &c."

Fawcett's Jack is not a hero. The play is, in fact, more concerned with the restoration of order and normalcy than with presenting the rebel who threatened that order in a heroic light. Fawcett clearly sympathizes with the planters; the play is presented from their point of view as a propaganda piece countering the reports of abolitionists who have decried the harsh cruelties suffered by the slaves and who, like Earle, have lionized Jack. Fawcett's Jack is a traitor who turns his ungrateful back on the happy life of a slave. His acts of unexplained violence are a result of his own savagery; he is not, for example, presented as being motivated by desire for revenge for any injustices done to him, such as the loss of his liberty. When Fawcett has Quashee's wife sing "We negro men and women meet / And dance and sing, and drink and eat", he is deliberately portraying an idealized version of plantation life, letting the pantomime audience know that this is what Jack has left behind, not days of back-breaking work, not whippings and rape. Fawcett's slaves, rather than admiring Jack and wishing to join him, are instead persuaded that Jack's depredations are harmful, not just to planters and the plantation system, but also to themselves. "By daily working their harms", Jack threatens their happiness. He is the enemy, not the slave-owner.

Fawcett had created a masterly pro-slavery work.

Stories, plays and pantomimes set in the Caribbean, such as *Inkle and Yarico*, *Blackbeard* and *Oroonoko*, had already proved popular with British audiences, and *Obi* was no different. It played to enthusiastic audiences and became a hit which dominated the theatre scene throughout the 1800s. One of the main reasons for *Obi*'s popularity was the music composed for the pantomime by Samuel Arnold, who died two years after it was first staged. George Colman Senior had hired Arnold as composer and music director of the Little Theatre, Haymarket, in 1777 (the two had collaborated on *Inkle and Yarico* in 1787, which may be why Fawcett took his *Obi* to them). Arnold held the posts of composer and musical director until his death in 1802. During his successful twenty-five years with the theatre, he supplied it with almost a hundred operas, pantomimes and other pieces.

It was George Colman Junior, however, not his father, who was in charge of the Little Theatre by the time *Obi* was staged. Among Colman and Arnold's previous collaborations was a highly successful production of *Inkle and Yarico*, based on the story of a shipwrecked English trader. The trader falls in love with the black woman who nurses him to health, but, like Earle's Harrop, he makes plans to sell her into slavery when he returns to civilization. According to Grove, "In imitation of Blackbeard, the younger Colman accepted from the actor, Fawcett, a scheme for an exciting ballet about voodoo and kidnapping in Jamaica, and Arnold's *Obi, or Three-Fingered Jack*, proved the most successful of his three ballets. The story was mimed mainly by actors, the dancing being mostly incidental; there were a few songs for variety."[28] One account relates:

> the little Theatre made a great hit with an interesting pantomimical drama, called "Obi; or, Three Fingered Jack". This production was decidedly the best of its class. It was arranged by Fawcett, who had accidentally met with a narrative on which it was founded – a historical fact recorded by Dr Moseley in his "Treatise on Sugar". The recital was highly exciting, and was very accurately followed in the action of the pantomime, which was original on the stage at the time. The incidents and situations were well contrived by Fawcett. Baron Trenck, Caleb Williams, Count Fathom and Gil Blas have met with adventures nearly as perilous; but they had not been previously so forcibly introduced to the eye. Difficulties gradually presenting themselves, had not been so demonstratively, and unexpectedly, yet naturally surmounted. It was justly denominated a pantomimical drama, for it had the merit of dramatic arrangement. Charles Kemble was the animated representative of Three Fingered Jack, and Miss Decamp displayed the graces of her figure and accomplishments, which, in this line of the drama, she at that period, incontestably possessed. Farley exhibited his usual cleverness. The music, principally composed by Dr Arnold, was most appropriate, and the scenery by Whitmore very much surpassed any former effort of the Haymarket Theatre.[29]

The reviewer for the *Lady's Monthly Museum* noted the presentation of

> a new Pantomimical Drama . . . under the title of "Obi; or, Three Fingered Jack". The scene is laid in Jamaica and the fable is founded on the real history of a runaway slave of that name, who was a man of great bodily strength, courage

---

28 *The New Grove Dictionary of Music and Musicians*, ed. Stanley Sadie (London: Macmillan, 1980), 1:617.

29 Richard Brinsley Peake, *Memoirs of the Colman Family* (London: Richard Bentley, 1841), 2:284.

244   OBEAH, RACE AND RACISM

and agility, qualities which, aided by the difficult nature of the country, enabled him to elude all pursuit for two years, from 1779 to 1781, during which time, as a free-booter, he was the terror of all the neighbouring inhabitants.

On a reward being offered, "two slaves" decided to

engage in this arduous undertaking. . . . Such were his strength and ferocity, that he was on the point of vanquishing them both, when the little boy wounded him with a pistol shot, and he was overcome. So far the composer of this Piece has faithfully adhered to fact, and retailed all the interest which a real possess over a feigned story . . . for the great body of interest and mass of embellishment the composer has drawn from his imagination. . . . Of all Pantomimes for some time produced there is not one superior to the present in intelligibility. In the whole progress of the story, in every incident, and every particular circumstance, the meaning forces itself upon the mind, and supersedes the necessity of all dialogue. In this performance, the graceful action of Miss De Camp, the heroine of the piece, was much admired . . . the prevailing beauty in the Piece is the scenery, in which the nature of the country and of the fable has afforded an opportunity of introducing a great variety of picturesque views of rocks and caverns richly coloured, the machinery of which is managed with the most perfect precision.[30]

The *Whitehall Evening Post* was equally fulsome in its praise. The critic notes that the "pantomimical novelty" was

avowedly founded upon a story respecting a famous Negro Robber, which Dr Moseley has introduced in his Treatise on Sugar. Obi is a supposed magical power exercised by some of the Negroes, which enables them to annoy their enemies – the hero of this drama, it seems, was really a formidable marauder in Jamaica, in 1780, who excited great terror among the Negroes, and committed many ravages, but always escaped punishment by his bravery, his artifice, and the supernatural powers which were imputed to him. . . . [This] Fable forcibly interests the feelings. The great defect of the piece, however, is that Jack exhibits no proof of the power of his Obi, but is merely a valiant robber, so that the title of the piece is a misnomer.

However, he concedes that "the scenery is beautiful, and the acting is calculated to give full effect to the fable. The music, partly selected, and partly original, by Dr Arnold, is well suited to the incidents, and is, on the whole, excellent.

---

30   *Lady's Monthly Museum*, 1 August 1800, 151.

... The house was crowded to its utmost extent, and the piece was received with very great applause."[31]

The *Morning Post and Gazetteer* observed that "the house overflowed at an early hour and we should suppose the repetition of the piece, will, for some time, be productive of a similar effect".[32] In fact, the pantomime was still being produced, in one form or another, up to the late 1800s. An announcement for the Royal Coburg Theatre in the *Morning Chronicle* of December 1818 "respectfully informed" the public "that the favourite serio-pantomime of *Obi or Three Fingered Jack* is in a forward state of revival and will be produced as soon as the new picturesque scenery and dresser are completed".[33] A review in the same paper several months later states: "Three Fingered Jack has lost none of its original popularity. The scenery is beautiful and the acting of Messrs Bradley, Paulo, and Howell, jun. with Smith, and Mrs W Barrymore as Jack and Rosa gave universal delight."[34]

In 1816, almost four decades after the real-life events which inspired Jack's legend, several British newspapers reported on the death of John Reeder, "the conqueror of that celebrated character Three Fingered Jack, on the 27th January, 1781". Reeder died in Hannah's Town; the newspapers reported that "he did not know his exact age but was a stout boy at the first peace with the Maroons in 1739 and must therefore be about 100 years of age".[35] The *Caledonian Mercury* of 4 November notes that "Reeder had received the reward of £100 offered by the proclamation of Major-General John Daling . . . and afterwards had an annual stipend of £25, which was increased of late to £30, and paid under the poll tax law". The paper goes on to recount Moseley's version of events, explaining that "though this subject has been dramatized, and was well-known in all its particulars at the time, yet there is so much chivalrous interest in the story, that it will bear repetition even to those of our readers to whom it does not bear the charm of novelty". The paper does not fail to repeat Bryant's etymology for *Obeah*, assuring readers that the practice was associated with the ancient Egyptians and with the demon Ob, "a spirit of divination and magic".[36]

---

31 *Whitehall Evening Post*, 1 July 1800.
32 *Morning Post*, 3 July 1800.
33 *Morning Chronicle*, December 1818.
34 *Morning Chronicle*, 6 August 1819.
35 *Hull Packet and Original Weekly Commercial*, 5 November 1816.
36 *Caledonian Mercury*, 4 November 1816.

"BY FLAME UNBODIED BURN HIM"

Almost three decades after the staging of Fawcett's *Obi*, another production made its way to theatres. On 13 March 1828, *Trewman's Exeter Flying Post* reported: "The Manager of Covent Garden Theatre intends to present his holiday visitors, at Easter, with a new version of the popular Pantomimic Drama of Obi, or Three Fingered Jack. O. Smith is to sustain the part of Obi."[37] Richard John "Obi" Smith had spent some time on the Guinea coast and had been acting in pantomimes since at least 1810, but it was his "singularly fortunate performance"[38] in the role of Fawcett's Three Finger'd Jack that earned him the nickname "Obi", by which he was known for most of his professional life. In fact, he played the part of Jack for several years. Much in the same way that certain actors nowadays are associated with the parts of villains and supernatural bad guys, the *Monthly Magazine* noted that Smith went over well in "wild, gloomy, and ominous characters in which a bold, or rather a gigantic, figure and a deep sepulchral voice could be turned to good account".[39]

Obi; or, Three-Finger'd Jack: A Melodrama in Two Acts begins in much the same way as the pantomime, with the slaves and the overseer singing, but the threat of Obeah and the fear of it is introduced almost right away, when the overseer, announcing the holiday because of Rosa's birthday, says, "Let the sugar canes take care of themselves, and hey for mirth and merriment. And a fig for Obi, and Three Finger'd Jack." The slaves draw closer to the overseer and, looking around cautiously, they entreat him to be quiet. "What the devil's the matter with you all?" the overseer responds. "Has the name of that three-fingered rascal power to stop your mirth so suddenly?"

Sam, as cautious as the rest, replies, "Oh, massa, take care, he hear us and make Obi woman kill us."

The overseer, predictably, dismisses their trepidation as foolishness. "Nonsense, nonsense! ye black ninny hammers", he exclaims. "Do you think an old woman, as great a noodle as yourselves, can stop your wind-pipes by cramming parrots feathers, dogs' teeth, broken bottles, rum, and egg-shells into a cow's horn, and then mumbling a few words over it, as incomprehensible as your own fears?"

---

37 *Trewman's Exeter Flying Post*, 13 March 1828.
38 "The Theatre: Its Literature and General Arrangements", *Monthly Magazine or British Register* 2 (July–December 1826): 54.
39 Ibid.

Quashee is not easily persuaded. "Oh, massa", he says. "You say what you please, but Obi woman know ebery ting from top of head to bottom of toe; and if once she put Obi on poor negro man, he no eat, he no drink, he no nothing, but pine, pine, pine, pine, pine and die away."

"Why, ladies and gentlemen, to judge from your aversion to work," the overseer says, "Obi seems rather a fashionable disorder, but as to not eating, drinking, or sleeping, I really discover no symptoms of the complaint, so set your minds at rest, and enjoy the sports."

Ormond, the plantation owner, then enters and the slaves surround him, "expressing great affection for him", before exiting the stage, shouting their joy at the holiday. Observing this, the overseer grumpily remarks, "Ay! they can shout loud enough now, though but a moment ago, the very name of Obi and Three-fingered Jack struck them as dumb as –." But Ormond interrupts him and gives a backstory to Jack that never appears in Fawcett's pantomime, or in any other known version.

Ormond tells the overseer that Karfa, as Jack was then known, possessed a "savage nature" and that each day he became more and more ferocious: "crime followed crime, until the villain dared to attempt the honour of my wife". Jack was apprehended but escaped during the night, broke into Ormond's bedroom and killed his wife before Ormond could stop him. Though attempts have been made to recapture him, Ormond says that "all have failed; the negroes dread his incantations, and many of our colour believe him possessed of some supernatural power".

Scene 1 ends with the arrival of Orford, and scene 2 is a brief scene between Tuckey and Kitty, a white servant woman whom Tuckey admires. Interestingly, Kitty asks Tuckey where he learned to forget the difference between white and black, and he responds, "in England". He later sighs to himself that "we poor blacks have a weary time of it, and are as much railed at as if the darkness of our skins were a sample of the colour of our hearts".

Scene 3 takes place in the Obeah woman's hut, as opposed to the traditional cave. A bench before the fire is covered in a white cloth, on which rests a figure. The Obeah woman possesses a "wand" with charms and a handful of feathers. An iron pot is suspended above the fire, near which sits the Obeah woman "forming an Obi. After performing several incantations, she speaks:

> Magic fire duly placed
> In square within a circle traced,
> Boil the mystic herbs I've brought,

> Till the Obi charm be wrought;
> Bones I've raked from the burial ground,
> When night and the storm were black around;
> Give strength to my work, till I've fixed my dart,
> Like a cankerous thorn in the white man's heart –
> Till I pierce him and wring him in nerve and spleen
> By the arrows felt, but never seen.
>
> Then by flame unbodied burn him,
> Then on racking windlass turn him,
>
> Till his sinews quiver and ache anew,
> And the cold sweat falls like drops of dew,
> Toil him and moil him again and again,
> Sicken his heart and madden his brain;
> Till strength, and sense, and life depart,
> As I tear the last pulse from the white man's heart.

Karfa/Jack knocks on the Obeah woman's door. "Well, mother", he greets her. "How work our charms? Do they hasten to an end or still, tortoise like, so creep to their completion, that the white man's breath is more like to waste with age than be stopped by my revenge?" When she remonstrates with him for his impatience, he forgets the courtesy with which he had greeted her and snarls:

> Impatience – impatience, hag! The gods of my fathers frown on my delay. Years have elapsed since I sacrificed the wife of the white man, a victim to the memory of my beloved Olinda, whom they tore lifeless from these arms as they dragged me from my native land; can I forget? Can I forgive? Never. And long ere this should vengeance have been satisfied, had not a mistaken faith in thy mummery restrained my arm.

So this Jack is no great believer in Obeah but views it as a tool to use against the superstitious. The Obeah woman, understandably, takes offence at his attitude and suggests that he "Rail not on Obi, lest [he] feels its power".

"Power?" Karfa/Jack scoffs.

> Thy power is in the fear of thy votaries – and fear I know not. As Africa receded from my gaze I swore that the first white man who purchased Karfa's services should also feel his hate. Ormond was that man. The wife of his bosom was my first victim, and long ere this should his bones have been mouldering in the grave, but that you promised a sweeter, though a slower vengeance.

The Obeah woman promises him that Ormond will die. "But here have I his image made in wax, and as it is molten by a blue fire kindled with dead men's eyes, so shall he waste, waste, waste."

Despite his avowed unbelief, Jack asks her how long the charm will take to work. When she tells him a month, he responds that not one more day will pass without his taking his revenge for his dead wife, Olinda, their "helpless infants, and the wrongs of my poor country". The Obeah woman puts some feathers into his horn and tells him to "trust that Obi" but is interrupted by Jack. "Obi!" he exclaims. "Here is the charm I trust!" and he holds up his dagger.

Scene 4 is brief and shows Orford, Ormond, Tuckey and others hunting. Foreshadowing what is to come, Tuckey preens with pride at Orford's praise for his shooting. In scene 5, Jack captures Orford when he becomes separated from the rest of the hunting party and takes him to his cave. In the following scene, Quashee sings as he prepares for the dance that night. Scene 7 opens with the slaves singing, but the festivities are interrupted by Ormond, who reports that Jack has killed Orford and asks for their aid in killing "the blood-stained villain, Karfa". The slaves shiver with alarm, drawing reproach from Ormond, who reminds them

> poor Orford was the black man's friend. Oft at his intercession has the hand of punishment been stayed; and with my Rosa, often has he stood by the bed of sickness, and soothed the sorrows of the poor negro; yet now, subdued by vain and superstitious terrors, ye tremble to avenge the murder of your benefactor. For shame! For shame! Be men; and by one bold effort, let us rid ourselves of this detested wretch.

The overseer then sings his song asking the slaves to swear to kill Jack, after which Quashee approaches Ormond with his wife and child in tow.

"Massa!" Quashee says. "You have been kind massa to me; and Missee Rosa been kind missee to wife and pickaninny here, and I now show you black man's heart beat warm as white. I will go; and if I meet this Jack, Quashee will kill him, or him kill Quashee, only if poor nigger die, you take care of wife and little Massa Quashee." Sam immediately signs up too, declaring that he will not let Quashee go alone. Ormond frees them on the spot and encourages them to "fear not his wily stratagems – his magic art – all will fail before the arm that's nerved by freedom and by gratitude. This night continue your feast; let not my sorrows taint the few moments you have of mirth. Nay, 'tis my command. Tonight celebrate your new-found liberty, tomorrow for vengeance!" Of course, a bit more than a simple declaration was necessary for a slave's freedom to be secured, but the passage removes any need for reference to the governor's proclamation or that of the House of Assembly.

Jack has been given a backstory and a reason to desire the downfall of whites, but his reasons are presented as originating in the distant past; what happened to Olinda and Jack's children happened in Africa, not in Jamaica, where slaves, however brutally they may have been torn from Africa, are depicted as living a life of comparative ease. The passage above makes clear the expectation of gratitude on the part of blacks for their removal from Africa. Unspoken is the suggestion that the lives of slaves in the Caribbean were an improvement over the lives they might have led back home. As in the pantomime, this is the unspoken message of the play, with its scenes of happy, singing slaves living a life of comparative ease and order on the plantation – a life that Jack and, by extension, other rebels have rejected.

The slaves go back to singing and dancing and Quashee sings:

> Jack have charm in Obi bag,
> Tom cat foot, pig tail, duck beak.
> Quashee tear the charm to rag,
> Make Three-fingered Jack to squeak.
> Now we dance, sing, and eat,
> With a yam foo-foo, with a yam foo-foo.

Act 1 ends and act 2 begins with Ormond finding out that Rosa has disguised herself to join Quashee and Sam's expedition against Jack. Ormond calls on his slaves to arm themselves and follow him in pursuit of Rosa. Scene 2 sees the storm burst on the mountains and Rosa, lost, enters a cave, seeking shelter. Jack captures Rosa, thinking her a boy, in scene 3 and tells her she will be his servant for life, since he cannot allow her to leave and tell others of his cave. In scene 4, Karfa/Jack shows off his cave and says to Rosa, "Your white man, I am told, can soar into the air, fathom the deep, ransack the mine, and enslave in every clime where his accursed arts find access. Here, here alone, no white man finds an entrance, but as Karfa's slave." He drinks some rum, commands her to sing for him and falls asleep as she sings "Lady in Fair Seville City". Rosa then discovers Orford. They are attempting to make their escape when Jack awakes, seizes Rosa and shoots at Orford, who falls. In scene 5, meanwhile, Ormond has caught up with Tuckey, who informs him that Quashee and Sam are in hot pursuit of Jack.

Rosa begs for her life in scene 6, but Karfa/Jack responds:

I had a daughter once; did they spare her harmless infancy? Where is my wife? Was she spared to me? No! With blood and rapine the white man swept like a hurricane o'er our native village, and blasted every hope! Can aught efface the terrible remembrance from my soul, how at their lordly feet we begged for mercy and found it not? Our women knelt, our infants shrieked in vain, as the blood-stained murderer ranged from hut to hut, dragging the husband and the father from their homes, to sell them into bondage! No more, no more! The vext spirits of my wife and child hover o'er me like a holy curse, and claim this due revenge.

Karfa/Jack is about to stab her with his dagger when Quashee leaps out from behind a rock, crying that he will not see her hurt. Jack contemptuously greets him with one word: "Slave!" But Quashee informs him that he has been freed. "Me no slave! Me free! Me gentleman, me Mr. Quashee now, and no care a button for you or Obi either." Rosa twists away and Quashee and Sam fall on Jack, who is shot by Tuckey and then finished off. The play ends with Quashee and Sam shaking hands and much celebratory shouting by the slaves and others.

The melodrama is interesting in several respects, not least in that, while it may boast a stronger role for Jack, the stereotypes of blacks that it presents are even more wide-ranging than those suggested by either the pantomime from which it borrows so heavily or the various chapbook editions. In addition to the superstitious blacks frightened of Obeah and the singing slaves making merry and being grateful for "kind massa", British audiences were also presented with a Karfa/Jack who, in his assault on the "honour" of Ormond's wife, conforms to European expectations about black men's lust for white women. Tuckey's liking for the white Kitty, a new twist, reinforces the stereotype. All in all, Karfa/Jack is equally as unsympathetic in this play as he is in the pantomime, though he has been given both a voice and a backstory to justify his enmity against Ormond. Audience-goers could hardly have failed to come away without the conviction that the planters and other whites of plantation society had been uniformly kind and generous. Any violence or cruelty associated with slavery had taken place back in Africa, by the traders who seized the captives from their homes. Ormond earned Jack's enmity not because of his cruelty but simply because he had been the one to purchase Jack. This was clearly irrational of Jack, but irrationality is only one of the stereotypes attributed to blacks presented by the play.

Again and again, the play drives home the point that blacks were lazy, superstitious, cowardly, ungrateful and savage. Jack, scornful of Obeah and determined to get revenge for the deaths of his wife and children, is not the hero; that designation belongs to Quashee, who, thinking Jack has killed Orford and grateful for the kind treatment he received from the latter, volunteers to avenge the white man's death. Quashee is then freed by Ormond. Having gained his freedom not by running away or becoming a rebel, but by being given it, Quashee can declare to Jack that he's a "gentleman" who cares nothing for the rebellious and violent Jack or for Jack's obi. Quashee, the play suggests, received his freedom legitimately while Jack did not. Quashee is the good slave, grateful and happy; he has made a contented life for himself with his wife and children on the estate. Jack, on the other hand, lost all that back in Africa and is the Outsider, violent and full of hate, who never found a place within plantation society; in the end he is killed, an anomaly removed.

Three-Fingered Jack continued to intrigue and haunt writers and their readers throughout the nineteenth century but it was not until Ira Aldridge assumed the role of Jack in 1830 that a black actor became part of the cast.

CHAPTER 8

Credulous Blacks and Faithful Mulattoes

POPULAR FICTION BEGAN TO TAKE OFF IN the early 1800s as literacy increased and printing methods enabled writers and publishers to put out ever-increasing numbers of books for the leisure class created by the Industrial Revolution. The West Indies was a popular setting for novelists, providing as it did an exotic backdrop against which themes of racial difference, religion and class could be explored.

"THE STORY OF HENRIETTA"

"The Story of Henrietta" appeared in volume two of *The Letters of a Solitary Wanderer: Containing Narratives of Various Descriptions*, by Charlotte Turner Smith. Though she was born into a wealthy family, by the time she was fifteen Charlotte's father was facing bankruptcy. She was forced into an early marriage to Benjamin Smith, the son of a West India merchant who owned plantations in Barbados. Benjamin was violent and unfaithful and the marriage was an unhappy one, though it produced twelve children. Charlotte later condemned her father for turning her into a "legal prostitute", a theme she returns to in "The Story of Henrietta".

Charlotte's first published work was a book of poetry which came out in 1784 and paid for her and her husband's release from debtor's prison. She left her husband in 1787 and published her first novel, *Emmeline*, a year later. Charlotte went on to write several other well-received novels and works of poetry and gained the admiration of contemporaries such as William Wordsworth, Walter Scott and Samuel Coleridge. Her correspondents also included Robert Southey, Erasmus Darwin, Thomas Erskine and Richard Brinsley Sheridan.

Her popularity was on the wane by the time *Letters* was published, however. Three years after its publication she was ill and on the verge of bankruptcy. She died destitute in 1806 and was then largely forgotten.

"The Story of Henrietta", published in 1801, is recounted by a narrator who informs readers that Henrietta herself and her fiancé, Denbigh, told it to him. After her mother's death, Henrietta's father, Mr Maynard, sends her away from Jamaica to live in England with her aunt, while he keeps her brother behind to grow up on the island. Years later, when the aunt dies, Henrietta decides to visit her father. Her suitor, Denbigh, also the owner of property in Jamaica, wants to go with her but is able to take passage only on another ship sailing at the same time. Denbigh's ship becomes separated from the main convoy during a storm, but Henrietta arrives safely in Jamaica.

Among Henrietta's surprises when she arrives is the discovery that she has several mulatto half-sisters who live in their father's house. Maynard, meanwhile, is often away fighting the Maroons, but, like Smith's real-life father, he has matrimonial plans for Henrietta and wishes her to accept the suit of a man by the name of Sawkins, whom the slaves know to be a bad and cruel man. Sawkins is poor and low-born but Henrietta's father wants him to be in his debt, which is why he supports the marriage. Maynard tells her that she must obey him and informs her that she should put Denbigh out of her mind, since his ship was captured by a French privateer. He hates the very idea of Denbigh because he is supposed to be a reformer, and thus, to Maynard, something of a traitor in supporting better conditions for the slaves. The only person on the plantation whom Henrietta trusts is Amponah, a male slave who once accompanied her brother to England and stayed at her aunt's house. She is frightened of and distrusts everyone else.

When a hurricane damages the estate, Henrietta's father sends her to another of his estates, a place in the north, where she comes in contact with Obeah. In this isolated place "there are times when the hideous phantasies of these poor uninformed savages affect my spirits with a sort of dread, which all my conviction of their fallacy does not enable me to subdue".

One of her mulatto half-sisters, Little Maria, would

> talk to me of their Obeahs, persons who persuade others, and perhaps believe themselves, that they possess supernatural powers, acquired by I know not what operations, resembling, as far as I could learn, those of the witches in Macbeth round the magic cauldron. I afterwards fancied that the two or three the little girl pointed out to me had something particularly horrid in their appearance;

> yet, as they are liable to severe punishment if their being Obi men or women is known, they carefully conceal any outward appearance of their profession. But the mulattoes, and the unfortunate children belonging to them and white parents, who are brought up amidst all the vices and superstitions of the negroes, are too apt to imbibe both the one and the other; and what attempts have been made to give them other ideas, seem to me only to have made in their minds a sort of "darkness visible". These Obi men and women are, as I have been informed, more numerous here than in other plantations: and I shudder involuntarily when I fancy, from the mysterious looks and odd gestures of some of them, that they are deeply initiated in these wild rites of superstition.[1]

Amponah tells her that her father plans to come with Sawkins and a clergyman and get her married off, something he says that has been foretold by the Obeah practitioners. At first Henrietta scorns their warnings: "The wretched creatures of whom I have spoken, that pass here for having the power to look into futurity, in vain declare that a marriage and great festival will soon happen here."[2] In true Gothic tradition, Henrietta is isolated in a distant part of the island, far from those who might offer their help, among people she terms "savages", while an atmosphere of growing evil closes in around her. "Misery so overwhelming as that which threatens me will destroy me. I hear again the gombay in the woods; I hear the strange yells as of savage triumph, and I shudder to think that there is no alternative" to the wedding.[3]

The next part of the story has been told to the narrator by Denbigh, who says that he finally arrived in Jamaica after about six months and hurried to Maynard's nearest estate. Maynard is not there and the slaves refuse to tell him where he can find the planter and his daughter. Desperate to save Henrietta from what he has learned of her father's machinations, Denbigh rides off into the mountains but is hurt when his horse falls. His black servant goes to look for help and finds a party of Maroons, who treat Denbigh well though they take him prisoner. "I was now their prisoner; yet a prisoner towards whom they were disposed to shew every sort of kindness, on the report of my servant, whose honest solicitude for me convinced them I was not one of those whom their unfortunate race have reason to pursue with execrations and with vengeance."[4]

---

1 Charlotte Turner Smith, "The Story of Henrietta", in *The Letters of a Solitary Wanderer: Containing Narratives of Various Descriptions* (London: Sampson Low, 1800), 2:96–98.
2 Ibid., 100.
3 Ibid., 101.
4 Ibid., 112.

The Maroon leader informs Denbigh that Maynard's northern estate has been destroyed in retaliation for the planter's cruelty towards them. The white women and the slaves found on the estate are now captives of the Maroons. Despite his avowed sympathy for the "unfortunate race", this news fills Denbigh with racial dread: "She was released from the power of Maynard only to fall into that of savages, always terrible in their passions, and in whom the fierce inclination for European women was now likely to be exalted by the desire of revenge on a man so detested as the father of my unhappy Henrietta!"[5]

Some time later, Henrietta's captors stop near a stream to refresh themselves and rest. Some began to cook, a few go to fill their calabashes with water and some began to drink their rum. In the scene that ensues, Smith employs the literary trope of "the devil's revelry", discussed earlier, as a way of underlining or highlighting the savagery of blacks and the extent of the danger Henrietta faces at their hands. "I shall never forget the group as they appeared beneath the bright light of the moon then at full. The strange dresses, where Indian nakedness was oddly intermingled with military ornaments; their dark faces, and that peculiar look of ferocity which the eye of the negro rolling in its deep socket gives to the whole race of Africans."[6]

The next day the Maroons who have captured Denbigh are set upon by the militia. Two Maroons are killed and the others stab Denbigh in retaliation, leaving him to die on the ground. Denbigh is badly injured and loses a lot of blood, but an Englishman, a hermit living in the mountains, finds him, takes him back to his cave and looks after him. After he recovers, Denbigh explores the cave, finds a door at the back and opens it. On the other side he finds Henrietta and is joyfully reunited with her. When the Englishman returns, Denbigh confronts him, fearing that he is in cahoots with the Maroons, but the man asks Denbigh to trust him and tells him that they all need to leave the cave. He says that the Maroons have gone on an expedition, so now is the safest time to go through the mountains. Denbigh is suspicious about the man's relationship with Henrietta but is persuaded to flee the cave.

The hermit leads them away from the mountain forest to the home of a widow, from where the military escorts them to St Jago de la Vega. Later, the hermit explains to Henrietta and Denbigh that he is actually Maynard's brother, whom Maynard has treated cruelly. He relates the sad story of his life and his failed marriages and tells them that, sometime after his son's death, he

---

5   Ibid., 114.
6   Ibid., 119.

came to Jamaica, hoping "to do some good for this miserable race". His lenient treatment of the slaves on his estate caused the other planters to consider him a lunatic who should be confined, lest his mercies to the Negroes stir them up. Before they could have him put in an asylum, he leased out his estates with ameliorative conditions and retired to a cave.

At the end of the story we learn from Henrietta how she came to be in her uncle's cave. When Amponah is warned by the Obeah women that Henrietta is in danger, he urges her to flee with him. "The Obi women had been in the woods employed on their spells, and they discovered that some great misfortune was about to happen to me, and would happen if I did not immediately leave the house and take shelter in some other place."[7] Amponah takes her away from the estate, but it turns out that he wants her for his own wife. "I saw his eyes roll, and his features assume an expression which still haunts my dreams. . . . 'Missy, I tell trute now – I love you. I no slave now; I *my* master and yours. Missy, there no difference now; you be my wife. I love you from a child!'"[8] Henrietta prepares to throw herself off a cliff rather than accept his advances but is saved by Maroons, who kill Amponah. Their leader then reveals that he rescued her from Amponah because he wants her for his wife himself. He describes her as "a beautiful white woman . . . to be added to the number of his wives".[9] Here we can see that Smith has laid on very thickly the theme of black men's desire for white women.

The leader and his men take Henrietta to their cave, where she is put in the care of the chief's wives while the men fortify themselves with "drink" before heading back out on a raid. "The oldest of the women turned and came towards me. I never beheld so hideous, so disgusting a creature; and such was the dread with which I was inspired as she hung over me that I was once more on the point of losing my misery in insensibility." The woman offers her a mixture of rum and goat's milk which Henrietta dares not refuse. "The menacing attitude and countenance assumed by the sorceress terrified me into immediate submission", so she drinks it.[10] Interestingly, Henrietta appears to have made up her mind that the old woman is a sorceress, based on nothing more, at this point, than the woman's age and "hideous" looks. Not interested in sharing their husband with yet another wife, the leader's two wives help her to escape.

---

7 Ibid., 297.
8 Ibid., 303.
9 Ibid., 307
10 Ibid., 309–10.

Henrietta finds her happily-ever-after ending when Denbigh marries her and they return to England.

Smith is credited with being one of the earliest writers to establish the conventions of Gothic fiction, and "The Story of Henrietta" employs many of the tropes that would become familiar to fans of the genre. Henrietta is a young and virginal heroine isolated in an exoticized and menacing country and tyrannized by an arch-villain, her father. Denbigh is the gallant hero, though a rather lacklustre one, since he himself becomes a captive and is not the one who rescues Henrietta. According to the conventions of the genre, Henrietta is set upon by various other villains, such as Amponah and the Maroons. Drums beat in the distance, servants and slaves whisper of obeah, and evil closes in on her from all sides.

Charlotte's father-in-law, Richard Smith, owned slave plantations in the West Indies and had taken a few of his slaves to England, where Charlotte may have met them. She describes the slaves as savages but slavery appears to have made her uncomfortable and she later expresses abolitionist sympathies in other works. Certainly in "The Story of Henrietta" she presents us with a father who rules over his daughter almost as tyrannically as he does over his slaves; it is likely that she recognized the power granted to slave-owners as not being very different from those assumed by white men (such as her real-life father) over their daughters. But, concerned with making her point about the "legal prostitution" into which Henrietta is being forced, Charlotte offers only caricatured portrayals of blacks, who are uniformly presented as superstitious and duplicitous, if not plain violent.

BELINDA

Maria Edgeworth's novel *Belinda* appeared in 1801, a year after "The Story of Henrietta" was published. Edgeworth's first book, *Letters for Literary Ladies*, was published in 1795, but it was not until the publication of *Castle Rackrent* in 1800 that she achieved commercial success. She was to go on to achieve even greater fame with *Patronage* in 1814, and wrote several novels and non-fiction works until her death in 1849. Though she may not be as well known today as Jane Austen or Sir Walter Scott, she was one of the leading novelists of her day and widely admired. Scott himself claimed to have been inspired by her. Austen was equally impressed. Of *Belinda*, she wrote that it was a "work in which the greatest powers of the mind are displayed, in which the most thorough knowledge of human nature, the happiest delineation of its varieties, the liveliest effusions of wit and humour, are conveyed to the world in the best chosen language".[11]

Edgeworth's writing was often praised. In an 1852 article in the *Ladies' Cabinet of Fashion, Music and Romance*, her writing is described as "diversified and striking takes of character and life", and she is extolled as evidence "that the intellect of woman may possess commanding influence". Edgeworth's "name still holds its high place, and her fame remains undiminished and unobscured",[12] but the woman who once mixed with such luminaries as Lord Byron and Sir Humphry Davy and counted Walter Scott among her friends was by then largely unknown.

Belinda Portman, the eponymous heroine of the novel, is a young woman sent by her aunt to live with Lady Delacour and her husband so that she might be shown in society and acquire a husband. Lady Delacour is fashionable and a great wit, but her husband drinks and their marriage is unhappy. Worse, like a woman Obeahed, Lady Delacour believes she is dying; her face, excessively made up, reveals the ravages once the makeup comes off: "Lady Delacour's eyes were sunk, her cheeks hollow; no trace of youth or beauty remained on her death-like countenance." "My mind is eaten away like my body by incurable disease – inveterate remorse", Lady Delacour says.[13] In reality, she is a hypochondriac who believes she has cancer, and she has fallen under the sway of a doctor repeatedly described as a quack, who, in the manner of an Obeah man, persuades her that she is nearly at death's door. He prescribes all kinds of medicines for her, including opium and laudanum, so she is sometimes out of her mind.

Interestingly, during a discussion of developments in the medical field, one of Lady Delacour's acquaintances reveals that she had heard

> an account of sundry wonderful cures that had been performed, to her certain knowledge, by her favourite concentrated extract or anima or quassia. She entered into the history of the negro slave named Quassi, who discovered this medical wood, which he kept a close secret till Mr Daghlberg, a magistrate of Surinam, wormed it out of him, brought a branch of the tree to Europe, and communicated it to the great Linnaeus.[14]

(This was the Quassi discussed in an earlier chapter.)

---

11 Jane Austen, *Northanger Abbey* (London: Richard Bentley, 1848), 23.
12 *Englishwoman's Domestic Magazine*, 1 July 1852, 65.
13 Maria Edgeworth, *Belinda* (London: J. Johnson, 1801), 1:57–60.
14 Ibid., 163.

Some of Lady Delacour's unhappiness stems from the fact that she married her husband to spite the man she really loved, while Lord Delacour, who was then a gambler, married her for her money. She had started spending wildly, which, in addition to his gambling, threatened to bankrupt them, so they sold off land and other possessions to pay their bills. Then a rich uncle of Lord Delacour's died, leaving him restored to wealth. He stopped gambling but turned to drink instead, under the impression that Lady Delacour loved another man. Two of her children died young and she was blamed for it. Her third child, a little girl, lived, but by then Lady Delacour had little interest in motherhood and had infrequent contact with her. More recently, Lady Delacour has become friends with Harriet Freke, another woman who is a great wit and much given to the social whirl. In the meantime, Belinda has met Clarence Hervey, with whom she falls in love. They determine to rescue Lady Delacour from her dissipation and save her relationship with her daughter.

In volume two, Belinda and the rest of the characters meet Mr Vincent, who has just returned from the West Indies and has brought the slave Juba with him. Everyone goes to Harrowgate House for an extended party, and there Juba has a confrontation with Mrs Freke's servants over the use of the coach house. Juba prevails but the whole argument has been overheard by Mrs Freke, who swears to punish him. As their stay at Harrowgate progresses, Juba becomes more and more morose and disconsolate. His mood improves only after they leave, but when Vincent asks him to go back to Harrowgate House for something he forgot there, Juba confesses his fears.

"'Oh, massa, Juba die! If Juba go back, Juba die!' and he wiped away the drops that stood upon his forehead. 'But me will go, if massa bid – me will die!'" Vincent says he will protect him, but Juba tells him he cannot.

> "Ah, massa, you no can! Me die, if me go back! Me no can say word more"; and he put his finger upon his lips and shook his head. Mr Vincent knew that Juba was excessively superstitious; and convinced, that, if his mind were not already deranged, it would certainly become so, were any secret terror thus to prey upon his imagination, he assured him that he should be extremely displeased if he persisted in his foolish and obstinate silence."[15]

So Juba, not only superstitious but clearly also highly emotional, breaks down in tears and tells him.

---

15 Ibid., 2:141–42.

With a sort of reluctant horror, he told that the figure of an old woman, all in flames, had appeared to him in his bed-chamber at Harrowgate every night, and that he was sure she was one of the obeah-women of his own country, who had pursued him to Europe to revenge his having once, when he was a child, trampled upon an egg-shell that contained some of her poisons.

Vincent reacts as one would expect.

> The extreme absurdity of this story made Mr Vincent burst out a laughing; but his humanity the next instant made him serious; for the poor victim of superstitious terror, after having revealed what, according to the belief of his country, it is death to mention, fell senseless on the ground. When he came to himself, he calmly said, that he knew he must now die, for that the obeah-women never forgave those that talked of them or their secrets; and, with a deep groan, he added, that he wished he might die before night, that he might not see her again. It was in vain to attempt to reason him out of the idea that he had actually seen this apparition: his account of it was, that it first appeared to him in the coach-house one night, when he went thither in the dark – that he never afterwards went to the coach-house in the dark – but that the same figure of an old woman, all in flames, appeared at the foot of his bed every night whilst he stayed at Harrowgate; and that he was then persuaded she would never let him escape from her power till she had killed him. That since he had left Harrowgate, however, she had not tormented him, for he had never seen her, and he was in hopes that she had forgiven him; but that now he was sure of her vengeance for having spoken of her.
>
> Mr Vincent knew the astonishing power which the belief in this species of sorcery has over the minds of the Jamaica negroes; they pine and actually die away from the moment they fancy themselves under the malignant influence of these witches. He almost gave poor Juba over for lost.[16]

Edgeworth finds this incident so significant that she footnotes it with a reference to the excerpt from the Fuller report contained in Edwards's *History of the West Indies*.

Vincent retells the story to Belinda, who remembers a trick of a head drawn in phosphorus which glowed by night and wonders if somebody has "terrified the ignorant negro by similar means". This makes Vincent remember that Mrs Freke swore to make Juba repent his insolence, and she becomes their main suspect. To dispel Juba's fears,

---

16 Ibid., 143–46.

Miss Portman proposed that a figure be drawn with phosphorus, as nearly as possible to resemble that which Juba had described, and that it be shown to him at night, to try whether it would excite his apprehensions. Mr Vincent drew the figure of a frightful old woman on the wall, opposite the foot of Juba's bed. In the morning he told his master that he had been again visited by the obeah-woman, and he exhibited all the signs of extreme terror.

Belinda suggests that one of the children should show him the phosphorus and draw some ludicrous figure with it in his presence. This is done and it has the effect that she expected. "Juba, familiarized by degrees with the object of his secret horror, and convinced that no obeah-woman was exercising over him her sorceries, recovered his health and spirits. His gratitude to Miss Portman was as simple and touching as it was lively and sincere."[17] Juba later composes a song that "described in the strongest manner what had been his feelings whilst he was under the terror of Mrs Freke's fiery obeah-woman, then his joy on being relieved from those horrors, with the delightful sensations of returning health".

In the first edition of *Belinda*, Juba courts Lucy, an eighteen-year-old white girl, one of the maids, who is at first a bit offended by his affection and frightened by "Juba's black face". Though this is again demonstrative of the conviction that black men were consumed by a desire for white women, it is significant that Edgeworth had none of the other characters object to this, not even Lucy's grandparents, who point out that Juba is an "industrious, ingenious, good-natured youth". They eventually get married with Vincent's blessing and the gift of a small house on his farm, and Juba disappears from the rest of the story. In the end, Harriet Freke gets her comeuppance and Lady Delacour, whose sickness was all in her mind, recovers her health and, with Belinda's help, is restored to the bosom of her loving husband and daughter.

Though Juba's courtship of Lucy also appears in the 1802 edition of the book, the interracial relationship was left out of subsequent editions at the instigation of Edgeworth's father, who edited her books. "My father says that gentlemen have horrors upon this subject, and would draw conclusions very unfavourable to a female writer who appeared to recommend such unions: as I do not understand the subject, I trust to his better judgement", Edgeworth wrote to the editor of a series of books by English novelists.[18]

---

17   Ibid., 146.
18   Kathryn J. Kirkpatrick, "'Gentlemen Have Horrors upon This Subject': West Indian Suitors in Maria Edgeworth's *Belinda*". *Eighteenth-Century Fiction* 5, no. 4 (September 2010): 342.

Though Juba is portrayed as simple and superstitious, he is a sympathetic character, grateful and eager to please, and is not described in the savagely derogatory terms used by Cynric Williams and Scott. Edgeworth's willingness to give Juba a relationship with a white woman (even a lower-class one) suggests a lack of racial feeling that was not shared by many of her contemporaries. In addition, the way in which Mrs Freke behaves – employing science to create a "supernatural" scare and recall Juba's fears of Obeah – makes Harriet herself into something of an Obeah woman, raising the possibility that Edgeworth may have consciously wanted to point out that evil people could also be white, a suggestion she makes more explicit in *The Grateful Negro*.

Interestingly, while in the first edition Edgeworth gives Belinda and Vincent their own budding love story and they come close to getting married, in the later editions she "esteems" him highly but feels nothing else for him. It is possible that Edgeworth's father also suggested this change. By the time the later editions of *Belinda* were published, the tide had turned decisively against West Indian planters and against continuation of the slave trade; this may have factored in the decision to scale back Belinda's relationship with the slave-owning Vincent.

"THE GRATEFUL NEGRO"

In Edgeworth's story "The Grateful Negro", which appeared in an 1804 collection, two planters in Jamaica, Jefferies and Edwards, treat their slaves very differently. Jefferies considers the Negroes "an inferior species, incapable of gratitude, disposed to treachery, and to be roused from their natural indolence only by force". His overseer, Durant, is of the same mind and "did not scruple to use the most cruel and barbarous methods of forcing the slaves" to work hard.[19]

By contrast, Mr Edwards, a neighbouring planter,

> treated his slaves with all possible humanity and kindness. He wished that there was no such thing as slavery in the world, but he was convinced . . . that the sudden emancipation of the negroes would rather increase than diminish their miseries. . . . [consequently] He adopted those plans for the amelioration of the state of the slaves which appeared to him the most likely to succeed, without producing any violent agitation or revolution.

---

19 Maria Edgeworth, "The Grateful Negro", in *Harry and Lucy, Lame Jervas, and The Grateful Negro* (London: W. and R. Chambers, 1804), 253.

Edwards's slaves are paid for extra work and, once they are finished their regular tasks, they can do as they wish. His overseer, Abraham Bayley, is a humane man who carries out Edwards's ameliorative instructions. In addition, Edwards is a paragon who does not gamble or get into debt as Jefferies does.

One day, Edwards discovers that Caesar, Jefferies's "best negro", is to be sold away from Clara, the woman he is planning to marry, from his cottage and from his banana field, in which he works so hard. Caesar and Clara beg Edwards to buy them and declare that they will serve him faithfully. He makes no promises but goes to see Jefferies. The two planters argue. Jefferies maintains that slaves are happier in the New World "than they ever were in their own country" and says he was told so by people "better informed than negroes". He points out that the planters "would be ruined if they had no slaves", but Edwards replies that sugar can be produced just as well by free men working for wages, and that Negroes work no harder under an overseer than a Birmingham journeyman toiling for himself and his family. "The instant a slave touches English ground he becomes free", Edwards points out. "Glorious privilege! Why should it not be extended to all her dominions?" But Jefferies will have none of it. "Do what you please for a negro, he will cheat you the first opportunity he finds."

Despite their argument, Jefferies agrees to the sale of Clara and Caesar and they become Edwards's slaves. This now poses something of a dilemma for Caesar, who knows that the slaves are plotting rebellion. "Their object was to extirpate every white man, woman, and child, in the island. . . . The confederacy extended to all the negroes in the island of Jamaica, excepting those on the plantation of Mr Edwards", who have not been told of it because of fears that their attachment to him will make them betray the rebels. The rebel leader is Hector, a slave on Jefferies's plantation, who is Caesar's friend and shipmate (they were brought over on the same slave ship). Hector is a man who "breathes vengeance". Even in his sleep he cries out, "Spare none! Sons of Africa, spare none!" The two men are both Koromantyns.

Now that he has been bought by the kind Edwards, Caesar wants to call off the revolt. This enrages Hector, who challenges him to betray the rebels' secret if he must. Caesar is in a quandary because he knows that if he reveals the plot, his friend will be executed in punishment. Hector, on the other hand, wants to persuade Caesar not to abandon the cause, so he goes to "one of those persons who, amongst the negroes, are considered as sorceresses". Here Edgeworth provides another footnote referencing Edwards.

The enlightened inhabitants of Europe may, perhaps, smile at the superstitious credulity of the negroes, who regard those ignorant beings called Obeah people, with the most profound respect and dread; who believe that they hold in their hands the power of good and evil fortune, of health and sickness, of life and death. The instances which are related of their power over the minds of their countrymen are so wonderful, that none but the most unquestionable authority could make us think them credible. The following passage, from Edwards' History of the West Indies, is inserted, to give an idea of this strange infatuation.

The sorceress Hector seeks out is an example of those discussed in the Fuller report:

> Esther, an old Koromantyn negress, had obtained by her skill in poisonous herbs, and her knowledge of venomous reptiles, a high reputation amongst her countrymen. She soon taught them to believe her to be possessed of supernatural powers; and she then worked their imagination to what pitch and purpose she pleased.
>
> She was the chief instigator of this intended rebellion. It was she who had stimulated the revengeful temper of Hector almost to phrensy. She now promised him that her arts should be exerted over his friend; and it was not long before he felt their influence.[20]

Clara becomes melancholy and takes to standing immobile, in deep reverie. Finally she tells Caesar that unless he does as Esther wants, he will die. Caesar responds that Esther wants him to kill Edwards. Clara is shocked; she knows nothing of the conspiracy, which has been hidden from her because of her timid nature. Clara is afraid, but Caesar reassures her that his hands will "never be imbrued in the blood of my benefactor".

Meanwhile, over on Jefferies's plantation, the overseer lashes a Negro who has allowed the sugar to ferment. After his whipping, the slave mutters, "It will soon be our turn!" while looking at Hector. The overseer suspects a rebellion is in the works; he has Hector and three others lashed unmercifully to get them to confess, but they say nothing. A few days later, Mrs Jefferies has Hector's wife whipped because she tears a dress which has just arrived from England.

Hector tries harder to get Caesar to re-join the plotters; he realizes that if he and Clara do not join them, they may have to be killed in order to prevent them from betraying the rebels. Esther sets "to work upon [Caesar's] mind

---

20 Ibid., 253–54.

by means of Clara. On returning to her cottage one night, [Clara] found suspended from the thatch one of those strange fantastic charms with which the Indian sorceresses terrify those whom they have proscribed."[21] ("Indian" suggests some racial confusion, as well as possible confusion between the religious practices encountered in India by the British East India Company and those associated with Africa.) Clara is terrified and hurries to see Esther, who tells her that she wants to see Caesar. He is sent for, but when he arrives he finds Clara lying on the ground.

"The sorceress had thrown her into a trance by a preparation of deadly night-shade. The hag burst into an infernal laugh" at the expression on Caesar's face. She tells him that he has defied her power and must now "behold its victim". Caesar goes to strangle her, but she promises to revive Clara if he obeys her. Esther reveals that she has already administered "the solemn fetish oath, at the sound of which every negro in Africa trembles" to Hector and the rest.[22] She says she will steep their weapons in poison and render them invulnerable. She points to where Hector and his confederates are advancing and tells Caesar he must join the rebellion or die with Clara.

Caesar decides to pretend acquiescence and asks Esther for permission to get his knife so it too can be dipped in the "magic poison". She grants it, and he manages to raise the alarm at Edwards's house, urging the planter to arm himself and all on his plantation. As Caesar leads them to Esther's hut, he begs for a pardon for Hector. "Mr Edwards looked through a hole in the wall; and, by the blue flame of a caldron, over which the sorceress was stretching her shrivelled hands, he saw Hector and five stout negroes standing, intent upon her incantations. These negroes held their knives in their hands, ready to dip them into the bowl of poison."[23]

Edwards sets fire to the hut and the leaders rush out. Edwards and Caesar cry to Hector that he is pardoned, but he stabs Caesar who, believing he is dying, asks to be buried with Clara. The wound is discovered not to be fatal, however, and he awakens from his faint to find Clara beside him, the opiate Esther gave her having worn off. But, though Edwards imprisons the chief conspirators, the rest of Jefferies's slaves rise up and kill Durant. They set fire to the canes but the insurgency is quelled before it spreads to the neighbouring estates. Ruined, Jefferies returned to England with his wife, "where they were

---

21 Ibid., 254.
22 Ibid., 256.
23 Ibid., 258.

obliged to live in obscurity and indigence. They had no consolation in their misfortunes but that of railing at the treachery of the whole race of slaves." But, says, Edgeworth, "Our readers, we hope, will think that at least one exception may be made, in favour of THE GRATEFUL NEGRO." (Edgeworth does not say what happened to Hector, or Esther, for that matter, beyond that the chief conspirators were taken prisoner.)

That Edgeworth was very taken with Bryan Edwards and his outlook on slavery and the West Indies is quite clear from the story. Not only does she name her ideal white planter after him, but the story itself is little more than a fictionalization of the information and prescriptions he presents in his *History Civil and Commercial*. Like her fictional Edwards, the real Edwards, for example, encouraged "allowing to such of [the slaves] as shall have finished their task within the time limited, the rest of the day to themselves, and pay them wages for extra labour".[24]

In this short story, Edgeworth continues to portray blacks in a relatively sympathetic manner, suggesting that any who became violent did so as a result of bad treatment by slave-owners. The greatest villains of the piece are Jefferies, Durant and, to a lesser extent, Esther. The first loses his riches, the second is killed and we presume the last to have been, at the very least, imprisoned, while Caesar, grateful and loyal, is given a happy ending. Edgeworth repeatedly refused to demonize blacks and consistently made some of her most sympathetic characters black, as with Quaco in the following story.

THE TWO GUARDIANS

Maria Edgeworth's comic drama *The Two Guardians* is about two men feuding over who will be in charge of young St Albans, a West Indian left a fortune by his father. Mr Onslow, one of the candidates for guardianship, wants to shape his character according to what is true and honourable, while Lord Courtington will leave St Albans to his wife, who seeks to ensnare him for her daughter, Juliana. Both Lady Courtington and Juliana are shallow people, unkind to their poor relation Mrs Beauchamp, a widow and a relative to whom they owe money they avoid paying. Quaco, St Albans' black servant, is the conscience of the play. When we are first introduced to him by one of the other servants, he is described as a "boy" and Lady Courtington calls him "little Quaco", but

---

24   Edwards, *History Civil and Commercial*, 151.

from what other characters say he appears to be perhaps only slightly younger than St Albans himself, who is probably in his early to mid-twenties.

"I don't know rightly what to make of that fellow, with the big whites of his eyes moving about so quick", one of the Courtington's servants says of Quaco. Even writers who did not dwell on racial differences or demonize black features found it hard to avoid mentioning the whites of black people's eyes, struck by the contrast, presumably.

Edgeworth wanted to show other whites that they had nothing to fear from blacks, that blacks, simple and child-like, would repay their good treatment by patient and benevolent whites with gratitude and devotion. This was the theme of the racial relations she explored in her books and it was carried through in *The Two Guardians*. In the following exchange, for example, St Albans' dialogue is refined and almost exaggeratedly mature, while both the stage directions and his dialogue reveal Quaco's childishness:

> *St Alb.* Well, Quaco, how do you like England? – How do you like London?
> *Quaco.* London *very* fine, Massa! – Quaco like England very much, Massa. – Very good country, England. – No whip for de slave, – nor no slave no where.
> *St Alb.* True. – No slaves in England. From the moment that you touched English ground, Quaco, you ceased to be a slave.
> *Quaco.* Me! – Quaco?
> *St Alb.* You, Quaco – you are as free this moment as I am.
> *Quaco.* (*Clapping his hands and capering.*) Free! free! Quaco? – But no, Massa – (*Changing his tone, and kneeling to his master*) – me will be Massa's slave alway.
> *St Alb.* My servant, henceforward – not my slave. Now if you stay with me, it is from choice. – You may go when, and where you please – you may chuse another master.
> *Quaco.* Quaco never have no other massa. – Good massa – love him – kind to Quaco, from time leetle piccinini boy. – Oh, let Quaco stay wid massa.
> *St Alb.* Stay, and welcome, my faithful fellow, – but remember you are at liberty. And here, Quaco, look at this little scarlet purse – it has my name marked on it – your mother marked it for me. – It contains, – what do you think it contains?
> *Quaco.* Gold guinea, Massa, me tink me see peeping.
> *St Alb.* All the money you have earned, Quaco, – the price of that provision ground, at which you used to work so hard, in every hour you had to yourself. – I told you, that if you trusted to me, and if you would come to England with me, you should not lose the value of your former labor.
> *Quaco.* Oh, Massa! how good you remember!

> *St Alb.* Here is all the money you have earned, and something more. – Now don't let it spoil you. – Don't spend this money in drinking.
> *Quaco.* (*Very seriously.*) Massa, no – me promise you – no rum – no drinky for drinky – but drinky for dry.
> *St Alb.* And don't throw away your money.
> *Quaco.* Throw! – Oh, Quaco never throw it away.
> *St Alb.* Shew me, Quaco, that you are a reasonable being, and fit to be free.

He leaves the scene and Quaco is alone.

> Quaco. (Alone.) Shew you Quaco fit to be free. – Yes, Quaco shall.
> (*He sings.*)
> Freedom! Freedom! happy sound,
> Magic land this British ground;
> Touch it slave, and slave be free,
> 'Tis the Land of Liberty.
>
> Indian *Obee*'s wicked art,
> Sicken slow poor negro's heart;
> English *Obee* makes the slave
> Twice be young, and twice be brave.
>
> Quick the magic, strong the pow'r –
> See man changing in an hour!
> For the day that makes him free,
> Double worth that man shall be.
>
> Massa, grateful Quaco do
> Twice the work of slave for you;
> Fight for Massa twice as long;
> Love for Massa twice as strong.[25]

Soon after, Mrs Beauchamp visits the Courtingtons once more to try to obtain what they owe her but is turned away. Distraught, she wonders what will happen to her as she is now on the edge of bankruptcy. Brought to tears by Mrs Beauchamp's plight, Quaco, unseen, slips all his money into her basket, wondering why St Albans cannot see through the Courtingtons.

Then St Albans is injured in a horserace through the machinations of Juli-

---

25 Maria Edgeworth, "The Two Guardians; A Drama in Three Acts", in *Comick Dramas* (Boston: Wells and Lilly, 1817), 160–63.

ana's brother and is taken to a nearby house in Park Lane. When Lady Courtington hears of the accident, she tries to hide the news from Mrs St Albans, the young man's mother. Juliana's brother is concerned only about the injury to the horse, while Lady Courtington does not want the incident to blight her husband's chance of being appointed guardian, with the access to all St Albans' money that guardianship would entail. When the Courtingtons go to the Park Lane house, they discover that it belongs to Mrs Beauchamp, who thanks Juliana for the purse of gold she put in her basket. When she holds up the purse, St Albans realizes it is the bag he gave to Quaco. The scales drop from his eyes and he rejects the Courtingtons for the Onslows.

Despite the popularity of Edgeworth's books, the play was not well received by the critics. The *Quarterly Review* sniffed that "many may be surprised that a writer, whose novels are read with mingled amusement and instruction, should have given to the world dramas of no higher merit than the three contained in the volume now before us. . . . The Two Guardians . . . is intended to exhibit a picture of the fashionable society of London." The reviewer then gives a brief outline of the plot and points out that "from this sketch of the fable, it is sufficiently obvious that the plot is meagre in the extreme. . . . [It] is deficient in what should constitute its most essential quality, abundance of incident; and this deficiency, of itself fatal to the interest of the piece, is aggravated by the loose and unartificial connection of the scenes."[26] The reviewer for the *Literary Gazette* was similarly unimpressed and dismissed *The Two Guardians* as "altogether uninteresting",[27] while the *Theatrical Inquisitor* pronounced Edgeworth's attempt at writing comedy a failure and added, cuttingly, "the dramatic interest of this piece is beneath consideration".[28]

The *American Monthly Magazine and Critical Review* was even more scathing:

> This has not even the recommendation of fidelity to offset against all its staleness and insipidity. It is intended as a representation of the corruption of what is termed high life and a negro boy, who would be turned out of any decent house on this side of the water for his impertinence, is virtually made the hero of the piece. He is, to be sure, endowed with many commendable qualities of the heart by the bounty of the author, but we cannot get over the absurdity of obtruding such a spectator upon the privacy of fashionable ladies and placing

---

26 *Quarterly Review* 17 (April–July 1817): 101–2.
27 *Literary Gazette, or Journal of Belles Lettres, Politics, and Fashion*, 24 May 1817.
28 *Theatrical Inquisitor and Monthly Mirror*, October 1817, 283.

him upon the familiar footing of confidential adviser to his master in the delicate scrupulosities of love.[29]

The other reviewers couch their criticisms in terms of perceived dramatic weaknesses and issues with scene transitions, but the *American Monthly*'s reviewer probably identifies the real problem for viewers: the depiction of an intelligent (though uneducated) black man as being morally superior to upper-class whites. Edgeworth had not given Quaco the stereotyped characteristics common at the time – he was not violent, thievish, lazy, clownish, irrational, stupid, deceitful or superstitious. The reviewers, and presumably her audiences, found it hard to forgive her for that.

CAPTAIN CLUTTERBUCK'S CHAMPAGNE

William George Hamley was a grandson of the founder of the toy store Noah's Ark, now known as Hamleys. He entered the Royal Corps of Engineers in 1833 and became lieutenant governor of Bermuda in 1864; he was also appointed to the Council of the Bermudas and served as acting governor. His first novel appeared in 1850 and he was a regular contributor to *Fraser's Magazine* and *Blackwood's Magazine*. The novel *Captain Clutterbuck's Champagne: A West Indian Reminiscence*, which draws from his experiences in the region and in Bermuda, was published in 1862 after being serialized in *Blackwood's*. It is set in Jamaica in 1861.

Like other writers, Hamley was well aware of other books set in the Caribbean. He refers once or twice to *Tom Cringle's Log* and happily includes a comedic funeral procession similar to that described in Scott's book. He also quotes extensively from Bryan Edwards.

Captain Clutterbuck follows the romantic travails of Arthur Brune, a young army officer who falls in love with Violet Arabin, the daughter of a plantation owner, on the ship that is taking them to the island. At first Violet's father, Christopher Arabin, is quite taken with Arthur but then hears disturbing news of a scandal back in Ireland. Arabin throws his support behind another young man, Manuel Melhado – his foreign name of course being a big clue that he is the villain of the piece. Manuel is also described as having an "olive complexion" and is part-owner of a shop, which means that the army officers

---

29 *American Monthly Magazine and Critical Review* 1 (September 1817): 396.

deride him as a mere merchant, not a gentleman. Violet is thus far above his station and too good for him. Manuel, however, has, through legal trickery, become the proprietor of several large estates and is expected to soon own a couple more. Arabin, though already rich and powerful, is delighted at the thought of joining his own considerable property to Manuel's.

The introduction of Obeah is gratuitous to the story, as it plays no part in the events, but at a dinner attended by the main white characters,

> the conversation . . . turned upon some superstitious excitement which was agitating the negroes, and leading them to hold frequent and large nocturnal meetings. The overseers and book-keepers on the estates thought that these assemblies might lead to mischief, and had represented their misgivings to Mr Arabin as proprietor of Crystal Mount, and to Mr Melhado as representing the owner of the Cinnamon estate, a little farther down the hill. Obi is the name of the religion, incantation, or devil-worship, whichever it may be, that prevails among the Negroes. Obeah men, their high-priests or professors, are always native Africans, so are the women who practise its crafts. Hence there is no doubt that the whole of its mysteries are of African origin. When their orgies are more than usually solemn, it is to be dreaded that they mask some insurrectionary move, and the whites are uneasy while they continue.

The dinner party had waited until the servants were out of the room to discuss the subject: "It is never wise to speak on this subject before black servants, as nearly all of them are in thraldom to the superstition, and they may be chiefs and ringleaders; for there is a peculiar mystery most carefully maintained concerning the rites, professors, and votaries of Obi, and the whites have never been able to sift it, though now and then they get a little insight into its abominations."[30]

Manuel decides to set some of his Cuban dogs on the Obeah gathering, or "the pests of the country" as he calls them, and a day or so later, two black men, Domingo and Snowball, are sent out on an exploratory mission with the dogs. Domingo reveals to Snowball "some of the local secrets of Obi, and the name of the most cunning Obeah man in the district – a patriarch originally from Congo, but now of great age and fame, and of surpassing power".[31] Snowball is interested to hear this and the two decide to visit him. The Obeah man "was seated on a tree-stump under a banana shade. A cloud of mosquitoes veiled

---

30 Hamley, *Captain Clutterbuck*, 98.
31 Ibid., 146.

his venerable person, which was otherwise imperfectly covered; the fingers of one hand scratched viciously among his hoary wool, the other held an empty calabash, from which he had lately eaten his evening meal, tokens of which clung about his oracular mouth."

The interior of the Obeah man's hut

> was decorated with symbols and natural products, such as would not have very powerfully impressed a European, but which seemed charged with weird meanings and unearthly influence to Snowball, who lifted his cap and thrice did obeisance on entering the sacred chamber, which, besides the daddy's bed, contained several shelves, on which were arranged rags and feathers, bones and teeth, worked into a hundred fantastic shapes. There were a few dried herbs, but the staple articles were cats' and alligators' teeth, bottles containing blood, earth from graves, egg-shells, skulls of cats stuffed with clay, so that the clay and bone together should form a sphere; balls of earth stuck with parrots' beaks, or with dogs' or even human teeth; claws of animals, glass beads, and a mucilage contained in egg-shells or broken bottles. There were likewise many little bags containing the above-mentioned ingredients in various proportions.[32]

When the mulatto Leander arrives, the Obeah man announces that he heard him coming from a mile off, but Leander responds that he has been to England, "where de people knows better!" and he does not believe a word of it. Shocked, the Obeah man responds, "You no 'fraid me make you eat dirt – you no 'fraid Duppy come choke you – you no 'fraid you find for youself change to one lilly pig, squeakee, squeakee?" Undaunted, Leander recounts what he has seen in England: sword-swallowing conjurers, fire-breathing magicians and others who were able to summon impressive ghosts, even though everyone knew it was "all a cheat". Leander informs the Obeah man that he cannot be taken in "wid your poor negar tricks" after all the wonders he has seen.

Despite his disbelief, Leander proceeds to bribe the daddy, as they call the Obeah man, with beads, feathers, rum and other things so he will not make a love potion for Nicholas Chitty, an older black man who is trying to woo the mulatto Rosabella. Leander wants the pretty Rosabella for himself. She returns his affections, but he is worried that, with the help of Obeah, Chitty might succeed.[33] Hamley takes the opportunity to display his knowledge of Obeah with a long exposition.

---

32 Ibid., 149.
33 Ibid.

The Obeah man, of whom we have just had a glimpse, is, it is believed, a sample of his profession in general. The reader has already pronounced him and his art ridiculous and contemptible beyond patience. But things must be regarded according to their estimation and effects in places where they exist; and the power of Obi over the negro mind has worked many a social and political convulsion, and caused sufficient anxiety to lawgivers. The statutes of Jamaica direct the severest penalties against it; and probably the other West India islands were equally anxious for its suppression. Its secret has never been fathomed by white men. The tricks and apparatus of the art are, as far as we can detect, the very grossest species of impostures, palpable even to a negro mind. But the terror which it inspires sufficiently attests its grasp on the imagination, and forces respect from those who cannot control it, much as they may contemn the means which it uses. The word Obi introduced in ordinary conversation will cause a black person to spring almost off the ground, and utter the "hi!" of reverence or terror. The negroes will undergo immense labour and privation at the dictation of the Obeah man; and, to break a spell, give anything short of life, as, if unbroken, it will probably destroy life itself. The superstition works by external symbols, the meaning of which has never been ascertained. These are to be seen in all directions – in fields, gardens, lanes, and houses. A man, on issuing from his house in the morning, recognises some token, which is without significance to the uninitiated, but which he knows to be a warning that Obi is set for him; whereupon terror takes possession of him, and he can see no hope except by propitiating the sorcerer who has wrought the spell, or by enlisting on his side a professor of superior power. Many a time the victim failing to do either has pined and died, so confirming the opinion of the irresistible power of Obi. Even where no animosity of race dictated the charms, and the intrigues related to internal affairs of the negroes themselves, Obi was a serious plague to the master, as killing and incapacitating his slaves.[34]

Be that as it may, nothing attributable to Obeah happens in the story; the references to it are mere window-dressing for the real story, which centres around Arthur and Violet's love affair and efforts to thwart Manuel.

Hamley is clearly a keen observer and has a rare ear for dialect, but his prejudices result in the familiar stereotypical characterizations. Chitty, for example, is a secondary villain who seeks to aid Manuel because of his dislike for Arthur. He is described as "black as de debil" with a "black visage" and woolly hair (the woolliness of their hair is invariably part of the description of all Hamley's black characters). Leander, on the other hand, is a Brune partisan

---

34 Ibid., 155–56.

and "a smart, intelligent, young mulatto", while the mulatto Rosabella, also on Brune's side, is "pretty" and "fair". Hamley has already characterized Africans as a weak race with "miserable beginnings"; later he notes that Lorton, a young English officer "compelled do duty with black troops", is bitterly disappointed and despondent over it (Lorton sickens and eventually dies).

Interestingly, in comparing creole blacks with African blacks, Hamley notes that the former "possesses a slight, a very slight, advantage in point of skill and intelligence, but morally he is, we grieve to say, by far inferior".[35] It is possible that with this comparison, Hamley may have been hoping, like Williams before him, to induce misgivings about the work of missionaries. If, after all their decades of preaching to the slaves and their descendants, Africans from Africa were their moral superiors, then the missionaries were clearly suspect and not credible informants on the "negro question". Hamley sympathized with the planters and clearly thought that emancipation had been premature.

> At the date of our story, the Negro question was creating its very fiercest contentions. Jamaica was being torn and ruined by excited factions. The planting interest, after years of domination, found itself suddenly overborne and trampled on, while upon its forehead were branded all the sins of oppression committed since the world began. The triumphant abolitionists, as if the sacredness of their grand object absolved them from all blame as to the means they might use, conducted themselves with a vindictiveness and rancour which disgraced their profession, and soon were blinded to the difference between truth and falsehood, right and wrong. . . .
>
> The state of dissension of course afforded openings for loud-mouthed agitators and demagogues to exhibit their stump-oratory, and to grasp at places and gains. Crowds of these appeared, all with liberal and philanthropic sentiments on their lips, but the lives of many of them characterised by greed and hate. Like Judas, they were eloquent concerning the claims of the poor, not that they cared for the poor. And in the very front of the political agitators stood the religious sects, the preachers acting as the leaders, and instilling their secular doctrines, and inciting to deceit and dishonesty from their pulpits.[36]

Hamley absolves the Church of England and the Wesleyan Methodists (via a footnote) from these accusations and says the state of affairs has resulted in an inevitable "wreck". The entire rant reads as if it could have been lifted straight from Cynric Williams.

---

35 Ibid., 127–28.
36 Ibid., 221.

At the end of *Captain Clutterbuck's*, Violet and Arthur are married, Manuel is in disgrace and no Obeah insurrection has surfaced. We are told that Chitty has "jined relijan" (became "attached to one of the denominations of Christians") and opened a liquor shop to serve both the army and his "religious connection (which was a thirsty one)". One of the black servants returns to England with his "master", becomes the darling of the "liberal and sympathising community" and marries a white woman, who seeks to profit from his fame as a member of a wronged race. When he refuses to enumerate the various forms by which he was oppressed, the wife is enraged, particularly when "a less scrupulous black man" raises a "heavy sum" at a huge meeting.[37] (It is interesting to speculate that this may have been a sideswipe at the abolitionist Frederick Douglass, who arrived in England in 1845 for a series of lectures on slavery that also served as fundraisers.) The wife physically attacks him, is arrested and jailed, and dies in prison, whereupon he returns to "the service of his old 'Massa'". Leander and Rosabella are also married and both work for Arthur Brune and his wife, Violet. British readers could not have failed to understand by all this that freedom was a burden for black people, who were better off with their "massas".

THE MAROON

Thomas Mayne Reid was a "man's writer" who wrote testosterone-charged stories of adventure and gallantry that were beloved by adolescent males such as Theodore Roosevelt and Arthur Conan Doyle.[38] In fact, his wide popularity in the United States, Britain, Russia and other European countries helped to influence perspectives on race and masculinity by successive generations of boys who then went on to influence others through their own writings and beliefs.

In his prologue to *The Maroon*, published in 1862, Reid describes the military post of Montego Bay and notes that fifty years ago it would have been a bustling place, "a scene of active, busy life", but now it was much quieter. Fifty years ago there was both great intellectual activity and commercial enterprise, then "[a] crisis had arrived . . . followed soon after by quick decadence. And

---

37   Ibid., 370.
38   Descriptions of Doyle's sole black character, Zambo, in *The Lost World* often come in the form of comparisons to animals. For example, he is "as willing as any horse, and just as intelligent" and "as faithful as a dog"; Arthur Conan Doyle, *The Lost World* (Rockville, MD: Arc Manor, 2009), 53, 57.

who need lament the downfall of a commerce whose most important commodity was *human flesh*? Rather let humanity rejoice in its ruin!"[39] Reid's math is a little off here, since slavery was abolished in 1834, twenty-eight years before. He may be confusing emancipation with the abolition of the British slave trade, which occurred in 1807, fifty years before the publication of his book. Reid suggests that the "decadence" is due to the end of the commerce in slaves, failing to note such factors as the depression in world sugar prices, the rise in competition and the failure of planters to adapt to changed circumstances. His stereotyped representations of black people in *The Maroon* suggest that whatever rejoicing humanity may have done, Reid considered it misplaced.

Reid, a military man who had served in the US Army, admired the Maroons, however, and made a distinction between them and other blacks. The prologue contains a paean of praise for them: "in the annals of the New World, there is none whose history possesses for me so powerful an attraction as that of the *Maroons of Jamaica*. No lover of liberty – no advocate for the equality of mankind – can fail to feel an enthusiastic admiration for those brave black men, who, for two hundred years, maintained their independence against the whole white population of the island."[40] The narrator claims that the story he tells was related to him by Quaco, a Maroon who was 110 years old at the time they met.

In chapter 1, Reid discusses the homes of sugar planters and introduces the estate of Mount Welcome, providing some foreshadowing with a description of Jumbé Rock and the titillating information that a black man was sacrificed there by "men of white skin and European race". We are barely into the story when Reid begins a discussion of "Obeah-ism":

> In the West Indies a few years previous to the Emancipation, there was much agitation on the subject of Obeah-ism. The practice of this horrid art had become appallingly common – so common that upon almost every extensive estate in the island there was a "professor" of it; in other words, an "Obeah man". "Professor", though often used in speaking of these charlatans, is not a correct title. To have *professed* it – at least in the hearing of the whites – would have been attended with peril: since it was punishable by the death penalty. *Practitioner* is a more appropriate appellation.[41]

---

39 Thomas Mayne Reid, *The Maroon* (London: Hurst and Blackett, 1862), 1:3.
40 Ibid., 4–5.
41 Ibid., 8–9.

Reid, who does not appear to have ever visited Jamaica or the Caribbean, gives a description of Obeah men which relies heavily on the Fuller report:

> These mysterious doctors were almost always men – very rarely women – and usually natives of Africa. Universally were they persons of advanced age and hideous aspect: the uglier the more successful in pursuit of their criminal calling.
>
> There was a class of them distinguished as "myal-men", whose chief distinction consisted in their being able to *restore life to a dead body*.
>
> Such was the belief of their ignorant fellow slaves, who little suspected that the defunct subject had been all the while only dormant, his death-like slumber secretly brought about by the myal-man himself, assisted by a prescription of the branched "callalue" – a species of *caladium*.[42]

The narrator notes that he cannot enter into "an explanation of the mysteries of Obi" but that he has met a variant of it in every land that he has travelled. Though "it holds a more conspicuous place in the social life of the savage, it is also found in the bye-lanes of civilization". In fact, he explains, "it is the first dawning of religion on the soul of the savage".[43]

Mount Welcome, it turns out, is also "blessed, or rather cursed, by a follower of the art, an old Coromantee negro – Chakra by name – a man whose fell and ferocious aspect could not have failed to make him one of the most popular of its practitioners".[44] Chakra, we learn, is suspected of poisoning his former master, a cruel man who was apparently not liked by many. Mount Welcome is then bought by another man, Loftus Vaughan, who puts Chakra on trial for "practising the arts of Obi". The trial is presided over by Vaughan as the justice of the peace, or *custos rotulorum*, and two other white men from the district. Vaughan presses for the death penalty, giving credence to a rumour that he wants Chakra dead, not for Obeah but because he knows certain things about the planter's own crimes. Chakra is convicted and sentenced to be chained to a palm tree at the top of Jumbé Rock and left to perish. Reid notes that such men were usually hung on the scaffold or burnt at the stake, but people wanted to make an example of Chakra.

> As already stated, at this particular period, much unpleasant feeling prevailed on the subject of obeah-ism. In almost every district mysterious deaths had

---

42 Ibid., 9.
43 Ibid., 17–18.
44 Ibid., 19.

occurred, and were occurring – not only of black slaves, but of white masters, and even mistresses – all attributed to the baneful influence of Obi.

The African demon was ubiquitous, but invisible. Everywhere could be witnessed his skeleton hand upon the wall, but nowhere himself. It had become necessary to make a conspicuous example of his worshippers. The voice of all planterdom called for it; and the myal-man, Chakra, was selected for that example – in the belief that his fearful fate would terrify the votaries of the vile superstition to their very heart's core.

The Jumbé rock suggested itself as the most appropriate place for the execution of the Coromantee. The terrors with which the place was already invested – added to those now to be inspired by the fearful form of punishment of which it was to be the scene – would exert a beneficial effect on the superstitious understandings of the slaves, and for ever destroy their belief in Obeah and Obboney.

Under this belief was the myal-man escorted up to the summit of the Jumbé rock; and, like a modern Prometheus, chained there.[45]

Sometime later, Vaughan receives two letters. After opening the first, he informs his daughter, Catherine, that Montagu Smythje, the owner of Montagu Castle, the neighbouring plantation, is about to arrive on the ship *Sea Nymph*. Catherine (usually called Kate) is described as having a "taint" of black blood and we later learn that she is a "mustee", someone of one eight black ancestry. Vaughan enjoins his daughter to entertain Smythje and make herself agreeable to him, since it is in his interest to be friendly with him. From previous conversations about Smythje, Kate suspects that her father is thinking of a marriage between her and the man, but she keeps her own counsel, already disapproving of what she has heard of Smythje's dandyish ways.

Vaughan is much less pleased by the contents of the second letter. His brother has died and, with his dying breath, made his son, Herbert, promise to go to Jamaica to his uncle. He too is travelling via the *Sea Nymph*. Vaughan expresses no sorrow over the death of his brother, merely saying that while he was alive he always wanted money and now, in death, is sending his son to trouble him. Vaughan is also dismayed to think that Smythje may meet the young man and learn that he is traveling steerage instead of first class, thus disgracing Vaughan. Kate, however, feels sympathetic towards the young man, her newly discovered cousin.

---

45   Ibid., 22.

Meanwhile, a slaver has dropped anchor near Montego Bay. A man goes on board:

> He appeared to be about sixty years old – he might have been more or less – and had once been white; but long exposure to a West-Indian sun, combined with the numerous dirt-bedaubed creases and furrows in his skin, had darkened his complexion to the hue of leaf-tobacco.
>
> His features, naturally of an angular shape, had become so narrowed and sharpened by age as to leave scarce anything in front; and to get a view of his face it was necessary to step to one side, and scan it *en profil*.
>
> Thus viewed, there was breadth enough, and features of the most prominent character – including a nose like the claw of a lobster – a sharp, projecting chin – with a deep embayment between, marking the locality of the lips: the outline of all suggesting a resemblance to the profile of a parrot, but still greater to that of a Jew – for such, in reality was its type.[46]

The description of this man, "Jacob Jessuron, the slave-merchant; an Israelite of Germanic breed", takes up two pages and is couched in such a way that we know he is to be at least one of the villains of the piece. To add to the image, Jessuron is given an awful accent that has him saying such things as "fushtrate" and "yourshelf".

On board the slaver is a young Foolah prince, Cingües, and his attendants. The prince's features are "not of a marked African type. . . . In truth, they were almost European." He has come over from Africa at the behest of his father, to find his sister, who was captured by Mandingoes and sold to slave traders. The prince has travelled with forty Mandingo slaves – twenty are the price of his passage and the other twenty he intends to trade for his sister. Jessuron persuades the captain that he can help find the girl and is later put ashore with the prince, his attendants and his slaves, as well as several girls Jessuron has bought from the captain as "breeding wenches".

Not only does Jessuron have an idea where to find the Foolah princess, Yola, it was he who sold her to Vaughan a year ago. The next day, he hurries over to Mount Welcome to make an offer for Yola, but Vaughan is not disposed to sell her, not even when Jessuron offers him the "doublish dear" price of two hundred pounds. Vaughan explains that he has given Yola to his daughter, who has grown attached to her and would not consent to her sale.

Jessuron's own daughter, Judith, (or, as he pronounces it, "Shoodith") is

---

46 Ibid., 53.

beautiful in looks but "in spirit . . . as devilish as he", and equally angered by Vaughan's refusal to sell Yola. She curses Catherine as a "conceited *mustee* – herself no better than a slave". Judith points out to Jessuron that he could simply strip Cingües of his royal robes and make him and the others his slaves with none being the wiser, since the captain never comes ashore and he is the only one who knows the truth. In any case, the captain will be offshore for only another day or so, at the end of which Jessuron and his daughter can obtain twenty-four slaves for free, including the prince.

Back at Mount Welcome, preparations are underway for the arrival of Smythje. As they wait for him, Yola tells Kate that she resembles Cubina, a Maroon man she knows (he is the Maroon of the title). Kate is quite put out at the thought and makes a joke about selling Yola, to which Yola responds, "Yola herself kill rather than she go back to Jew slave-dealer!"[47]

Vaughan goes to meet Smythje in his best carriage, with a cart for the luggage behind and the overseer riding as escort. He makes no effort to meet his nephew. Instead, Quashie, a young slave boy, has been deputized to meet Herbert and take him to the overseer's house, which is some distance from the Great House. When Herbert realizes the insult, he gallops to the Great House, where Vaughan, Kate and their guest are at dinner. Vaughan tells his domestics to have Herbert wait for him in the summerhouse, and Kate goes there to meet him.

Kate tells Herbert her mother was called Quasheba, but he is apparently too new to the West Indies to realize what this means; he makes no response to this revelation. (Quashie and Quasheba were popular slave names in literature and in reality. In Twi, the name is taken to mean somebody born on a Sunday, but in certain Caribbean countries *quashie* is now taken to mean any black man "who is considered gullible or stupid". As Allsopp points out, this latter-day connotation "may have grown out of the surviving use of original African names by later arrivals", who were often despised by the creole slaves for their African ways and their ignorance about plantation life.[48]) No white creole would ever be named Quasheba.

When Vaughan realizes where Kate is, he comes outside and orders her back into Smythje's company. Vaughan offers Herbert a bag of gold coins to leave Mount Welcome and to keep quiet about their being related, but Herbert throws

---

47 Ibid., 121.
48 Richard Allsopp, ed., *Dictionary of Caribbean English Usage* (Oxford: Oxford University Press, 1996), 459.

it at his feet. As he is leaving, Kate offers him a purse of her own money, but he gives it back to her, first detaching the ribbon from it and fixing to his chest as a token of the estimation in which he holds her. Not knowing what to do, Herbert heads into the forest to spend the night there while he decides what his next step will be. As he is walking through the forest, he hears people talking and hides in a tree, but he drops his gun as he is clambering up the branches.

Meanwhile, on Jessuron's plantation, once called Happy Valley but now known simply as the "Jew's Pen", Cingües has been stripped of his clothes and is brought forward for branding. He meets the brand unflinchingly but then launches himself at Jessuron and tries to strangle him to death. He is pulled off by Ravener, the overseer (also noted as a Jew), and some Cuban slave-hunters whom Jessuron has with him. Later, Cingües escapes into the woods and meets Yola's Cubina, a mulatto who lives in the mountains as a Maroon. When the mulatto sees the prince's wounds, he says to himself, "God of the Christian! ... if this be your decree, then give me the fetish of my African ancestors."[49] It is their conversation that Herbert overhears, and he keeps an eye on them from his perch.

The slave-hunters and their dogs are hard on the prince's heels, but Cubina finds Herbert's gun and gives it to the prince while he defends himself with a machete. Herbert, a true Englishman dedicated to the notion of fair play, sees that Cubina and Cingües are outnumbered by the slave-hunters; he jumps down to join them and make the numbers more even. The overseer and the slave-hunters demand the prince back but decline to fight. They leave, threatening to take Herbert to court for obstructing the recapture of a slave. After the departure of the slave hunters, Herbert and Cubina cement their friendship over a meal of barbecued pork. They part company afterwards and Herbert makes for Montego Bay, but he is arrested on the way for aiding a runaway slave.

Herbert is brought before Jessuron, who happens to be the nearest justice of the peace. Judith, observing the proceedings, is quite taken with the newcomer. Jessuron, when he realizes that Herbert does not get along with his uncle, is prepared to take him to his bosom and forgive him for interfering with the Cubans. He sentences Herbert to have dinner with him that evening and says that no harm was done, since the slave has been returned to him by a Maroon and Herbert, being new to the island, is probably unaware of its laws. He is lying, however; Cingües has not been brought back, as Cubina is reluctant to return him to Jessuron.

---

49   Mayne Reid, *The Maroon*, 1:239.

At dinner, Jessuron offers Herbert a position on his estate as bookkeeper, and Herbert accepts. Jessuron reveals to Judith that he has plans for the young man but does not tell her what they are, simply asking her to make herself agreeable to him so that he will fall in love with her. He tells her that his plans could make her the richest woman on Jamaica. He also cautions her that Herbert must see no ill treatment of the slaves, since young men newly come from England are usually upset by the sight.

We learn, meanwhile, that Cubina is hoping to raise one hundred pounds as Yola's purchase price, which is why, though he regrets having to turn Cingües over, he fully intends to do so. When Yola goes to meet Cubina, he presents the prince to her. They greet each other joyfully, and Yola explains to the surprised Cubina that Cingües is her brother. Sometime later, Cubina goes to see the custos and informs him that he proposes to buy Yola but does not have the full sum yet. Vaughan promises him that Yola will not be sold to anyone else in the meantime. Cubina then tells Vaughan about Cingües and how treacherously Jessuron dealt with him. The prince is still with the Maroons, who are reluctant to turn him over to Jessuron, given how he got him in the first place. Vaughan promises to think about the matter and see how he can help the prince; he advises Cubina not to turn him over to Jessuron.

At a ball held in Smythje's honour later, Kate cold-shoulders Herbert at her father's behest and is rewarded by the sight of him pretending gaiety with Judith, whom he has escorted to the dance. Rumours fly that Herbert and Judith are engaged and that Kate and Smythje are soon to be married. The guests snigger that Vaughan has done well by his "nigger" daughter. After the ball, Vaughan discusses Smythje's proposal with Catherine, who informs him that she does not love the man and has no desire to marry him. Her father is taken aback but tells Smythje that he consents to the union.

We are halfway through volume two of *The Maroon* before we encounter the Obeah man again. Chakra, it turns out, is alive and well and living near Jumbé Rock, in a remote valley called Duppy's Hole. He has constructed his hut among the roots of a giant cotton tree, which serve as its walls. We are told that there is very little furniture, but

> against the walls hung a variety of singular objects – some of them of ludicrous and some of horrid aspect. Among the latter could be observed the skin of the dreaded galliwasp; the two-headed snake; the skull and tusks of a savage boar; dried specimens of the ugly gecko lizard; enormous bats, with human-like faces; and other like hideous creatures.

> Little bags, suspended from the rafters, contained articles of still more mysterious import. Balls of whitish-coloured clay; the claws of the great-eared owl; parrots' beaks and feathers; the teeth of cats, alligators, and the native agouti; pieces of rag and broken glass; with a score of like odds and ends, forming a medley as miscellaneous as unintelligible.
>
> In one corner was a wicker basket – the cutacoo – filled with roots and plants of several different species, among which might be identified the dangerous dumb-cane; the savanna flower; and other "simples" of a suspicious character.[50]

The enumerated list is essentially a compendium of the ingredients listed in the Fuller report and in Jamaica's 1760 act.

Reid writes that a stranger to Jamaica might be puzzled by the hut's contents, but "not so, one acquainted with the forms of the serpent worship of Ethiopia – the creed of the Coromantees. The grotesque objects were but symbols of the African *fetisch*. The hut was a temple of Obi: in plainer terms, the dwelling of an *Obeah man*."[51] And truly, where better for an Obeah man to live than a duppy hole?

After this set-up in chapter 19, Reid titles the very next chapter "Chakra, the Myal-Man", demonstrating the confusion writers and others felt about the distinctions between Obeah and myalism. Chakra, "a man of dread aspect", is described in typical terms:

> He was a negro of gigantic size; though that might not have appeared as he sat squatted in the canoe but for the extreme breadth of his shoulders, between which was set a huge head, almost neckless. His back was bent like a bow, presenting an enormous hunch – partly the effect of advanced age, and partly from natural malformation. His attitude in the canoe gave him a double stoop: so that, as he leant forward to the paddle, his face was turned downward, as if he was regarding some object in the bottom of the craft. His long, ape-like arms enabled him to reach over the gunwale without bending much to either side; and only with these did he appear to make any exertion – his body remaining perfectly immobile. . . .
>
> The countenance of the negro did not need . . . terrific adornment to inspire those who beheld it with fear. The sullen glare of his deep-set eye balls; the broad, gaping nostrils; the teeth, filed to a point, and gleaming, shark-like, behind his purple lips; the red tattooing upon his cheeks and broad breast – the latter exposed by the action of his arms – all combined in making a picture that

---

50   Ibid., 2:179–80.
51   Ibid., 180.

needed no reptiliform addition to render it hideous enough for the most horrid of purposes. It seemed to terrify even the wild denizens of the Duppy's Hole.[52]

If all that is not enough to give him away as an Obeah man, his clothes confirm it:

> The dress of this individual was at the same time grotesque and savage. The only part of it which belonged to civilized fashion was a pair of wide trousers or drawers, of coarse Osnaburgh linen – such as are worn by the field hands on a sugar plantation. Their dirty yellowish hue told that they had long been strangers to the laundry: while several crimson-coloured blotches upon them proclaimed that their last wetting had been with blood, not water.
>
> A sort of *kaross*, or cloak, made out of the skins of the *utia*, and hung over his shoulders, was the only other garment he wore. This, fastened round his thick, short neck by a piece of leathern thong, covered the whole of his body down to the hams – the Osnaburgh drawers continuing the costume thence to his ankles.
>
> His feet were bare. Nor needed they any protection from shoes – the soles being thickly covered with a horn-like callosity, which extended from the ball of the great toe to the broad heel, far protruding backward.
>
> The head-dress was equally *bizarre*. It was a sort of cap, constructed out of the skin of some wild animal; and fitting closely, exhibited, in all its phrenological fulness, the huge negro cranium which it covered. There was no brim; but, in its place, the dried and stuffed skin of the great yellow snake was wreathed around the temples – with the head of the reptile in front, and two sparkling pebbles set in the sockets of its eyes to give it the appearance of life![53]

All in all, Reid's description of Chakra is impressively horrific. Even the Obeah man's lamp is no ordinary lamp but made from "the carapace of a turtle".

Chakra has a night-time visitor, Cynthia, a mulatto housemaid from Mount Welcome. Seeing that he frightens her, he tells her that she need not fear him, though "the Devil himself could hardly have appeared in more hideous guise than the human being who stood before her".[54] Awed, Cynthia asks him how he comes to be alive, when his skeleton is visible on Jumbé Rock.

> "You sabbey ole Chakra? You know he myal-man? Doan care who know now – so long dey b'lieve um dead. Wha for myal-man, ef he no bring de dead to life

---

52 Ibid., 185–88.
53 Ibid., 186–87.
54 Ibid., 191.

'gain? Be shoo Chakra no die hisseff, so long he knows how bring dead body to de life. Ole Chakra know all dat. Dey no kill him, nebber. Neider de white folk nor de brack folk. Dey may shoot 'im wid gun – dey may hang 'im by de neck – dey may cut off 'im head – he come to life 'gain, like de blue lizard and de glass snake. Dey did try kill 'im, you know. Dey 'tarve him till he die ob hunger and thuss. De John Crow pick out him eyes, and tear de flesh from de old nigga's body – leab nuffin but de bare bones! Ha! Chakra 'lib yet – he hab new bones, new flesh! Golly! you him see? he 'trong – he fat as ebber he wa'. Ha! ha! ha!"[55]

Like other fictional Obeah men, Chakra likes his rum and demands the bottle he has asked for. When Cynthia gives it to "the hideous negro", he sticks the neck down his throat and drinks a half-pint, "stroking his abdomen with his huge paw".

Cynthia is in love with Cubina and thought he returned her affections, though we later learn that this is pure fantasy on her part. In any case, she wants a love spell from Chakra that will make the Maroon captain forget Yola and cleave to her. She is prepared to pay almost any price and to steal anything Chakra wants in order to get the spell. Chakra begins to prepare his potion.

> His mysterious behaviour as he passed around the hut; now stopping before one of the grotesque objects that adorned the wall, – now fumbling among the little bags and baskets, as if in search of some particular charm – his movements made in solemn silence only broken by the melancholy sighing of the cataract without; all this was producing on the mind of the mulatta an unpleasant impression; and, despite her natural courage, sustained as it was by the burning passion that devoured her, she was fast giving way to an indefinable fear.
>
> The priest of Obi, after appearing to have worshipped each *fetisch* in turn, at length transferred his devotions to the rum-bottle – perhaps the most potent god in his whole Pantheon.[56]

Chakra explains that, in order for the love spell to work, he also has to work an Obeah spell to make somebody sick. Cynthia is alarmed at the thought that he means to sicken Cubina, but Chakra explains that he does not mean him. He asks her for the name of her greatest enemy; she names Yola, but Chakra tells her that it cannot be a woman or even a slave man: "Obi god tell me so jess now." No, it has to be a white man. "If buckra man hab de obeah-'pell, Cubina he take de lub-spell 'trong."

---

55   Ibid., 192–93.
56   Ibid., 257–58.

Chakra reminds Cynthia that "Massa Loftus" abused her when she was young and that Vaughan is his enemy too, and so the matter is settled: the Obeah will be set on Loftus Vaughan. "Obi god say so – muss be de planter ob Moun' Welc'm", Chakra reiterates to remove any of Cynthia's doubts. She sets her mind on the prize of Cubina and promises that she will do whatever needs to be done, if only it will make the Maroon captain love her. But when she asks Chakra what is required of her, he tells her that "Obi god" does not do everything at once, even for him, and she must await further instructions. He warns her that if, in the meantime, she reveals that "de ole myal-man" lives, she will "soon feel de obeah-spell" herself. In Cynthia, Chakra has found a willing accomplice, but what Cynthia does not know is that Chakra plans to "put the death-spell upon the Maroon himself: to 'obeah' young Cubina" in the same way that he had Obeahed Cubina's father.

After Cynthia has left, we learn that it was "not to an African god [that] the priest of Obi [was] indebted for his resuscitation, but to an Israelitish man – to Jacob Jessuron".[57] Jessuron had merely substituted a dead body from his baracoon for the myal-man so that Chakra would be in his debt. Since his "resurrection", Chakra "had pursued his iniquitous calling with even more energy than of old; but now in the most secret and surreptitious manner". He has also developed a network of confederates and informers, but none of them know his identity, since he disguises himself and never lets them come to his hideaway. "Although the confederates of the obeah-man rarely reveal the secret of his whereabouts – even his *victims dreading to divulge it* – Chakra knew the necessity of keeping as much as possible *en perdu*; and no outlaw, with halter around his neck, could have been more cautious in his outgoings and incomings." To Reid, as to most Europeans writing about Obeah, only black West Indians were superstitious, so "the reputation of the Jumbé Rock, as well as that of the Duppy's Hole, kept the proximity of these noted places clear of all dark-skinned stragglers".[58] When the slaves *do* see Chakra, they are of course convinced that they are seeing a duppy.

Gratified that his plans for revenge are coming together, Chakra's face is filled with "demoniac joy" and his laughter is "wild" and "maniac-like". After Cynthia's departure, Jessuron comes to visit; by his lack of surprise at the contents of the hut, he is revealed as having "worshipped" at the temple of Obi before. They begin their deliberations with swigs from the bottle of cognac

---

57 Ibid., 211–12.
58 Ibid., 213–14.

that Jessuron has brought with him. Jessuron informs Chakra that another of the three justices who sat at his trial has died and suggests that Providence may have had a hand in dispatching him, to which Chakra replies with a leer, "Or de Dibbil, mo' like, maybe?"

Jessuron enquires about Cynthia.

> "And she saysh she will help you to set the obeah-shpell for him?"
>
> "Hab no fear – she do all dat. Obi had spell oba her, dat make her do mose anythin' – ah! anythin' in de worl' – satin shoo. Obi all-powerful wi' dat gal."
>
> "Yesh, yesh!" assented the Jew; "I knowsh all that. And if Obi wash to fail," added he, doubtingly, "you hash a drink, goot Shakra – I know you hash a drink, ash potent as Obi or any other of your gotsh."[59]

Chakra and Jessuron proceed to discuss the specifics of Vaughan's murder.

> "How long dosh it take your shpell to work?" inquired the penn-keeper, after an interval of silence, in which he seemed to be making some calculation.
>
> "Dat," replied the negro, "dat depend altogedder on de saccomstance ob how long de spell am *wanted* to work. Ef 'im wanted, Chakra make 'im in tree day fotch de 'trongest indiwidibble cla out o' 'im boots; or in tree hour he do same – but ob coorse dat ud be too soon fo' be safe. A spell of tree hours too 'trong. Dat not Obi work – 'im look berry like pisen."
>
> "Poison – yesh, yesh, it would."
>
> "Tree day too short – tree week am de correct time. Den de spell work 'zackly like fever ob de typos. Nobody had s'picion bout 'um."
>
> ...
>
> "You say de word, Massr Jake. Obi no like to nigga. Nigga only brack man: he no get pay fo' 'im work. Obi 'zemble buckra man. He no work 'less him pay."
>
> "Yesh – yesh! dat ish only shust and fair. Obi should be paid; but shay, goot Shakra! how much ish his prishe for a shpell of thish kind?"
>
> "Ef he hab no interest hissef in de workin' ob de 'pell, he want a hunder poun'. When he hab interest, das diff'rent – den he take fifty."
>
> "Fifty poundsh! That ish big monish, good Shakra! In thish case Obi hash an interest – more ash anybody elshe. He hash an enemy, and wants refenge. Ish that not true, goot Shakra!"
>
> "Das da troof. Chakra no go fo' deny 'im. But das jess why Obi 'sent do dat leetle *chore* fo' fifty poun'. Obi enemy big buckra – 'trong as you hab jess say – berry diff'cult fo' 'pell 'im. Any odder myal-man charge de full hunder poun'. Fack, no odder able do de job – no odder but ole Chakra hab dat power."

---

59 Ibid., 222.

"Shay no more about the prishe. Fifty poundsh be it. Here'sh half down." The tempter tossed a purse containing coin into the outstretched palm of the obeah-man. "All I shtipulate for ish, that in three weeks you earn the other half; and then we shall be shquare with the Cushtos Vochan – for I hash my refenge to shatisfy ash well as you, Shakra."

"Nuff sed, Massr Jake. 'Fore tree day de 'pell sha' be put on. You back come to de Duppy Hole tree night from dis, you hear how 'im work. Whugh!"[60]

After Jessuron leaves and Chakra has conducted him across the lagoon, the Obeah man mutters to himself, "ole villum Jew wuss dan Chakra – wuss dan de Debbil hisself!'" But Chakra does not just want revenge on Vaughan; years ago Chakra's suit was rejected by Catherine's mother, and now the Obeah man has his eye on her daughter. With Vaughan out of the way, he thinks Catherine will "sleep in de arms ob Chakra de myal-man."[61]

Kate, as we have already noted, is so light-skinned as to be able to pass for white. In making her his heroine, Reid has invested her character with the qualities normally reserved by white writers for white women. She carries herself modestly and she is generous and kind; in short, she possesses a certain nobility. Additionally, Kate appears to have little awareness of her black heritage and does not identify in any way with the blacks around her. The slaves call her "Lilly Quasheba" but Kate identifies completely with her white parent and with white society. In Chakra's desire for Kate's quadroon mother and for Kate herself, Reid, far from subverting the conventional wisdom of the day, which held that black men desired white women, reinforces it. When thinking of Catherine, "a lurid light glared up in [Chakra's] sunken eyes, while his white, shark-like teeth were displayed in an exulting grin – hideous as if the Demon himself were smiling over some monstrous menace".[62]

Jessuron, on the other hand, desires Vaughan's death so that Herbert will inherit his estate along with Judith, whom Jessuron is hoping Herbert will marry. Jessuron knows that under Jamaica's laws, only the children of whites or mustees can inherit their father's property if it is willed to them. Kate, though herself a mustee, is the daughter of a quadroon and thus can inherit only up to fifteen hundred pounds worth of her father's estate, even if he were to will her the whole thing. Had Quasheba been a mustee, then her child by a white man would have been considered white and could have inherited her father's property. Jamaican

---

60 Ibid., 222–24.
61 Ibid., 225.
62 Ibid., 225–26.

planters did all in their power to ensure that property remained in white hands and white power was maintained. A planter wanting to will his property to his coloured child had to request the passage of a special act in the Assembly; though Vaughan fully intends to do so, he has not yet submitted his request.

Chakra begins his preparations the night after Jessuron's visit.

> As he bent over the fire – like a he-Hecate stirring her witches' cauldron – his earnest yet stealthy manner, combined with his cat-like movements and furtive glances, betrayed some devilish design.
>
> This idea was strengthened on looking at objects that lay near to his hand – some portions of which had been already consigned to the pot. A cutacoo rested upon the floor, containing plants of several species; among which a botanist could have recognized the branched *calalue*, the dumb-cane, and various other herbs and roots of noxious fame. Conspicuous was the "Savannah flower", with its tortuous stem and golden corolla – a true dogbane, and one of the most potent of vegetable poisons.
>
> By its side could be seen its antidote – the curious nuts of the "nhandiroba": for the myal-man could *cure* as well as *kill*, whenever it became his interest to do so.
>
> Drawing from such a larder, it was plain that he was not engaged in the preparation of his supper. Poisons, not provisions, were the ingredients of the pot.
>
> The specific he was now concocting was from various sources, but chiefly from the sap of the Savannah flower. It was the *spell of Obeah!*
>
> For whom was the Coromantee preparing this precious hell-broth?
>
> His mutterings as he stooped over the pot revealed the name of his intended victim.
>
> "You may be 'trong, Cussus Vaugh'n – dat I doan deny; but, by de power ob Obeah, you soon shake in you shoes."[63]

But Mayne Reid's Obeah man is too cunning to believe in it himself. For Chakra, Obeah is simply a tool with which to frighten other blacks. "Obeah!" he shouts in scorn. "Ha! ha! ha! Dat do fo' de know-nuffin niggas. My Obeah am de Sabbana flower, de branch calalue, and the alligator apple – dem's de 'pell mo' powerful dan Obi hisseff – dem's de stuff dat gib de shibberin' body and de staggerin' limbs to de enemies ob Chakra. Whugh!"[64]

When Cynthia returns and asks if the bottle full of the poison is the love spell, Chakra tells her, "Dat bottle . . . am de obeah-'pell.'" From the ceiling thatch he pulls out a coconut containing a paste made from the sapotamam-

---

63   Ibid., 235–37.
64   Ibid., 237.

mee and tells her that's the love mixture, the one which will make Cubina love her and only her. It will make them "like two turtle dove in de 'pring time". He gives the bottle to Cynthia and tells her it is for Vaughan. Not a complete fool, she asks whether it is poison. No, he replies, because it will not kill him off right away, but maybe "long time atterward". When she seems reluctant, he tells her that if she refuses to give it to Vaughan he will not put the love spell on Cubina. More than that, he will set Obeah on her! Cynthia is terrified and agrees to do as he asks. Chakra has chosen his agent well, since it is Cynthia who is responsible for making the rum punch Vaughan drinks every night before he goes to bed. Chakra tells her how she is to mix the concoction into the rum punch and in what quantity.

To further impress Cynthia, Chakra goes into a small room to invoke the god Accompong, whom he says no woman must see but who comes whenever he calls. Cynthia hears weird sounds coming from the room and then two voices, one of which she readily recognizes as Chakra's. Sometimes they talk in an "unknown tongue" and she cannot understand them, but what is in English or "negro *patois*" fills her with dread.

> Chakra, chantant:–
> "Open de bottle – draw de cork,
> De 'pell he work – de 'pell he work;
> De buckra man muss die!"
> *"Muss die!"* repeated Accompong, in a voice that sounded as if from the interior of an empty hogshead.
> "De yella gal she gib 'im drink;
> It make 'im sick – it make 'im sr'ink,
> It send 'im to 'im grave!"
> *"Him grave!"* came the response of Accompong.
> "An' if de yella gal refuse,
> She 'tep into de buckra's shoes,
> An' fill de buckra's tomb."
> *"Buckra's tomb!"* echoed the African god, in a sonorous and emphatic voice, that told there was no alternative to the fate hypothetically proclaimed.
> There was a short interval of silence, then the shrill, conch-like sound was again heard – as before, followed by the long-drawn bass.
> This was the exorcism of the god – as the same sounds, previously heard, had been his invocation.
> It was also the *finale* of the ceremony.[65]

---

65 Ibid., 248.

When Chakra comes out, he advises Cynthia to do what she has been told or, as the god has suggested, her life will be worthless.

As Cynthia is hurrying back through the woods that night, she is met by Jessuron and informs him that Vaughan is planning to go to Spanish Town the following morning. Jessuron instantly understands that this means the custos plans to petition the Assembly for the special act to make Kate his heiress, and he realizes he must act quickly to prevent it. What they do not know is that Yola and Cubina, trysting nearby, have overheard them. Though Cubina does not understand why Jessuron would want to stop Vaughan, he knows it can be for no good reason, so he follows them after bidding Yola goodbye.

At the Duppy's Hole, Jessuron signals his arrival to Chakra, watched in amazement by Cubina, who is startled to see someone approaching across the lagoon: "Midships of the craft, a form was crouching. Was it human or demon? The aspect was demon – the shape scarce human. Long, ape-like arms; a hunched back; teeth gleaming in the moonlight like the incisors of a shark; features everything but human to one who had not seen them before!"[66] Cubina recognizes Chakra and remembers something Quaco said about seeing Chakra's ghost. "Quaco, like most of his colour, a firm believer in 'Duppy' and 'Jumbé', had believed it to be Chakra's ghost he had seen"; terrified, he fled the area "instead of making an attempt to pursue the apparition, and prove whether it was flesh and blood".[67]

Cubina, however, is a mulatto and thus, according to Mayne Reid, "less given to superstitious inclinings". He follows Jessuron down the cliff and sneaks his way to Chakra's hut as Cynthia turns to make her way back to Mount Welcome. As Cubina listens to the conversation inside the hut, he wonders if there exists on Jamaica or even in the whole world "two such villains as Chakra, the Coromantee, and Jessuron, the Jew". Reid has earlier admitted that it was not only Jews who were slave-dealers or slave-traders, but the constant repetition of the appellation "Jessuron, the Jew", along with his description of the man himself, suggest he was an anti-Semite.

Chakra, though larger and presumably stronger than Jessuron, cowers before him. Jessuron is upset that Vaughan is going to act before he can do anything about it and also upset because Cynthia has told him that Cubina and Vaughan are plotting against him and that Cubina told the planter about the Foolah prince's capture. During the conversation Jessuron reveals that

---

66   Ibid., 269.
67   Ibid., 271.

Quasheba, Kate's mother, had loved a Maroon and that Cubina is their son. Cubina is shocked at the news, never having known his mother. He is overjoyed to realize that he has a sister, but what he hears next is not so edifying.

Jessuron wants Chakra to put an Obeah spell on Cubina, but Chakra replies that it took him twenty years to spell Cubina's father and that it is not so easy to spell a Maroon. Nevertheless, Chakra promises to do what he can to put a death spell on Cubina. Even more urgently, Jessuron wants Chakra to see to Vaughan's death; he threatens to tell officials that the Obeah man is alive and well and living in the Duppy's Hole if he does not effect Vaughan's demise before the planter has a chance to reach Spanish Town. Chakra swears his Obeah spell will work and that Cynthia will play her part, but Jessuron is not completely convinced. When he returns to his estate, he goes to see the Cuban slave-hunters and tells them he wishes the custos to be intercepted on the road to Spanish Town. Jessuron wants to prevent Vaughan from applying for the special act and also from instituting an investigation into the case of the Foolah prince.

Meanwhile, back at Mount Welcome, Vaughan is getting ready to set out for Spanish Town, despite how ill he feels. Before he goes out, Cynthia offers him a "swizzle" drink in which is a strong infusion of the "baneful *Savannah flower* . . . one of the deadliest of vegetable poisons".[68] On his way, Vaughan falls sick and is conveyed to a nearby abandoned hut while his servant goes for aid. As he lies there, Chakra makes his appearance, "the shoulders, surmounted by the hideous hump – the arms long and ape-like". Vaughan screams in fear, but Chakra laughs and tells him that he will soon be dead by his death spell and that he, Chakra, saved Vaughan's death for the last after killing the other two justices. Vaughan begs for mercy and tells Chakra he will give him anything he wants, but Chakra says he cares nothing for money, that he has enough for his wants, and that the only thing the custos has that he cares about, he will take anyway, and that is "Lilly Quasheba". At those words, Vaughan dies, overcome by horror.[69]

That night, Jessuron and Chakra meet in the woods and Jessuron pays the Obeah man the rest of the money he promised for Vaughan's death. Jessuron offers another fifty for Cubina's death and Chakra undertakes to see to the Maroon captain's demise. When Jessuron asks if he will use Cynthia for that purpose, Chakra indicates that she has outlived her usefulness; as a talkative

---

68 Ibid., 3:35.
69 Ibid., 118–22.

woman, she will have to die in order for him to keep his secrets. Neither realize that Cynthia has been listening to them, but after Jessuron leaves, she sneezes and Chakra discovers her hiding place. He strangles her to death.

Chakra abducts Kate after setting the Great House on fire. Cubina and Herbert, returning to Mount Welcome with Vaughan's body, arrive too late to save the estate, but Cubina blows his horn to summon his Maroons and they set off in hot pursuit of the abductors. They come upon Yola, who followed Chakra and is able to tell them where the Obeah man went. But when they arrive near Chakra's hut, Kate is lying there as if dead, and Chakra is nowhere around.

Quaco, it turns out, is the bush-doctor of the Maroons and knows something of myalism. Observing the remains of the phial containing the sleeping draught Chakra has given the girl, he begins rummaging around the hut to find its antidote.

> In addition to being Cubina's deputy on all important occasions, Quaco was the doctor of the band; and in his medical experience he had picked up some knowledge of the system of Obeah – more especially of the trick by which, in the belief of the ignorant, a dead body can be brought to life again – that dread secret of the Coromantee charlatan, known in the West Indies as myalism.[70]

Quaco finds what he is looking for and, in no time, Kate is restored to herself and she and Herbert declare their mutual love.

Finally, after a few more misadventures – Judith accidentally kills herself while trying to shoot Kate and both Chakra and Jessuron drown – Yola and Cubina become husband and wife and Herbert and Kate are married. Like the main villains of the story, Jowler, the slaver captain who turned over Cingües to Jessuron, also meets an unhappy fate: when he returns to the Foolah kingdom to negotiate the purchase of more slaves, he is killed and eaten! On hearing this news from Cubina, who has gone to Africa to meet his new in-laws, Kate expresses her happiness that Cubina will be leaving such a country where "such scenes are too common".[71]

Reid, of course, has presented a rather sanitized version of slavery, so one can certainly see how the West Indies would come across as a more favourable place for blacks than Africa. This was, of course, the argument that the planters were making, and it is no great leap to arrive at the conclusion that Mayne

---

70   Ibid., 293–94.
71   Ibid., 351.

Reid himself subscribed to this opinion. His Jamaica is a fairly innocent place, marred only by the machinations of a Jew and his co-conspirator, an Obeah man. Other than that, life on the island is not portrayed negatively. The slaves we meet who do not belong to Jessuron are presented as fairly happy. Yola is happy. Cynthia would be happy if only Cubina still loved her. Kate, though the daughter of a slave, leads a comfortable and pampered life.

Mayne Reid only hints at the darker side of a slave society when he describes the attempted execution of Chakra and Jessuron's enlistment of the Cuban slave-hunters after Cingües runs away. He fails to offer any observations about the backbreaking work done by plantation slaves, the cruelties they suffered, the families torn apart or the horrific whippings and other punishments to which they were subjected. A runaway like Cingües, for example, would have been severely whipped and/or would have lost an ear in punishment, but Reid ignores all of this. Slavery is merely a backdrop for this story of Semitic greed, thwarted love and Obeah.

It is worth noting that Maroon communities were established by runaway slaves who fought off all efforts to re-enslave them. They took great pride in their African blood, yet Cubina is presented as light-skinned – an honorary white in appearance and behaviour who does not subscribe to the superstitions of blacks like Quaco. If whites (that is, British whites) were at the top of the evolutionary pyramid, as was the accepted wisdom of the day, then to people like Mayne Reid, mulattoes with their white blood were not far below. Certainly, they were above both creole blacks and African blacks but Mayne Reid had a fuzzy understanding of Jamaica's Maroons. The real ones, though they may have felt themselves superior to slaves, would surely have rejected this notion of white or mulatto superiority. In addition, Reid appears to have forgotten all about Nanny, the Maroon leader and Obeah woman.

HAMEL, THE OBEAH MAN

Though published anonymously, it appears to have been an open secret that *Hamel, the Obeah Man* was written by Cynric Williams, the author of *A Tour Through the Island of Jamaica*. In fact, several reviews of *Hamel* refer to the travel narrative, which was published earlier. For example, the *Westminster Review* recorded its pleasure "that the author, who last year published an amusing *Tour in Jamaica*, has selected that island for his scene".[72]

---

72   *Morning Chronicle*, 11 June 1827.

In *Hamel*, Williams gave free rein to his animosity for Methodists and abolitionists and lays bare his support for (as he saw it) the beleaguered planters. In *Hamel* he repeats, again and again, his admiration for quadroons, his conviction that all black men desire white women, that most slaves rejoiced in their enslavement, and that slavery was essentially a benevolent institution under which the blacks were well taken care of. More to the point, he fleshes out the argument he only hints at in *Tour*, that, as the enemy of missionaries, Obeah practitioners had reason to make common cause with the planters. In *Hamel*, Williams presents us with an Obeah man, a slave, so grateful to a white man for removing him from his servitude to another black man that he undermines a slave rebellion.

Hamel, the Obeah Man begins with a description of an unnamed man riding in the countryside who comes across a group of black women. He flirts with them and asks about other women on the various estates, but he confuses them by also enquiring after their souls and whether they exist in God's grace. (Stories of the scandalous behaviour of West Indian planters and their mulatto progeny had already made the rounds in Britain and were decried by abolitionists and missionaries. Williams here turns the criticism back on them by accusing them of the same lechery.) Shortly after the man moves on from the group, a sudden heavy rainfall forces him to find shelter in a cave.

The cave appears to be inhabited but nobody responds when he calls out and he explores its contents:

> In a recess stood a couple of spears, one solely of hard wood, whose point was rendered still harder by fire; the other was shod with iron and rusted apparently with blood; a bamboo rod, ten feet in length and about an inch in thickness, leaned against the rock beside them, carved or tattoed [*sic*] from end to end. In another angle of the vault was a calabash filled with various sorts of hair, among which it was easy to discriminate that of white men, horses, and dogs. These were huddled together, and crowded with feathers of various birds, especially those of domestic poultry and wild parrots, with one or two of the spoils of a macaw. A human skull was placed beside this calabash, from which the teeth were missing; but on turning it up, the traveller found them with a quantity of broken glass crammed into the cerebellum, and covered up with a wad of silk cotton, to prevent them from falling out. There were several other skulls in a second recess, some perfect, some which had been broken apparently with a sharp pointed instrument, and many of them serving as calabashes or boxes to hold the strange property of the master of the cave; one was a receptacle for gunpowder, which the inquisitive traveller narrowly escaped inflaming; a

second contained bullets and shot of various sizes, mixed with old nails and pieces of rag; and from a third he saw with no little horror a black snake uncoil itself the moment he touched it. There were three muskets, all old and out of order; a pistol and two cutlasses, disposed on different ledges of the rock; a large conch-shell fitted with a belt of mahoe bark, to be worn over the shoulder, hung from a projection, with several other pieces of rope made of similar materials, to which were attached rings of wood and hollowed stones, perhaps intended for amulets or charms. A lamp of clay at last arrested his attention; it had carved on it some rude figures, and was filled with oil of the Palma Christi, having a wick formed of the fibres of the plantain stalk.[73]

Roland, for such we now learn is the traveller's name, falls asleep in the cave and has a nightmare, from which he awakes in

> amazement, not to say horror, on perceiving before him the very figure of the demon of his dream. . . . Of his features little or nothing could be seen, except the light gleaming from his eyeballs. He stood in an attitude which the dreamer's fears quickly determined to be the menacing posture of the demon from which he had shrunk; the forefinger of his right hand elevated, the left hand leaning on a bamboo staff. "In the name of God or Devil," cried Roland impatiently, "who or what art thou?"[74]

Williams writes that "a less experienced person" might suppose, at least for the moment, that it was the devil himself before him, but Roland does not think he is important enough for the "Enemy of mankind" to pay him personal attention. Roland questions the newcomer about the cave and the Obeah implements and about who lives there, but receives only oblique answers.

Hamel, a "dealer in magic, for he was no less a personage, was of a slight and elegant make, though very small of stature, being considerably under the middle size. His age was at least sixty; but the lines which that had traced on his features indicated, notwithstanding his profession, no feeling hostile to his fellow-creatures, at war with human nature, or dissatisfied with himself."[75] Despite Roland's first apprehensions about him, born out of his nightmare, Williams wants readers to think of this Obeah man as a sympathetic figure, so he is not depicted as someone who would inspire terror.

Roland and Hamel, who is also the slave watchman on an estate owned

---

73 [Cynric Williams], *Hamel, the Obeah Man* (London: Hunt and Clarke, 1827), 1:19–20.
74 Ibid., 24.
75 Ibid., 28–29.

by the absent Fairfax, embark on something of a philosophical discussion. It turns out that Roland is a passionate abolitionist who may be hoping to stir the slaves of a nearby plantation to rebellion and, perhaps, "in turn apply the whips and chains to their oppressors". Hamel argues that there are whips and chains in England too, and that white men should leave Negroes alone, but Roland retorts that white men are needed "who shall teach your children to read, to write, to pray to the only true God". The following passage gives an idea of the flavour of the argument between the two:

> "Your God," interrupted Roland, "has left you slaves; the Christian's God will make you free."
>
> "Ah!" cried the wizard, "is it so? Will your God make the Negroes free? ... Will he leave us unencumbered with white parsons? What security can you give us of that? It were better I belonged still to a tyrannical master, than that I was subjected to a tyrannical white priest, who should take from me one of my ten fingers."
>
> "Your master," cried Roland rather exultingly, "takes the labour of all your ten fingers."
>
> "Not so," rejoined Hamel: "we work, it is true, for our masters; but they feed us, clothe us, give us land and houses, attend us in sickness and old age, and leave our minds, our thoughts, to ourselves."
>
> "They leave you to the Devil," said the white man. "If you had a spark of courage, you would emancipate yourselves; if you had one glimmering of the greatness of our God, you would take up the cross, and devote yourselves to his service."[76]

Hamel pours some white powder on Roland's palm. He tells him to close his hand tightly and that, if he is guilty of murder, when he opens it again, the powder will be stained with blood. Roland's heart races but, when he opens his hand, the powder is still white. While he is still feeling happy with relief, Hamel seizes his hand and rubs the powder with his finger. It turns "crimson as the sun-setting in a storm", and "the Methodist" trembles with shock. Clearly he has a dark secret. He accuses Hamel of being "in league with the fiends of hell", but Hamel tells him his secret is safe with him, that he will tell no one.

Soon after, another black man, Combah, enters the cave. Roland knows him and is clearly dismayed to find that he is a friend of the Obeah man. "Are you too leagued with the Prince of Darkness?" he asks the newcomer.

---

76 Ibid., 32–33.

"Is it for this you have been baptized, and made a member of the church of Christ? Have you redeemed your soul from hell, to cast it headlong into the bottomless pit again? And have you faith even in Obeah spells, philtres, and charms? . . . I quit you; I renounce you; lead me from the cave; let me leap into one of your abysses; hurl me down the rocks; kill, murder me. My soul shall never testify to such abominations, nor my efforts for your temporal and eternal salvation be blasted by the breath of those who tamper with the Devil."[77]

Hamel replies that they "do not tamper with the Devil" and do not know him. Neither, he observes, do they attack Roland's religion or his god, though they had a religion before they knew about Christianity. Hamel also points out that their aims are similar and that, just as Roland has promised to aid Combah in his rebellion, he, Hamel, has sworn to make him king. Combah tells Roland that, at present, the white people, mulattoes and quadroons believe in Christianity but the Negroes believe in Obeah. When they are free, he says, they will be able to choose what religion to follow. (Williams's portrayal of Combah is intended to show that the conversion of blacks to Christianity was not a real conversion and that, contrary to the protestations of the missionaries, black people retained their core belief in Obeah.)

Roland contemplates leaving and denouncing the Obeah man to the authorities, but, on second thought, he decides it might be more "prudent after all to give or appear to give way to the Obeah man, who had such a strange and perverse power over the minds of the Blacks".[78] After all, he thinks, once the rebellion is in full swing, it will be easy to get rid of Hamel. And then again there is the fact that, for the treacherous Roland, the planned rebellion is mere cover for his plans to abduct a young woman who has no love for him but with whom he is obsessed. The missionary is counting on the fact that if the rebellion fails, the whites and those who hold Roland in high esteem will not believe he was one of the conspirators; if it succeeds, then he will be Combah's right-hand man, his viceroy.

Meanwhile, on Mr Guthrie's estate in St Mary's parish, a band of black and brown men has shown up claiming to have been shipwrecked and seeking shelter from the storm. Their real object, however, is to raid the house and abduct a young white woman by the name of Joanna, the same young woman on whom Roland has designs, but they plan to take her to be Combah's wife,

---

77 Ibid., 41–42.
78 Ibid., 50.

not Roland's. They are accompanied by Sebastian, a mulatto (actually the white planter Fairfax, in disguise), whom they have rescued from a shipwreck. He claims to be a fugitive from Cuba, but Guthrie notes that his speech is far above that of other blacks and mulattoes. The quadroon servant Michal is quite taken with him. For her part, Joanna reveals that she harbours an affection for Fairfax, who has been denounced by Roland as a buccaneer and a murderer. Sebastian and the robbers leave the next day, the storm having foiled their plans.

In the meantime, Combah, Roland and the others have been preparing for the rebellion by making their way to an abandoned great house where the rebels are gathering. There Combah takes one of his followers aside and instructs him to bring back some dirt from the grave of a child buried about eighteen months before. As Combah is waiting, Roland begins preaching about the perils he has endured in order to save their souls and help them to know about God and the Christian religion, which makes no distinction between masters and slaves. Roland's sermon contains one of the novel's more curious passages:

> "You will perhaps say I am a white man. So I am outwardly – my skin is white; but my heart is like yours; and if that is black as your skins, so is mine. I am an exception to the white men; I have never flogged you, nor ravished your daughters." Here a loud demoniac sort of laugh was heard from the cellar below, where, as Roland at the sound recollected, his Obeah rival was at work.[79]

As Roland continues his sermon he tells his audience that there are many white people in England who want to make them free, including a great lord whose ancestors were very rich because they stole lands and treasure from others. "He has lands and slaves – no, not slaves, poor men – to work for them and for him. . . . He gives them no clothes, and nothing to eat; but he is a great, wise man, and very religious and virtuous." Williams may be alluding to the abolitionist William Wilberforce, who became independently wealthy while still a young man and later turned deeply religious. But the reference is more likely to Bennet Langton, a Lincolnshire landowner born to an Anglican minister who was partly responsible for recruiting Wilberforce to head the campaign against slavery in the British Parliament.

Roland goes on to point out that the masters give the slaves "houses, and clothes, and fish, and grounds to cultivate" only so they will work harder. "Did

---

79 Ibid., 111.

not those of St Domingo make themselves free? *They* were brave men: they had white wives when they were free; for they loved their mistresses, and shed only the blood of their oppressors."[80] He also launches into a condemnation of parsons and bishops, presumably as representatives of the Church of England, and tells the rebels that when they are free, they must continue to hearken to the missionaries and not to parsons.

Suddenly there is a small explosion from below Roland's improvised stage in the dilapidated great house. He falls through the floor and into the cellar, where Hamel is conducting his Obeah ceremony.

> he found himself among a dozen or more of wild-looking negroes, most of them naked to the waist; or if they had garments, they were more or less stained with blood. There was likewise a human skull on a table in the midst of them, filled with earth; and a calabash, containing a filthy-looking mixture, placed beside a small iron pot which flamed with burning rum, whose blue and ghastly light, sufficient to illuminate the cellar, cast a glare of deeper hideousness on the faces and persons of these practitioners.[81]

Combah stations people around the ruins to ensure that no one surprises them at their Obeah rites, since their punishment would be either death or banishment. He castigates Roland for not proclaiming him king of Jamaica during his sermon and for not instructing the rebels to come and kiss his hand. Combah tells Roland that he trusts neither him nor his religion, and that what he promises today, he is afraid of tomorrow.

Combah calls on Hamel to administer the oath, which draws a pious protest from Roland, who begs to be spared "the sight of such atrocities, which your religion may justify, but mine contemplates as a sacrifice to the Devil, an acknowledgment of the power of Satan". Combah tells Roland that, as someone who has "witnessed the rites of Obeah, the mysteries of the enslaved Coromantins", he has to swear to secrecy. He must either participate in the ceremony or die. One of Combah's men, a Moco, "a people known . . . to be cannibals", offers to kill the missionary, but Roland hastily agrees to take the oath:

> Upon this, the skull was handed to him by Hamel; and he repeated without delay the words dictated to him; imprecating curses on his own head, that it might speedily become like that which he held in his hand, filled with dirt, if he ever mentioned to any man, woman, or child, of any colour, what he had

---

80   Ibid., 114.
81   Ibid., 117.

seen this night, or at any other time, of Obeah. The skull was then deposited again on the table; and Hamel, taking the calabash containing, as was related, a filthy-looking mixture, held it close to the Missionary's face, and bid him see that it was blood – blood drawn from their own veins, and mixed with gunpowder and with the grave-dirt of the skull. He dipped his finger in the mess, and crossed the face and the breast of Roland; finally holding it to his lips, and commanding him to taste and swallow a portion, and then to say after him as follows: – "If I lie, if I am treacherous, if I mean to deceive in way those whose blood I have tasted, may the grave-dirt make my heart rot, till it bursts and tumbles out before my face! May I die, and never awake in the grave, or awake to everlasting pain and torment, and become the slave of the white man's devil for ever and ever!" Having repeated this, the mixture was again put to his lips: he tasted it, and sunk to the ground in an agony created by his horror and disgust.[82]

While he is in his faint, the rest take the oath. When he wakes, Roland wars with his conscience, distraught at having to recommend as king a man linked with a necromancer, a man who has taken an oath "of a nature so diabolical" as to preclude all adherence to Christian tenets. Roland also realizes that Hamel is his rival for Combah's allegiance and, by extension, that of Combah's followers, the Negroes.

Seeing that he has the upper hand, Hamel is contemptuous of Roland and his pretensions and points out that the missionary could commit "ten thousand crimes", because no one in Jamaica will dare punish him while he has his "Bible-books" and preaches his Methodist religion.

"Though you were convicted of rebellion and murder, of rape, incest – hear me if you please, master Roland – though you combined with thieves and assassins, preached murder to them, and drank blood from an Obeah cup in token of your contract with them; and though all the inhabitants of this island knew it, believed it, and could prove it, – aha! none dare prosecute you; or if they did, and proved you guilty, they dare not punish you. They would condemn you, and send to England for advice, or let you escape; and if they sent to England, are there not thousands like yourself to vindicate you, to prove you innocent, to swear your crimes are imputations, lies, inventions; and that you are, were, and must be, a holy, virtuous, man – a martyr, at the worst? Ah, Roland! yours is a fine religion; but what will become of me? – The very mention of mine damns me, with your great friends, to everlasting fire and torment – to a level lake of

---

82 Ibid., 122–25.

Scotch brimstone. I should be hung and quartered, and my head stuck on a pole, or on the top of a mill-house – the Christians one and all would gibbet me – although I had never committed one crime beyond that (if it be a crime) of selling or giving away puntees, feathers, or glass bottles, to scare thieves from the orange or shaddock trees. Would the white men in the island believe I could be innocent of deeper crimes?"[83]

Hamel accuses Roland and the other missionaries and parsons of doing nothing all day but eating and drinking and making love to the mulatto and quadroon girls. Roland ignores this and asks Hamel if he knows who the mulatto Sebastian is. Hamel replies that he should avoid him, for he is a dangerous man and his bitter enemy. Hamel then warns Combah that if the alarm is given, Jamaica will be put under a state of martial law, so he must do whatever he needs to do quickly. With Hamel and Roland at his side, and in front of his "sable" subjects, Combah is quickly, if farcically, crowned.

While Roland and Hamel argue about the unction to be administered, Combah places the crown on his head himself, but it has been bent out of shape by the drunken man who carried it during the brief procession, and it sits askew. When Roland finally takes the oil from Hamel and is about to pour it over Combah's head, the clear oil turns red. Roland throws the phial from him in horror, and Combah, thinking the missionary seeks to insult him, grabs him by the throat. Their struggle is interrupted when Sebastian appears on a cliff above them and yells that the Maroons, hostile to rebels, are coming. Everybody runs away and Sebastian comes down to survey the empty scene. He is still there when Hamel returns. The Obeah man greets him joyfully, but Sebastian (Fairfax) asks him whether he is part of the plot to abduct Joanna, overthrow the whites and make Combah king.

Hamel was enslaved in Africa by a black man who sold him off the continent, apparently to another black man. Thus he feels himself indebted to Fairfax, the white man who he claims saved him from "the fangs of a tyrant, from the basest slavery, from the dominion of one who was a slave in my own country". There follows what must surely be one of the strangest speeches put into the mouth of a black character by a white author:

"Why do your friends in England send Missionaries to preach here? Are the merchants and mortgagees there the slaves of the Methodists? And why does King George want to make the slaves free for nothing, after the white men have

---

[83] Ibid., 151–52.

paid for them? You know, master, there must be something wicked here, if the king says we should be free; but what will be our freedom? What are we to do – the ignorant, nasty, drunken Negroes, who were born slaves in Congo, and Coromantin, and Houssa, and Mundingo. Some will make the others work: there will be slaves for ever, unless the white men stay with soldiers and cannons to keep the strong ones from beating the weak ones, and making the women do all the work . . . your great men in England must be very silly or very wicked, or all must be wrong here: for they will make Jamaica ten times worse than my own country was ever made by war, and fighting, and robbery, and murder."[84]

When Fairfax charges him again with being an Obeah man, Hamel answers that all he does, he does in Fairfax's service: his power serves Fairfax.

Over the next few days, the tide of events begins to turn in Fairfax's favour as Roland's former servant (who has gone into hiding) is discovered by Hamel, singing a mournful song about the man who looks so fair and smells so sweet but was sent to Jamaica by the "white man's devil". This servant tells Hamel and Fairfax (disguised as the mulatto, Sebastian) that it was Roland who, years ago, set fire to Guthrie's estate, then used the diversion to break into the house and rape Mrs Guthrie, Joanna's mother. No friend to Fairfax because of Joanna's attachment to the young man, he later managed to convince Mrs Guthrie that it was Fairfax who had raped her.

Several adventures later, Roland complains about Hamel to Guthrie and Fairfax: "He is a dabbler in Obeah. . . . I denounce him to you, Mr Guthrie; I will prove upon oath that he deals in philtres and charms; that he practises; that he is looked on as a wizard; that he practises the most – that he dwells in a cave full of abominations."[85] But Guthrie tells Roland that he is merely angry because, after he abducted Michal, Hamel rescued the quadroon from him. Roland is incensed that the word of a Negro is believed over his.

Things go rapidly downhill for the conspirators. The militia is called out to hunt for Combah and the truth about Roland is revealed. Roland is wanted for the murder of a child, for the attempted abduction of Joanna and for preaching sedition. Combah and Roland come to rely on each other as fugitives from justice, but neither trusts the other. Though Roland racks his brains to come up with a way out of his predicament, he realizes he is trapped. Too many people know of his misdeeds. Hamel finds Roland, offers him ten doubloons and advises him to flee the island and take Combah with him. Combah tells

---

84   Ibid., 197–98.
85   Ibid., 2:17.

Roland he should indeed fly, for he has no more use for him. "Do you think we were blinded with your religion, with your pretences, your psalms, and hymns, and prayers?" Combah asks Roland. "Do you think we could not see the wild boar dressed up in all this trumpery – the cunning, plotting, cheating, merciless, murderous priest – the sensual hypocrite? Yes, yes, I grant you, you deceived many; but think not you deceived me."[86] Roland shoots at Combah but only manages to set his own house on fire.

Both Combah and Roland are apprehended and Fairfax's estate is restored to him. But everything is not over yet. Hamel has a telling encounter with Fillbeer, the attorney who tried to steal Fairfax's estate from him.

> "Accursed villain!" cried [Fillbeer]; "you are that dabbler in spells and Obeah, who caused the turkeys to lay rotten eggs, and the chickens to have the pip. D—n you! I'll pheeze you, rascal! You shall grace a gibbet yet."
>
> "Thankye, master. Master's too kind – master likes hanging himself. He grease the gibbet well."
>
> "Scoundrel, do you mock me?" said Fillbeer, riding up as if to strike him with his whip. "It is you, you black monster, who bewitch the cows, is it? – who cause abortions among the women – who make your fellow-creatures eat dirt?"
>
> "Dirt!" said the Obeah man, emphatically – "dirt, master Fillbeer? It is such as you and preaching Roland who make my countrymen eat dirt. Who brought us from Africa? Who made slaves of us? Who treated – and treat us still – as the dirt they buy and sell? And while they affect to be for making us free, and for saving our *souls*, are cramming us with dirt, and trash, and filthy foolish lies?"[87]

It is intriguing to speculate on the character of Fillbeer. In *Tour*, Williams claims that blacks referred to the abolitionist Thomas Buxton as "the brewer or beerman". At the time, Buxton was a partner in the London brewery Truman, Hanbury, Buxton and Co. It must have provided Williams with a particularly vindictive pleasure to name one of his villains "Fillbeer". Most readers of the day would have recognized exactly who is being caricatured, though portraits from that time do not suggest that Buxton was fat, as Fillbeer is described. Constantly characterized as a "man-mountain", Fillbeer is a figure of scorn and ridicule and never comes off well in his exchanges with Hamel, Williams's mouthpiece. (Fillbeer's first name, Quinbus, is taken from *Gulliver's Travels* and is the name by which the Lilliputians called Gulliver; it means "man-mountain".)

---

86 Ibid., 54.
87 Ibid., 129–30.

Roland is arrested and imprisoned, but Hamel sends him a poisoned dagger to use on the gaoler and he escapes. The gaoler's wife, in a frenzy of grief for her husband, begs Combah for an antidote to heal her husband and frees him to get the herbs. He flees to the mountains, where he finds his associates of "the Obeah cup". They tell him that men from St Domingo have pulled into a nearby bay to advise enslaved in Jamaica on their insurrection. If the rebellion fails, the Jamaicans can escape in their boat.

Hamel, meanwhile, tells Joanna that the whites will be punished for taking him from his homeland, and that they are being punished already. "Is it not a crime now-a-days to be the master of slaves?" Hamel asks Joanna.

> "Who sends the Missionaries here to tell this to the Negroes? All the planters hate and fear the Missionaries. They are the ministers of vengeance, the agents of men blinded by vanity, who, without knowing anything about the matter, send them here to torment the Whites – aye, and the Blacks too. They will have vengeance in their turn."
>
> "Who? The Negroes?" said Joanna.
>
> "Yes, mistress – the Negroes; – look at Hayti. And they will again be punished for what they do. Look still at Hayti."
>
> "There are few Negroes who think as you do", said Joanna. "Most of them are too fond of the Missionaries."
>
> "If they knew them, as I have seen them! Look on the grave before you. I tell you that some of them are worse than devils – but God is just."[88]

Shortly after this exchange, Hamel reveals that he is there to protect Joanna from the men who still want to carry her away to be Combah's wife. He assures her that his presence will scare them away, but the men come on nevertheless; when he curses them, they smile at him and tell him they have been christened, so his curses mean nothing to them. Hamel fells several of the men with poisoned darts but the rest carry off Joanna and Michal.

Hamel regrets setting in motion the chain of events that led to Joanna's abduction. "I was wrong", said the Obeah man [to himself],

> to give Roland the means of escape, for it had been better that Combah had died on the scaffold, than that my friend – my friend? – yes, yes, he has been my friend – my friend Mr Fairfax should be injured in life, or property, or happiness, or hope. Combah was a minister of my revenge, but master Fairfax

---

88   Ibid., 185.

redeemed me from a tyrant. For his sake I had forgiven – I forgive – the white men, and will do for them all that can be done by Hamel before he dies."

He confesses to Guthrie and the militia.

"I can tell you, I was at the bottom of this plan of insurrection – yes – never start nor stare. I am determined to yield up myself – my life – everything. I would have revenged myself on the buckras for bringing me away from my own country, and selling me to a Negro. I would have made Combah king of the island, to revenge myself on the missionaries, and secured to him your daughter, and half-a-dozen more white women, to teach the buckras that black men have as much courage, and power, and knowledge, and strength, and right, as white ones. They will repay one day on all your heads. There is justice upon the earth, though it seems to sleep; and the black men shall, first or last, shed your blood, and toss your bodies into the sea!"[89]

Guthrie and the militia follow after the women's captors, but Hamel somehow manages to get to the cliffside where they are first. Guthrie can see him remonstrating with the rebels from where he is across the gorge. "'She lives, she lives yet!' he exclaimed, his agony of passion dissolving into tears. 'The Obeah man has saved her honour and her life! See, see how the rebellious cutthroats cringe before him! *Instar Jovis!* He treats them like the dirt they are. And ah! he kneels to Fairfax, and lays his master's hand on his own head!'"[90] (This passage recalls Grainger's wistful hope in an earlier section that Obeah practitioners could be put to good use by their white masters, once they were kept in their place.)

After Joanna and Michal's rescue, two of the women who were with the rebels go to Guthrie "not to supplicate for themselves, but to intercede for many who, they said, had been induced by Roland and others to take up arms in support of the rights which Mr Wilberforce had obtained for them. . . . 'they told the Negroes so, who were slaves'", Hamel says. "'They preached to us that the king of England had given liberty to all, had paid for their freedom; and they read out of big books, and little books, and Scotch books, that we should put the knives to the throats of the buckras, who then would own it was true.'"[91]

---

89 Ibid., 192–97.
90 Ibid., 271.
91 Ibid., 313.

The rebellion is all over, but before he sails off into the sunset, Hamel has more to say to the whites. Some of the rebels are slain, some have run away to the mountains, some will come in to surrender, and some, says Hamel, have gone back to

> "St Domingo, where they were invited to come from. . . . Your Missionaries have persuaded the Negroes that they are free; and they believe the king's proclamation, telling them they are still slaves, to be a forgery! It will not be long, therefore, before they rise again; and they will take the country from you, except the king of England, and the governor here, keep these preaching men in better order. What do you want with them? You have a bishop and regular parsons; good men, who tell the Negroes their duty as slaves, and try to keep the poor ignorant things quiet and happy. If you let any other people turn their heads, believe me, they will twist off yours. I declare to my God, I never saw such trumpery. Your king, your governor, and all yourselves (forgive me, gentlemen) are afraid of these white Obeah men. What a fuss is made with them, and what strange nonsense they preach! . . . If you or your king wish to make the Negroes free, do it at once; say they are free. Your white man's country has room for you all, and land and nyam-nyam enough. They are rich, and can pay the planters for their slaves, and houses, and estates, and works; but if they are not to be free by the law – forbid anybody to deceive them, on pain of death. I would hang or shoot the cunning, sneaking, fawning, fanatical, murderous villain, who tampered with the passions of my slaves, or dared to hint at such a circumstance as that of master Quashie holding a knife to his master's throat. [This was another furious arrow directed at radical abolitionists such as Stockdale and Shepherd, who urged the violent overthrow of slavery by the slaves themselves.] But you are no worth – (forgive me, gentlemen – I spoke without caution) – I mean you are afraid of the white Obeah men."[92]

Williams cannot resist taunting the Methodists again before the close of the book. He has Filbeer recall to himself that "he had often adverted to the resolutions of the Wesleyans in September 1824; and remembered that the ministers who subscribed to them were censured and recalled by the rest of the society – the gang (as he termed them to himself) in England [as per the events noted in an earlier section]".[93]

The *Westminster Review* declared itself pleased with Williams's fictional effort:

---

92   Ibid., 315–17.
93   Ibid., 317.

This is an entertaining, we may say instructive, novel. . . . We are glad, therefore, that the author, who last year published an amusing Tour in the Island of Jamaica, having the advantage of personal acquaintance with it, has selected that spot as the scene of his novel. . . . The author is no friend to the emancipation of the slaves, and he has evidently had an object beyond that of the mere novel-writer: that object is, to show that the slaves do not really want emancipation, and that, if it were granted, they are, in fact, not qualified to make a good use of it; and secondly, that much mischief has been done by the zealous missionaries who have been transported thither to convert them; that they have caused fear in the planter, and discontent in the slave, without improving the moral or intellectual condition of either. These are important topics; and instead of treating them in the way of argument, which would not be read, he has given a practical illustration of their working. . . . The author has a considerable respect for the clergy of the Establishment; . . . but a methodist missionary is the object of his detestation. . . . As far as the slaves are concerned, he has, we should suppose, presented us with a tolerably faithful picture of our black brethren, with the exception of two sable heroes, who, notwithstanding their complexion, are too highly coloured; but of the principal missionary, the author has been influenced by some degree of prejudice to draw an exaggerated picture. That such a creature may exist in nature, we do not deny, but he must be a rara avis, and it is the business of the novelist to deal rather with the probable than the possible. . . .

Both the Obeah man and the Missionary are the oracles of their followers, and they propose to lead them to the same end, viz. rebellion; but the means they take are somewhat different and inconsistent.

The author has invested the African magician, although by no means a scrupulously moral person (according to our code), with a superiority of character and conduct over the Missionary . . . Roland is throughout represented as an execrable villain, whereas the Obeah-man is distinguished by some fine traits of character . . . the author's work would have been less liable to suspicion, if his tone had been more moderate; . . . The immediate object of the author, must be in a great measure defeated by this violent portraiture. The work will be said to be the production of a slave-owner, perhaps a slave-driver, and that he is actuated by prejudice and malice, and other evil qualities with which very zealous people are apt to load their adversaries. It is so far, therefore, injudicious. An accurate representation of the state of the negroes morally and intellectually, as well as physically, and of their immediate masters, embodied in the action of a novel, is not a bad idea, and might have been so managed as to make both parties view each other in a somewhat more charitable light; it might have

> removed some misconception and a great deal of ill-will, with respect to the important question of the abolition of slavery. . . .
>
> The characters are upon the whole well drawn: . . . Combah is really a very reasonable specimen of royalty – a sturdy, brave, and shrewd sort of person, with the usual carelessness of life which belongs to royal conquerors as well as savages; though we believe the latter quality is not very characteristic of the negro race. The Obeah-man is also peculiarly well done, his shrewdness and his self-possession, with manners as polished as his skin, set off with no small quantity of the marvellous, make him a very respectable hero. In short, he is a very wonderful and amiable wizard.[94]

The critic then launches into a paean of praise for the "beautiful" Jamaican scenery. He notes, "It is pretty clear that the danger to human life in these climates is exaggerated in much the same way as the misery of the slaves."

> We do not think of the every-day maladies which are the scourge of our own country, and which are unknown there, any more than we consider the misery and ignorance, and the degraded condition, of our own peasantry, when we are taking so much pains to ameliorate that of the negroes. In this respect we act contrary to a much-used, and frequently abused, maxim: our charity does not begin at home. In the present state of things, the free negroes (except those who are themselves slave-owners) are neither so happy nor so well off as the slaves; and we are told that when a slave wishes to convey an idea of extreme hunger, it is not unusual for him to say he is as hungry as a free negro. The greater part of the population of every country are in fact in some degree slaves in reality, though not in name. West-India slavery is indeed a servitude of more extended duration than any other: yet there is scarcely a negro who may not have it in his power to purchase freedom for himself and his offspring. When we look at the unceasing toil of large classes of our own countrymen, at their poverty and misery; when we consider the state of our criminal law, the heavy punishments attached to trifling offences against the rich or their property; when we reflect on our marine and military servitude, we are induced to think that greater importance is attached to a name, than properly belongs to it; and that we should probably do more good, both to the West-Indies and England, by emancipating the colonies, than by giving freedom to the slaves.[95]

According to an advertisement for the book in the *Chronicle*, *The Atlas* noted that

---

94 *Westminster Review* 7 (October 1826–January 1827): 444–64.
95 Ibid.

the descriptions of scenery are alive and striking; the portraits of character are true and vigorous; the sketches of manners lively and instructive. Many of the situations are well conceived, and produce a deep interest in the reader, while the effect of the whole is heightened by the novelty of the subject. The Author is on entirely new ground, and – let us add, ground which abounds in objects of great and powerful interest.[96]

In fact, for all its acknowledged faults, many critics received the novel well, indulgently even, but Williams had expressed himself too forcefully for others, who clearly found his caricatured portrayals distasteful and thought he had overplayed his hand to the detriment of his position. The critic for *The Examiner* calls the novel a "racy and singular production . . . [with] a high degree of descriptive power, and an arch feeling of humour", but notes that "were this fiction as fairly as it is pleasantly and forcibly written, our approbation would go much farther than at present we can allow it to do. But, in truth, our author is a West Indian partisan, and what Dr Johnson called 'a good hater', who deals out his antipathies with no sparing hand. His spleen is particularly excited by African Associations and Methodist Missionaries." The reviewer expresses his reservations about the imputation of evil design to missionaries, doubting that "either Missionary or African Associations wish to produce Negro supremacy or insidiously seek to promote discontent and insurrection". Having gotten that qualm out of the way, however, the review goes on in a more genial fashion, the reviewer declaring himself pleased with the "descriptive power and energy" displayed in the conception of the characters and the description of the scenery.[97]

Williams did antagonize some critics who had little use for his novelized tirade and wanted readers to be in no doubt that he was hand-in-glove with the planters, if not one of them himself.

> We should not be surprised to hear that the Jamaica Assembly have voted the thanks of the house in a hogshead of sugar, to the author of Hamel. The warmth of its sentiments seem exactly to correspond with the temperament of that angry convention, and the temperature of the Antilles. Writers on slaves and coffee, methodists and planters, seem to draw their inspiration from the liquor of the islands: such wrath against missions, such virulence against ministers, can only be bred of rum. We can picture the author of Hamel in a house

---

96 *Morning Chronicle*, 11 June 1827.
97 *The Examiner*, 1 April 1827, 194.

of bamboo, with a hurricane behind him, and a tall green bottle of rum before him; flourishing his pen with one hand, and lashing his legs with a cat-o'-nine tails in the other. The rum, the hurricane, and the scourge together, excite a storm of passion, which fortunately finds a vent at the point of his pen, or an earthquake in Jamaica might result, more serious in its consequences than the importation of a ship-load of tracts, or a convulsion of slaves. There are mild animals that, on hearing some obnoxious sound, will instantly become furious, gnash their teeth, and howl. The author of Hamel we take to be an agreeable, good-natured man, placid and tolerant on common occasions, but still we know one word that would at any moment throw him into fits. Let some of his friends try the experiment on this well-meaning planter, for such we take him to be . . . let them whisper Methodist in his ear – and watch how his eyes will begin to roll – his teeth to grind – his hands to clench, – listen – how he will call for his tablets. – See, how he will brandish his pen, and write down the canting rascals. . . . This good man . . . believes the devil to be the principal missionary, and all those who go roaring about the islands seeking whom they may convert, to be his liege imps. That this was his creed we saw in his Tour in Jamaica; but then he was not so angry but that we could laugh with him – in Hamel, we confess we laugh at him. In the former work he charmed us by his specimens of canting slaves, spluttering a jumble of gospel and gibberish – but here he has taken a burnt stick, and daubed a grimy outline of the devil as parsons paint him, and written under the figure of blackness the name of Roland, the missionary. This is a pity, for the author is an exceedingly clever fellow when he is not in a rage, and no writer has described the manners and the climate of the country of the Antilles so well as he has done, and we trust will continue to do. But he must permit himself to cool, and he must concoct his story with a little more care.[98]

Nothing is known of Cynric Williams. Was he a Jamaican planter? Tim Watson has speculated that the name is the pseudonym of the coffee planter Charles White Williams, but we do not know this for sure. In *Hamel* and *Tour*, however, he presents us with the views and attitudes of many of the planters in the West Indies and their supporters in Britain. These whites considered black people ignorant and savage and saw the missionaries who tried to help them as traitors to their race. What else are we to make of Roland's declaration to the rebels that they too could have white wives, like the revolutionary Haitian blacks? This was a false claim, but even whites uncomfortable with slavery were

---

98 *London Magazine*, n.s., 30 (June 1827): 182–84.

offended by the idea of miscegenation, so who among them would support missionaries who espoused interracial relationships?

But in addition to Methodist missionaries and Obeah workers, writers also drew on other prejudices to flesh out their stories. Mayne Reid's depiction of the grasping, treacherous Jew Jessuron and his equally villainous daughter derive from stereotypes even more ancient than the derogatory ones attributed to blacks. Edgeworth was an exception who did her best to consistently present positive images of blacks, but, too often, writers were unable to overcome their racism. Their depictions and portrayals of Obeah workers painted an unflattering picture of those people in particular and of blacks in general. In fact, writers employed Obeah to emphasize the Otherness of blacks over and over again, creating an enduring image of black people and of black West Indians that, even today, has not been completely eradicated.

CHAPTER 9

Black Sorceresses and Mulatto Vampires

EVEN AS THE NINETEENTH CENTURY DREW TO a close, the fascination with Obeah continued, ensuring that new generations became aware of the practice and the horrors associated with it.

THE WORLD WENT VERY WELL THEN

Walter Besant's novel *The World Went Very Well Then* is told in the form of a memoir by Luke, the son of a pastor, who is attempting to correct what he says are misapprehensions and lies by people who know of the events in the book but were not involved in them and so could not know what really happened as well as he does. He begins by describing Mr Brinjes, an apothecary in the British city of Deptford, who is very old and wrinkled, though not frail, and has only one eye; in fact, he has the appearance of a conventional Obeah man, save for the fact that he is Caucasian.

When the local herb women cannot help people, they turn to Brinjes, who owns a very interesting object:

> in the corner of the room . . . there was a very fearful and terrible thing, until you grew accustomed to it, when you ceased to fear it. This was nothing less than a stick painted red and black, with bright-coloured feathers tied round it, and surmounted by a grinning human skull. It was a magic stick, called, we were told, the Ekpenyong, or skull stick, by the Mandingo sorcerers – a thing only to be handled by an Obeah man, the possession of which is supposed by negroes either to confer or to proclaim wonderful powers, and cut from a juju or holy tree. . . . This stick it was which caused the apothecary to be greatly respected by the Admiral's negroes. . . . He who has such a stick can catch the

shadow, as they say – that is, the soul of a man; and set Obi upon him – that is to say, bring suffering, sorrow, and shame upon him. So that the possessor of a skull-stick is a person greatly to be feared and envied.[1]

Some suspect Brinjes of having made a pact with the Devil, the "Great Potentate". He appeared in the city in 1725 and has been there fifteen years. Like any Obeah man, he can cure as well as inflict harm and distributes charms for various afflictions or to meet a range of desires. His amulets are made of such things as the tooth of a poisonous snake (protection from drowning) and the head of a frog wrapped in silk (protection from the gallows). In addition, he can tell his patients if they will be cured or if they will die.

> there was no physician in London itself more skilful than Mr Brinjes, and that by certain preparations, the secret of which he alone knew, and had learned in his voyages in foreign parts, especially the West Coast of Africa, where the negroes possess many strange secrets of nature, he had acquired a singular mastery over every kind of disease. . . . It was also whispered of Mr Brinjes that by magic or witchcraft he could bring diseases upon those who offended him, and that he could avert all the misfortunes to which mankind are liable in shipwreck, drowning, wounds, and death. . . . Further, it was said of him, that he could, also at will, command these diseases to seize upon a man and torture him. . . . [People] came to him also for amulets and charms, which he did not always refuse to give, for protecting those who carried them from drowning, hanging, burning, the shot of cannon, and the stroke of steel.[2]

Jack and Bess are youngsters who visit Brinjes regularly and to whom he tells stories of his travels and of the sights he has seen. Jack became a Deptford resident at age nine when he came to the city to live with Rear-Admiral Sayer after the death of his father. Described as "handsome" and "masterful", he was given into the care of Bess's father, Mr Westmoreland, to learn penmanship, arithmetic and navigation. Brinjes is Westmoreland's next-door neighbour.

Jack is desperate to be a sailor like his father, and when he is thirteen, the Admiral signs him up on a ship headed to the West Indies. Many of the denizens of Deptford, including all the leading characters, come to the harbour to see Jack off. "And here a singular thing happened", Luke recalls. "There is no man more free from superstitious terrors, I think, than myself. Yet I cannot

---

1 Walter Besant, *The World Went Very Well Then* (London: Chatto and Windus, 1887), 1:4–5. The story first appeared in the *Illustrated London News*.
2 Ibid., 10–12.

but remember . . . the old witch-woman – she was nothing less – this Mandingo prophetess, whose powers were as real as those believed to belong to Mr Brinjes – began to shiver and to shake and her teeth to chatter." He supposes it could have been a cold wind that caused it, "but, to Philadelphy, everything unexpected was full of prophetic warning, could she read it aright". The West Indian woman Philadelphy had been Castilla Westmoreland's nanny, and she continued to work in the Westmoreland household after the girl got older.

> "What does it mean?" [Philadelphy] murmured. "I dun know what this shiver means: Mas'r Jack come home again, I think, and play mischief with some of us. There's trouble sure, for somebody – trouble and crying. Dun you be afraid, miss Castil, old Philadelphy know plenty words to keep off the Devil."
>
> She meant that she had plenty of incantations or charms by which to avert and ward off evil. I am sure there was never a witch-woman or Obeah man on the African coast or in Jamaica had more spells and secrets of magic and unholy craft than this old negress.[3]

Jack is away for about two years, fighting the Spanish in Cuba and other places, and rises to the post of midshipman. On his return, he gives Bess a coral necklace, surprising the narrator, who had thought he would be sweet on Castilla, the Admiral's daughter. Jack gets into a fight with a young man, Aaron, his nemesis from schoolboy days, as Bess and the narrator watch. Aaron is enamoured of Bess, who has eyes only for Jack.

For his part, Jack wants nothing more than to go back to sea and rise to the post of lieutenant, so the Admiral secures him a place on a ship sailing to the Pacific. Before he leaves, Brinjes tells him a strange story of how, when he was in the area to which Jack is going, their ship came across another drifting on the sea, full of wine, silks and treasure but completely unmanned. Brinjes and the other men brought the treasure aboard their own ship and set the galleon on fire. They celebrated by becoming drunk, and a fight broke out over the treasure. The fight lasted all night and only 150 men survived. The next night, they quarrelled again, and so on for the next three days and nights, until only fifty men were left. The captain, the helmsman and most of the officers were dead. Each share had now risen from two thousand to four thousand pounds, but the ship was becalmed for weeks, unable to move.

"One day, while we were still becalmed, the [compass] needle began to turn all ways, as if the witches had got hold of it – the Jamaica Obeah men know

---

3   Ibid., 111.

that secret", Brinjes tells the young people. But finally, the winds took them to islands where, Brinjes says, people "have no religion, and therefore are not afraid".[4] According to him, the natives do not murder or rob each other, do not gamble or commit adultery. The sailors stayed there for about three years, until twenty-five of them decided to leave; but they had not gone far before they realized they needed to keelhaul their ship. They offloaded the treasure, but before they could start work on the ship, it sailed off, with only some of the men aboard. Brinjes speculates that a current may have caught the ship and that the men on board were drunk or sleeping or bewitched. The remaining men decided to leave the treasure behind and try going from island to island until they could be rescued and come back for it, but Brinjes alone survived. He tells Jack and Bess that he bequeaths the treasure to them and that he will sail with them to find it one day.

Brinjes is also keen to find the secret of longevity. He tells Jack and Bess that if he could have only fifty more years on the African coast among the Coromantyns, he would find "the secret which their wise women know. It is in the African forests that the herb grows which can cure all disease, even the disease of old age."[5]

Philadelphy is confident that Jack will come back safely, but this time he is away for six years. As time passes, people begin to think he is dead. "Witchcraft and magic were proved of no avail", the narrator says. Only Brinjes and Bess still believe in Jack's return. "Philadelphy, at my request, hath proved in many ways", Brinjes assures the Admiral, "by the bowl, by the cards, by the mirror, and by the glass ball".

Both Bess and Castilia have grown into beauties and Bess is much pursued, particularly by Aaron, but she is holding out for Jack. One day, a gaunt man, his hair long and wild, turns up in the town, and everyone takes him for a beggar. Not even Philadelphy, "though a witch and a sorceress, and an Obeah woman", recognizes him as Jack. When Bess sees him, however, she calls out to him by name, and Jack weeps because she remembers him. He is deeply moved by this and later tells her that he loves her. She tells him she loves him too, and that she always knew he would return, since Philadelphy had said so.

Luke is less sanguine. "Well, in the event the forecast proved true; but, if we are to trust to such an oracle, where is religion?" he laments. "If an ignorant negro woman is permitted to find out, by her witchcraft, the secrets of the

---

4   Ibid., 160–61.
5   Ibid., 179.

future, and to foretell them, what shall become of religion? Then, farewell, faith; farewell, prayer; farewell, trust in Divine Providence; farewell, learning, since ignorance succeeds where wisdom fails!"[6]

Jack passes his seamanship examinations and becomes a lieutenant. He and Bess continue to meet secretly in the apothecary's shop, prompting Aaron to confront Bess and tell her that Jack is a gentleman and will never marry her. When Bess complains to Jack, he decides to fight Aaron at the Horn Fair, where Aaron challenges people to fight for a guinea or a groat. Jack wins and later swears before Luke and Bess that he will think of no other woman but Bess, and that he will marry her when he comes back as a commissioned officer. But Aaron and his accomplices capture Jack; they are making off with him, planning to have him put on an East Indiaman, when the Admiral comes upon them. At first the Admiral does not realize what is happening, since it is night-time, and he walks on. When he discovers evidence of a fight, he sends his Negro servants after the group, but Luke points out: "negroes are in essentials all alike. No man ever yet found courage in the black African, any more than industry, patience, or honesty, unless the white man was behind him with Father Stick for encouragement. The night was dark. Nothing more daunts a negro than darkness, because to him the night is peopled – especially when there is no white man present – with all kinds of fearful and terrible creatures."[7] So the blacks stop their pursuit once out of the Admiral's sight and the men make their escape with Jack. Later, one of the men who is not as bad as the rest frees Jack, and the rest of the accomplices are themselves pressganged. Jack confronts Aaron, who agrees to pay Jack back what he stole. In turn, Jack promises to take no further action against him, but Brinjes warns Aaron that misfortune will come his way.

Before Jack sails away again, Bess procures a charm from Philadelphy for him to turn away bullets and cutlasses:

> That evening Bess did a thing which is forbidden by the Church. . . . She went to seek the advice of a witch. The sailors and their wives sometimes importuned Mr Brinjes to bestow upon them, or to sell to them if he would, some kind of charm or amulet, either to maintain constancy in separation . . . to prevent drowning, against incurring the wrath of the captain, and punishment by the cat-o'-nine tails, against being killed or wounded in action, and against hanging.

---

6 Ibid., 205–6.
7 Ibid., 2:115.

Luke notes that he himself never really knew if Brinjes believed in his charms, but,

> Whatever his belief concerning his own powers, Mr Brinjes, without doubt, entertained a high respect of those of Castilla's black nurse Philadelphy – a true witch if ever there was one. . . . Mr Brinjes would talk to her in her own Mandingo language. . . . She it was who assisted him in the compounding of those broths which he used to simmer on his hob. . . . By these and other secrets of which he was always in search, and forced the woman to reveal by terror of his magic stick with the skull, he hoped to cure disease, to arrest decay, and to prolong life.[8]

Bess goes to see Philadelphy, who "crept closer to the [cooking] fire, the light of which seemed to sink into her skin, and there to become absorbed (the blackness of Philadelphy's cheeks not being shiny, as is that of some negresses, but dull); while her eyes shone by the firelight like two balls of fire".[9] Philadelphy tells Bess:

> "I sell very fine charm – proper gri-gri charm. Eh! When Massa Brinjes wants pow'ful charm for gout and toothache he sends for Philadelphy, and puts his skull-stick on the table. Then I give him what he wants. I got charm for most everything. Massa Brinjes very good Obeah Doctor: he learn in Mandingo country when he live among the rovers. . . . But he dunnow so much as ole Philadelphy. When he want to learn mus' come to de ole woman. . . . " As she spoke, her eyes rolling about so that the whites in the firelight were glowing red, she held out her hand for the money

and "clutched the money greedily". Philadelphy asks Bess what kind of charm she wants – for true love or to stop her lover from drowning – but Bess decides she wants one to turn away "shot and cutlass".[10]

> Then the old woman rose slowly, being, in spite of her magic powers, unable to charm away her own rheumatism, and fumbled in her pocket. . . . From the rubbish lying in its vast recesses she produced a small leather bag, apparently empty, tied with a long string, which, after securing the bag with half a dozen knots, was long enough to be slipped round the neck. To untie these knots and to open the bag was to destroy the charm. More than this, it was to invite the

---

8   Ibid., 199.
9   Ibid., 201.
10 Ibid., 202–4.

very danger which was sought to be averted. Two or three years afterwards I was present when the bag was opened. It contained nothing more than a small piece of parchment, inscribed with certain characters, which I believe to have been Arabic, and very likely a verse of the False Prophet Mohammed's book, the Koran; there was the head of a frog, dried; the leg-bone of some animal, which may have been a cat or a rabbit; the claw of some wild creature, a nutmeg, and a piece of clay. This was a famous collection of weapons to interpose between a man's body and a cannon-shot.[11]

Even so, Philadelphy has Bess take the bag in her hand, go down on her knees and keep her eyes closed while repeating after Philadelphy,

> Shot and bullet pass him by;
> Pike and cutlass strike in vain;
> Keep him safe though all may die;
> Bring my sweetheart home again.

As Bess does so, "there was a rushing and whirling of the air about her ears and a cold breath upon her face, and, which was strange, though she held the bag tightly by the neck, she felt that things were being dropped inside it". Afterwards, Philadelphy tells her the gri-gri is made up and the bag, which had been empty, is now filled with something. She instructs Bess to hang it around Jack's neck while chanting the same incantation. She warns her that he is never to take it off or look inside it or tell anybody about it. Philadelphy also reads Bess's fortune and tells her that, whatever may come, she will marry her lover.[12]

Bess is hard put to get Jack to wear the Obeah bag, however. At first he laughs, then he asks her only for a lock of her hair to tie around his wrist. The narrator admits that many sailors believed such a wrist-tie would keep them safe from harm. Bess says she would give him all her hair if it would protect him and finally gets him to agree to wear the bag. When she has finished tying it around his neck, she says with satisfaction that he is now well protected, to which Jack replies, "'Tis woman's foolishness, Bess. Yet have I heard strange stories about these old negresses. They are sold to the Devil, I believe . . . no man knows what power these old women may have acquired." The narrator muses that it is

> most certain that this superstition concerning amulets is vain and mischievous. How can a witch by any devilry preserve a man from lead and steel? How can

---

11 Ibid., 205–6.
12 Ibid., 206–7.

a leopard's claw and a verse from a so-called sacred book stand between a man and the death that is ordered for him? To think this is surely grievous sin and folly. Besides, it is strictly forbidden to have any doings with witches; and what was forbidden to the people of old cannot be lawful among ourselves. Yet one cannot but remark, as a singular coincidence, that in all his fighting Jack had never a wound or a scratch.[13]

Two years after he sails away, Jack returns. The ship on which he sailed has captured several French prizes and he has gotten richer, but he leaves again. When he returns, he is in command of a ship, but he no longer feels the same way about Bess. Brinjes offers to compel Philadelphy to give Bess a charm which will bring Jack back to her. He offers to trade his Obeah stick for the charm, though "all my Obi [will leave] me, and I shall cause and cure diseases no better than the quacks of Horn Fair".

"The old negro woman gave thee a charm to keep him safe from shot and steel. She will give thee one, if I compel her, to bring him to thy knees. Nay, she will not at thy bidding. And for why? Because she wants Miss Castilla to marry the Lieutenant. Yet, if I compel her, she will make thee such a charm. Then he must needs come straight to thee, his heart mad with love, though a hundred fine ladies tried to drag him back."

"I know not what you mean."

Mr Brinjes took up his famous magic stick, the stick with the skull upon it. "It is by virtue of this stick, which gives its possessor, she believes, greater Obeah wisdom than she hath herself attained unto. Wherefore, if I order her to do a thing she cannot choose but obey, else I might put Obi upon her. She hath given me the secrets of all her drugs, by means of which, if I live long enough, I may find out the greatest secret of all, and be like unto the immortal angels."[14]

But Bess stops Brinjes from getting the charm, believing that Jack will come round. Instead, he begins courting Castilla. Meanwhile, the misfortunes that Brinjes predicted for Aaron begin to plague him: his shipyard burns down, his boat is lost at sea and his business fails.

Bess sends Luke with a letter to Jack, who responds that there is nothing more hateful to a man than a woman he once loved and now loves no more. Bess is devastated by his rejection and goes to see him herself, but he rejects her. When Jack tells Philadelphy that he means to marry Castilla, she tells

---

13 Ibid., 210–13.
14 Ibid., 297–98.

everyone. Aaron offers to help Bess kill him, but she changes her mind at the last minute and warns Jack of the ambush. Bess tells Jack that, while she will harbour no more animosity towards him, God will punish him in a way that will deeply hurt him.

Without Bess's knowledge, Brinjes goes to Philadelphy to offer her his stick in exchange for the charm. "The old woman clutched it and kissed it, with the unholy light of witchcraft in her eyes. I wonder if the Sorceress of Endor had a skull-stick."[15] Brinjes points out to Philadelphy that Bess can testify how he put Obi on Aaron, who had formerly thrived, but then he got a toothache, his ship was captured by the French, his boat-building shed burned and he went bankrupt. "'If you have enemies, you could put Obi on them, and go sit in the sun and watch them slowly dying", he tells her. "Those who possess this stick . . . can do whatever they please."[16]

When she learns the charm is for Jack, Philadelphy is reluctant, but Brinjes points out that, with "the great Obeah stick", she can get any other lover for Castilla. Philadelphy offers him the secret of longevity instead, but though he has long sought it from her, he replies, "Jack or nothing." She responds that it will be "nothing", since Castilla has her heart set on Jack and she loves the young woman. As he leaves, Brinjes taunts her, saying, "I do not believe you know any charm at all. You know nothing. You are only an ignorant old negro woman. In Jamaica they would laugh at you. You are not a wise woman."[17]

Jack sails away again as the captain of his ship, and nothing is heard of him for a long time, until rumours start flying that, during an engagement with the French, "he struck his colours", that is, surrendered without fighting. The rumour is that he was bewitched, but Bess says she knew something like this would happen and that she loves him still. The rumours are substantiated by reports in the newspapers. Brinjes curses Philadelphy: "Devil take all black negro witches with their lying prophecies!"[18]

Jack is brought back to stand trial after having retaken his ship from the French. When Luke goes to see him, Jack tells him that he heard Bess's words – "Thou shalt be struck where thou shalt feel the blow most deeply" – and then it was as if something possessed him and drove him up the mast to haul down the flag and surrender. He can now think of nobody else but Bess. Luke

---

15 Ibid., 3:130.
16 Ibid., 128.
17 Ibid., 137.
18 Ibid., 144.

tells him that Bess loves him still, but he can hardly believe it after the way he has treated her.

When Jack is court-martialled, Brinjes says to Luke that Bess "must have put Obi upon him by the help of some, though I knew not that there were any other Obeah men in this country, besides myself". The president of the court-martial sentences Jack to be shot to death on the quarterdeck of his ship, the *Calypso*. The day before his execution is scheduled, Jack escapes with Brinjes's help. Jack, Bess and Brinjes say goodbye to Luke and sail to the southern seas to find the treasure. In time, Luke marries Castilla, Aaron is transported to the West Indies and dies there, and the Admiral dies. Many years later, Luke hears that Jack is now the captain of a privateer ship crewed mainly by blacks, and that he, Bess and Brinjes are all happy and doing well. Nothing is said of Philadelphy.

Besant was born in 1836 and was expected to become an Anglican clergyman like Luke, but he chose instead to teach and write. He became a senior professor at the Royal College of Mauritius and remained there for six and a half years before returning to England, where he became the secretary of the Palestine Exploration Fund and at first confined his writing to scholarly works on French culture and history. A collaboration with James Rice produced the novel *Ready-Money Mortiboy* in 1872, and several other novels and stories followed. Rice's death saw Besant strike out on a profitable literary career of his own, with his first, *All Sorts and Conditions of Men*, remaining popular for years. At the time that *The World Went Very Well Then* was published, Besant was a member of the Freemasons, the Savile Club, the Athenaeum and the Rabelais Club. He was well connected and well known, and his books would have been widely read. An indefatigable social reformer who established evening schools to help promote handicrafts, founded the Women's Central Bureau of Work to help women find jobs, and campaigned for sweatshop workers, the poor, free public libraries and more, he was knighted in 1895 for his charitable work. He died in 1901.

YOUMA: THE STORY OF A WEST-INDIAN SLAVE

Lafcadio Hearn emigrated to the United States from Ireland when he was nineteen years old. There he settled in Cincinnati and became a reporter for various newspapers. He ignited a scandal when he married a black woman (at that time, interracial marriages were against the law), but he later divorced her.

Hearn moved to New Orleans in 1877 and developed a reputation for covering stories often ignored by the mainstream media of the time, such as his story on Filipino emigrants who had made their home in Louisiana. It was probably a combination of the eccentricity of his reporting and his submissions to a magazine about voodoo practices that inspired *Harper's Monthly* to send him to Martinique in 1887. He spent two years there; both his fictional *Youma: The Story of a West-Indian Slave* and his autobiographical *Two Years in the French West Indies* were published in 1890.

Youma is the story of a coloured girl brought up on Martinique as the companion and friend of Aimée, the daughter of Madame Peyronette. When Aimée dies from pleurisy after being married and having a child, Youma becomes *da*, or nanny, of the little girl she left behind, Mayotte. Mayotte is sickly, so Mme Peyronette sends her and Youma to live on the father's plantation in the country. There Youma falls in love with Gabriel, a handsome slave, but Mme Peyronette thinks he is too coarse for her. Youma "had received a domestic training that gave her a marked superiority above her class, and she had moral qualities more delicate by far than those of Gabriel".[19]

When Gabriel's owner, Monsieur Desrivières, asks Mme Peyronette for Youma on his behalf, she refuses. Desperate with love, Gabriel asks Youma to run away with him to one of the British islands, where emancipation has already occurred. She is torn but thinks that the "good God would never forgive her". He begs her again; she wants to go and tells him she will think about it, but again decides not to. "Once more the darker side of her nature was quelled", and she resolves to tell him no. She cannot leave Mayotte or those who have been kind to her, she tells him. Disturbed by Gabriel's persistence, Mme Peyronette brings Youma and Mayotte back to live in St Pierre.

Soon after, the slaves become convinced that they have been freed by the government in France but that the planters are withholding their emancipation. Tensions begin to rise: "strange negroes were mingling with the rioters, – savage-looking men, whom the city domestics had never seen before, and who replied to the assurance '*C'est yon bon béké*' (this is a *good* white) only by abuse or violence".[20]

Things that for two hundred years had been done in darkness and secrecy were

---

19   Lafcadio Hearn, *Youma: The Story of a West-Indian Slave* (London: Harper and Brothers, 1890), 78.
20   Ibid., 146.

now being done openly in the light. An occult power had suddenly assumed unquestioned sway, – the power of the African sorcerer.

Under the tamarinds of the Place du Fort, a *quimboiseur* plied his ghastly calling, – selling amulets, selling fetiches, selling magical ointments made of the grease of serpents. Before him stood an open cask filled with tafia mingled with gunpowder and thickened with bodies of crushed wasps. About him crowded the black men of the port . . . "*Ça qui lè?*" shouted the quimboiseur, serving out the venom in cups of tin, – " . . . Who will drink it, the Soul of a Man? – the Spirit of Combat? – the Essence of Falling to Rise? – the Heart-Mover? –the Hell-Breaker?" . . . And they clamored for it, swallowed it – the wasps and the gunpowder and the alcohol, – drinking themselves into madness.[21]

The uprising begins with the "blowing of a hundred lambi-shells. . . . And from the market-place, where by lantern-light the sorcerer still gave out his *l'essence-brisé-lenfè*, and his amulets and grease of serpents, began to reverberate ominously the heavy pattering of a *tamtam*".[22] Youma, Mayotte, Mme Peyronette and M Desrivières take refuge in the home of some other whites who are deemed to have a strongly built house. Despite the strength of the house, the mob breaks in. They kill a young white man and set the house on fire. The whites are hoping for rescue from the soldiers, but the governor has confined them to their barracks. Among the crowd, some call for the women to be allowed to escape, but another answers them, "they burned poor negresses for sorcery".[23]

Youma emerges on the balcony of the house with a stirring plea for the lives of the whites, but the mob is not impressed. Gabriel breaks through the crowd and urges her to save herself, promising his help, but she will not go without Mayotte and he refuses to save the child as well. The crowd also refuses the child safe passage. Youma and everyone inside the house perish in the fire.

In the character of Youma, Hearn presents us with the classic tragic mulatto, loyal to the whites who deny her the possibility of love, and willing to sacrifice her happiness and her life to stand at their side. Youma turns her back on love to affirm her solidarity and identification with whites. This is something to which Hearn also alludes in *Two Years*, that blacks considered mulattoes the allies of whites and plotted their combined downfall. In *Youma*, black people are associated with Africa and African sorcery, ignorance and

---

21 Ibid., 151–52.
22 Ibid., 153.
23 Ibid., 183.

coarseness, savagery and superstition. The mulattoes, on the other hand, are superior, less superstitious, more refined, and thus more like the whites.

A WITCH'S LEGACY

Hesketh Bell was twenty-nine and already about ten years into his career in the British colonial service when *A Witch's Legacy* was published. There seems to be some doubt about whether he was born in the West Indies and later assigned to the Barbados government or born in France and entered the British colonial service with a first appointment to the Bahamas. Whatever his early history, Bell served in several Caribbean posts: he was administrator of Dominica and acting governor of the Leeward Islands between 1895 and 1905, and again, after an appointment in Nigeria, served as governor of the Leewards from 1912 to about 1916. He retired from the Colonial Office in 1925. When his book *Obeah: Witchcraft in the West Indies* was published in 1889, he was either still working in Grenada's inland revenue department or had just finished his time there before being appointed supervisor of customs on the Gold Coast. He completed *A Witch's Legacy* during the latter assignment.

A Witch's Legacy is set on the island of Grenadilla (obviously a thinly veiled reference to Grenada), where Jack Moresby, a young planter, is threatened with having his estate, Palm Vale, foreclosed. Moresby is in love with Violet Lee of the Belvoir estate but despairs of ever having the money to woo her properly or successfully. One day, Mammy Quamina, whom Jack refers to as "the old Obeah woman", sends for him. As in his non-fiction work, Bell explains:

> In the old days of slavery, every plantation in the West Indies possessed one or two Africans, male or female, who enjoyed an unenviable reputation for working "Obeah", the West Indian term for witchcraft. These people were popularly supposed by the credulous blacks to be in league with his Satanic Majesty and to have wondrous mysterious powers not vouchsafed to the majority of mortals. The Obeah men and women obtained an extraordinary influence over their neighbours, through an intimate knowledge of the poisonous plants which grow in every tropical forest, and the frequent fatal uses they made of their knowledge. Sixty or seventy years ago, the slaves on an estate would sometimes be mysteriously decimated by the machinations of these wretches. The poisons which they used worked in a manner so gradual, and their effects were so different from those known to medical science, that crimes of this sort were very rarely brought home to the sorcerers, and they frequently practised

their fatal proceedings for years before the planter was even aware that such miscreants lived on the estate.

There was, however, a less deadly branch to their business, and one which, while being less risky, brought them considerable profits. This was the preparation and sale of love-spells, medicines and charms, and even at the present day the credulous negroes frequently stint themselves of necessaries and save all they can put away, in order to be able to pay the exorbitant price of some spell, charm or potion, with which they firmly believe that the Obeah woman can supply them.[24]

Jack goes to see the Obeah woman and recognizes her as "one whom he had frequently seen hobbling about the estate, and who had been pointed out to him by labourers and tenants as an Obeah woman, and unmitigated vampire".[25]

This particular old sorceress, Quamina, was popularly supposed to be very nearly a hundred years old, and she had imbued her coloured neighbours with great respect and fear for her mysterious powers. Jack, on looking at her now, could hardly believe that she was even human. The shrunken old frame appeared to be almost void of flesh, and was covered with black wrinkled skin that looked quite unearthly. She seemed the personification of age and decay, her shrivelled black arms and hands looked like the bones of a skeleton dyed black, while her wizened knotted face, sunken jaws, and almost sightless eyes reminded him of a badly preserved mummy.[26]

Quamina is ill and Jack offers to bring a doctor to help her, but she responds that her "bush medicine be better past all your white doctor's stuff".[27] Mammy Quamina tells Jack that she was brought from Guinea in a slave ship as a young girl and has been on the plantation since before emancipation. She tells him his grandfather treated her badly and had her flogged, but nine days later he was dead – she had poisoned him. "He nebber know dat my mammy in Guinea was plenty strong fetish woman, and dat she teach me how to work Obeah, even when I was quite small", Quamina tells Jack. "It be more than seventy years ago since I give your gran'fader de bush medicine what take him to his grave."[28] But she later regretted poisoning him, because both Jack and his father were kind to her.

---

24   Hesketh Bell, *A Witch's Legacy* (London: Sampson Low, Marston and Co., 1893), 41–43.
25   Ibid., 41.
26   Ibid., 43.
27   Ibid., 45.
28   Ibid., 46, 47.

She relates how pirates came one day and raided Palm Vale and stole his grandmother's diamonds and other jewels, but a hurricane struck and the pirate ship was destroyed. Only one man managed to survive and make it back to shore, though crippled and badly hurt. Quamina looked after him. She was able to harbour the pirate because her reputation for Obeah meant nobody pried into her business. When people heard voices in her cottage, they assumed she was speaking to the Devil and stayed far away.

The pirate recovered and persuaded Quamina to look for his captain's treasure chest where Jack's grandmother's jewellery and other stolen items had been secured. Another slave helped them to recover the chest but was later killed by the pirate for his trouble. The pirate himself died also, possibly with Quamina's help, though she does not say. Quamina tells Jack that the chest should be his and gives him its location. Childless and with no living relatives, she makes Jack her heir before she dies, telling him about a tin where she keeps her money.

When she is dead, Jack inspects her hut.

> The walls of the miserable shanty were hung round with the mysterious implements and stock-in-trade of the dead witch. Small bottles full of some mysterious compounds, supposed to be sovereign charms against thieves and evil-doers, were lying ready to be handed over to some foolish negro in exchange for their weight in silver. In every corner was the most heterogeneous collection of rags, feathers, bones of cats, parrots' beaks, dogs' teeth, broken bottles, grave dirt, rum and egg-shells, all ingredients which went to form the fearful and wonderful mixtures which old Quamina had sold to her credulous neighbours in the guise of charms, potions, and love-spells.[29]

Despite all the magical clutter, Jack unearths the tin she told him about. Inside he finds about three hundred pounds in silver coins, gold pieces and colonial banknotes – her Obeah earnings. Jack arranges a proper burial for her and tells Sam Brett, his mulatto overseer, the story of the treasure chest. The two men find the chest and take it back to Palm Vale, but before they can examine it, a fire breaks out in the cane fields. When they get back, the chest is gone.

Jack learns that Sandy Sneat, a white man he once thrashed for his cruelty to a dog, has been in the area and he suspects him of the theft. Sam and Jack ride after him but Sneat has caught the boat to Trinidad in the company of a black man by the name of Josiah Sampson, his accomplice. The police are unable to help Jack, so he and Sam pursue Sandy and Josiah to Barbados,

---

29 Ibid., 64.

where they find out that the men have boarded yet another ship, a Royal Mail steamer bound for England.

Meanwhile, back in Grenadilla, Violet Lee is in trouble, as Belvoir is about to be foreclosed. Violet's mother blames her for the looming loss of the estate, because she would not accept richer suitors over Jack. Not knowing what to think about Jack's hasty departure, Violet accepts Joseph Nettley's offer of marriage in order to save her mother and herself from destitution. In London, after many shenanigans, the chest is recovered and Jack and Sam return to Grenadilla in time for Jack to stop Violet's wedding and marry her himself.

A Witch's Legacy was fairly well-received, with the *Publishers' Circular and Bookseller's Record* calling it "a highly interesting and very well written romance".[30] The only mulatto in the story, Sam, is a loyal friend of the white hero, but Josiah, described as black, is in cahoots with the villain. The information presented about Obeah and the Obeah woman seems almost superfluous to the story but allows Bell to present a fictionalized version of more or less the same information given in his earlier *Obeah*. Anyone who had failed to read his non-fiction work but had picked up this novel would still be exposed to the same information.

THE INTENDED

Bell's *A Witch's Legacy* was followed the next year by Henry De Vere Stacpoole's horror novel *The Intended*. It tells the story of Roger Jeffries, who has been sent from Jamaica by his father and is living in London in rather miserable lodgings. He writes home, pleading for money, but a lawyer writes back to inform him that his father, James Jeffries, has died and left the bulk of his money to charity. Roger's only legacy is a cheque for one guinea, which he promptly uses to pay his overdue rent. Destitute, he makes up his mind to kill himself that night, but he is accosted by a stranger who follows him home from the British Museum and asks him to perform a service for him. They exchange clothes but not names. The stranger gives him gold and tells him to meet him at an address in Chelsea that night but still does not reveal his name.

Roger goes to the meeting, puzzled about the fact that the stranger looks so much like him. At the house in Chelsea he meets a beautiful woman, who,

---

30 *Publisher's Circular and Bookseller's Record of British and Foreign Literature* 59 (July–December 1893).

he realizes, is the stranger's mother. He is quite taken with her. Everybody in the household mistakes him for the stranger, so Roger acts the part of the missing man. While he is at the house, the woman laments that her husband has tried to hit her and Roger is outraged, vowing to kill him. The woman entreats him not to kill his own father and asks why he has never defended her from him before.

Later, Roger catches a glimpse of a "black face peeping into the room – a hideous face". The butler tells him it's Mammy, apparently seeing nothing strange in the son of the house failing to recognize one of his servants: "The face he had seen was the face of a mulatto woman – hideous, wrinkled and old – crowned with a turban of ochre-coloured cloth. . . . A cold finger from the past seemed laid upon him for a second – a finger of evil augury – touching him and pointing through him to the future."[31]

A day or so later when Roger sees Mammy again, it is "in the full light of day", which reveals a face "marvellous to look upon. With most negresses, old age and ugliness go hand-in-hand, but Mammy's countenance possessed a third attribute that chilled the gazer upon it in a weird and uncanny fashion – its dryness. It was inhuman from want of moisture. The skin is not a parchment; one may grow old and wrinkled, but one's skin always retains the form of skin. But Mammy's face said 'No!' to this."[32] (The dryness of Mammy's skin mirrors the medieval belief about the condition of witches' skin mentioned in previous chapters.)

Mammy calls him aside and tells him that she recognizes him, since she looked after him as a baby. She informs him that he is really Roger Tyrell, whose mother left James Jeffries for "Massa Will Tyrell". The man with whom Roger has exchanged clothes is his brother, George Tyrell, whom his mother took with her when she left Jeffries; Roger was left with Jeffries. Roger is shocked that the woman he has been so attracted to is his own mother. He recalls the kiss on the lips he gave her: "The libertine was blown heavenward by his own petard. Never had the devil been so duped, duped by his own liege servant, the hideous black bag of bones, Mammy."[33]

Roger decides he wants to continue to play the role of George and to live in the house until he can learn more about what is going on. Mammy responds that she is leaving it "all to Obeah; she [has] done the waiting; [let] Obeah do

---

31 H. De Vere Stacpoole, *The Intended: A Novel* (London: Richard Bentley and Son, 1894), 84.
32 Ibid., 122.
33 Ibid.

the work". Roger demands to know more about Obeah and about his family, but an old white man comes half crawling, half walking along the corridor, blind drunk, "a man fearfully and wonderfully like a brute". This is Will Tyrell, his real father. Roger views him with disgust but does not reveal his identity. "A planter was the product of the highest Western civilization, brought into juxtaposition with African savagery", but to Stacpoole this does not mean that the planter himself is the ideal representative of that civilization. Planters "undoubtedly . . . were somewhat noble, somewhat aristocratic, but utterly monstrous and utterly rotten".[34]

Roger goes to Will Tyrell to ask for money but Will accuses him of being a forger; he shows Roger a letter in which George admits to forging a cheque for seven hundred pounds on the Bank of England in his father's name. Roger knows he has been caught in George's trap and considers suicide again, but his mother calls him to her. He suggests to her that they run away from Will, but she replies that it is too late, that he should have agreed to the idea when she first suggested it a year before. She shows him a pulsing swelling on her neck and tells him that she has loved him and only him always. When he asks her how she feels about Roger, she responds that he belongs to her sinful past and assures him that she forgives all George's transgressions.

Later, Mammy offers to lend Roger as much as one hundred pounds and tells him she has lots of money. He is tempted to take it when his mother's doctor reveals that she may have only a few months to live. Roger also discovers that his brother broke into the house during the night and stole back the fine clothes he lent Roger, a valuable statuette, and several other things. Roger learns where George may be living and decides to confront him, but he keeps his plans to himself. In the meantime, he tells Mammy that he wants to know everything. "It was like hearing a man addressing blandishing words to a snake, and snake-like mammy made answer: 'Yiss.'"[35] Stacpoole likens Mammy to a snake more than once. For example, on page 170 he notes that "like the torpid snake, [Mammy] seemed encased in an impenetrable drowsiness".[36]

Mammy reveals to Roger that the fathers of Laura Beauchamp and Will Tyrell, both of New Orleans, had decided that their children should wed to cement their business alliance, but the couple fell out during Will's visit to the Beauchamp house. As she is talking, Roger is thinking that "Mammy seemed

---

34   Ibid., 200.
35   Ibid., 125.
36   Ibid., 170.

a person for ever deadly in earnest. One could never imagine a joke issuing from that black pucker of a mouth, or a smile curving those dry, withered lips."

Will bought Mammy's pretty young mulatto daughter, Prue, from Beauchamp. The girl had rejected his advances before and when Mammy found out about the sale, she went looking for Will with a knife. She heard Prue screaming in the grounds and ran towards the sound, but by the time she arrived, the screams had stopped. Will emerged from a shed bathed in blood. Mammy hid herself and saw him begin to dig a hole. Filled with grief and rage, Mammy went straight to the Obeah woman Sue, "a very old negress".

> "Ho, Mammy!" said this black Witch of Endor. . . . Mammy sat down on a basket-chair and told the beldam she wanted Obeah against a man's body and soul. . . . Then the Obeah woman took a foetus in a bottle and placed it on the table, and burnt some powders before it in a saucer, and commenced incantations in strange tongue; the powders burnt with a blue flame. . . . Raising her voice to a shrill falsetto, the sweat running down her face, she altered the rhythm of her incantations. Suddenly the powders burst into a blood-red flame, and terrible to tell, the foetus in the bottle began to writhe. "It wuks!" cried Sue. At the sound of her voice, the powders went out and left them in darkness.[37]

Mammy was told to put a snake-like mark on Will's first-born son, but the Obeah woman warned her that her revenge might take years – "but yo' be in at him death, and the child will be in at him death, an' the snake, an' Obeah will hab him soul".[38] As Mammy tells her story, Roger thinks about the curving mark he bears on his leg.

Mammy goes on to explain that a Yellow Jack (yellow fever) epidemic killed off old Mr Beauchamp and old Mr Tyrell and Laura was left in the guardianship of James Jeffries, who fell in love with her, not knowing that she was already pregnant by Will. James proposed and, when Will failed to respond to her plea to come get her, she quickly married him. Seven months later, Roger was born and James realized he had been duped. He became cruel. Will finally put in an appearance but James forbade Laura to have anything to do with him. Instead, she ran away with Will, taking George and Mammy with her and leaving Roger behind.

"Mammy left yo' too, but Mammy knew yo'd turn up ag'in sure an' suttin

---

37 Ibid., 211–12.
38 Ibid., 213.

for yore 'pinted work, de Obeah works, de Obeah works, works, works!" cried Mammy, snapping her long fingers, clacking her bony joints, writhing, undulating, and commencing a strange epileptiform dance in front of Roger. . . . "Hell shall have him, shore an' sutin. . . . Radger shall send him down down, down, down, int' de pit he drove Prue. Prue, Prue, Prue!" raved Mammy, now absolutely like a demon dancing before the astounded Roger.

Mammy then falls to the ground in an epileptic fit, "writhing, twisting . . . blood running from her nose, foam from her mouth".[39] Stacpoole later informs us that Mammy "could have killed William Tyrell by poison over and over again but she had faith in Obeah. She wanted not only the body but the soul. Surely if faith in God can move mountains, faith in the devil can move men."[40] But when Roger goes to bed, he looks at the mark like a wriggling snake on his inner heel and dismisses its meaning: "Bah. I don't believe in all that rubbish."[41] (No fictional white British character ever believes in Obeah, and it is the rare creole white who does.)

Mammy, however, has given herself over to her belief in Obeah's ability to avenge the death of her daughter. It is her reason for being.

> An idea fixed in the brain, an idea lived with for years, slowly grows to a terrible stature, and slowly assumes a terrible power. The man with a fixed idea becomes either a lunatic or a power. Mammy had slowly assumed the form of a power; she had become like a whirlpool endowed with the powers of selection. She had drawn together elements capable of crushing the thing she wanted to crush. . . . It is this power of will . . . that made Mammy more terrible than a tigress.[42]

Mammy's shadow looms menacingly over the family. She gives Roger a photo in which she is pictured standing at the edge.

> Beyond [her] lies Mammy's past, a terrible black country, older than Egypt, treasuring faiths old as are the hills; holding a people who, from time immemorial, have warred against evil with evil, and have righted their wrongs with wrong. There stands Mammy, her eyes upon you all; and you all stand your eyes upon each other. What is she? Only a servant, an old black woman who makes good coffee and laces madam's stays, and who has been waiting for you, Roger Jeffries, to come for months and years, who told you last night of this long and

---

39 Ibid.
40 Ibid., 217.
41 Ibid., 219.
42 Ibid., 263.

anxious waiting, without exciting any surprise in your mind. . . . You said to yourself, "She was my old nurse; niggers are queer folk."[43]

Things fall apart from this point. A man comes to the house and identifies Roger as the man who tried to sell him the stolen statuette. Will declares that he will call the police, but Roger accuses him of Prue's murder. They are at a stalemate when Will bribes Mammy with four hundred pounds to poison Roger's tea. She turns over the money to Roger and he tells her he wants to leave the house but finds he cannot. She attributes it to Obeah, but he says that it is his affection for his mother. "Same thing", Mammy replies.

In the final pages, Will attacks George, who has broken into the house to steal his mother's diamonds. Mammy gives Roger a knife and he stabs Will. Mammy then bears Will away to her room and Roger hears him shout, "Who are you between me and Roger and the light?" "The mother of Prue", Mammy answers, and then there are no more sounds from the room.

A fallen candle sets the house on fire. The scene of Mammy's death appears to owe *Jane Eyre* a debt. "Away upon the parapet, black against the glow, appeared a wild outline dancing – epilepsy outlined on flame. 'Prue, Prue, Prue!' came a voice, thin and hard like a parrot's. . . . Something flew through the air like a shot eagle. A thing lay stretched on the ground like a hideous rag doll. It was Mammy! The flames roared up as if bidding speed to her passing soul."[44]

Roger tries to save his mother but she dies in his arms after he reveals his identity to her and confesses that he has killed George. He is mistaken, however, for George is still alive, though badly wounded. Will has left everything to Roger, who becomes a rich man and marries the woman who nurses him back to health after these events.

The Intended was Stacpoole's first novel but, by the time it was published, he was friends with such literary luminaries of the time as Aubrey Beardsley, Pearl Craigie and Alfred Noyes. Stacpoole had trained as a doctor and had even been employed as one aboard a cable-laying ship, but he did not appear greatly interested in pursuing a medical career. Still, early literary success evaded him. Though several books quickly followed *The Intended*, he did not begin to achieve commercial success until the publication of *Fanny Lambert*, a comic romance, in 1905. His most popular work was *The Blue Lagoon*, about a pair of children who are shipwrecked on an uninhabited island, fall in love

---

43 Ibid., 143.
44 Ibid., 312.

over the years, and have a child. *The Blue Lagoon* went through several reprints and was made into a film three times. Few people might have expected such an outcome for his literary career, given the critical and commercial failure of *The Intended*.

In its review of the novel, the *Pall Mall Gazette* writes that

> Mr H. de Vere Stacpoole's horrors are really quite refreshing. . . . The flesh creeps in joyful anticipation. But the plot is too preposterous . . . , the construction too woefully feeble. The author has a certain ingenuity, but he knows not the value of restraint. The parricide, madness, epilepsy, flinging about of corpses, blood and thunder, fire and revenge, crowded into one short chapter would scarce go down even with the gallery at the Surrey or Britannia. And to follow these horrors with a silly little afterthought of a love scene savours of the clumsy amateur. Careful study of Poe and Mr Stevenson and their methods might help Mr. Stacpoole to do better next time.[45]

By the end of the nineteenth century, the menacing Obeah man or woman had become a stock character, employed by authors who wanted to inject an exotic note into their plots. The black Obeah worker was shorthand for frightening Otherness. Interestingly, while Stacpoole may have introduced Mammy as a mulatto, everywhere else he describes her as "black" and a "negress". Since nothing is made of her mulatto-ness, of her half-black, half-white nature, it is probably safe to assume that to Stacpoole himself she was black. Certainly, the Obeah woman to whom Mammy went to apply for the spell was black so the only black characters are Obeah adherents. Mammy's daughter, the desirable and pretty Prue, is a mulatto who dies early on. As noted before, mulatto characters were often used to signify or enhance the contrast between blacks and whites – the darker they were or the more evil they were reflected the extent to which their natures were given over to their "dark blood". The lighter-skinned and the more loyal to whites and less superstitious they were, the more it was seen as evidence of the "white" blood in them being dominant.

THE BLOOD OF THE VAMPIRE

Florence Marryat, author of *The Blood of the Vampire*, was the daughter of adventure novelist Captain Frederick Marryat. During her first marriage she briefly lived in India but returned to England when she became ill. She turned

---

45 *Pall Mall Gazette*, 19 October 1894.

to writing to support herself and became a successful novelist who also wrote for newspapers and took up acting. A Roman Catholic, she became interested in spiritualism after interviewing a clairvoyant in 1874, and this interest is reflected in *Blood of the Vampire*, published in 1897, two years before her death. In *Blood*, Marryat presents us with a mulatto so tragic that not even her ability to pass for white is enough to save her from the supernatural doom which is her inheritance as the daughter of a mad white scientist and a bloodthirsty black Obeah woman.

As with *The Intended*, *Blood of the Vampire* takes place in England, not the Caribbean. At the story's opening we meet Baron and Baroness Gobelli and the Englishwomen Mrs Margaret Pullen and Miss Elinor Leyton, who are on vacation in the Hotel Lion d'Or in Heyst. A young woman, Harriet Brandt, joins them in the dining room; she is described as "a remarkable-looking girl ... her skin was colourless but clear ... her nose was straight and small. ... Not so her mouth however, which was large, with lips of a deep blood colour, displaying small white teeth."[46] Several pages on, Harriet's eyes are described as "deeply, impenetrably black ... there was no sparkle nor brightness in them". Unlike the other ladies, she "devours her food" and calls for more.

The Baroness, by contrast, is described as an "enormous woman of the elephant build" with coarse skin and features – obesity, then as now, serving as code for greed, sloth and other undesirable qualities. Marryat does not describe the other two women in the first few pages but later tells us that Elinor, the daughter of Lord Walthamstowe, has "attractive features" and is "pre-eminently a woman for a man to be proud of as the mistress of his house [who] could be trusted never to say or do an unladylike thing". These were, of course, qualities much desired in the Victorian woman.

As the diners converse, we learn that Margaret's brother-in-law, Ralph, is engaged to Elinor, who takes a dislike to Harriet. Harriet is a creole who attended a convent school in Jamaica for ten years but now, at age twenty-one, has decided to see the world. Harriet becomes quite clingy with Margaret, which Elinor finds off-putting, but Margaret is more forbearing.

Harriet confides in Margaret: "When I was a little thing of four years old, Pete used to let me whip the little niggers for a treat, when they had done anything wrong. It used to make me laugh to see them wriggle their legs under the whip and cry!"[47] She talks of other cruelties, saying, "We think nothing

---

46   Florence Marryat, *The Blood of the Vampire* (London: Hutchinson, 1897), 21.
47   Ibid., 23.

of that sort of thing, over there", and describes Pete, the African overseer, as the "only creature" who ever loved her.

While black slaves often served as drivers, the post of overseer, responsible for the day-to-day running of the plantation, was almost always filled by trusted whites. In the unlikely event that a slave was made overseer, he would probably have been a creole, not an African, but Marryat was writing decades after slavery was abolished and may not have been aware of these distinctions. In any case, simply by making Pete black – and not just black but African – she imbues him with a sense of menace and dread and alerts readers that Harriet is not to be trusted. Marryat's audience, whom she undoubtedly envisioned as white and British, would immediately have identified with Margaret and Elinor out of a sense, however vague, of race loyalty.

Later that day, at a café, Harriet puts her arm around Margaret, who suddenly feels faint, "as if something or someone were drawing all her life away". She tries to disengage herself from Harriet "but Harriet Brandt seemed to come after her, like a coiling snake". Olga Brimont, who came over from Jamaica in the same cabin as Harriet, describes a similar feeling of "a terrible oppression as though some one were sitting on my chest". Olga found it difficult to sleep and was very ill throughout the voyage and in London. She reveals that Harriet kept her company night and day, but it is only now, at the Lion d'Or, that Olga has begun to feel better.

As the story continues we learn that the Baroness is cruel and abusive towards her son, Bobby, and to her servants, but she tries to make friends with Harriet and invites her to visit them in London. Harriet begins to spend more time with the Baroness, which pleases Margaret, who often felt listless and depressed around her and who disapproves of all the gifts Harriet has showered on her baby daughter, Ethel. Harriet gushes: "'I love little white babies! I adore them. They are so sweet and fresh and clean – so different from the little niggers who smell so nasty, you can't touch them!"[48] With this outburst, as well as with her behaviour at the dinner table, Harriet is revealed as uncontrolled; she says what others might think but not say and is the opposite of the Victorian ideal of modest and demure womanhood.

Later, baby Ethel takes a turn for the worse. She begins sleeping all day and is no longer restless or lively. Ralph arrives and Elinor denounces both Harriet and the Baroness to him, but he is charmed by Harriet's liveliness and by her beautiful singing. When Dr Phillips arrives to attend to Ethel he sees Harriet.

---

48 Ibid., 36–50.

The doctor spent some time in Jamaica with the Thirteenth Lancers and knows of Harriet, her family and Helvetia, their plantation. He warns Margaret that she must have nothing more to do with Harriet, that she comes "of terrible parentage". He explains that Mr Brandt, Harriet's father, was expelled from Swiss laboratories for "barbarity" and went to Jamaica. He never married Harriet's mother. Brandt's character may be very loosely based on Lewis Hutchinson, a Scotsman who studied medicine before emigrating to Jamaica in the 1760s and embarking on a career of torture and murder which was ended only by his capture by Admiral George Rodney.

"She was a revolting creature", the doctor says of Harriet's mother. "A fat, flabby half-caste, who hardly ever moved out of her chair but sat eating all day long." Again, Marryat marries obesity with greed and grossness – Harriet's mother is like a black and more malevolent version of the Baroness. Intriguingly, a portrait of the obese Barbadian tavern owner Rachel Pringle raises the intriguing possibility that she was the inspiration behind Marryat's description of Harriet's mother. Like Harriet's mother, Rachel was a mulatto, the daughter of William Lauder, a Scottish schoolmaster, and his African slave, but she was not associated with any murders or with Obeah. By making one of her characters, Judge Carey, a Barbadian, Marryat may be giving readers a nudge and a wink, prompting them to make the connection, however. An illustration of Rachel by Thomas Rowlandson was printed by William Holland in London in 1796.

"I can see her now", the doctor continues,

> with her sensual mouth, her greedy eyes, her low forehead and half-formed brain, and her lust for blood. It was said that the only thing which made her laugh, was to watch the dying agonies of the poor creatures her brutal protector slaughtered. But she thirsted for blood, she loved the sight and smell of it, she would taste it on the tip of her finger when it came in her way. Her servants had some story amongst themselves to account for this lust.

The servants claimed that her own mother had been bitten by a vampire bat, "which are formidable creatures in the West Indies".[49]

Margaret asks the doctor what became of Harriet's mother and is told

> She was killed at the same time as Brandt, indeed the natives would have killed her in preference to him, had they been obliged to choose, for they attributed all the atrocities that went on in the laboratory to her influence. They said she was "Obeah" which means diabolical witchcraft in their language....

---

49 Ibid., 121–38.

> Brandt was a brute – the perpetrator of such atrocities in vivisection and other scientific experiments, that he was finally slaughtered on his own plantation by his servants, and everyone said it served him right . . . he had been known to decoy diseased and old natives into his laboratory, after which they were never seen again, and it was the digging up of human bones on the plantation, which finally roused the negroes to such a pitch of indignation that they rose *en masse*, and after murdering both Brandt and his abominable mistress, they set fire to the house and burned it to the ground.

Pete saved Harriet from the fire, however. "We medical men know the consequences of heredity, better than outsiders can do", the good doctor assures Margaret. "A woman born in such circumstances – bred of sensuality, cruelty, and heartlessness – cannot in the order of things, be modest, kind, or sympathetic."[50]

Margaret confesses her concern about Ralph, who is spending a lot of time with Harriet and the Baroness, so the next day the doctor warns Ralph about Harriet and tells him her history. He points out that he can tell "by the way she eats her food, and . . . uses her eyes, that she has inherited her half-caste mother's greedy and sensual disposition".

> The mother was the most awful woman I have ever seen. . . . She was the daughter of a certain Judge Carey of Barbadoes by one of his slave girls, and Brandt took her as his mistress before she was fourteen. At thirty, when I saw her, she was a revolting spectacle. Gluttonous and obese – her large eyes rolling and her sensual lips protruding as if she were always licking them in anticipation of her prey. She was said to be "Obeah" too by the natives and they ascribed all the deaths and diseases that took place on the plantation, to her malign influence. Consequently, when they got her in their clutches, I have heard that they did not spare her, but killed her in the most torturing fashion they could devise.[51]

Ralph responds angrily that he has given Harriet his word that he will visit her in Brussels, but the doctor tells him that he suspects she is infected "with the fatal attributes of the Vampire that affected her mother's birth". He tells Ralph that he thinks she draws health and strength from those around her, rendering her love fatal to those upon whom she bestows it. When Ralph dismisses these suggestions, the doctor reveals his belief that Harriet was

---

50 Ibid., 121–38.
51 Ibid.

responsible for the baby's decline and Margaret's vague sickness. He also points out that Ralph is not looking too well himself.

Baby Ethel dies soon after. Ralph takes what the doctor said to heart and returns to England with the grieving Margaret, half ashamed of his acquaintance with Harriet. When Harriet and the Baron and Baroness come back to Heyst, they learn that the baby has died and the others have left for England. Harriet is in a frenzy at the thought that Ralph has forsaken her. Bobby has a crush on her and tries to console her, but he is no substitute for Ralph. The Baroness notices that Harriet expresses no regret about the baby even though she spent so much time with the child. (Strangely, neither the Baron nor the Baroness sicken from Harriet's proximity, an immunity that Marryat does not explain.)

The Baroness decides to return to England and invites Harriet to come with her family. Now that she's in England, Harriet wants to get in touch with Ralph, but the Baroness counsels against it. Bobby sickens. The great visitors of whom the Baroness boasted in Heyst come to the house to conduct business, not for parties or dinners, as she claimed; they go up to her rooms and are shut in there with her. Bobby spends most of his time draping himself over Harriet, though he is getting weaker and weaker.

Elinor comes to see Harriet and brings three letters Harriet wrote to Ralph, which he threw away while staying at his future father-in-law's house. Elinor demands that she stop writing to him and informs Harriet that they are engaged, but Harriet responds that she will go see him if she wants and take him from her. Elinor hurries off to tell Margaret and Dr Phillips about her encounter with Harriet. Margaret summons Anthony Pennell, Ralph's cousin, and Dr Phillips tells him that Harriet "inherits terrible proclivities, added to black blood. She is, in point of fact, a quadroon, and not fit to marry into any decent English family".[52] However, he does not tell Pennell anything about Obeah and the vivisections. So Anthony goes off to see Harriet at the Baroness's.

"Harriet Brandt entered the room, moving sinuously across the carpet as a snake might glide to its lair." Anthony is struck by Harriet's beauty but manages to tell her that she should stay away from Ralph. After dinner, he is enchanted by Harriet's singing. He invites her to his house in Piccadilly and later reports back to Margaret. When Ralph arrives, he points out that he could not

---

52 Ibid.

have married Harriet because she has "black blood in her". Anthony, a kind man (said to be a socialist), begins to view her as someone in need of rescue from the bad influence of the Baroness and the malicious thoughts of others. He dismisses Ralph's warning, "The girl wishes intensely to be married, and she is not a girl whom men will marry." He predicts that she will soon figure among "the free lances of London", particularly given the Baroness's example. It is unclear what exactly Marryat means here, as the Baroness earns her living by fortune-telling, owns a house, is married and maintains her household with the proceeds of her occupation – an arguably dubious one but plainly profitable. But being a "free lance" is clearly not a worthy characteristic; Marryat may in fact be suggesting a future as a prostitute or courtesan.

Anthony starts visiting Harriet regularly and brings her improving books, while Bobby grows weaker and weaker. The Baroness grows less fond of Harriet and the latter begins to feel unwelcome. Anthony is alarmed and proposes to Harriet, offering to find her a home until they can marry. "And yet he knew all the while that the savage in her was *not* tamed – that at any moment, like the domesticated lion or tiger, her nature might assert itself and become furious, wild and intractable."[53]

In the meantime, Miss Wynward, the old governess, and the Baroness fall out; the Baroness threatens her, saying, "You know that those I 'ate, *die!*" That same evening, however, it is Bobby who dies. The Baroness turns her fury on Harriet. "'This is all *your* doing, you poisonous, wicked creature!'" Harriet is astounded by the charge, but the Baroness reveals that she knows "your mother was a devilish negress, and your father a murderer". The Baroness rants that Harriet "has the vampire's blood in 'er and she poisons everybody with whom she comes in contact".[54] She lists Margaret Pullen, Olga Brimont and Bobby among Harriet's victims and threatens to kill her. Miss Wynward, who has lost her fear of the Baroness, tells her she should not accuse the girl of unholy dealings, given all the money she herself has made professing "to hold communication with the spiritual world" – and thus do we learn that she is a spiritualist. Later, Harriet asks Miss Wynward if what the Baroness said could be true, but the governess puts it down to the Baroness's grief and temper. Harriet moves out.

Determined to find out more, Harriet goes to see Dr Philips, since the Baroness has said that he knows all about her past. The doctor resists telling her

---

53 Ibid.
54 Ibid.

the truth because he does not want to hurt her. He tells her that no good comes of speaking ill of the dead, but she persists and from his answers deduces that the Baroness was telling her the truth. She asks him if she was responsible for Bobby's death and he tells her that she exerts a "weakening and debilitating effect" on her friends and that she will have "*sucked them dry*". He advises her against ever marrying. Forlorn, Harriet asks the doctor if he has told her the truth, "medically and scientifically". He says that he has and advises her to find other pleasures and interests beyond marriage or love:

> if there is any one person in the world whom you most desire to benefit and retain the affection of, let that be the very person from whom you separate, as often as possible. You must never hope to keep anyone near you for long, without injuring them. Make it your rule through life never to cleave to any one person altogether, or you will see that person's interest in you wax and wane, until it is destroyed![55]

Despondent, Harriet goes back to the hotel and summons Anthony. She tells him all but he dismisses it as mere superstition. She recounts that her wet nurse died, and another little girl, before she went into the convent. A nun who befriended her was eventually sent to a sanatorium. She rebuffs Anthony's embraces and wails that it is all true and that she must part from him so that she "will not sap [his] manhood and [his] brains". Anthony leaves but promises to return the next morning with the marriage licence. During the sleepless night that follows, Harriet curses her fate and her parents but wonders if the doctor was telling her the truth or if he just wanted to deter her from pursuing Ralph.

The next day, Anthony will not accept no for an answer, so she marries him and they travel to Paris and Nice. He gets steadily weaker and dies in his sleep after they arrive in Florence. Harriet, grief-stricken, is invited to stay in a nearby convent to which she has given money. Despondent, she takes a drug overdose and dies, leaving everything to Margaret Pullen, for her kindness to her in Heyst and for being "the best woman Tony said that he had ever met". In her note to Margaret, Harriet has written: "Do not think more unkindly of me than you can help. My parents have made me unfit to live. Let me go to a world where the curse of heredity which they laid upon me may be mercifully wiped out." [56] And thus the story ends.

Fictional stereotypes of mulattoes or mixed-race people fall into three broad

---

55 Ibid.
56 Ibid.

categories: the tragic mulatto, exemplified by Youma, who identifies with whites and is willing to die with or for them; the heroic mulatto, such as Cubina, in whom "white" qualities predominate, more intelligent than blacks, more noble and brave and never superstitious; and then the degenerate mulatto, such as Harriet's mother and Harriet herself, disgusting, despicable and despised, given to gluttony and treachery and subject to all forms of depravity. Condemned by their black parentage, mulattoes either surrender to their "darker natures" or adopt the manners and customs of whites, thence being depicted in de-racialized ways, as is Mayne Reid's Kate, for example. Presented with no counterbalancing portrayal, readers would have understood that nothing good can come of miscegenation. As usual with books of this sort, the only characters in Marryat's story who come off well are the British ones. The Baroness may be Caucasian, but she is certainly not a sympathetic character. In fact, her portrayal as something of a charlatan suggests that Marryat may not have been quite as dedicated to spiritualism in her later years as she once had been.

THE WOOINGS OF JEZEBEL PETTYFER

The author of *The Wooings of Jezebel Pettyfer*, Major Haldane MacFall, was born in 1860, which means that he was about twenty-five when he was gazetted to the West India Regiment in 1885, serving in Jamaica and West Africa. He retired as a lieutenant in 1892. Clearly he drew on his experiences while in the Caribbean for *Jezebel Pettyfer*, which was his first novel. It was reprinted in the United States under the title *The House of the Sorcerer* and he went on to write several other novels and books.

Jehu Sennacherib Dyle is the son of Virginia Dyle, a mulatto, who left him behind on Barbados as a boy when she ran off to Panama with a white captain. Dyle grows up stealing and making do with odd jobs but, when he is older, he becomes a butler in George Lonnett's household. He loses his job, however, when Mrs. Lonnett catches him flaying and burning her dead black dog for its fat, which he was planning to give to the beautiful dressmaker Jezebel. Turned out of Lonnett's house, he moves in with Jezebel, who refuses his offer of marriage, pointing out that they do not have the money and that either of them might get to liking someone else.

Before she goes to sleep at night, Jezebel always throws "a bowlful of corn and rice across the threshold, to keep out ghouls that would otherwise enter in a ball of blue flame under the door . . . and, taking the human shape of corpses, with cold and clammy lips suck the blood and sap the strength from the sleeping folk within the house".⁵⁷ Dyle begins keeping chickens and does good business, but one day the fowls refuse to set and Jezebel discovers an Obeah charm on her doorstep:

> As she had kissed Dyle she had seen over his shoulder a hideous evil face leering into the doorway, and her blood turned chill. . . . [She feels under the front step and finds] a little ball of mud with four crossed hairs and a feather sticking out of it; on it was set a bird's eyeless white skull, and the whole was wrought about with string and other dirty odd ornament. [She also finds] a little glass phial full of a green liquid with some dead insect floating in it.
>
> "Me Gahd!" she said hoarsely. Her hands shook. "De obeah-man he's put de curse of Obi upon de house; de bad luck are bound to come."⁵⁸

Things do, in fact, go from bad to worse, though Macfall fails to suggest a reason for the Obeah man's enmity. Dyle sets out to steal Mrs Lonnett's sewing machine for Jezebel and takes hankies and some money as well, but he is almost caught by the police and leaves the sewing machine behind. His inability to show it to her and prove what happened makes Jezebel suspect him of carrying on with "yaller gals" and she summons the police for him. He is jailed. Later, Jezebel drops a "conjure bag" that was supposed to keep off bad luck into the fire. It cost her four dollars, but she denounces Obeah:

> "What are de point of all dis obeah?" She flung out her arms impatiently; then gathered them in, and rested her chin in her palms again. "Dis here sorcerer feller's tricks dey is no good to bring de evil to me enemy – he's charms dey is no good to keep de bad luck from meself. What de good of de feller anyway? I is never goin' to believe dis nigger trash about luck and charms and such any more. It are all graven images and blasted idolaturry. De Scriptures deirselves is mighty strong agin dese here carryin's-on and weakness o' de flesh. Dat blamed old nigger obeah-man he are a ole rum-swillin' egg-suckin' graven image heself – dat what I call he. Huh! de amount o' good money I has given dat feller for all he's trash! Dar was dat piece o' de rope dat Portugee feller hanged heself wid. 'Burn dat into ashes and drink 'em in milk,' says de fool obeah-man, 'den yo' is bound to get de sartin' good luck to make yo'r enemy yo'r footstool,' says he,

---

57 Haldane Macfall, *The Wooings of Jezebel Pettyfer* (London: Simkin, Marshall, Hamilton, 1898), 58.
58 Ibid., 65.

'and de price o' dat is five dollars,' says he. And a heap o' good luck dat bring'd me, exceppin' fillin' me belly wid charcoal!"[59]

Jezebel believes that the woman Dyle likes intends to marry a Jamaican rum-store keeper by the name of Huckleback, and she decides to take Huckleback for herself. When Dyle is released, he joins the West India Regiment and they go to Jamaica. In Jamaica, Dyle becomes involved with Huckleback's previous woman, Melissa Haslap, who is cast out when Jezebel marries Huckleback. Going home one night, Melissa sees an Obeah man outside Huckleback's house.

> Before the door, in the deep dusk, the ape-like filthy-looking figure of a foul old man in rags and tatters was jigging on silent feet, with bendings of the knee and wavings of his arms, mumbling an incantation in some strange tongue. He smiled evilly at the startled woman, and held out a threatening arm over the house. "Death! – death! – death! – de swift death!" he barked, and in the saying of it passed away with a leer into the dusk.

Melissa finds "a little miniature wooden coffin [lying] on the step, and [fouling] the air with the sour smell of the dead".[60]

When Melissa goes into the rum shop, Huckleback tells her that Jezebel is running around on him and that he is planning to sell his business and move to Panama. He wants her to come with him. Later, Jezebel comes into the rum shop with an English sailor, Anak Streke, with whom she has taken up. A rum-shop customer is holding forth on race; he declares that all a white man has to do is call and coloured women will leave black men for them. Streke is drunk and makes a fool of himself but Jezebel shows how little she cares for Huckleback by kissing one of the men on the mouth. Huckleback demands to know if she has been with Streke, but she spits in his face, so he hits her and rips her dress open to the waist. He then attacks Streke with a knife and is killed by the sailor. Jezebel holds a wake for Huckleback to make sure his duppy does not come to haunt his store or his house. His shade makes an appearance on Third Night, but they send it back. On Ninth Night they hold another wake but the shade does not appear, though the sexton sees a Rolling Calf, a ghostly apparition trailing a rusty chain. (At present the Ninth Night tradition is still alive in Jamaica but is on the wane, as is belief in the Rolling Calf.)

Jezebel gets a new man, Boaz, whose wife, Deborah, and mother-in-law,

---

59   Ibid., 92.
60   Ibid., 145.

the widow Tiffles, naturally object to the relationship. Deborah decides to use Obeah to get him back and asks her husband to get her some grave dust, a shred of some corpse's burial shroud, and a chip off the gallows tree. He does it and later scares his mother-in-law, who is digging up another grave. When Boaz does not come back to her, both Deborah and her mother become convinced that stronger steps are needed; separately, they decide to seek out the Obeah man King Ardah.

The scenes in which the widow Tiffles and, later, Deborah petition King Ardah for a curse on Jezebel are the most gripping in the book. Deborah creeps through the swamp to a hut from which emanates "a strong gust of rum and the sour smell of negroes". A "negress" yells: "Mamaloi – little queen mother! make she's body covered wid boils and sores by day; make de black dog of de witches get into she's throat and steal she's breath and strangle she by night; make all de evil come to Jezebel Huckleblack!" There is a fire, drums boom, pipes wail and a circle of "chanting black women, naked to the waist", whose shadows dance and leap on the wall. Every now and then, a black bottle is passed to the dancing women, "who would tilt it up to their lips, and, drinking from it, pass it back again . . . old African negresses whose withered breasts hung pendulous against their lean ribs, stout middle-aged black women with full breasts, Jamaican negro girls with budding breasts – all bowed themselves and sang and stamped their feet". The drummers are also half-naked; one has a "shelving forehead and ape-like head", while another musician is dirty and dressed in rags.[61]

The widow Tiffles sits enthroned on a stone slab stolen from a grave. Wearing a richly embroidered robe, she sits "munching her toothless gums", with "the headless bodies of several white cockerels" at her feet. Behind her, on a ledge, "a blind little wooden image stood on his little bandy legs in an ungainly straddle and smiled. . . . He stood before a crude little print of the Virgin Mary in a tawdry frame, and a little crucified sorrowing Christ. . . . A bleached human skull gleamed white" to complete the arrangement. The widow Tiffles also has a black bottle, from which she occasionally drinks. When she enters the chalk circle, she falls to the ground, "foaming at the mouth".[62]

McFall follows the description of the dance with a portrayal of King Ardah which employs all the standard conventions and includes a few colourful additional details, such as body-paint and earrings.

---

61 Ibid., 278.
62 Ibid., 279–81.

Out of the darkness beside the tomb a vile-looking old negro stepped into the dim light. . . . His stooping black body was naked except for a loose pair of man-o'-war's-man's duck trousers. . . . His head was bound down to his eyes with a bright red cloth, and from under the cloth his villainous black face peered out like a great ape's. In his ears were large gold earrings that glittered in the light. His face was streaked with white paint, and streaks of white paint were on his bare black chest. He stood masterfully before the tomb, as a king might stand before his throne; and as he faced the people his great lips opened over the red gap of his mouth, showing a couple of snaggy pointed yellow teeth in the red gums. . . .

The old sorcerer's bloodshot eyes looked evilly over the circle of silent women, then glanced calmly down at the old woman where she lay struggling in a fit at his feet upon the floor. He licked his lips and spoke, picking his words and phrases with the pretty precision of a man who speaks in an acquired tongue:

"De spirit of Obi has passed out of its dwelling-place in de body of de snake and entered into dis woman."[63]

King Ardah then delivers himself of one of the most remarkable speeches in literary Obeah.

"Obi is great. The Spirit of Evil is mightier than the spirit of good – mightier and more eternal. All else perishes and passes into dust – hearsay – a dream – and is not. But evil is without end – evil endureth for ever. That which is good can do us no hurt. Therefore the Controller of evil is more fearful than the Maker of good. . . . The white man believeth there is a God, not because he can prove it, but because he cannot. But evil requireth no proof. This is the longest remembered story of the ages, that the first man and the first woman and their firstborn did evil; in the white man's book of life it is so written, that the first man and the first woman did evil, and their firstborn slew his brother: for these things are they chiefly remembered, but the good that they did is forgotten. For the spirit of evil is mightier than the will of God; Obi in his habitation in the snake destroyed the design and the handiwork of God and sullied Paradise. . . . The white preacher ordereth that we overthrow our gods; yet . . . he raiseth up altars to his God . . . but he maketh the law of life to his own desires, and in his own house he forgetteth charity and even pulleth down his neighbour's Christ. For evil overcometh good. The white man preacheth the Son of God but feareth to follow the laws of the Son of God. For evil is stronger than good. Take no heed to the tattling of fools, but remember that you have your passions and your desires given to you that you may use them. Evil endureth for ever. You

---

63   Ibid., 282.

> have called to Obi for a sign, and he hath given it. We have called to the devil of hate that hath his dwelling-place in the body of the snake, and it has passed into this woman where she lieth upon the house of the dead. Her soul is become the soul of Hate – her breath the breath of Hate."[64]

Cocks crow and momentarily silence the "hideous ruffian". "Obi will have no further prayers tonight", he says. "Obi loveth the darkness; but the cockerel loveth the light." He enjoins his listeners not to speak of what they have seen and done. "That which is once spoken has lost its mystery, and the secret strength of evil that was in the unspoken thing hath utterly gone out of it. That which is known killeth mystery – but we are born in mystery and die in mystery, and mystery keepeth us for her own. Obi acts through mystery alone; he punisheth always the breach of this ritual – and hath no mercy."[65]

King Ardah then beheads another rooster, whose blood is caught in a glass vessel and placed on the tomb.

> He stepped behind the tomb again, brought out a bottle of rum, and filled up the glass vessel, mixing the spirit with the red blood that was already in it; and, standing at the foot of the tomb whereon lay the still figure of the woman, and gripping in his right hand the gleaming knife, its blade dripping blood, his wicked little eyes glittering under the black projecting brows, he lifted the glass vessel and drank a mouthful of the blood and spirit; placing the vessel back on the tomb again, he called to Obi, crying out that leprosy, and foul disease, and madness and sickening death should fall upon whomsoever broke the oath of secrecy; then ordering the people each to swear the oath, he cried "Go!"[66]

They all leave except for the widow Tiffles, who awakens slowly and proclaims, "De liver of a pussun four days buried, and de little finger of a little child dead in the borning." King Ardah nods, instructs her on how these are to be procured and tells her to hurry, for the night is nearly over. After she leaves, he walks "behind the stone seat, and from amidst the strange jumble of odds and ends, bleached skulls of cats and parrots, polished human finger-bones, and other piled-up rubbish and foul-smelling charms and spells, he took the black bottle of rum, uncorked it, and putting it to his mouth, tilted it up and took a long pull at it".[67]

---

64 Ibid., 283–84.
65 Ibid., 285.
66 Ibid., 285–86.
67 Ibid., 287–88.

Deborah then announces herself and reproaches Ardah for "havin' dis here foreign Hayti trash kickin' around and yellin' here dis evening". She warns him that if he keeps on in their company he is "bound to get into plenty trouble" (she makes no mention of her own mother's part in the ceremony). Deborah tells him that she wants Jezebel killed and that her mother, the widow Tiffles, has "laid a heap o' wangas and tricks agin Jezebel", to no avail. "And she make'd a heap o' charms to keep de strength o' me love over Boaz Bryan", also to no avail. The widow Tiffles finally confessed herself at a loss and recommended Deborah seek out King Ardah.

King Ardah acknowledges that "'de widow Tiffles she are a mighty strong sorcerer sheself, de most vig'rous in dis island – excepping' only meself. She's been tryin' and tryin' – but she don't able to raise de devil of Hate. She's magic it don't got de strength to call upon de spirits out of Africa. She was bound to come to de ole obeah-man' – he drew himself up proudly – 'and she come'd.'" Another soliloquy follows in which Ardah again loses the broken English which he uses in conversational speech.

> "We have met together and made sacrifice to the four corners of the earth – to the rising of the sun, where the night dies amongst the mists; to the setting of the same, where the night is born out of the darkness; to the south where the four stars sink amidst the waste of waters; to the north where barren places are – and we called to the places under the earth, in the fifth place where the dead sleep – and we made sacrifice, slaying white cockerels, which are the enemies of Obi." He swept his hand towards where the four candles guttered upon the ground. "And they that had the desire of Hate in their hearts bowed themselves down to Obi in his habitation in the body of the snake, and prostrated themselves in the dust, and called aloud to Obi to send the devil of Hate into the body of the woman that sat in the fifth place, that it might manifest itself and accomplish their desire. And the four women that stood in the places towards the four corners of the earth bit each the arm of the other, and sucked the blood the one of the other, and cried out to Obi with lips of blood, and danced before the fifth place. And with music and dancing the frenzy of the strong willing of evil came upon us, and we called with the might of our desire upon Obi, with the blood of cockerels upon our lips. And of a sudden the devil of Hate that was in the snake came out of it and entered into the woman where she sat in the fifth place upon the house of the dead. And she leaped up and fell upon the ground – and the devil of Hate rent her body so that she foamed at the mouth."[68]

---

68 Ibid., 291–92.

King Ardah informs Deborah that the widow has gone to "de buryin'-grounds" to get the "evil spell" to put on her enemy, and that once the spell is laid, "evil and madness, and after de madness sores and agony and a dreadful death, shall come", unless one of Jezebel's friends smites Deborah on the back before she can lay the spell. If that happens, the spell will turn on her and what she desires to happen to Jezebel will happen to her. Ardah then tries to ensorcell Deborah herself.

> As the gaze of the snake-like eyes pierced into hers, Deborah Bryan felt the grip of the excitement of this venomous ruffian fasten upon her. Her senses thrilled unwilled to the words he spoke, and she now of a sudden knew with speechless certainty the force of his unspoken desires. . . . The snake-like play of his tongue between the raw-red gums, as he darted it between the yellow fangs of his eye-teeth and licked his great lips, usurped her imagination and fascinated her with terror.

But she is not the daughter of the widow Tiffles for nothing and repulses his attack on her consciousness; "the fierce thrusts of his stabbing gaze weakened". Thwarted, he threatens to curse her, but she responds that his curses have not hurt her enemies, so how can they hurt her? He advises her to come back at the next moon, but Deborah will hear none of it.

She draws out a handful of charms from her bosom and throws them on the ground. "Curse yo'r tricks and conjurin's and spells and charms and all dese here wangas and child-toys – curse 'em all!" she shrieks.

> Dese here dry lizards, and forty-legs, and hopper-grasses, and cockroaches, and locusts, and fireflies, and scorpions, and frogs, and bedbugs, and a piece o' de skin offen of one o' dem stingin'-snakes from St Lucia, and a piece o' de lungs of a jackass, and a hair out o' de head o' dis Jezebel female – dey was all dried up, and I see you beat 'em fine into a powder before me two eyes – wid dat I see'd yo' mix four pinches o' de grave-dirt from offen of de grave o' dat mulatter fellow dat suicided heself – de fellow dat hanged heself and was buried widout a funeril . . . and yo' spitted four times into de midst o' de powder, "put a four pinches o' dat dust on to de person's head," says yo, "and all dese things I tell yo' is bound to come to pass," says yo'. "She's flesh it bound to dry up and lose its plumpness and freshness," says yo', "and she's hair it's goin' to drop off," says yo'.[69]

But instead, Jezebel's hair had grown straighter and longer and shinier since

---

69 Ibid., 293–95.

she managed to put the powder on it: "de female, she's all de better for dat powder".

This is more than King Ardah can stand and he tells her that she will never get another sign from Obi and that she will lose all she has. Madness will afflict the last house she was in before sunset, and Death will come to the first house she steps into after midnight. Deborah is unimpressed and begs him for a little poison. Ardah knows her for something of an Obeah woman herself, with "a wide reputation amongst the women", and he decides to give her what she wants.

> He walked round behind the tomb, mumbling and bending the knee as he moved; took up an empty black rum-bottle; put something into it with great care, crooning a strange incantation the while, and bowing, and bending the knee. He brought the bottle round to where the woman sat upon the tomb, and taking up the black bottle of rum which stood beside her he divided the small remaining liquor about equally between the two bottles. He put back the rum-bottle upon the tomb, and carefully shaking up the poisoned drink, he set that down also on the stone seat.
>
> The sorcerer turned to her:
>
> "Dis here are a mighty powerful poison, Deborah Bryan – de gall of de alligator is full of hate for man – yo' is got to remember yo' can give too much poison for killin,' and yo' can give too little poison for killin'. . . . I tell yo' de pusson dat drinks dis poison done bound to die a drefful death.". . .
>
> "Yo' has got to be keerful. When de woman has drinked off de poison yo' is still got to remember Obi are mystery – de poison don't goin' to begin to act till yo' done fill'd de empty bottle wid water four times and emptied de bottle on to de thirsty sand four times, and den yo's got to break de bottle and trow de pieces into de sea. . . . Obi gives signs and strikes, but Obi is never seen."

He charges her sixteen "pieces of silver", which she pays, though she protests that it is almost all her savings.[70]

Deborah then attempts to poison Jezebel again, but Jezebel is none the worse for it. Instead, Deborah's mother goes mad, and Deborah curses: "*dat* fool feller call heself a obeah-man!" Outraged, she wants her money back and crosses the mangrove swamp to "the ruin where the old sorcerer had his dwelling".

> There was a beating of many wings. It came to the ears of Deborah Bryan like the fluttering sound of the headless bodies of fresh-killed cockerels, flung upon

---

70 Ibid., 296–300.

the floor by the old African, making sacrifice.... She knew the accustomed smell of the dirty ill-kept place – the bitter scent of stale tobacco, together with the other sickly unclean stenches, but out of the midst of it all there now came to her nostrils a strange odour, the faint sour smell of the dead.

Inside the hut, she sees dead vultures on the floor and calls out, "Is yo' there, king?"[71] But Ardah is dead and disembowelled. As Deborah leaves the Obeah man's hut she sees the idol on its ledge smile. Meanwhile, the children stop jeering at Deborah's mad mother after she calls "down the curse of Obi" on one of them and the boy contracts leprosy.

> Dyle, now a member of the West India Regiment, is informed by his lieutenant, the story's narrator, that he's leaving for Africa and that his replacement will not be as lenient with Dyle as he has been. He says Dyle should not forget that he is a man and has been a corporal, though he was demoted because of his troubles. Before he leaves, the lieutenant also has an encounter with the Obeah man, who now appears to have become a duppy: Suddenly I saw before the blackness of an open doorway near at hand an old ragged negro ... he turned his black ape-like face upon me ...
>
> "Hee-hee!" he cackled ... "de white man comes to de land of de black man and puts de black man in de gutter – but he kisses de black woman upon de mouth – and so he shall rot – and rot – and rot!"
>
> Here he spat at me.... I stepped up to the foul rogue, and swung my cane to lay it upon him –
>
> There was nothing where he stood.
>
> But out of the dusk there came a husky cackling.[72]

In the epilogue of this somewhat confusing novel, Melissa and Deborah are both living in town. The former has had a son with Dyle, who went to Panama, made his fortune there and then returned to Jamaica to live.

The author of the *Longman Companion to Victorian Fiction* calls *The Wooings of Jezebel Pettyfer* a "lively picaresque novel" with a "densely documented depiction of black life"[73] and the editor of the *Negro Year Book: An Annual Encyclopedia of the Negro, 1931–1932*, describes it as "a fascinating story of rather free and adventurous natives in Barbadoes" with "accounts of [their] superstitious

---

71 Ibid., 341.
72 Ibid., 380.
73 John Sutherland, *The Longman Companion to Victorian Fiction*, 2nd ed. (London: Pearson, 2009), 339.

practices".⁷⁴ The book drew fire, however, from a prominent black American, Emmett J. Scott. Scott, who had worked as a journalist for the *Houston Post*, went on to co-found the *Texas Freeman*, Houston's first African-American newspaper. He later became Booker T. Washington's chief aide, serving as his personal secretary, speechwriter and ghost-writer; he also assisted Washington with the founding of the National Negro Business League in 1900. Years later, President Woodrow Wilson appointed Scott as special advisor on black affairs to Newton Baker, Wilson's secretary of war.

Scott denounced *Jezebel* as having a tone of "sustained contempt, almost hatred, for Negroes.... About midway through the book, Macfall abandons [his] labored attempts at humor, puts aside all sympathy for his characters, and begins to show himself a genuine Negro-hater. From this point on, all Negro women are 'slipshod Negresses', or 'slattern gossips', or something equally offensive. Negro men are ape-like."⁷⁵ In responding to a questionnaire on the representation of blacks in literature sent out by the editors of *The Crisis* in 1926, MacFall admitted that Scott had "every right to pour contempt on my literary gifts" and to find *Jezebel* "feeble in wit and humour", but he denied that Scott had any grounds for calling him a "Negro-hater". To explain that he was certainly not one, MacFall launched into an account of an incident that happened when he was "left in command of a company of Zouaves at Port Royal in Jamaica [when he] was a mere boy", sidestepping the question entirely.⁷⁶

In Britain, no objections or questions about the depiction of blacks were raised by a populace long accustomed to reading about violent, superstitious, ape-like, thieving, drunken black people. Instead, the reviewer for the *Pall Mall Gazette* sang the book's praises:

> Let us freely admit that this book is strikingly clever, funny, strong, and worth reading. It is a bundle of loosely strung incidents and very unequal, but on the whole it really merits those complimentary adjectives.... But it is not for edification that you should read this book. Other excellent things you will find. You will find a telling series of pictures of the comically, pathetically, naughty

---

74 Monroe N. Work, ed., *The Negro Year Book: An Annual Encyclopedia of the Negro*, 1931–1932, http://www.archive.org/stream/negroyearbookana00workrich#page/n7/mode/2up.

75 Martha Jane Nadell, *Enter the New Negroes: Images of Race in American Culture* (Boston: Harvard University Press, 2004), 16.

76 Henry Louis Gates Jr and Gene Andrew Jarrett, *The New Negro: Readings on Race, Representation, and African-American Culture, 1892–1938* (Princeton, NJ: Princeton University Press, 2007), 198–99.

and childish life of the nigger, laid on with a vivid and bold brush. You will find really powerful stories such as . . . the fate of the obeah man, squalid but strong and effective. . . . You will find immensely funny sketches of the light-hearted darkies with their "prognostications" and their "supe' law" and their delightful misapplications of the Scriptures. In short, with all its deliberate breaches of taste and its scrambling inequality, it is a vigorous book by a man with stuff in him.[77]

In other words, the reviewer was gratified that the characters had fully conformed to his expectations, given the stereotypical conventions to which he was accustomed.

Praises for the book continued long into the next century. In 1923 the American writer and book reviewer Vincent Starret declared that "few better novels have been written in the language" and pronounced it "deserving of immortality".[78]

A decade later, the critic Paul Jordan Smith noted that Starret's admiration for "this picaresque narrative of West Indian life" had raised its value among book collectors. Smith was also a fan, observing that the book "was a highly amusing account of a people who are happily without morals of any kind whatever. Specifically it relates the adventures of one Jehu Sennacherib Dyle and Jezebel Pettyfer, both of whom knew tricks that might have astonished Casanova: a background of witchcraft lends color, and the unconscious knavery of the protagonists gives the tale that rich flavor seldom found in fiction since the 18th century."[79] The book's racist depiction of black people and its contribution to the perpetuation of negative stereotypes is completely overlooked as unworthy of mention. Smith and the rest, conditioned by centuries of stereotyped portrayals of blacks, were unfazed by the book's racism and accepted the depiction of black people as accurate and factual. This acceptance pervaded British society and still exists today, though now somewhat muted by the advent of political correctness.

---

77 *Pall Mall Gazette*, 14 July 1898.
78 Vincent Starret, "Haldane Macfall: Novelist", in *Buried Caesars: Essays in Literary Appreciation* (Chicago: Covivi-McGee, 1923), 170–78.
79 Paul Jordan Smith, *For the Love of Books: The Adventures of an Impecunious Collector* (Oxford: Oxford University Press, 1934; repr., 1963), 125.

CHAPTER 10

Fictional Adventurers and Real-Life Travellers
Obeah in Boys' Papers and Travel Narratives

BLACK DEMONS AND WITCHES: BOYS' ADVENTURE PAPERS

As the printing process grew cheaper in the 1800s and literacy rates improved, the appetite for cheap literature exploded. The demand for chapbooks and "penny dreadfuls", which spawned the unique form of literary entertainment knowns as boys' adventure papers, took off. Devoted to lurid tales of highway robbery, true crime, vampires and ghosts, the penny dreadfuls were popular among Britain's working classes but were a source of anxiety for reformers worried about what they perceived as vulgarity and moral decline. That many of the stories presented criminals in a heroic light was of particular concern to the middle and upper classes and the religious establishment. As the nineteenth century progressed, however, and British imperialism gained ground, the subject matter began to change: the preoccupation with stories set in domestic locales gave way to tales of adventure in faraway lands.

Dixon has written that "anyone interested in how ideas – political ideas in the broadest and most important sense – are fostered and grow up in a society cannot afford to neglect what children read".[1] And in the 1800s and early 1900s, what white children – or, more particularly, white boys – were reading was cheap adventure papers with names like *Chums*, *Union Jack*, *Boys of England* and *Pluck*, titles that, like bugle calls, evoked a certain response, both inspiring and reinforcing a public-school *esprit* in the service of crown and country. Some of the papers, such as the *Boy's Own Paper*, started in 1879

---

[1] Bob Dixon, *Catching Them Young 2: Political Ideas in Children's Fiction* (London: Pluto Press, 1977), xv.

by the Religious Tract Society, arose from their publishers' desire to lift the tone of current offerings and present boys with inspirational stories of gallantry and courage. Team spirit, patriotism, grit, pluck and fair play were the main themes of the stories which often featured heroes who were engaged in big-game hunting, sporting competitions, criminal investigations and exploration in exotic lands.

Orwell notes that the favourite subjects in boys' adventure papers were the "Wild West, Frozen North, Foreign Legion, crime . . . tropical exploration, historical romance (Robin Hood, Cavaliers and Roundheads) . . . and the Tarzan motif in varying forms".[2] He could also have listed Obeah or African sorcery as a frequent or popular subject. For example, a story in *Pluck*, "Through Fire and Flood", set in Jamaica, features a character by the name of Ben Obeah, while "The Wire and the Wave", in the *Boy's Own Paper*, describes Quaga, who has set himself up as an Obeah man to acquire influence among his fellow blacks. *Baily's Magazine of Sports and Pastimes* contains the "Memories of an Old Soldier" who had a run-in with Obeah. Moseley's account of Obeah and the obi-bag of Three-Fingered Jack was reproduced in *Peter Parley's Annual*.[3]

As in adult literature, the descriptions of Obeah men and women were suitably gruesome. In *Pluck's* "The Secret of Grenville Towers", the Black Goblin – in reality, a Jamaican Obeah man – wears a "fiendishly diabolical" mask, but when he removes it, his face is "scarcely less repulsive and hideous". When Sable Gross, the villain of "Black Demons of Hayti", variously described as an Obeah man, Papaloi, savage or monster, throws his head back to laugh, he displays "his gleaming white teeth and the lurid redness of his prominent gums and swollen tongue, contrasting hideously with the ebony-black of his complexion". The hero of another story in *Young England* meets an Obeah woman who is just as horrible.

> Ha! what was this shapeless coil of black, writhing limbs that lay before him, in which the only thing plainly seen was a bony, shrunken, ghastly face – hideous in itself, and doubly so from its look of fiendish malignity – which spat at him and cursed him with impotent fury as he came near. Brave as he was, our hero

---

2 *The Collected Essays, Journalism and Letters of George Orwell*, ed. Susan Orwell and Ian Angus (Harmondsworth: Penguin, 1968), 1:521.

3 "Through Fire and Flood", *Pluck* 276 (n.d.): 11; T. Munro, "The Wire and the Wave", *Boy's Own Paper* 606 (23 August 1890): 744; "Memories of an Old Soldier", *Baily's Magazine of Sports and Pastimes* 445 (1 March 1897): 207.

felt his bold heart stand still as he recognized a horrible old negro beldame whom all the local blacks held in awe as an "Obeah-woman", which on their lips, meant all, and more than all, that the most superstitious English-man could have conveyed in the days of witchcraft, by calling any old woman "a downright witch". Apart from her supposed supernatural powers, and her venomous hatred of all white people whatever, the wretched old creature was darkly credited with crimes at which even the lowest and most brutalized of the negroes dared only to hint in shuddering whispers.[4]

While most of the stories take place in Jamaica or one of the other islands, a few are set in England. For example, in *Pluck's* "The Secret of Grenville Towers", a former governor general of Jamaica has returned to his family's ancestral seat in England, but we are told that, while he was in Jamaica, "he had condemned many negroes to death for offering human sacrifices to Obeah, the demon-god". In fact, one of his servants, Cynthia, who was brought from the island, was the wife of "a prominent worshipper of Obeah" described as "an undersized being of phenomenal strength and unparalleled ferocity". He was convicted of being "the perpetrator of untold villainies" and Sir Rupert sentenced him to hang. Feeling sorry for the man's destitute widow, Sir Rupert then took her into his employ and she "proved a kindly, affectionate nurse to his newborn babe". When it begins to appear that Grenville Towers is haunted by a black goblin, Sir Rupert questions Cynthia, who says it is "what my people call Obeah, the black demon-man".

A couple of nights later, the Black Goblin appears in Sir Rupert's bedroom, sinks a pitchfork into him and his wife and sets the place on fire. "Vengeance is good", the Obeah man whispers to himself, happy that "the man who caused me to be hanged is a charred corpse. His wife and child have shared his fate". As the story winds on, various Grenvilles suffer tragic fates, Cynthia begins to "openly worship Obeah" and "croon incantations", and her husband continues to wreak havoc until both meet their ends.[5]

Whatever the name of the adventure paper, it was never targeted at non-white readers. The editor of *Peter Parley's Annual* addressed his editorials "To all the Boys and Girls in England, Scotland and Ireland".[6] Meanwhile, his counterpart at *Boys of the Empire* explained:

---

4 "Corn from the Foundations", *Young England*, n.d., 5.
5 G. G. Green, "The Secret of Grenville Towers", *Pluck* 218 (n.d.): 1.
6 *Peter Parley's Annual*, 1840, 1.

> By the phrase "Boys of the Empire" we mean not only the Boys of England, Ireland, Scotland and Wales, but the Youth of Britain's noble dependencies – of the splendid continent of Australia – of the equally large and wealthy Dominion of Canada, with its immense prairies and forests, the Boys of the luxurious and glowing East Indies (itself an Empire) – not forgetting those of the smaller states which own allegiance to our Empress Queen.[7]

It is unlikely that the black boys of Africa, which was still largely unsettled by Europeans, and of the West Indies, where schools were often of a low standard (where they existed at all), were included in those "smaller states".

Selling for one penny or only slightly more, these papers were extremely popular among boys, many of whom probably read two or more regularly. Orwell himself estimates that "nearly every boy went through a phase" of reading at least one paper. Figures are difficult to obtain, but at one point the circulation of the *Boy's Own Paper*, which lasted from 1879 to 1967, reached as high as one million.

The enduring popularity of the papers over a number of decades ensured their influence over successive generations of boys, shaping and reinforcing their view of themselves as young Englishmen and their perception of their rightful roles in the world vis-à-vis other races. Malchow has argued that "as the nineteenth century progressed, racism became ever more widely diffused and achieved an acceptability, almost a consensus, in educated society as well as at deeper levels of popular culture".[8] As we have seen, this racism was certainly on display in much of the adult fiction that touched on the West Indies, but it was also quite evident in the boys' papers, arguably the most popular form of literature among children.

Invariably, the role of whites in adventure-paper stories was one of leadership and dominance over other races; whenever a hero came into contact with black people, they would be downright stupid, superstitious, cowardly, vain and credulous at best, or savage, murderous and plain evil at worst. As the former, they were often the agents of a dastardly white villain who used their ignorance and credulity for his ends. As the latter, their aim was often to overthrow and exterminate the white race and establish on whichever island they happened to be (usually Jamaica), a black republic on the order of Haiti. Of course, a similar fear permeated many adult books.

---

7 *Boys of the Empire* 1 (1 July 1888), n.p.
8 Malchow, *Gothic Images*, 39.

Dismissive of Obeah themselves, quick-thinking and resourceful whites could display their superiority by using the terror of it to hold rebellious blacks at bay. For example, in "The Black Demons of Hayti", a story in the *Big Budget*, two white men are being hotly pursued by a gang of blacks when one of the white men remembers a rag doll that he found. "An inspiration flashed upon him, a ridiculous idea, but one worth a trial. The fetish bogey, the rag doll! These child-minded murderers feared the fooling thing; he would try its effect upon them. Almost smiling at the notion, despite the desperate crisis, Stephen drew the bundle from his pocket, and held it full in view of the wolfish pack, at the same time yelling some words of gibberish." He throws it at one of them, who falls to the ground dead, and the others run away. "The white men were masters of the field."

Later, when Stephen wants to know where Sable Gross has gone with his white captives, a woman and a young child, he

> resolved to further test the power of Obeah. He, himself, was credited with the possession of that dread influence (how simple these murdering fools were), perhaps he might exercise it again.
>
> "Attend to me", he said harshly. "Answer my questions straight, reply truthfully or dread your doom. You have said, you have seen, that I am a powerful Obeah-man, answer me truthfully or I will put a curse upon you. I will blast you, will wither you, your flesh will dry and shrivel, then drop from your aching bones."

"The terrified black . . . his black visage blanching to a hideous pallor", tells him everything he knows.

Similarly, when a fight arises between a white man and a black, the former always wins. Blacks may have had brawn on their side, but whites had brains and could call on their skills to defeat brute strength. In "The Black Demons of Hayti" the protagonist is attacked by a black overseer and Obeah man who is "Herculean in bulk and muscle, the white but a stripling; but what the latter lacked in power, he more than made up in skill"; he knocks down "the hercules . . . like a ninepin".[9]

Unlike adult books, however, the boys' papers only rarely allude to black men's perceived desire for white women. In "The Black Demons of Hayti", Sable Gross first fixes his unwanted attentions on the mulatto Elsa. Only after he captures the sister of one of the main white protagonists does she become

---

9 "The Black Demons of Hayti", *Big Budget* 121 (7 October 1899): 274.

his goal: "'As for Missy,' [Sable] proceeded, smacking his lips lustfully, 'she one dainty piece, far more better dan Elsa. She my prize – mine, mine alone – I deal wid her myself. She be my queen, yet my slave. Oh, it is grand, grand, grand!'" Conscious of the sensitivities of parents and middle-class critics, most stories avoid plot lines around this particular trope, however.

Like the adult books discussed earlier, the boys' papers depict blacks (and people of other non-white races) in stereotypical ways. An evil person is readily identifiable by the way he or she looks, dresses and acts, and evil is explicitly associated with blackness. The blacker the skin, the uglier and more evil the villain. In "Forecastle Tom", a *Boys of the Empire* story, a white character describes a Papuan as "positively hideous. . . . He was nearly jet-black, and his features were exceptionally large and ill-favoured. His huge ears were drawn down by ponderous earrings, while a bar of metal was thrust through his nose. His body was tattooed in various colours, and his limbs were . . . without the slightest grace. "Why, he's like Satan", exclaims one of the whites. "'And he'll show himself as evil as Satan, too,' said Tom."[10]

In some of the stories, the racism is overt and proud. "I do not like niggers", says the protagonist of "A Naval Officer's Yarn", which appears in an 1893 issue of *Chums*. "I have seen them wild and I've seen them tame, and I object to them under either aspect. Yes, perhaps I'm prejudiced against them, and if you'd seen as much of them as I have, perhaps you would be prejudiced too." The fictional events of the story take place during Jamaica's 1865 Morant Bay uprising. The rebellion and its suppression polarized British public opinion and resulted in the recall of Governor John Eyre, who was vigorously condemned for his actions by men such as John Stuart Mill and Charles Darwin. He was defended equally strenuously by such celebrities as Charles Kingsley and Charles Dickens. In the Britain of the late 1800s, it would have been hard to find someone who had no opinion on Governor Eyre.

The author of "A Naval Officer's Yarn" is among Eyre's many fans. "You are a bit too young to remember the revolt among the niggers in Jamaica, which was only saved from becoming a massacre of the whites by the presence of mind and firmness of Governor Eyre", the narrator says, going on to relate that he was serving on HMS *Wolf*, which was in Port Royal, Jamaica, at the time. They hear gunshots and see fire inland, so they land under the command of Lt Bright, who, along with the narrator, is courting the daughter of a "large sugar

---

10 "Forecastle Tom", *Boys of the Empire* 1 (19 March 1888): 106.

grower", Charlie Lanchester. They make their way to Lanchester's house and are met by Slewin, the overseer, who begs them to protect him because "the niggers have sworn to have their revenge on me".

"In another minute a disorderly crowd of niggers, armed with every imaginable description of a weapon from a shot gun to a carving knife, and the majority of whom were evidently more than half-drunk, advanced towards the house." The group is headed by a "tall buck nigger" who confronts the white men and demands that Slewin be handed over. Bright refuses and says he will shoot if they do not leave, so they go. Miss Lanchester tells Bright afterwards that the blacks hate Slewin because "he's very severe with them", and she confesses that her father would have let him go but "he's so clever with the sugar". Of course, the word *severe* raises an image of schoolmarmish firmness with recalcitrant children, not the outright cruelties to which black people were commonly subjected.

The black people then set fire to the boiling house and the armed sailors rush there. "A strange sight met our gaze. The niggers had all joined hands and were dancing and leaping round and round, while they chanted one of their infernal Obi songs, and the savage exultation on their countenances made them look more demoniacal than ever." The narrator hears Slewin's cries for help and, sword in hand, leads the way towards the "black savages", who run away, fleeing in all directions – "and yet only an hour before these inhuman brutes had robbed, beaten and murdered two unprotected women". This is the first and only mention of these victims in the story, leading the reader to wonder who the women were, since they were not Lanchesters and the sailors are not reported as having encountered any other women.

The blacks have somehow captured Slewin and thrown him into the largest boiler. He dies, but not before identifying "Three-fingered Jumbo" as the perpetrator. The narrator claims to have "had the pleasure of forming one of the party who assisted in his execution at Morant Bay".[11]

In another *Boys of the Empire* story, "Ross Billings' Banjo", the author claims to have been on a plantation in the American South when emancipation was declared and gives the following account of what transpired. "On the third day after the slaves had been declared free . . . about ten or a dozen of the blacks [rushed] into the room. They were half-crazy with drink, and looked and acted like mad, yelling devils." The blacks seize the plantation owner, his daughter

---

11 "A Naval Officer's Yarn", *Chums*, 1893, 440.

and the writer himself, bind and gag them and drag them out. To save themselves, the narrator (the eponymous Ross Billings) lays open his host's wine cellar to get the "niggers" properly drunk. He then plays the banjo for them, cringing with distaste all the while as they dance.

"I shall never forget the scene as long as I live. It was like some one of Dante's infernal regions. The room was illuminated by the glare from the burning barrels outside, and their dark forms moving to and fro seemed like grotesque imps going through some fiendish dance." When the group of whites finally manages to escape, the slave-owner swears "to fight the negroes and against their cause till the last"; Billings relates that he later died in the fall of Richmond.[12]

That writers were fascinated by the whole idea of these Tam O'Shanter revelries is clear by how often the scenes recur. In the *Big Budget's* "The Black Demons of Hayti", whose author, W. Shaw Rae, confuses Obeah with voodoo with reckless abandon, one of the characters describes the Salthous:

> the great annual festival of that horrible Vaudoux sect of which we were speaking, during which many people . . . retire to some secret spot, there to indulge in the most hideous, most horrible wickedness. These people are cannibals. Quiet and submissive as they appear during ordinary season, they become fiends incarnate at the Salthous. Children are sacrificed on their altars, the mutilated little bodies afterwards devoured, even grown men and women are killed and eaten in the course of that awful saturnalia. It makes me sick with horror even to think of it; no wonder God's curse lies heavily on the Black Republic, which permits such frightful wickedness.

Later we are given another, similar description. "The large congregation, excited by drink and lust, were in a state of delirious frenzy. The 'Chica' and 'Colenda' had been danced with all their voluptuous wantonness; many animals had been slaughtered, the blood drank warm, yet still large wine-skins containing goat's blood freely dashed with rum, passed from mouth to mouth in hideous glee, alternated with jars of fresh, raw spirit liquid-fire. . . . 'Twas a living picture of the Inferno."[13]

Even where the papers do not resort to stories of drunken bacchanalias, the stereotypical depictions they offer are no less offensive. *Chums*, for example, often features cartoons of barefoot, thick-lipped, half-naked black people with

---

12 "Ross Billings' Banjo", *Boys of the Empire* 1 (14 May 1888), 239.
13 "Black Demons of Hayti", 274.

big hoops in their ears being made fools of by European technology and products such as the cinematograph. Only rarely are blacks depicted as getting the best of whites, and this is usually more by error than by intent. While the papers may indeed have instilled patriotic and heroic values, they also helped successive generations of children to absorb and internalize racist stereotypes and attitudes that continue to find their way into print even today.

More than a century after the first boys' adventure paper hit the streets of London, Maddy and MacCann write that "many Western writers for children promote a damaged image of Africa and the African personality . . . media coverage typically treats Africa as uncivilized and African people as incapable of manging their own affairs. Books for children instill this idea at the earliest stage of life – the time when it can become deeply embedded in consciousness."[14] Arthur Conan Doyle; Jules Verne; R.M. Ballantyne; the founder of the Scout movement, Robert Baden-Powell; Max Pemberton; and the famous cricketer W.G. Grace were perhaps the most well-known of these writers. What follows is a more in-depth exploration of a few of these stories.

"Morgan's Head"

"Morgan's Head", a *Boy's Own Paper* story which ran as a serial over the course of five issues, was based on the events of Jamaica's 1865 Morant Bay uprising. It begins with an old Negro, Sam, warning Mr De La Cour, the custos of St Thomas and owner of the Cool Shades estate, one of the largest in that part of Jamaica, that trouble is brewing. Sam informs De la Cour that the "niggers" are meeting every night at Ephraim Bingo's rum shop. De La Cour affects not to think much of it, since he believes that the blacks are content with their lot and have nothing to complain of, but he decides to talk the matter over with a Captain Walker.

Before he can visit Walker, a man-o'-war sails into the harbour and sets anchor. A naval officer comes ashore and gives De La Cour a letter from the governor in which the governor says he has had reports that blacks in the southern part of the island are planning to rise and that the uprising will begin in Port Morant, which is why he has sent the warship. He encloses a warning sent to him which reads "Better let the Buccra redcoats get em gun ready. Hungry fowl wake soon. Make big noise down Morant first."

---

14 Yulisa Amada Maddy and Donnara MacCann, *African Images in Juvenile Literature: Commentaries on Neocolonialist Fiction* (London: McFarland, 1996), 4.

De La Cour discounts this as well and does not plan to keep the ship around, but he invites the naval officer, Mr Charteris, to his house, where he meets Julia and Amy De La Cour. Walker arrives later and joins De La Cour in dismissing the idea that the blacks might rise. "As to the niggers rising, they haven't the pluck. . . . I have served with the rascals all my life; know 'em well, sir; give 'em plenty to eat and little to do and they won't take no trouble to fight", he assures De la Cour. (These repeated assertions about the cowardliness of blacks are, of course, amazing in light of the numerous revolts that took place during slavery and then in the post-emancipation era, not only in Jamaica but throughout the region.)

De la Cour writes back to the governor that he will make enquiries but that he does not think there is any cause for alarm, and Charteris goes back to the ship. Meanwhile, the mulatto Ned Teacke, also known as "the Spider", goes to Ephraim Bingo's rum shop with a list of names of possible conspirators he wants Bingo to vet for him. Teacke has been sent by the ringleaders "to Morant Bay to light the torch of insurrection, which it was hoped would set the whole island ablaze, and on its ashes phoenix-like was to rise a new black republic like that of the sister island of Hayti". Teacke is an example of the "degenerate mulatto", perhaps meant to represent the racially mixed George William Gordon, one of Governor Eyre's most vocal critics, who was hanged for his alleged role in the uprising.

Bingo is described as a "dark-complexioned man of forbidding aspect, shabbily dressed, and well besprinkled with dust". He tells Teacke that all the people on the list can be trusted except Sam. Teacke is "engaged in assisting to stir up the black population; not that he cared for the welfare of the negro, whom he cordially hated, but he hoped to make a good thing out of the business, whichever way it went".

The conspirators meet and discuss plans to murder the whites, as well as the rules which will govern the appropriation of land afterwards. Teacke plans to take over Cool Shade.

A storm comes up quickly and, before he can help himself, Sam – who has been eavesdropping – falls through the roof. (We later learn that Sam was in the woods when he overheard an Obeah man discussing the planned meeting.)

> Sam had recognized one of his country-men, of whom he had a particular dread, a certain Obeahman, who dwelt in the hills some considerable distance from the bay – for, notwithstanding the stringent laws against the practice of Obeah in Jamaica, the practisers of this system of witchcraft still carried on

their trade of terrifying their enemies and influencing the passions of those who consulted them, and there is little doubt that many of the deaths occurring from time to time in the country villages were caused by poisonous draughts administered under the directions of those wretches.

Sam had heard the "witch-doctor say to his companion '. . . soon dere'll be no white massas left in dis place. . . . I know sart-in sure that the Spider gwine to make fire blaze.'" He then made it his business to go by the rum shop and climb an overhanging tree so he could listen in on the conspirators, but has the misfortune to fall when the branch broke. The blacks lock him up in a closet and leave with Teacke/Spider, who is going to a meeting with the Obeah man.

The warship leaves the harbour just as Amy and De La Cour come to the realization that they have not seen Sam in a little while. Nobody can find him, but De La Cour decides to leave for the courthouse in Morant Bay, where he has work to do. On his way there, an old Negress warns him and Walker not to go but, like Caesar, they continue on. When they are inside, the uprising breaks out; a mob descends on the courthouse, and Captain Walker is hacked to pieces. The police and volunteers try to hold back the rebels but are "shot down and mutilated by the crowd". The blacks shout, "Come out, you white trash", and then set the courthouse on fire. De La Cour is shot and killed and the building burns to the ground.

Teacke rides to Cool Shade, but it too is burning, "surrounded by a number of drunken, excited negroes, many of whom had worked on the estate from boyhood and had received nothing but kindness at the hands of their unfortunate master". Teacke is angry at the destruction of the property he covets, but Bingo asks him if wants to be massa now: "guess dis Spider more buccra than black", he says, and threatens to "burn de yaller skin". Spider escapes on his mule to the hills. He thinks of going to Morant Bay, but when he meets the Obeah man, the latter warns him not to go.

> "Don't go that way, Massa Spider. You take my advice, clear out; not much time for to lose. Africans bold up now. Yaller skin go same way as white. 'Cockroach eber so drunk him no walk past fowl-yard.'" (Negro proverb). The Spider took the hint, and muttering imprecations on the heads of all the black-skinned sons of Ham for their ingratitude, once again turned the animal's head towards the mountains and rode off.

Before Cool Shade is destroyed, the loyal Sam manages to break free of his prison and rescues Amy and Julia, whom he hides in a mountain cave while he goes to look for help. He brings back Charteris and the other naval officers, who tell the girls of their father's fate and take them back to the warship. One year later, there is a double wedding as Amy and Charteris marry at the same time as Julia and her sweetheart. Sam also gets an optimistic ending, with the opportunity to look for his woman, Dinah.[15]

"The Slaves' Fetish"

"Let the white men die!" shouts the Obeah priest in the first line of "The Slaves' Fetish", a story which appeared in the 21 August 1897 issue of the *Big Budget*. The unnamed author wastes no time in introducing the action: the story opens with another version of the drunken bacchanalia. In a gathering in the Jamaican forest, an "Obeah priest" is standing on a stone conducting an Obeah ceremony.

> He had the marks of a slave's manacles upon his wrists and ankles, but many curious and horrible ornaments were hung around his neck, carved images, bits of glass and dead men's bones and teeth. Around him, hands locked in hands, stood a throng of worshippers, men and women, slaves all, yet free to hate and plot and pray to awful gods in whom they put their faith. And they took up the priest's words, and began to dance around him, at first, very, very slowly, with a swaying, serpent-like motion. The moon shone upon their dark, ferocious faces and the naked writhing limbs and the heated air vibrated with the burden of the chant of death. Monotonous and low at the beginning, the chant sounded, not in the debased English of the slaves, but in a tongue that had once voiced the words of life and death in Africa. Faster it grew, and faster yet, and rose into an infernal scream that trembled with hate and devilry, and the unholy dance increased in degrees until every living link in the human chain was possessed of a mad frenzy. Then, not till then, the Obeah priest raised in his hand a grim fetish, a hideously carved figure in blackened ivory. At sight of it, the slaves flung themselves upon their faces, uttering cries of terror.
>
> "Let the white men die!" said the Obeah priest. "Let steel slay them, let fire burn them, let water drown them! Let them fall before the spirit of Obeah, so that their hearts turn to dust and their limbs rot! Let the chains be broken, and the slaves be free. Jamaica belongs to the black man!"[16]

---

15   "Morgan's Head", *Boy's Own Paper* 6 (1883).
16   "The Slaves' Fetish", *Big Budget* 10 (21 August 1897), 3.

Suddenly a white man appears and the dancers vanish. "The priest would have followed them, but a pistol glittered, and a command in English rang out: 'Stand, you black dog, on your life!'"

The white man advances on the Obeah man, boasting that he has caught him at last, but the Obeah man is unsurprised and tells him that he is expected. In fact, "'Obeah tell me some one come, massa' . . . and it was curious how, in the presence of the white man, the dignity lent by his superstition deserted him utterly." The white reveals that he does not believe in Obeah himself – "no, nothing shall make me believe in it! But fools do, and your trickery has made you the master of many niggers who'd stick at nothing if you gave 'em the word."

The white man continues.

> "Do you remember . . . how, years ago, the niggers of Jamaica had what they called a Great Fetish, which they kept in a hidden fetish hut in the mountains, and how they believed that if they could plunge it into a white man's blood, at a certain hour, in a certain place, every master in the island would die and every nigger be free? . . . Do you remember, too, how the Great Fetish was stolen in the night, and has not been recovered! You niggers have no courage to do anything till you get it back."

It turns out that the man who stole the Great Fetish is the white man's enemy, whom he wants killed: "He is the man I hated. Swear, you black fiend, by your Obeah, never to tell a soul of what has passed between us to-night."

The Obeah man complies. He holds up "his fetish in the moonlight, [he] crooned over it, and made strange passes in the air. His features were so convulsed with idolatrous madness that they lost almost all human semblance. 'It done, massa!' he said at last. 'Obeah know all 'bout it. De man dat stole the Great Fetish will be dead in a month. No good try to trick fate.'" When the white man scoffs at Obeah, again the Obeah man reveals that he knows something about a murder he committed, so the planter shoots and kills him, telling him he will take his knowledge with him into the other world. What neither knows is that they are being observed by another white man.

Later we are introduced to the main characters in the story: Wilfred Sand, a young man who owns Goldensand, a large plantation which is coveted by Lupus Royland, whose niece, Mary, is in love with Wilfred. Lupus is cruel to his slaves but Wilfred is kind to his and means to free them. Wilfred's grandfather, who left him the estate, "had discovered that blacks dabbled a good deal in Obeah and had punished them with great severity. In this he had been perfectly justified, for the heathen rites were full of cruelty and ghastly horrors"; but the black people had hated him for his persecution of Obeah, and some also hate Wilfred.

Wilfred stops Randolph Holles, Lupus's overseer, from giving Pompey, a slave, a worse beating, but when Pompey tells Holles that he is a coward, the two men fight. "They were equally matched, and struggled fiercely, the muscles standing out upon their arms like whipcords. But the white man was the best man and, suddenly, calling into play all his skill and strength, raised the negro bodily from the ground, held him poised in the air for a second, and hurled him down with stunning violence." When Pompey rises to continue the fight, Wilfred trips him up and he is taken away to the prison hut. Holles points out that Pompey will have it in for both of them now. "There's nothing so spiteful as a spiteful nigger."

That night Wilfred follows a man in a red cloak to a clearing in the forest, where another Obeah dance is being held. This time the Obeah priest is

> Pompey, savage, grim, and too portentous to be aught save horrible as he stood in his ghastly paraphernalia, and held up the fetish. Wilfred watched breathlessly, and saw the man in the cloak advance slowly to the Obeah-man, but in such a way that his face could not be seen, and speak to him. Then Pompey threw up his arms and gave a loud yell. It was the command to the slaves to rise.

On his way back to his estate, somebody clouts Wilfred from behind, and by the time he recovers consciousness and makes it back to his house, it has been taken over by the slaves. "He saw [the] dead bodies of [the other white men] flung from one of the windows by the blacks, whom superstition and suddenly acquired freedom had changed into fiends."

There are further adventures, but Wilfred, his cousin Cyril Harden, Holles and Mary are eventually captured by the rebels and taken to the Negro quarters at Goldensand, where a platform has been built on which Pompey sits "with a big hat on his head, and all the fetishes of the Obeah man arranged about his person. He was the new master of Goldensand – he was King Pompey." Pompey informs Wilfred that he was the master yesterday but "black man massa now – for ebber. Black man have Jamaica for himself and make white man slabe, or kill him."

Pompey demands the Great Fetish of Wilfred, who has no idea what he is talking about. He makes up his mind "to suffer like a man whatever was inflicted on him", but it is Mary who they mean to torture in order to make him talk. Holles persuades the rebels that he knows where the Great Fetish is and will tell them if they free him. They untie his bonds, whereupon he seizes a powder keg and throws it into the fire, causing an explosion. "Dead and writhing black bodies" fall to the ground but, except for Holles, the whites are unharmed. He frees the captives and they escape into the forest.

Harden leads them into what appears to be a trap and the whites are re-captured, except for Holles, who falls into a pit. The captives are taken deep into the heart of the mountain, but Holles manages to save himself and, with Lupus, goes after them with a band of loyal slaves. This last group discovers a hidden cavern full of gold coins and treasure, which distracts Lupus until he remembers the danger Mary is in; they press forward with their search and come upon an amazing sight.

> Below them, at a depth of some thirty feet, was a great amphitheatre, which had been hewn out of the solid rock, and to which countless steps led down. In the centre was a black slab of stone. Near this stone was a throne-like chair of gold, in which sat a figure in crimson, decked with fetishes and strange ornaments in metals and jewels – and this figure was the embalmed body of a dead man. Around him were grouped more than a hundred blacks, many of them fantastically dressed.... Upon the stone, bound fast with cords, lay Wilfred Sand and Mary Royland side by side, and over them stood Pompey, ghastly in his insignia of the Obeah-man, and with the withered hand of a negro held aloft. He stood there, black, pitiless, awful, with the torchlight playing upon him – a sable angel of death.... "Here is the Great Fetish, O brothers!" said Pompey, speaking in the African tongue, and in a loud voice. "You know the will of Obeah – that on the day that the head of the great chief, Uzulman, which is now the Great Fetish, should be bathed in white blood, the isle of Jamaica from shore to shore should belong to the black men! So now is the day of fate come."[17]

Pompey raises his knife, but "at the same second, Lupus Royland, levelling a pistol with a steady hand, fired". Lupus and the rest then rush down and free Mary and Wilfred as the blacks stand around, held in a "spell of inaction".

> "You hab won, white man," [Pompey] said, "but Obeah beat you yet." He pointed to the dead man on the throne. "I saw him shot by white man in the forest, but I no go see white man's face. And when white man fly, I go to him, for him my father. And him tell me how him make Obeah's spell, and him try tell me more, but him die too soon. But this me know, de man dat stole de Great Fetish am here, and him am doomed."

---

17 Ibid., 4.

> And then, dying though he was, he rose and raised the awful fetish once again, and began to chant in a hoarse voice that was choked with death and hate; and advancing slowly, he pointed at Wilfred Sand, who never moved, at Lupus Royland, who spat upon him, and at Cyril Harden, who flung up his hands with an awful cry, and staggering forward, fell dead at the feet of the Obeah man whom he had murdered.
>
> And Pompey fell with him, and a terrible fight followed, for the slaves were mad with desperation and fierce for blood. And in the end the white men won the victory.[18]

Finally, we learn that it was Lupus who witnessed Harden's murder of Pompey's father, and that it was Harden who was "working on the superstitions of the negroes ... who were his tools" in order that he could obtain Goldensands for himself. Wilfred frees the slaves and leaves for England with Mary as his wife.[19]

The Obeah Tree and Current Novels

While the taste for boys' papers may have declined after the first couple of decades of the twentieth century, Obeah remained a fascinating subject for writers of books for boys. *The Obeah Tree*, by Frederick Guthrie Skey, for example, was first published in 1932 and then went into a second print run in 1939. A look at the story will demonstrate how well the familiar stereotypes were preserved, received and imparted to another generation of British boys.

As the story begins, we meet a Roman Catholic priest at a dinner party who is giving his opinion on blacks.

> "I know they believe in sorcery, which they call Obeah, and live in great dread of the men and women who practice it. But they are very secretive, and it is not easy to find out where Obeah is being practised, or by whom. Your old femme de chamber, Dido, Madam, has some knowledge of it. She practises the healing art, and, although she is steeped in superstition, her spells are all beneficial, and, as you know, some of her cures are truly marvellous."[20]

Skey has attempted to make some distinction between herb women and Obeah by attributing positive qualities to the former, but as is clear from other infor-

---

18 Ibid.
19 Ibid., 8.
20 F.E.G. Skey, *The Obeah Tree: A Tale of the West Indies for Boys* (London: Thomas Nelson and Sons, 1932), 2.

mants, Obeah could be used both for good and for harm. "But most of the workers of Obeah are undoubtedly criminal and harmful in the extreme", the priest continues.

> "I remember when I first came to these parts there was some man on this estate who was working Obeah against his fellow-slaves. We found that he was making little cakes of clay – they said it was taken from graves – with hair and various horrible ingredients, and sticking them on the doorposts of the huts at night and many of the slaves died mysteriously. He became very idle and worthless, and the seigneur decided to get rid of him. He was bought by a planter in the north of the island. More than a year after it was discovered accidentally that he was the Obeah man. There were no more mysterious deaths, and the seigneur took no more notice of it."
>
> "Do you believe that these Obeah men have any real mystical power?" asked the lieutenant.
>
> "I believe that most of it is merely terrorism," answered the *abbé*, "but curious coincidences do occur that are hard to explain. I prefer to leave these things alone."[21]

As the story continues, we learn that a dying pirate had told the American captain who was at the dinner party that he and his crew came ashore to bury their treasure in a valley and came across an Obeah man preparing his poisons under a silk-cotton tree (the Obeah tree of the title). They were about to kill him when they decided to let him live if he would put a spell on the place so none would go near it. The pirate died from the bite of a fer-de-lance, a poisonous snake, before he could reveal more about the treasure's location.

The captain decides to search for the tree but is warned by Dido: "Captain very foolish to go to Obeah tree. Snake defend Obeah tree! Demons defend Obeah tree! Obeah tree giving much trouble and calamity." The *abbé* explains that "all the Africans are afraid of silk-cotton trees, they believe them to harbour evil spirits". Cakes of "sun-dried" clay hang from the tree. We learn that black people stay away from the valley, but those who venture into it suffer scorpion bites, avalanches or earthquakes.

The Obeah man who put the spell on the treasure is still alive. He is described as a "little wizened creature who might well have been an African Methuselah, thin to starvation and bent with age, toothless, his woolly hair a dirty white, his deeply lined face and sharp, beady eyes wearing an expression

---

21   Ibid., 3–4.

of the wickedest cunning". Caught and sentenced to execution, he is mysteriously helped to escape. Soon after, there is an uprising among the slaves. "The Obeah man who, after his rescue, had been almost forgotten . . . was triumphantly placed at the head of the rioters in the north" and the rebellion grows. "In every part of the island, the Africans rose against their masters and spread over the estates, burning, destroying, butchering", but some planters escape with their families.[22]

One night, when the rebels have gathered under the silk-cotton tree, the hero planter of the story shoots and kills the Obeah-man. "Accursed sorcerer . . . thus shall your many victims be revenged." But a Frenchman remonstrates with the planter. "I had rather have lost my right hand than this old man", he says, explaining that the Obeah man worked for him and was his secret agent among the blacks.[23]

Skey's story blends many elements – piracy, slave rebellion, war – and clearly owes a lot to its predecessors, particularly *Hamel*, from which it borrows many of the stereotypes and stock characters noted previously, including the superstitious non-Anglo-Saxon white, the Roman Catholic *abbé*. It is also telling that the lieutenant working with the Obeah man is French, suggesting that such an alliance would have been considered beneath a proper Englishman.

Racist, imperialist literature like that found in the adventure papers had an undeniable impact on young, impressionable British minds. To this day, these stories are being recycled in new forms of literature and under different guises. In David Gemmell's *The First Chronicles of Druss the Legend*, for example, Druss, the white-skinned hero, and his small band of warriors are beset by a "horde" of "black-skinned Panthians" whose "feet drum a savage beat" before their charge.[24] The Panthians fight with spears and wicker shields while the white Drenai have more advanced weapons – axes, short swords and barbed javelins. They also have body armour, so it is no surprise that, at the end of the day, the Drenai have lost only forty men while the Panthians have lost more than eight hundred. The battle and the phrasing employed by Gemmell recall the swashbuckling stories based on imperialist adventure heroes of the previous century and clearly owes them a great debt.

Similarly, in Wilbur Smith's *Warlock*, published in 2001, the would-be queen begs Nubian soldiers to rape an Egyptian princess, saying, "I know you

---

22   Ibid., 23.
23   Ibid., 67–69.
24   David Gemmell, *The First Chronicles of Druss the Legend* (London: Random House, 1993), 315.

black animals, you have prongs big as that of a bull elephant and you love to give them employment."[25] The soldiers refuse, but in this little snippet Smith has projected modern racist stereotypes back thousands of years.

Both Smith and Gemmell, the former born "of British stock" (as he describes himself on his website) in 1933 and the latter in 1948, would have been exposed to books and stories of the type I have discussed. On his website, Smith, who grew up in what was then Northern Rhodesia with "small black boys" as his companions, recalls being a great fan of C.S. Forester, Rider Haggard and John Buchan, themselves acknowledged fans of colonial adventurers who subscribed to the theory of black inferiority. Influenced by the books and stories they read as children, many of which depict blacks as savage, primitive, violent and superstitious, authors have gone on to perpetuate those stereotypes in their own books, even in the twenty-first century.

ILLUSTRATED NEWSPAPERS

The stories in the boys' papers were matched in gruesome horror by similar stories published in cheap illustrated papers such as the *Penny Illustrated Paper*, *The Graphic* and others, which were meant for adults and tended towards the sensational. Like the boys' papers, these had a wide audience.

"The Obi Man"

"The Obi Man", a story by Eden Phillpotts, appeared in the 1 July 1893 issue of *The Graphic* and is set on the then little-known island of Tobago. Tobago is also mentioned, to one degree or another, in several of Phillpotts's novels and short story collections, for example, in *The Poacher's Wife*, *Lying Prophets*, *The Folk Afield* and *Black, White, and Brindled*. He was an author, poet and dramatist whose play *The Farmer's Wife* was made into a movie by Alfred Hitchcock in 1928. A friend of Agatha Christie, he also collaborated with writers such as Jerome K. Jerome and Arnold Bennett and was well-known to his contemporaries, including Arthur Conan Doyle, George Bernard Shaw and Henry James.

In his travelogue *In Sugar-Cane Land*, Phillpotts describes blacks as "lazy and good-tempered". "Quashie – by which title one means the bulk of the

---

25 Wilbur Smith, *Warlock* (London: Macmillan, 2002), 682.

present snuff-coloured and brown people rather than the full-blooded blacks – Quashie is simple-hearted, unambitious, and intellectually poor. These qualities produce a happy man of an inferior sort." Further on he notes that Quashie is "warm-hearted, untruthful, feline, and more feminine in [his] moral fibre than masculine". Phillpotts draws similarities between blacks and the Irish, whom he says the former "strangely resemble in qualities of superstition, excitability, idleness, and lack of all logical perceptions".[26] Later, Phillpotts writes: "Superstition is deeply rooted in the black man's nature", explaining that "Jumbies and Obi are still as much a part of Quashie's beliefs – as sacred and as real – as anything the missionaries have taught him".[27]

In "The Obi Man", Phillpotts resurrects the story of the fingernail poison but adds a twist which makes the Obeah man an assassin in the hire of a white overseer. He begins his story with a beautiful description of the "tropical tangle" of vegetation in which the Obeah man's hut is hidden. The "secluded, ragged hut" is

> adorned with strange fragments of things dead. Two eyeless bullocks' skulls ornament the entrance of our Obi Man's dwelling, and his land is fenced with a fantastic ribbon, whereon hang empty bottles, bright feathers, and fragments of gaudy rag. . . . Obeah is a real and terrible business still – a creed beyond the power of missionary to shatter or destroy; and the African negro would no more speak disrespectfully of it than of his own grandparents.[28]

This passage is little changed from *In Sugar-Cane Land*, in which he notes: "The cult of Obeah certainly dies hard. In fact, it does not die, for a negro would as soon speak disrespectfully of his grandparents as criticise an Obi man."[29]

Inside the hut,

> dried mummies of beasts and men haunt the place, hang against its walls, and sit propped in corners, with a loathsome semblance of living about them. Festoons of birds' eggs and curious seeds and empty bottles hang across the roof. Skins of animals and birds litter the floor; strange malodorous smells greet the nostrils. There is a piece of red glass in the roof, and, thrown down through this, falls a round flaming eye of light. The illumination centres upon

---

26 Eden Phillpotts, *In Sugar-Cane Land* (London: McClure, 1894), 74–75.
27 Ibid., 165.
28 Eden Phillpotts, "The Obi Man", *The Graphic*, 1 July 1893, n.p.
29 Phillpotts, *Sugar-Cane Land*, 167.

a little three-legged table, scattered over which lie strange, uncanny-looking fragments. Filth and mystery and darkness blend in grim combination here.[30]

The Obeah man himself "appeared very ancient. His old ribs made a gridiron of his lean breast; his limbs were skin and bone; his scanty wool was grey; a tangled net-work of furrows and deep lines scarred and seamed his face in every direction; and, curiously wide apart, on either side of a flat Ethiopian nose, the man's eyes gleamed from his withered head-piece like the eyes of a toad or other reptile."

The Obeah man's name is Jesse and he appears to be digging a grave, but while he is doing so he digs up "a flat-browed negro skull with low receding forehead". The skull belonged to a man by the name of Jephson whom "Massa Ford" had wanted "rub out". Ford had sent Jephson to Jesse, who had obliged, but what is more, we learn that Ford now wishes him to inflict the same fate on a white man.

Phillpotts then tells us a bit more about "Massa Ford", who turns out to be the nephew of the owner of the Pelican Sugar Estate. Ford was overseer for about twenty years and worked hard for his uncle on the understanding that when the older man died, he would inherit. John Ford was under the impression that his uncle was ailing back in England, but when William Ford comes for a visit, it is clear that he is in excellent health and likely to be around for a long time. William's good health disconcerts John, who covets the estate and now realizes that "desperate troubles need equally desperate remedies". John hatches a plan to murder his uncle and induces Jesse to help him. Under the pretence of wanting to introduce his uncle to a real Obeah man, John persuades his uncle to accompany him on a trip to Jesse's house.

In preparation for the visit, Jesse places on his head

> a fur cap with long black horns, between which hung tinkling trophies of empty medicine-bottles and beads. Over his lean body and legs he drew hairy garments, coarsely painted with daubs of crimson and white. These things were girt upon him with a waist-belt of feathers. His lean black arms remained bare, but upon wrists and ankles he tied links of snake-skin and elaborate bracelets of red and black "crab's-eye" seeds. About his neck he festooned a chain of human teeth, and upon his breast he fastened a loathsome amulet – a shrivelled-up mummy baby – the hideous ghost of a thing that had never lived. He next painted sundry blue hieroglyphics over his wrinkled face.[31]

---

30 Philpotts, "Obi Man".
31 Ibid.

A little "brass-bound Bible" and a big jack-knife also hang round his neck. Jesse looks himself over in the mirror and proclaims himself pleased with the results: "Yes, Obi somebody dis day." Phillpotts drew heavily from his real-life experiences while in the islands. According to *Sugar-Cane Land*, while on Martinique during Carnival, Phillpotts had observed a "weird creature with huge horns; a string of empty medicine bottles hung between them, and extraordinary raiment of beads and fur".[32]

The "human monster" then retrieves a small box within a box hidden in one corner, containing "a thick, glutinous, grey substance". He "pulled back the ball of his left-hand middle finger until a space was left beneath the nail. Into this he carefully plastered his compound from the box. All his nails were particularly long and dirty, so this strangely anointed middle finger was not calculated to attract the least attention."

When John Ford, his son, and William arrive, Jesse pretends to have been caught unawares but offers them fruit and rum. Ford then regales William with a story about the theft of tons of sugar cane from the estate. According to Ford, he had gone to both "the parson and the police", to no avail. It was only when he sought Jesse's help that the thievery stopped. In *Sugar-Cane Land*, Phillpotts notes that

> only recently, an estate-owner, in self-defence, had to summon Obeah to his aid and consult a professor of it. Nocturnal thieves were stealing this gentleman's sugar-canes in tremendous quantities, and Christianity and the eight commandment went for nothing. Then a black wizard put the entire plantation under Obi: a high-sounding performance, which merely consisted in tying empty bottles and bright-coloured rags to the outlying canes. But the purpose was effectually answered: not another sugar-cane disappeared.[33]

Back in the Obeah man's hut, "Jesse put your lands under Obeah, Uncle William", Ford says, going on to admit that he did not "believe in all that rubbish any more than you do, but Obeah is a real terrible thing to the niggers. Our friend here just threw a spell over the place, and hung red rags, and empty bottles and feathers about on the skirts of the plantations, and not another cane went."

Jesse gives them a brief tour of his garden and points out a silk-cotton tree, which he calls an Obeah tree, explaining that this is the tree "loogaroos" –

---

32   Phillpotts, *Sugar-Cane Land*, 202.
33   Ibid., 167.

"a sort of vampire", John's son explains – put their skins under before going abroad at night. Finally, Jesse washes out "four split calabash-bowls" and, "endeavouring to get a look of cheery hospitality into his bright toad's eyes", pours out some rum. "A very acute observer might have noticed that the long bony middle finger of Jesse's left hand rested for a brief while in one of those calabashes – that destined for Mr William Ford." Knowing what will follow, John makes a hasty exit from Jesse's house, explaining to his son that the uncle will follow soon after a brief rest. Back at the hut, William drinks half of his rum-and-water and falls at Jesse's feet. Jesse tells him his nephew will be back soon and that he is probably just suffering from the hot sun. He offers him the calabash, and "again a long black finger touched the liquid in it".

Later, when William fails to meet Ford and his son or to arrive at his estate, a party goes to search for him. Jesse tells them that he left soon after Ford and his son did, intending to meet them at the beach and bathe. Ford fakes uneasiness about this, given the older man's unfamiliarity with the safe areas of the coast. The next day, William's horse is found tethered to a coconut tree near the beach. William's clothes are nearby and footprints lead to the sea. His body is never found and Ford goes into mourning. The Pelican estate now becomes Ford's and we are told that "harmless old Jesse continues to be a great institution in Tobago". He often sings a strange song to himself:

> Low him lie; low him lie,
> Where de worms dey crawl in de white man's eye;
> But only de snakegard and Jesse know
> Where him sleep so still in de hole so low.
> Obeah – die – Obeah – Obeah – do,
> Obeah – die – Obeah – Obeah – do.[34]

"Hobbling Mary"

"Hobbling Mary", a story by Grant Allen, appeared in an 1897 issue of the *Penny Illustrated Paper and Illustrated Times*. Allen was a Canadian-born British science writer and novelist who came out to Jamaica to teach at Queen's College between 1873 and 1876. A friend of Herbert Spencer, Arthur Conan Doyle and H.G. Wells, he produced several books on science subjects but also wrote science fiction and detective novels. An interesting side note to Allen's

---

34   Phillpotts, "Obi Man".

brief sojourn in Jamaica is that, in his wife's absence, he apparently fathered an illegitimate child by a black woman, a son by the name of Hamilton. Hamilton grew up to be great friends with Herbert G. de Lisser, the editor of the *Daily Gleaner* and author of the famous West Indian Gothic classic *The White Witch of Rose Hall*, about a white voodoo priestess.

One of the nineteenth century's most prolific authors, Allen published scores of books and short stories. His novel *An African Millionaire* was serialized by the BBC and a stage version was produced in New York. Another book, *The Woman Who Did*, about a woman who has a child out of wedlock, became a bestseller. Many of his books and short stories were written to appeal to audiences that craved sensationalism, and many were tales of derring-do set in various places around the world.

In "Hobbling Mary" we are introduced to old Aunt Mary, described as "a wizened old crone" and "toothless", who is grumbling about the imperious summons of her young mistress, Rosa. "Him more trouble, dat one gal, nor all de udder pickney in de house put togedder. Him don't got white man's temper; him got black man in him heart. . . . I wish I rid ob dat pickney. White people is a blessed people – had blessed temper; dat dar pickney got black heart." Aunt Mary resolves to do something about Rosa, telling herself "me fadder don't be Obeah man from Calabar for nuffin". The narrator explains: "Obeah is the West African and West Indian form of witchcraft, dreaded almost as much by the whites as the black people. Aunt Mary was universally regarded as a witch. . . . And she believed in her own power."[35]

Two days later, when a young boy drowns, Aunt Mary seizes her chance. "De pickney jumby am de ting for to settle Miss Rosa!" Later that evening, Rosa yells for Aunt Mary to come and comb her hair and derides her as a "lazy, idle, good-for-nothing nigger woman". Rosa's hair is in a tangle; when Aunt Mary snips some of it off, Rosa realizes what has happened and demands the hair. Aunt Mary gives it to her but keeps a few strands. Rosa rolls up the cut hair in a piece of paper, burns everything in the candle flame and then throws the ashes out the window. The narrator notes that "it is dangerous to let a witch or wizard get a lock of your hair or a paring of your nails, for if they once possess themselves of anything that has formed a part of your body, they can do dire witchcraft with it afterwards, as they will upon the remainder".

That night, at the wake for a little boy, "men talked and smoked: women

---

35 Grant Allen, "Hobbling Mary", *Penny Illustrated Paper and Illustrated Times*, 10 July 1897, 20.

wailed and keened; and rum flowed. It was a most gruesome carouse, a melancholy rejoicing – the chief public amusement of the Jamaican negro. They love the excitement." Aunt Mary arrives and is greeted with momentary silence. "As the daughter and representative of a genuine acknowledged Obeah man of true Fanti origin, she had a place of importance in all such funeral ceremonies. She moved over to the coffin and admired the corpse with professional ardour." The other mourners do not realize that when she leans over the coffin, she thrusts the lock of Rosa's hair into the boy's hands and whispers in his ear, "Remember!"[36]

Days later, the washerwoman informs Rosa that all of Port Antonio is talking about how the gravedigger saw a lock "ob buckra hair in de nigger pickney's fingers".

> "What sort of hair?" Rosa cried, clapping her hand instinctively to the part of her own head where she had felt the cold touch of Aunt Mary's scissors.
> "Dem sayin' it yaller, like Missy Rosa's own," Martha answered, staring hard at her.
> Rosa's face was white as death. She knew what it meant. The Obeah woman had dispatched the black boy's ghost to wander over the world, with a magic command that he should trouble the soul of the man or woman whose lock of hair had been placed in his hands to give him power over them.

Rosa's suitor, Captain Galloway, proposes to her, and she is wildly happy. But that night when she goes to bed, a fruit bat enters her room as a turkey buzzard screams from nearby. "She trembled and shivered, and hid her head under the bed-clothes. Could this be the visible form of Isaac Cling's jumby?" She lies there in "unspeakable torment" and sobs in terror until she falls asleep in the early morning.

> From that evening forth, every night of the year, Rosa Mackonochie saw or fancied she saw, in one form or another, Isaac Cling's jumby. It pursued her everywhere. Sometimes it was visibly present as bird or beast, or lizard on the wall; sometimes – and that was worse – she did not behold it, but felt its presence. Silently, inaudibly, it stood by her bedside and grinned and jabbered at her. It never left her.

She grows wan and distracted. Within eight months, the Colonial Asylum at Half-way Tree receives a new inmate "who looked perpetually around her

---

36 Ibid.

as though something or somebody were dogging her footsteps". Aunt Mary congratulates herself and the jumby on a job well done as the asylum doctor offers his diagnosis: "insanity due to superstitious fright", or, as the Negroes put it, "de jumby troublin' him".

Allen's story is unique in that the Obeah woman triumphs over Rosa, the white woman, but Allen's sojourn in Jamaica was not a completely happy one. The school of which he became principal folded after only three years and he left in the midst of some bitter acrimony. Rosa's downfall may well symbolize his contempt for white creoles. It is unlikely that he would have put an English heroine in the same predicament or had her experience the same outcome. After all, in a later story, Harry Tristram, the hero of Allen's "The Beckoning Hand", early on expresses his preference for "simple little English prettiness" over an exotic southerner whose looks betray black or "Moorish" blood.

In fact, "The Beckoning Hand" was published as part of a collection of short stories in 1887, a couple of years after "Hobbling Mary". Its story of Césarine, a strange Haitian beauty who exerts a mysterious pull on the infatuated English hero, Harry, is very similar in tone and plot to *The Blood of the Vampire*, which it predates by ten years. The usual tropes – African witches, child sacrifice, cannibalism and poisoning – all make an appearance in the story, which ends with Césarine's death and Harry's return to the arms and affections of the English woman who was his first love.

Harry gives thanks that Césarine died childless, leaving no one to inherit her curse. It is unclear whether Allen is referring to the curse of African blood or the curse of voodoo worship, but given his earlier reference to "the sinister half" of her pedigree, one suspects that for him it is all one and the same. At any rate, "sweet, simple" Irene willingly forgives Harry's abandonment of her, pointing out that it was all due to poison, witchcraft and "sheer African devilry".[37]

The influence of "The Beckoning Hand" is obvious in the American writer Henry S. Whitehead's "Sweet Grass", published in 1929, in which the protagonist, this time a white Dane, Cornelius, is overcome by the sensual pull of the islands' scents and scenery and is momentarily attracted to a mulatto girl. When he first sees the fifteen-year-old girl from the verandah of his Great House one moonlit night, he turns "suddenly cold at the unexpected, wraith-like sight of her. Her amber eyes are wide and an "eery light" shines from them.

---

37 Grant Allen, "The Beckoning Hand", in *The Beckoning Hand and Other Stories* (London: Chatto and Windus, 1887), 24, 32.

He invites her to come in, and the very moonlight seems to usher her into the house. Cornelius is "entranced, bewitched" by the scents of jasmine, sweet grass and the sea, and by the moon, too. Then "his fastidiousness" reasserts itself and he escorts her back out of the house. The next day, he announces his engagement to the daughter of one of the local white families.[38]

CULTURAL CURIOSITY AND REAL-LIFE ADVENTURERS: TRAVEL NARRATIVES

As the Empire expanded, so also did the British appetite for more and more information about the exotic lands and peoples encountered by travellers. Travel books, a genre not completely new in the eighteenth century, flew off bookstore shelves and did their part to shape and mould Britishers' understanding of the world. Like the boys' adventure papers, travel books presented readers with a narrative in which a Briton – someone who looked like the reader and shared his or her values – found himself in an alien landscape among alien peoples with strange religions and bizarre customs and habits. The travelling Briton interpreted what he saw and heard for the benefit of those back in the comfort of their homes, and did so in a way that either furthered or calmed their fears, depending on his or her prejudices. Travellers well-disposed towards blacks and persuaded of the efficacy of both Christianity and education to effect upliftment of the race tended to see evidence of this happening, while others, not quite as convinced that blacks were capable of advancement, tended to take a gloomier view.

For those in the latter group, even simply travelling in the West Indies felt fraught with danger. Kingsley, for example, may have longed to visit the West Indies, as he acknowledged, but his discomfort and unease among the black people he met there were palpable. On a purely intellectual level he accepted that blacks had legitimate grievances against whites and was even prepared to allow for a certain "rudeness", but he was petrified that it might turn into something more:

---

38 Henry S. Whitehead, "Sweet Grass", *Weird Tales*, July 1929. Whitehead was an American episcopal minister who spent eight years in the US Virgin Islands, from 1921 to 1929, and got much of the inspiration for his tales of horror there. A collection of his work, *Jumbee and Other Uncanny Tales*, was published posthumously in 1944.

> As long as the Negros are decently loyal and peaceable, and do not murder their magistrates and drink their brains mixed with rum, nor send delegates to the President of Hayti to ask if he will assist them, in case of a general rising, to exterminate the whites ... we must remember that we are very seriously in debt to the Negro, and must allow him to take out instalments of his debt, now and then, in his own fashion. After all, we brought him here, and we have no right to complain of our own work. If, like Frankenstein, we have tried to make a man, and made him badly; we must, like Frankenstein, pay the penalty.[39]

Kingsley, fresh from his defence of the embattled Governor Eyre, viewed blacks as dangerous and violent and considerably inferior to whites. Obeah signified and highlighted all that was wrong with the race:

> It appears to me, on closer examination, that [Obeah and fetish worship] is not a worship of natural objects; not a primaeval worship; scarcely a worship at all: but simply a system of incantation, carried on by a priesthood, or rather a sorcerer class. ... The Negro does not, as the primaeval man is supposed to have done, regard as divine (and therefore as Fêtish, or Obeah) any object which excites his imagination; anything peculiarly beautiful, noble, or powerful; anything even which causes curiosity or fear.

According to Kingsley, then, black people were not animated by the same motivations that animated Europeans; unlike whites, blacks were immune to beauty and nobility and too brutish "even" for curiosity or fear. No, he explains,

> a Fêtish is no natural object at all; it is a spirit, an Obeah, Jumby, Duppy, like 'Duvvels' or spirits of the air. ... That spirit belongs to the Obeah, or Fêtish-man; and he puts it, by magic ceremonies. into any object which he chooses. ... In a case which happened very lately, an Obeah-man came into the country, put the Obeah into a fresh monkey's jaw-bone, and made the people offer to it fowls and plantains, which of course he himself ate. Such is Obeah now; and such it was, as may be seen by De Bry's plates, when the Portuguese first met with it on the African coast four hundred years ago.

He also notes that some whites, "not two generations ago", believed in Obeah too, though of course not as whole-heartedly as the blacks. To Kingsley, "the most practically important element of Obeah, is poisoning", a "habit" which he claims was imported from Africa.[40]

---

39 Kingsley, *At Last*, 2:150–51.
40 Ibid., 134–37.

Whatever his feelings about black people, Kingsley felt much more well-disposed to "the educated and civilized coloured population of the towns – they stand to us in an altogether different relation. They claim to be, and are, our kinsfolk, on another ground than that of common humanity. We are bound to them by a tie more sacred, I had almost said more stern, than we are to the mere Negro. They claim, and justly, to be considered as our kinsfolk and equals." He saw the coloured policemen as a "focus of discipline and civilization amid what would otherwise relapse too soon into anarchy and barbarism".[41]

As noted before, many white writers viewed blacks with suspicion while regarding mulattoes or the mixed-race population as their natural allies, closer to them not just in complexion but also in values and outlook. "Between the black and mixed peoples prevail hatreds more enduring and more intense than any race prejudices between whites and freedmen in the past", Hearn writes. "And the true black element, more numerically powerful, more fertile, more cunning, better adapted to pyrogenic climate and tropical environment, would surely win. All these mixed races, all these beautiful fruit-coloured populations, seem doomed to extinction: the future tendency must be to universal blackness, if existing conditions continue – perhaps to universal savagery."[42]

Centuries had passed since the Middle Ages, but Europeans still associated the colour black with darkness and evil and were unable to rid themselves of the notion that blacks were incapable of advancing in civilization (as understood by whites). Hearn points out that Père Labat "regarded the negro as a natural child of the devil, – a born sorcerer, – an evil being wielding occult power".[43] Blackness and, by extension, blacks constituted wildness, savagery, ignorance and primitivism; their superstition was perhaps the most obvious marker of how very different from whites blacks were. Hearn, for example, says of his housekeeper's belief in zombies that it was a "part of her inner nature, – something hereditary, *racial*, ancient as Africa".[44]

The more racist and the less benevolent the writers, the more likely they were to point with relish to evidence of Obeah's continued existence. Even those writers who were unable to gain any first-hand information about it did not resist the temptation to speculate about its existence, knowing full well that readers at home were interested in anything they could find to say about it. "I regret that I have been able to acquire but little reliable information about

---

41   Ibid., 150, 163.
42   Hearn, *Two Years*, 97–98.
43   Ibid., 168.
44   Ibid., 369 [emphasis added].

the Obeah superstition, but I have no doubt it is still widely prevalent, though the people are heartily ashamed of that to which they have habitual recourse", writes Chester in his *Transatlantic Sketches*. His lack of access to information did not stop him from declaring that "few districts are without its Obeah doctor", and producing the intriguing news that the "'new lights' are certain privates of a West Indian regiment, lately arrived from Africa with a knowledge of the latest doctrinal quackeries".[45]

Conversely, for some writers – those more benevolently disposed to black people and more likely to wish them well – Obeah was a thing of the past, or at the very least, a fading superstition. Monk Lewis, for example, notes that "the belief in Obeah is now greatly weakened, but still exists in some degree".[46] Similarly, Revd Ellis, concerned with promulgating the view that missionaries had accomplished great things in the West Indies, stresses that Obeah is a thing of the past and criticizes the travel writers who say different. Discussing the case of the oft-described Obeah man discovered to have been poisoning scores, if not hundreds, of people, Ellis writes that "this indicates to a great extent the impression conveyed to many home-readers by tourists, with a turn for writing and a desire to write something tasty and spicy, who bring back with them thrilling stories of the prevalence of the practice of Obeah".[47]

The examination of three travelogues below illustrates how differing viewpoints on the character of blacks were highlighted and emphasized by the respective authors' different perspectives on Obeah. They also illustrate its continuing fascination for writers.

The Wonders of the West Indies

Theodora Lynch was born in Sussex but her father, Arthur Foulks, managed a sugar plantation in Jamaica, and that is where she most likely grew up. In 1835 she married the Jamaican-born Henry Mark Lynch at her father's plantation. Lynch studied law at the Middle Temple and was called to the bar in 1840; he returned to Jamaica to practise law but died in 1845. Theodora returned to England, where she began her writing career with a book of poetry, *Lays of the Sea, and Other Poems*, which appeared in 1846. Though she published several books before her death in 1885, little was known about her during her own time and even less today.

---

45 Chester, *Transatlantic Sketches*, 82.
46 Lewis, *Journal*, 93–94.
47 Ellis, *Diocese of Jamaica*, 218.

Theodora's *The Wonders of the West Indies* was published in 1856, a couple of decades after emancipation. As with other authors, Lynch owed much of her understanding of Obeah to earlier writers, including Jacob Bryant. In the introductory paragraph to her chapter "Superstitions", Lynch writes: "The great superstition amongst the negroes in the West Indies is that of Obeahism. The witch of Endor is called in the Hebrew language Obi; the word therefore has reached Africa through the Arabic of the Mohammedans. In Hayti, the term Obeah is not known."[48] A student of Bryant, she goes on to explain:

> Amongst the Egyptians, a serpent is called Obion; and Moses in the name [of] God, forbad the Israelites ever to enquire of the demon Obi, translated in the Bible, Wizard.
>
> At first sight this Obeahism appears but a harmless delusion; and it is only when we look closely into it, that the dark mischief it works becomes apparent. The Obeah Chief is on all occasions looked up to as an oracle. He is considered potent to heal diseases; to discover crime, and for the bribe of gold, he will through risk and danger find means to satisfy the applicant's wildest thirst for revenge.[49]

Lynch asserts that Obeah "was by no means an unprofitable employment" and that the Obeah man or woman "assumed a power over health and illness, life and death".

As we've seen in the earlier section on poisons, several practitioners were apparently driven by thoughts of their imminent demise to confess to unsuspected poisonings. Lynch also offers one of those stories:

> A fair young girl from England became perhaps unsuspectingly the bride of some creole planter. She thought that her husband had been free to seek her affections; and little dreamed she had, by her marriage, displaced from the situation of housekeeper one of Africa's dusky daughters; who with a burning jealousy at her heart, was plotting with the Obeah man a scheme for her rival's destruction. So baneful was the nature of this Obeah practice, that the negro woman, who would have stood aghast at the very thought of murder, fancied herself quite justified in "turning the eyes", as the expression is, of her young mistress; and to accomplish this would not hesitate to set Obi for her, or in other words to receive from the Obeah man a slow poison which she dexterously inserted in the food of her unsuspecting victim, a mission which she is

---

48 Lynch, *Wonders*, 160.
49 Ibid., 160–61.

> generally most careful to fulfil, having received from the old man the prophetic assurance, that by thus acting, she will regain the lost affections of her master. The bodily disease, the natural consequence of poison, is immediately attributed by the infatuated slave to the power of the Obeah chief; and if the agent of this sin-stained man feel any latent compunction, any sharp pang of conscience, when she looks on the success of her scheme in the drooping form and sunken cheeks of her mistress, on the very system of papal indulgences, for a little more money given to the Obeah man, she is assured that all is right, and she watches calmly her helpless rival sink into the grave.[50]

It is tempting to speculate about this story – is she relating something from her own marital experience in Jamaica? Would that explain both her decision to leave Jamaica right after her husband's death and her deep religiosity? Or is the mysterious story simply a generalized expression of the sexual rivalry between white and black women? Certainly, this theme of a black woman jealous of a white received little attention from male writers, Madden being the notable exception.

Lynch relates another story she claims to be familiar with, about

> the grand-daughter of a lady who lost her life from the practice of Obeah. . . . This lady noticed a mysterious community of interest amongst some of the negroes on the estate. In the hut of one of the slaves was found a collection of feathers, bottles, rags, alligator's teeth, fish bones, and egg shells; and whilst her husband passed them by with a laugh, as symbols of a harmless superstition, she felt convinced that some deep and terrible mischief lay hidden under these fantastic emblems. As if consumption had marked her for its own, the lady passed away from life, withering as a summer flower sometimes does, with sunshine gleaming around it; and many long years afterwards when she was but imperfectly recollected as a dream of the morning, a dying negro woman revealed the terrible fact to her startled master, that she had long, long ago poisoned his fair English bride. Knowing her mistress' practice of taking every morning a fresh egg for breakfast, she had contrived to insinuate poison through the shell, and thus to work out the Obeah which had been put on her mistress. The woman died a few hours after this confession.[51]

Lynch does not make it clear whether this is a repetition of the same story she has already told, but the similarities would suggest that it is.

---

50 Ibid., 161–63.
51 Ibid., 163–64.

While poison may have been necessary to dispatch unbelieving whites, Obeah practitioners did not generally need it when dealing with fellow blacks, according to Lynch. Poison was

> not necessary to deprive [the negro] of life. The effect of this superstition on his mind is most astonishing. If a garden or poultry yard has been robbed, the proprietor, himself a negro, applies to the man of witchcraft, to set Obi for the thief. It is talked of among the neighbours, and as soon as the culprit discovers that he is under Obi, his imagination conjures up a thousand horrors, which playing riot in his heart, work a real ruin on the physical part of his nature. A settled despondency overshadows him, and the terror in his soul saps the very springs of life. The negro is peculiarly susceptible and credulous, and the anticipation of indefinite evil hurries the emaciated victim to his grave.[52]

Echoing Edward Long and the other writers who came after him, Lynch notes "if a negro is taken ill, he enquires of the Obeah man, whether the sickness be unto death. Should this dire prophet give a chance of recovery, all is well. But if on the contrary . . . he receives an indefinite or doubtful answer, terror and fear become the able ministers of disease, and the poor man finds himself in a very short time standing on the very confines of life." She then recounts the hoary old story first trotted out by Fuller.

> Many years ago, the proprietor of a fine low-land estate in Jamaica observed that there was a great mortality amongst his negroes. There was no fever prevalent; neither was there any epidemic at that time in the island. Sometimes two or three persons were buried in one day, and the doctor began to suspect, that Obeah was practised on the place. At length in the extremity of her fear, a young woman told her master that all the negroes who had died, had previously been put under Obi, and this led to further investigation. The house of the accused was searched; a variety of articles belonging to the practice of the superstition were found in her house, and her master feeling persuaded that she was an Obeah enchantress, sent her off to one of the other West India islands. This punishment had the desired effect. She never again followed those evil courses, and the negroes on the estate from which she was banished were soon restored to their usual health and tranquillity.[53]

Lynch gives no attribution, but the story is very similar to Fuller's.

---

52   Ibid., 164–65.
53   Ibid., 165–66.

Lynch goes on to observe that while myalism offered itself as an alternative to or "disenchanter" of Obeah, "their impositions are very nearly related to each other". She relates that the "Myalmen by means of a narcotic potion made from a species of calalue, pretend to be able to reanimate dead bodies, and assert, that they can at any time keep the stern messenger death from themselves". She notes once again that "these superstitions are, with the dark ignorance fostered by slavery, passing gradually away in the West Indies", but she recounts the story of Dr T—, who "some three or four years ago, . . . travelled through Jamaica successfully practising Myalism, and actually pressing out of the credulity of the negro not less than fifteen or twenty pounds a day".

Apparently, it was not only the Negroes who were credulous, because the proprietor of a country estate suffering from drought

> drove Dr T— in his own carriage to the [nearby] river side. There was a well near its banks into which the doctor was let down; when he appeared again, he brought an alabaster doll from his bosom, and told the negroes who crowded round him, for he had not quite hardihood enough to look at the proprietor, that he had brought up in his arms the mermaid who kept the waters from flowing. He received a handsome fee for thus capturing the spirit of the drought, and though some time passed away before the stream again bore its burden of waters to the ocean; yet when the drought ceased it was attributed with solemn gravity to the influence of Dr T— over the mermaid, and He who sends the early and the latter rain was unthought of.[54]

Sometime later, according to Lynch, Dr T— was prosecuted and convicted of obtaining money under false pretences. Still up to his old tricks, he apparently "contrived to impress his fellow convicts with an idea of his control over the last enemy", but "they were soon made sensible of the folly of their credulity by the circumstance of his sudden death from a large stone which fell on him".[55]

Never mind all that, though, as "with the advance of civilization attendant on freedom, this obeahism has almost passed away from the British West Indies", Lynch assures us. She then goes on to deliver one of those back-handed compliments too common with even the most liberal English writer:

> The present race of English negroes, though still listless and idle, and almost entirely devoid of enterprise, are comparatively an enlightened set, as the ignorance

---

54 Ibid., 166–67.
55 Ibid., 167.

which was justly considered an indispensable requisite for slavery is unnecessary for free labour; the blacks are no longer shut out from the means of improvement; schools are established throughout the West Indies, and the rising generation in many instances, excels in knowledge the village poor of England.[56]

Despite all she has to say about the terrors of Obeah and the mischief wrought by it in previous years, Lynch, a devout Christian, is careful to emphasize that, through the work of missionaries and the progress of education, it was a dying practice. Obeah may have been common prior to emancipation, but according to her, it was already fading by the time she wrote this book. Of course, this was essentially the missionaries' party line, which declared that because of their Christianizing work, and because emancipation meant they now had a free hand to preach and teach, blacks were making progress.

Letters from Jamaica

Charles Joseph Rampini was born in Scotland on 20 July 1840, but apart from that, very little is known about him. A Scottish lawyer, he appears to have been appointed to serve as a district judge in Jamaica sometime late in 1866 or early in 1867; he retired from the colonial service in 1877 and returned to Scotland. It would appear that *Letters from Jamaica: Land of Streams and Woods* was originally published anonymously while Rampini was still in Jamaica. In the book, he describes Jamaica's vegetation, the different towns, the birds and the fish and provides a couple of Anancy stories. Obeah, along with other "superstitions", naturally comes in for quite a bit of attention.

Rampini explains that his "first introduction to negro superstitions" came when he was about to hurl a stick at a cotton tree to bring down an orchid. His servant, Bob, a man he earlier describes as having the "face of a baboon", stayed his hand. The following is the exchange that ensued.

> "Cracious! . . . Don't do dat, massa, if you please!"
> " . . . Nonsense!"
> "For true, massa! No, massa. I beg you quite hard."
> "But why not, Bob?"
> "Massa don't understand dese tings: but cotton tree bery comical tree, an' if you did trow dat stick I an' you wouldn' lib to de end of de year!" . . .

---

56   Ibid., 163.

> [The servant asks him,] "Massa eber hear de nigger proverb 'bout cotton tree?"
> "No, Bob...."
> "Well, you know, 'when cotton tree fall, billy-goat jump over him'; ... 'By am by buckra (gentleman's) dog catch billy-goat by him ear, an' mek him cry Ba-a-a!'"[57]

In essence, Bob was saying that when the great (cotton) tree falls, anyone can jump over it, but those jumping might themselves be caught or destroyed by a greater force than they.

As with other writers, Rampini's racism is close to the surface, and it emerges frequently to display his conviction that blacks were a lower species.

> A man's estimate of the negro character varies according to the length of time he spends among them. The first year, his opinion of them is a high one. He is amused by their merry faces, their broad grins, their apparent good nature, their seeming simplicity of character. He looks upon them as happy children, for whom the song, and the dance, and the church constitute the essentials of life. The second year his ideas are somewhat modified. He regards them as children still, but now as spoiled children, who give a great deal of trouble; and by the third or fourth year he has begun to talk about the "irrepressible nigger", and to speak of them in very much the same language as the planters get the credit of doing.
>
> A surface polish of civilization the negro can attain, and is attaining; but beyond this it seems doubtful whether he can ever advance.... The native springs of civilisation, the quick working brain to conceive, the prompt energy to execute, knowledge of other countries, and of races besides his own, from which to gather ideas, are wanting to him. Without these, the negro will ever remain a race apart.[58]

Rampini goes on to list the "moral defects of the negro" – to wit, "his propensity" to steal, to lie and to be promiscuous. He is "too lazy to work". Among defects he lists are his superstition and his lack of understanding of eternal life as propounded by Christianity: "Death to the negro has no terrors. He dies because his time has come. But he dies, like a dog, without a regret and without a pang.... Fatalism is itself a superstition, and the negro is superstitious in the extreme."[59] Rampini enumerates several of these superstitious beliefs,

---

57 Rampini, *Letters*, 42–43.
58 Ibid., 80–81.
59 Ibid., 82.

from duppies to the Rolling Calf to the notion that the sight of bats crossing each other in flight at sunset will bring conflict between friends. Strangely, he appears quite unaware of English and Scottish superstitions that thrived in those countries in tandem with Christianity.

> Professedly a Christian, it may be doubted whether one negro in a thousand attaches a correct meaning to even the most simple ordinances of religion. In some districts of the island, indeed, these are travestied at midnight meetings held under leafy booths erected for the purpose, which are carefully concealed from the knowledge of the parish minister. At these "singing meetings", a woman sanctifies the bread and administers the elements. Hymns are sung, words are spoken, mysterious rites are observed. The worshippers grow more and more excited as the fires burn out and the night grows old; and the meeting ends as might be expected in license and debauchery.[60]

Indeed, the idea of a woman performing the sacred rites may have been even more alarming to his readers than the description of the rites themselves!

Rampini finds little to admire about black people, particularly country blacks, whom he describes as "the true, unadulterated, and genuine Quashie". In addition to the failings listed above, he considered blacks to be generally lazy unless working on their own provision grounds and claimed that they also eat cats and rats and are litigious.

But it is to Obeah that Rampini attaches the greatest importance. His first line in the chapter devoted to the practice reveals his convictions: "Of all the motive powers which influence the negro character, by far the most potent, as it is also the most dangerous, is that of Obeah." According to him – and readers acquainted with his identity would have considered him in a position to know – "the obeah man or woman is one of the great guild or fraternity of crime. Hardly a criminal trial occurs in the colony in which he is not implicated in one way or another. His influence over the country people is unbounded."[61]

> Under the style and title of a "bush doctor", he wanders from place to place, exacting "coshery" from his dupes on all hands: supplied with food by one, with shelter by another, with money by a third, denied nought, from the mysterious terror with which he is regarded, and refused nothing from fear of the terrible retribution which might be the consequences of such a rash act. His pretensions are high: but he has means at hand to enforce them. He can cure

---

60   Ibid., 84.
61   Ibid., 131.

all diseases; he can protect a man from the consequences of his crime; he can even reanimate the dead. His knowledge of simples is immense. Every bush and every tree furnishes weapons for his armoury. Unfortunately, in too many instances more potent agents are not wanting to his hand. His stock-in-trade consists of lizards' bones, old egg-shells, tufts of hair, cats' claws, ducks' skulls, an old pack of cards, rusty nails, and things of that description. "Grave-dirt", that is, earth taken from where a corpse has been buried, is also largely used. "It is supposed that if an obeah-man throws it at a person he will die." But ground glass, arsenic, and other poisons, are not unfrequently found among the contents of the obeah-man's "puss-skin" wallet; and it is not difficult to conjecture for what purposes these are employed.[62]

Rampini observes that "serpent or devil worship is by no means rare in the country districts; and of its heathen rites the obeah-man is invariably the priest". He refuted the notion that Obeah had died out or was dying out and notes that "the practice of Obeah amongst the humbler classes is still, unfortunately, as prevalent at the present day, despite the severely penal laws against it, as it was in the beginning of the century".[63]

He includes a fascinating story that appeared in the *Daily Gleaner* on 26 January 1869, which quoted it from a smaller paper, the *Falmouth Post*.

During the past week, the town of Lucea was kept in a state of considerable excitement, in consequence of a report which was circulated and believed, not only by the lower but middling classes, that a Spanish jar, containing a large quantity of gold coins, had been discovered in the yard adjoining the premises of a black man, named Johnson. . . . The report of the discovery was strengthened by the assertion of several persons, male and female, that preparations on an extensive scale, and commensurate with the stated value, were being made for the purpose of taking up the jar and its contents. We instituted an inquiry, and ascertained that many of the friends of the man Johnson were assisting in doing all he suggested, – that obeah-men were employed by the parties immediately concerned, – that the obeah-men were supplied with an abundance of food and liquor, – and that nights were passed in the performance of superstitious rites which disturbed the Christian-minded villagers in the neighbourhood. A white cock was killed on one occasion, for the purpose of carrying out one of the objects that was declared necessary, and there were sacrifices of goats and pigs, the spilling of blood in all directions, and the commission of other abominations, which we have neither time nor inclination to mention.

---

62   Ibid., 131–32.
63   Ibid., 133–34, 140.

On Sunday, 17th instant, the excitement was greater than on preceding days. One of the crowd remarked, that all attempts made to take the jar from the earth would be unavailing, until human blood was sprinkled on the land, – "that human blood must be used, for nothing else would answer". . . . On arriving in front of Johnson's house, where upwards of 400 men, women and children, were assembled, an inspection was made of the piece of land where the treasure was said to be, and one of the constables . . . found a clayed cooking utensil, called a yabba, and a common water jar, both of which had been evidently placed in the newly-excavated earth by Johnson and his associates. At the discovery of the imposture, a shout of indignation was raised by some of the assembled people, and between them and Johnson's family there was a violent altercation. Upon a gentleman remarking that the whole affair was a compound of Obeahism, Myalism, and Revivalism, some of the bystanders observed, that if the white people had not interfered the jar and money would have been found. One of the black lookers-on said, "The jar began to sink down as soon as the white people began to trouble it." . . . on inquiry being made, the fact was ascertained that Obeahism had been at work for several days and nights. We are informed that three Obeah-men, who were not apprehended at the time we left Lucea, had received £10 for their services, and that for some months past they have had other and well-paying customers in Lucea, some of whom are among the most earnest in professions of Christianity.[64]

Rampini also observes that myalism was still around. According to him,

> The Obeah-man must not be confounded with the Myalman, who is to the former what the antidote is to the poison. He professes to undo what the other has done; to cure where the other has injured; but it must be confessed that, both in its operation and its results, the cure is often worse than the disease. In truth, the boundary line between the two classes of professors is oftentimes but a shadowy one.

"Obeah", he concludes, "is not destined to die an inglorious death".[65]

As usual, reviewers took particular note of the fascinating Obeah information. In reviewing *Letters from Jamaica*, for example, "The Reader" describes it as "[a] very entertaining and well-written book about a comparatively little known corner of the globe. . . . The chapter on Obeah would in itself render the book worthy of notice, had it no other good points."[66]

---

64 Ibid., 140–42.
65 Ibid., 142.
66 *The Graphic*, 12 August 1873, n.p.

Love and the Caribbean

Alec Waugh, older brother of Evelyn Waugh, the famed author of *Brideshead Revisited*, visited the Caribbean frequently over a period of more than thirty years. *Love and the Caribbean: Tales, Characters and Scenes of the West Indies*, published in 1958, is a collection of articles Waugh had written about the region and, in his words, "tell of my own love for the island and of love in the islands". As such, some of the articles had appeared at least twenty years earlier.

In the twentieth century, Obeah continued to hold an enduring fascination for European writers, and Waugh did not prove the exception. In a 1951 piece for *Holiday* magazine, he wrote of Antiguans that "the fetishes of the bush" remained and that "their belief in obeah – a kind of necromancy – persists". A year later, *The Times* published his article "Change and Tradition in the Caribbean", in which he writes that, "though church attendances are large ... Obeah flourishes". He describes an incident in which his hosts returned from off-island and

> found their cook prostrate with terror and despair. The daughter of a neighbour had been drowned while in her own daughter's company and the bereaved mother, in revenge, had placed Obeah on her. She insisted on returning to her own island of Anguilla. On the morning after her departure we found the mosquito netting over the windows draped with white feathers and a semi-circle of white feathers drawn round the front steps. Later in the day, the dogs unearthed the neatly severed wings of white duck. The carcass and the head were missing. It was, we presumed, counter-Obeah.[67]

"Much has been written in recent years, about Obeah men and voodoo rites, and there can be little doubt that in the last analysis most West Indians have more faith in their own witch-doctors than in the priests whom their education has approved for them", Waugh writes in "The Sugar Islands", published in 1939 and excerpted in *Love*. He goes on to explain that "the authority of the 'Obeah men' is little questioned" and recounts a story told him by a Grenada planter whose labourers said they were being troubled at home by spirits. The planter went to investigate for himself.

Things flew around the dark room: "A shower of nutmegs out of the basket under the bench flew into the air and fell all round us. My hair felt like

---

[67] Alec Waugh, "Change and tradition in the Caribbean", *The Times*, 18 October 1952, Iss. 52446.

standing on end and when, a few minutes later, the bottle jumped off the table, hit the roof and fell at my feet, I thought it time to go", the planter admits to Waugh. The labourers brought in the Anglican parson but the spirits continued as before, so they brought in "the African Shango Dancers" and paid them five pounds. The dancers consisted of an old woman and a teenager who were accompanied by a drummer. The ritual started at seven a.m. on Friday morning, and the next afternoon the planter went back to see what was going on. While he was there, the old woman fell to the ground and rolled out of the house, down the hill and back up. The planter was amazed. "It looked impossible and the whole thing was so inhuman and beastly that we left." Yet, he reports, the house was not disturbed by the spirits again.[68]

In the excerpt from "Most Women", Waugh relates a strange incident when he and his friend Eldred Curwen were staying in Martinique at a small hotel. Their waitress at the old restaurant spilt sardine oil on Waugh's trousers and gave generally poor service, so on their second night, they asked for a change of table. The maître d'hotel "became flustered" and the waitress, Floria, got angry, but Waugh and Curwen stuck to their guns. That night neither slept. The following night was also sleepless. They asked someone if the waitress was poisoning them and were told that she did not need poison.

Twenty years before, Floria had apparently met and fallen in love with a French civil servant who invited her to come live with him. "My love will be a chain about you: a chain between you and me: a chain that will hold you fast, hold you for ever to this little island", she told him, but after three years of their living together, he got news that he was to be transferred off-island. Floria took it badly but then regained her usual good spirits. She sang to him the night before he was to leave.

That night "there was a new temper to her singing: it was less crooning, more barbaric, almost terrifying ... in a tongue he had never learned". When he questioned her about it, she had replied, "They are the songs of my people. They are very old." On the day he was to leave, the man experienced blinding pain and decided to postpone his departure. Five weeks later, when he was on the dock about to board the ship, the pain returned. Men took him back to the house he shared with Floria.

"There was on her face a strange, rapt brooding look, as though she was looking at things – dark things that were many miles and centuries away." The

---

68 Alec Waugh, *Love and the Caribbean: Tales, Characters and Scenes of the West Indies* (1930; repr., New York: Farrar, Straus and Cudahy, 1958), 151–53.

doctor who attended the man told him: "you will think I am romancing: but I have lived all my life among these people. They have secrets that are dark to us. When they want to commit suicide they do not shoot themselves or cut their throats. They lie upon their beds and die." The civil servant was doubtful. "It was impossible to believe that contiguous with this merry, familiar, sunlit world existed the dark mysteries of Obeah." But the doctor was not finished.

> "They can will mischief or death upon their enemies. They have philters that will win them the love of the stubborn-hearted. It would be no hard task for them to make one who wishes to leave them incapable of movement." . . . Sorcery and sorceress were one. Even sorcery could not outlive the snapping of the thin thread of life that bound it to its origin. It was his life or hers. As long as she lived, he was her slave.

The man remained on Martinique until he died. Now, the restaurant kept her on as a waitress because "they just daren't not". Waugh reported that he and Curwen changed back their table and slept peacefully for the rest of their stay.[69]

Waugh returned to the story of the French civil servant at least once, in a novel, *The Fatal Gift*, which is set on Dominica. It also concerns a white colonial who believes himself unable to leave the island because of an Obeah woman's spell. Waugh's 1955 commercial success *Island in the Sun*, about a black labour leader fighting sugar interests, also makes several references to Obeah and features a white man who claims superior Obeah to that of the black Obeah man.[70]

---

69 Waugh, *Love*, 154–69.
70 A 1957 movie based on the book stars Harry Belafonte, James Mason, Dorothy Dandridge, Joan Collins and Joan Fontaine; it was filmed in Grenada and Barbados.

Conclusion

IN 1845 THOMAS DE QUINCEY MADE AN analogy in *Blackwood's Edinburgh Magazine* between grief and the "ignoble witchcraft of the poor African Obeah", which prompted the editor to offer this footnote:

> Thirty years ago it would not have been necessary to [explain] Obi or Obeah magic; because at that time several distinguished writers (Miss Edgeworth, for instance, in her *Belinda*) had made use of this superstition in fictions, and because the remarkable history of Three-finger'd Jack, a story brought upon the stage, had made the superstition notorious as a fact. Now, however, so long after the case has probably passed out of the public mind, it may be proper to mention – [that] when an Obeah man, i.e., a professor of this dark collusion with human fears and human credulity, had once woven his dreadful net of ghostly terrors, and had thrown it over his selected victim, vainly did that victim flutter, struggle, languish in the meshes; unless the spells were reversed, he generally perished; and without a wound except from his own too domineering fancy.[1]

Yet, as we have seen, Obeah never passed out of the public mind. On the contrary, successive generations of British writers kept it very much in the forefront of British consciousness, continuing to write about the practice and to debate its prevalence and its hold on black people well into the twentieth century. "In spite of the gradual spread of education in all the British West Indian islands, the great majority of coloured people of the lower classes are still much affected by a belief in witchcraft", writes Hesketh Bell in a 1936 letter to *The Times*. "The superstitious negro peoples the darkness with a host of fearsome spirits. . . . It is not sufficient to declare to uneducated and simple-minded people that witchcraft is 'absurd'; it must be proved to them, if possible, that it does not exist."[2]

In his response to Bell's letter, the Anglican churchman John Levo acknowledges that "the Obeah-man's activities invariably issue in offences ranging in gravity from comparatively harmless psychomancy to plain murder" and

---

1 *Blackwood's Edinburgh Magazine* 57 (January–July 1845): 491–92.
2 Bell, letter to *The Times*.

calls it a "grave social evil". While Bell ascribes Obeah's harm to poisoning rather than supernatural agency, Levo is more inclined to leave some room for doubt, noting that though he can provide a rational explanation for most of the "phenomena of witchcraft which have come under my notice in the West Indies", he cannot do so for all of them. Rather, Levo understandably believes that evil has a supernatural basis and that one can drive out the "strong evil" of Obeah only "with a stronger good".[3]

Hundreds of years after Obeah's first literary appearance, two British men were debating its continued existence in the pages of one of Britain's most prestigious newspapers. Like many writers over the previous couple of centuries, Bell and Levo subscribe to and perpetuate a stereotyped image of black people as childish, violent, ugly and prey to sinister superstitions.

In fact, European racial theory owed much of its development to the works of writers on Obeah. Black people's belief in Obeah was the yardstick by which they were judged. Were black people capable of becoming Christians? Were they capable of understanding Christianity? Could they become people of reason or would they always be prey to superstition? Was not superstition part of their character, as unchangeable as the face of the moon? These questions were asked by both planters and their opponents, the missionaries and the abolitionists. The latter were convinced that they could be answered in the affirmative, and eventually they managed to persuade enough of their fellow citizens to their way of thinking to finally make emancipation a reality. But while the British public *did* become convinced that slavery was wrong, the debate, the flurry of writing, and the masses of books and pamphlets had left an impression – founded on early Christian writing – which equated the colour black with evil and with sorcery.

Obeah, the blackest of black traditions, symbolized disorder. It was outside white control. It set up the Obeah practitioner as a shadow power on the plantations, able to dispense justice, exact vengeance and treat the sick in mind or body. More significantly, Obeah gave the slaves the confidence to launch frightening revolts against the plantation system. Age-old fears of blackness and witchcraft blended with the terror of violence, of black retribution for captivity and slavery. To soothe their panic, British writers wrote and rewrote narratives in which either heroic white individuals triumphed over credulous and savage blacks or white civilization itself triumphed, gaining adherents to

---

3   John Levo, letter to *The Times*, 31 July 1936, 10.

Christianity and turning black people away from their traditions. In story after story, narrative after narrative, blacks are defeated by either the sword or the Word.

Earlier books, such as those by Long, Smith and Hearn, employed an almost hysterical tone when discussing Obeah, but by the late 1800s, white attitudes to Obeah had taken on a more amused and condescending tone, as in "The Black Demons of Hayti" and *The Wooings of Jezebel Pettyfer*. Slavery and resistance to slavery were no longer issues and British imperialism and colonialism were in full flower, accompanied by a gung-ho adventurism that exemplified what was seen as the best of white masculinity. White men were penetrating the heart of darkness and conquering it.

The story "How We Caught the Obeah Man", which appeared in the 19 June 1900 issue of the *Pall Mall Mall Gazette*, embodies the spirit of the times. In it, three white Jamaicans are having a conversation when they are interrupted by a man, "his black face shining with excitement and terror". He was apparently passing by the house of John Awful, an Obeah man, who was at his incantations when the man saw him. Outraged, the Obeah man seized his machete and gave chase, but the man has run straight to the white men. They immediately decide to do something about John Awful. "The resident magistrate gave him twenty lashes and gaoled him for twelve months" last year, but he was recently freed and "ever since then he's kept the countryside in terror", one of the white men explains to another. "We'll have him tomorrow", they promise each other, a dialogue which invites frightening comparison to the spirit in which the Ku Klux Klan carried out lynchings in the American south.

The next morning, a troop of local constables shows up to assist in the capture, and one of the men asks the justice of the peace who summoned them, "What do you mean by bringing in Her Majesty's troops to spoil the show? I thought we were going to have a quiet picnic on our own!" The justice of the peace responds that he has a duty to call in the troops, but that in any case, "you fellows know jolly well the 'constabs' will bolt when things get hot. They always do. We'll have the show to ourselves after all."

Near the Obeah man's hut they hear loud noises; "the negro 'constabs' turned a sickly green, and wanted to do an incontinent bolt". One offers to go and get more constables but is told, "You stay where you are, you black devil!" They emerge into a clearing and begin to fight the men that the Obeah man has with him. Two of the white men are described as having a "lovely scrimmage with half a dozen strapping niggers". By the time the fight is over, most of the black attackers have run off and four lie on the ground, injured.

Then the door to the hut flies open and "the most villainous-looking negro I ever clapped eyes on" emerges. "His eyes shone with madness, his face and hands were smeared with the blood of a cock he had just sacrificed, and round his throat was a ghastly necklace of teeth and bones." The Obeah man puts up a good fight but the white men subdue him and have him taken to jail.[4] Again, blacks are presented as cowardly and barbaric while the whites are brave and heroic, clearly members of a superior race.

"The Pardoner's Tale", written by Colin Mares, appeared more than half a century later, in the 3 January 1961 issue of the *Guardian*. It is very different in tone from "How We Caught the Obeah Man", but it too subtly reinforces the message of white superiority and black inferiority. The story revolves around Mares's two servants, Laxton, the handyman, and Dorothy, his common-law wife, who happens to be pregnant. When Mares returns to his home one evening, Laxton asks him if he has seen a duppy in the form of a "little yellah dog". Mares informs readers that "Duppy is the Jamaican word for spirits returned from the dead [which] are conjured up by Obeah-men". He assures readers that "to many Jamaicans, they are as real as royalty".

Laxton and Dorothy appear convinced that someone has set Obeah on them because Dorothy, though "an old hand at pregnancies", is twice her usual size at seven months. Their fears are confirmed when the baying yellow dog appears outside their door on two successive evenings. "The first appearance of a duppy is basically similar to the serving of a legal writ. It causes immediate consternation, it forebodes trouble and necessitates some definite action. For legal writs one consults a rival solicitor. For duppies, the Jamaican consults a rival Obeahman."[5]

It turns out that another woman desires the position of maid in Mares's household and has retained the services of "Old Man Touch 'n' Feel, a blind and somewhat decayed practitioner, to put an Obeah on Dorothy". Laxton and Dorothy have no faith in Mares's dismissal of their concerns; they hire "the Pardoner", so named because of his constant apologizing for his "frequent regurgitations" caused by chronic indigestion. The Pardoner advises Laxton to confront the yellow dog "wearing a repulsively dirty mask and waving a sort of totem pole festooned with old rags, skins, feathers, and pages torn from *Hymns Ancient and Modern*". Over the next few days, however, Dorothy's size increases noticeably.

---

4   "How We Caught the Obeah Man", *Pall Mall Gazette*, 19 June 1900, n.p.
5   Colin Mares, "The Pardoner's Tale", *Guardian*, 3 January 1961, 5.

> "It is Old Man Touch 'n' Feel, missus," Dorothy wailed. "He's been at me again."
> "It is absolute nonsense!" I snapped. . . .
> "You cannot understand Obeah, sah," Laxton groaned. "It is a science."
> "It is twins," said my wife decisively."

A doctor confirms Mrs Mares's diagnosis, but "modern medicine was of no comfort to the Obeah patients".

The next afternoon, when Mares and his wife return to their house, they find that the Pardoner has visited and has nailed "the feathered skeleton of a large John Crow, the ubiquitous turkey buzzard and the chief scavenger of the West Indies", above Dorothy's door. Mares orders its removal, summons the Pardoner and issues "dire threats about what would happen if any other masks, totem poles, dead John Crows, or other manifestations of Obeah appeared" on the property. The next day, the Pardoner comes back "with a potion guaranteed to keep the carcass free from termites and fleas" and sprinkles it around, muttering incantations.

> "You see, sah and missus," he said proudly as numerous insects perished instantly. "It is a science."
> My wife sniffed suspiciously. "It is Dettol," she said.
> "No, missus," explained the Pardoner, patiently and loftily. "Dettol, pyrethrex, and rum."

The neighbours place bets on who will win out, but then Mares's wife involves herself in the affair and procures huge amounts of orange juice and vitamin pills, which she administers to Dorothy. "Wondering watchers muttered about White Man's Obeah."

The Pardoner arrives to check out "his new rival's methods" and is given "rum liberally doctored with cascara". He stays away for several days and Mares's wife gains new admirers.

When Dorothy is about to give birth, the Pardoner reappears and tries to reassert his authority but loses it completely when twins are born. He begs Mares for ten shillings "for the idea, the patent idea". At first Mares has no idea what he is talking about, but then he goes to the verandah, where a growing heap of fruits has appeared and where his wife is doling out vitamin pills. "Much more powerful than this other Obeah", she tells one client as another approaches to ask for a remedy for a straying boyfriend. Mares pays the Pardoner and carries the fruit inside when his wife is finished.

> Silently, we carried the fruit inside and regarded it with lustful anticipation.
> "It's a bit of a fraud," I began, lamely and hypocritically.
> "It is a science," my wife said firmly. "You would not understand."

Wry and gentle in tone, this story nevertheless, depicts West Indians as superstitious and ignorant. By its failure to offer a critique of the shortcomings of colonial education, it also implies that West Indians are innately so. The white Mares and his wife represent reason, and the Pardoner and the other blacks, unreason.

So, as we have seen in story after story, influential and widely read British writers of one generation after another presented racialized stock characters in their works, which predisposed the British public to view blacks as savage, stupid, credulous, conniving, lazy and violent. In their stories and narratives Obeah was almost always present, proof positive that the stereotypes were true and, perhaps, even worse than imagined. Over and over, the British literati, shuddering deliciously, repeated what they had heard or read about blacks and Obeah.

Only a few noticed the startling similarities between the various reports and anecdotes offered. Kingsley's retelling of the hoary story about the servant who confesses on his or her deathbed to multiple Obeah-related murders may, for example, have prompted this reaction from the good Revd Ellis:

> Many of these [Obeah] stories are as old as the old days of sailing ships, and may be found in old and almost forgotten books and pamphlets; many of them are ubiquitous; their narrative, like history, repeats itself with but slightly different geographical settings. What was told, and probably truthfully told, in Antigua a hundred years ago was related fifty years ago as having quite recently happened in Trinidad and thirty years later a modern traveller in Jamaica was regaled with the same story of what took place "on this very estate, I assure you, my dear sir". No dates are mentioned and the guileless tourist fills his note-book with century-old yarns which he believes to be present day happenings.[6]

Eden Phillpotts concedes the point in *Sugar-Cane Land* when a fellow traveller scoffs at him: "That's right; believe everything you hear: all literary people do in the West Indies. They miss facts, and collect rubbishy fiction from any idiot who opens his mouth to them."[7] Yet this "rubbishy fiction" played a key role

---

6   Ellis, *Diocese of Jamaica*, 218–19.
7   Phillpotts, *Sugar-Cane Land*, 114.

in creating and perpetuating racialized theories about black people, even as those stories changed in tenor over time.

During slavery, stories of Obeah focused on violence and savagery, but by the end of the 1800s, Britain's growing confidence as an imperialist power resulted in a change of tone. The hysterical themes of the earlier narratives were replaced with condescension and amusement. Superstitious and violent blacks were no longer to be feared by members of a superior race who belonged to an empire on which the sun never set. Scientific racism, including the now discredited science of phrenology, assured whites that they stood head and shoulders above blacks. The sense of menace vanished from Obeah stories; Obeah practitioners were defanged, made into objects of ridicule, not fear. But, though they once again became the harmless blacks of the very earliest reports, the hold Obeah men and women had on successive generations of popular British writers underscores Obeah's impact in shaping racist perceptions of blacks for more than two hundred years. Viewed through the prism of Obeah, those perceptions were rarely benign and continue to affect race relations and racist ideas today.

Selected Bibliography

PUBLISHED SOURCES

"An Account of Moses Baker, a Mulatto Baptist Preacher near Martha Brea in Jamaica". *Evangelical Magazine*, September 1803, 365–71.

Allen, Grant. "The Beckoning Hand". In *The Beckoning Hand and Other Stories*. London: Chatto and Windus, 1887.

———. "Hobbling Mary". *Penny Illustrated Paper and Illustrated Times*, 10 July 1897, 20.

Allsopp, Richard, ed. *Dictionary of Caribbean English Usage*. Oxford: Oxford University Press, 1996.

Anolik, Ruth Bienstock, and Douglas L. Howard. *The Gothic Other: Racial and Social Constructions in the Literary Imagination*. Jefferson, NC: McFarland, 2004.

Arnold, Sam. *The Overtures, Songs, Choruses and Appropriate Music in the Grand Pantomimical Drama Call'd Obi; or Three Finger'd Jack, as Performed at the Theatre Royal, Haymarket*. London: John Longman, Clements, 1800.

Ashton, John. *Chapbooks of the Eighteenth Century*. London: Chatto and Windus, 1882.

Astley, Thomas, ed. *A New General Collection of Voyages and Travels: Consisting of the Most Esteemed Relations Which Have Been Hitherto Published in Any Language, Comprehending Everything Remarkable in Its Kind in Europe, Asia, Africa and America*. 2 vols. London: Thomas Astley, 1745.

Atwood, Thomas. *The History of the Island of Dominica*. London: J. Johnson, 1791.

Austen, Jane. *Northanger Abbey*. London: Richard Bentley, 1848.

Avery, Gillian. *Childhood's Pattern: A Study of the Hero and Heroines of Children's Fiction, 1770–1950*. London: Hodder and Stoughton, 1975.

Banbury, Thomas. *Jamaica Superstitions; or, the Obeah Book: A Complete Treatise of the Absurdities Believed in by the People of the Island*. Jamaica: Mortimer C. de Souza, 1894.

Barclay, Alexander. *A Practical View of the Present State of Slavery in the West Indies*. London: Smith, Elder, 1826.

Barham, Henry. *Hortus Americanus*. Kingston, Jamaica: Alexander Aikman, 1794.

Barnet, Miguel [Esteban Montejo]. *The Autobiography of a Runaway Slave*. London: Macmillan Caribbean, 1993.

Barrett, Leonard. *The Sun and the Drum*. Kingston, Jamaica: Sangster's Book Stores, 1976.

Bartels, Anke, and Dirk Wieman, eds. *Global Fragments: (Dis)Orientation in the New World Order.* Amsterdam: Rodopi, 2007.

Barthelemy, Gerard Anthony. *Black Face, Maligned Race: The Representation of Blacks in English Drama from Shakespeare to Southerne.* Baton Rouge: Louisiana State University Press, 1987.

Baxter, Richard. *The Practical Works of Richard Baxter.* Vol. 3. London: George Virtue, 1838.

Beckwith, Martha Warren. *Notes on Jamaican Ethnobotany.* Poughkeepsie, NY: Vassar College, 1927

Bell, Hesketh J. Letter to *The Times*, 27 July 1936, 8.

———. *Obeah: Witchcraft in the West Indies.* London: Low, Marston, Searle and Rivington, 1889.

———. *A Witch's Legacy.* London: Sampson Low, Marston, 1893.

Bellers, John. *An Essay Towards the Improvement of Physick, in Twelve Proposals.* London: J. Sowle, 1714.

Bentley, Richard. *Bentley's Miscellany* 30 (1851).

Bernheimer, Richard. *Wild Men in the Middle Ages: A Study in Art, Sentiment and Demonology.* New York: Octagon, 1970.

Besant, Walter. *The World Went Very Well Then.* 3 vols. London: Chatto and Windus, 1887.

Bisnauth, Dale. *History of Religions in the Caribbean.* Trenton, NJ: Africa World Press, 1996.

Bourdillon, Hilary. *Women as Healers: A History of Women and Medicine.* Cambridge: Cambridge University Press, 1988.

Boyd, Kelly. *Manliness and the Boys' Story Paper in Britain: A Cultural History, 1855–1940.* London: Palgrave MacMillan, 2003.

Brantlinger, Patrick. *Rule of Darkness: British Literature and Imperialism.* Ithaca, NY: Cornell University Press, 1988.

Bratton, J.S. *The Impact of Victorian Children's Fiction.* London: Croom Helm, 1981.

Bray, Thomas. *Missionalia; or, a Collection of Missionary Pieces Relating to the Conversion of the Heathen.* London: W.B. Roberts, 1727.

Brereton, Bridget. *Social Life in the Caribbean, 1838–1938.* London: Heinemann Educational, 1985.

Bridges, George Wilson. *The Annals of Jamaica.* London: John Murray, 1827.

———. *A Voice from Jamaica; in Reply to William Wilberforce.* London: Longman, Hurst, Rees, Orme, Brown and Green, 1823.

Briggs, Katherine Mary. *Pale Hecate's Team: An Examination of the Beliefs on Witchcraft and Magic among Shakespeare's Contemporaries and His Immediate Successors.* London: Routledge and Keegan Paul, 1962.

Broderick, Dorothy M. *Image of the Black in Children's Fiction.* New York: R.R. Bowker, 1973.

Bronkhurst, H.V.P. *The Colony of British Guiana and Its Labouring Populations.* London: T. Woolmer, 1888.

Brown, Robert. *Demonology and Witchcraft*. London: John F. Shaw, 1889.
Browning, Robert. *The Complete Poetic and Dramatic Works*. Boston: Houghton Mifflin, 1895.
Brunton, Deborah. "Moseley, Benjamin (1742–1819)". *Oxford Dictionary of National Biography*, edited by Lawrence Goldman. https://doi.org/10.1093/ref:odnb/19387.
Bryant, Jacob. *A New System; or, an Analysis of Ancient Mythology*. 3 vols. London: T. Payne, P. Elmsly, B. White and J. Walter, 1774–76.
Buchner, J.H. *The Moravians in Jamaica: A History of the Mission of the United Brethren's Church to the Negroes in the Island of Jamaica from the Years 1754 to 1854*. London: Longman, Brown, 1854.
Burdett, William. *The Life and Exploits of Three-finger'd Jack, the Terror of Jamaica*. 5th ed. London: A. Neil, 1802.
Burns, Robert. "Tam o' Shanter: A Tale". In *Eighteenth-Century Poetry: An Annotated Anthology*, edited by David Fairer and Christine Gerrard, 575–76. 3rd ed. Chichester, UK: John Wiley and Sons, 2015.
Canot, Theodore. *Memoirs of a Slave Trader*. London: Jonathan Cape, 1940.
Carmichael, Mrs [Alison Charles Carmichael]. *Domestic Manners and Social Conditions of the White, Coloured and Negro Population of the West Indies*. London: Whittaker, Treacher, 1833.
"Cassecanarie, Myal Djumboh". *Obeah Simplified: The True Wanga!* Port of Spain: Mirror, n.d.
Caulker, Tcho Mbaimba. *The African-British Long Eighteenth Century: An Analysis of African-British Treaties, Colonial Economics and Anthropological Discourse*. New York: Lexington, 2009.
C.B. "Obeah and Vaudoux: The Magic of the West Indies". *Manchester Guardian*, 12 March 1907, 8.
Chester, Greville John. *Transatlantic Sketches in the West Indies*. London: Smith, Elder, 1869.
Clark, John, Walter Dendy and James M. Phillippo. *The Voice of Jubilee: A Narrative of the Baptist Mission, Jamaica*. London: John Snow, 1865.
Clarkson, Thomas. *Letters on the Slave Trade and the State of the Natives*. London: James Phillips, 1791.
Coleridge, Henry Nelson. *Six Months in the West Indies*. London: Thomas Tegg, 1841.
Cooper, John, and Jonathan Cooper. *Children's Fiction, 1900–1950*. Aldershot, UK: Ashgate, 1998.
Cooper, Thomas. *Correspondence between George Hibbert Esq. and the Rev. T. Cooper, Relative to the Condition of the Negro Slaves in Jamaica, Extracted from the Morning Chronicle*. London: J. Hatchard and Son, 1824. http://www.recoveredhistories.org/pamphlet1.php?catid=131.
Corry, Joseph. *Observations upon the Windward Coast of Africa*. London: G. and W. Nicol, 1807.

Dallas, Robert Charles. *The History of the Maroons*. 2 vols. London: T.N. Longman and O. Rees, 1803.
Dancer, Thomas. *The Medical Assistant; or Jamaica Practice of Physic: Designed Chiefly for the Use of Families and Plantations*. Kingston, Jamaica: Alexander Aikman, 1701.
Daraul, Arkon. *Witches and Sorcerers*. London: Tandem, 1965.
Davy, John. *The West Indies Before and Since Emancipation*. London: W. and F.G. Cash, 1854.
de Lisser, Herbert G. *Psyche*. London: Ernest Benn, 1952.
———. *The White Witch of Rosehall*. London: Ernest Benn, 1929.
"A Description of Guinea and Benin, Including the Geography with the Natural and Civil History". In Astley, *New General Collection*, 2:520–732.
Dixon, Bob. *Catching Them Young 2: Political Ideas in Children's Fiction*. London: Pluto Press, 1977.
Dixon, Mary. *Tacky: Freedom Fighter and Folk Hero*. Jamaica: Handprint, 1990.
Doyle, Arthur Conan. *The Lost World*. Rockville: Arc Manor, 2009.
Drury Lane Theatre. *Furibond; or, Harlequin Negro*. London: J. Scales, 1807.
Duncan, Peter. *A Narrative of the Wesleyan Mission to Jamaica*. London: Partridge and Oakey, 1849.
Earle, William. *Obi; or, The History of Three-fingered Jack, in a Series of Letters from a Resident in Jamaica to His Friend in England*. London: Isaiah Thomas, 1800.
Edgeworth, Maria. *Belinda*. 2 vols. London: J. Johnson, 1801.
———. "The Two Guardians". In *Comick Dramas*. Boston: Wells and Lilly, 1817.
———. "The Grateful Negro". In *Harry and Lucy, Lame Jervas, and the Grateful Negro*. London: W. and R. Chambers, 1804.
Edwards, Bryan. *An Historical Survey of the Island of Saint Domingo*. London: John Stockdale, 1801.
———. *The History, Civil and Commercial, of the British Colonies in the West Indies*. New York: Arno Press, 1972.
———. "An Introductory Account Containing Observations on the Disposition, Character, Manners and Habits of Life of the Maroons". *Proceedings of the Governor and Assembly of Jamaica in Regard to the Maroon Negroes*. London: John Stockdale, 1796.
Ellis, J.B. *The Diocese of Jamaica: A Short Account of Its History, Growth and Organisation*. London: Society for Propagating Christian Knowledge, 1913.
Falconbridge, Anna Maria. *Narrative of Two Voyages to the River Sierra Leone during the Years 1791–1793*. London: L.I. Higham, 1802.
Fawcett, John. *Obi; or, Three-Finger'd Jack! A Serio-Pantomime in Two Acts*. London: T. Woodfall, 1800.
Fermor, Patrick Leigh. *The Traveller's Tree: A Journey Through the Caribbean Islands*. 1950. Reprint, London: John Murray, 1965.

Finucane, Ronald C. *Miracles and Pilgrims: Popular Beliefs in Medieval England*. London: J.M. Dent and Sons, 1977.
"Folklore of the Negroes". *Folklore: A Quarterly Review* 15 (1904): 87–94.
Froude, James Anthony. *The English in the West Indies; or, The Bow of Ulysses*. London: Longmans, Green, 1888.
———. *Essays*. London: John Long, 1924.
Fuller, Stephen. *Report to the Lords of the Committee of the Council Appointed for the Consideration of All Matters Relating to Trade and Foreign Plantations*. London, 1789.
Gardner, William J. *A History of Jamaica from Its Discovery by Christopher Columbus to the Present Time*. London: Elliot Stock, 1873.
Gates, Henry Louis, Jr, and Gene Andrew Jarrett. *The New Negro: Readings on Race, Representation, and African-American Culture, 1892–1938*. Princeton, NJ: Princeton University Press, 2007.
Gemmell, David. *The First Chronicles of Druss the Legend*. London: Random House, 1993.
Grainger, James. "The Sugar Cane". In Hutson, *Treatment*, 143–46.
Green, G.G. "The Secret of Grenville Towers". *Pluck* 218, n.d.
Hamley, William George. *Captain Clutterbuck's Champagne: A West Indian Reminiscence*. London: William Blackwood and Sons, 1862.
Harvey, Alison. "West Indian Obeah and English 'Obee': Race, Femininity and Questions of Colonial Consolidation in Maria Edgeworth's *Belinda*". In *New Essays on Maria Edgeworth*, edited by Julie Nash. 1–30. Aldershot, UK: Ashgate, 2006.
Hearn, Lafcadio. *Two Years in the French West Indies*. London: Harper and Brothers, 1890.
———. *Youma: The Story of a West-Indian Slave*. New York: Harper and Brothers, 1890.
The History and Adventures of Jack Mansong, the Famous Negro Robber and Terror of Jamaica. Otley, UK: William Walker, n.d.
Hoogbergen, Wim S.M. *The Boni Wars in Suriname*. Leiden: Brill Academic, 1997.
Hopkins, Matthew. *The Discovery of Witches*. London: R. Royston, 1647. http://www.gutenberg.org/files/14015/14015-h/14015-h.htm.
Hughes, Griffith. *The Natural History of Barbados*. London, 1850. Reprint, New York: Arno Press, 1972.
Hutson, Edward, ed. *On the Treatment and Management of the More Common West India Diseases, 1759–1802*. Kingston: University of the West Indies Press, 2005.
Hutton, J.E. *A History of Moravian Missions*. London: Moravian Publication Office, 1922.
Hutton, William. *A Voyage to Africa: Including a Narrative of an Embassy to One of the Interior Kingdoms in the Year 1820*. London: Longman, Hurst, Rees, Orme and Brown, 1821.
Jamaica. *The Laws of Jamaica*. Vol. 6. St Jago de la Vega: Alexander Aikman and Son, 1816.
Jekyll, Walter. *Jamaican Song and Story: Annancy Stories, Digging Sings, Ring Tunes, and Dancing Tunes*. London: Folk-Lore Society, 1907.
Johnston, Harry H. *The Negro in the New World*. London: Methuen, 1910.

Jordan, Winthrop D. *White over Black: American Attitudes Toward the Negro, 1550–1812*. Chapel Hill: University of North Carolina Press, 1968.

[King, William]. *The Present State of Physick in the Island of CAJAMAI*. London, 1710.

Kingsley, Charles. *At Last: A Christmas in the West Indies*. 2 vols. London: Macmillan, 1871.

Kingsley, Mary H. *West African Studies*. London: Macmillan, 1901.

Kirkpatrick, Kathryn J. "'Gentlemen Have Horrors upon This Subject': West Indian Suitors in Maria Edgeworth's *Belinda*". *Eighteenth-Century Fiction* 5, no. 4 (September 2010): 331–48.

Kramer, Heinrich, and James Sprenger. *Malleus Maleficarum*. 1487. Reprint, New York: Dover, 1971.

Labat, Jean-Baptiste. *The Memoirs of Père Labat, 1693–1705*. Translated by John Eaden. London: Constable, 1931.

[Lanaghan, Frances]. *Antigua and the Antiguans: A Full Account of the Colony and Its Inhabitants*. 2 vols. London: Saunders and Ottley, 1844.

Langton, Edward. *Satan, a Portrait: A Study of the Character of Satan Through All the Ages*. London: Skeffington and Son, 1973.

Lee, Debbie. *Slavery and the Romantic Imagination*. Philadelphia: University of Pennsylvania Press, 2002.

Lehner, Ernst, and Johanna Lehner. *Picture Book of Devils, Demons and Witchcraft*. New York: Dover, 1971.

Lewis, Matthew "Monk". *Journal of a West India Proprietor, Kept During a Residence in the Island of Jamaica*. London: John Murray, 1834. Reprint, Oxford: Oxford University Press, 1999.

Ligon, Richard. *A True and Exact History of the Island of Barbadoes*. London: Peter Parker, 1673.

Livingstone, William Pringle. *Black Jamaica: A Study in Evolution*. London: Sampson, Low, Marston, 1899.

Lloyd, William. *Letters from the West Indies During a Visit in the Autumn of 1836 and the Spring of 1837*. London: Darton and Harvey, 1838.

Long, Carolyn Morrow. *Spiritual Merchants: Religion, Magic and Commerce*. Knoxville: University of Tennessee Press, 2001.

Long, Edward. *Candid Reflections upon the Judgement Lately Awarded by the Court of the King's Bench in Westminster Hall on What Is Commonly Called the Negroe Cause*. London: T. Lowndes, 1772.

———. *The History of Jamaica; or, A General Survey of the Antient and Modern State of That Island*. 3 vols. London: T. Lowndes, 1774. Reprint, Montreal: McGill–Queen's University Press, 2002.

Lorimer, Douglas A. *Colour, Class and the Victorians: English Attitudes to the Negroes in the Mid-Nineteenth Century*. Leicester: Leicester University Press, 1978.

Loyer, Godfrey. "Abstract of a Voyage to Iffini on the Gold Coast in 1701". In Astley, *New General Collection*, 2:417–45.
Lynch, Theodora [Mrs Henry Lynch]. *The Cotton Tree; or Emily, the Little West Indian: A Tale for Young People*. London: John Hatchard and Son, 1847.
——. *The Mountain Pastor*. London: Barton, 1852.
——. *The Wonders of the West Indies*. London: Seeley, Jackson and Halliday, 1856.
[Macaulay, Zachary]. *Negro Slavery; or, a View of Some of the More Prominent Features of That State of Society*. London: Hatchard and Son, 1823.
Macfall, Haldane. *The Wooings of Jezebel Pettyfer*. London: Simkin, Marshall, Hamilton, 1898.
Mackenzie, John M. *Propaganda and Empire: The Manipulation of British Public Opinion, 1880–1960*. Manchester: Manchester University Press, 1984.
Madden, Richard Robert. *A Twelvemonth's Residence in the West Indies*. 2 vols. London: Carey, Len and Blanchard, 1835.
Maddy, Yulisa Amada, and Donnara MacCann. *African Images in Juvenile Literature: Commentaries on Neocolonialist Fiction*. London: McFarland, 1996.
Malchow, H.L. *Gothic Images of Race in Nineteenth Century Britain*. Stanford, CA: Stanford University Press, 1996.
Mares, Colin. "The Pardoner's Tale". *Guardian*, 3 January 1961, 5.
Marryat, Florence. *The Blood of the Vampire*. London: Hutchinson, 1897.
Mather, Cotton. *On Witchcraft*. New York: Peter Pauper Press, 1693.
Matthews, John. *A Voyage to the River Sierra-Leone on the Coast of Africa*. London: B. White and Son, 1791.
Mayne Reid, Thomas. *The Maroon*. 3 vols. London: Hurst and Blackett, 1862.
McLeod, John. *A Voyage to Africa, with Some Account of the Manners and Customs of the Dahomian People*. London: Frank Cass, 1820.
Melville, James. *The Memoires of Sir James Melvil of Hal-Hill*. London: George Scott, 1683.
Mirzoeff, Nicholas. *The Visual Culture Reader*. London: Routledge, Taylor and Francis, 2002.
Montgomery, James, James Grahame and Elizabeth Benger. *Poems on the Abolition of the Slave Trade*. London: R. Bowyer, 1809.
Moore, Francis. "Travels into the Inland Parts of Africa". In Astley, *New General Collection*, 193–233.
Morrish, Ivor. *Obeah, Christ and Rastaman: Jamaica and Its Religion*. Cambridge: James Clarke, 1982.
Moseley, Benjamin. "Miscellaneous Medical Observations". In Hutson, *West India Diseases*, 105–6.
——. *Obi; or, the History of Three-Finger'd Jack*. Newcastle: M. Angus and Son, 1800.
——. *A Treatise on Sugar; with Miscellaneous Medical Observations*. London: John Nicholls, 1799.

Mosto, Alvide da Ca' da [Alvise Cadamosto]. "A Voyage". In Astley, *New General Collection*, 1:572–91.

Munro, T. "The Wire and the Wave". *Boy's Own Paper* 606 (23 August 1890): 744.

Murray, Hugh. *Discovery and Adventure in Africa*. London: T. Nelson and Sons, 1857.

Nadell, Martha Jane. *Enter the New Negroes: Images of Race in American Culture*. Boston: Harvard University Press, 2004.

Nash, Julie, ed. *New Essays on Maria Edgeworth*. Aldershot, UK: Ashgate, 2006.

The New Annual Register; or, General Repository of History, Politics and Literature for the Year 1807. London: John Stockdale, 1808.

Nissen, Johan Peter. *Reminiscences of a Forty-Six Years' Residence in the Island of St Thomas*. Philadelphia: A.H. Senseman, 1838.

Nugent, Maria. *A Journal of a Voyage to, and Residence in, the Island of Jamaica, from 1801 to 1805*. London, 1839.

"The Obeah Man". *Pall Mall Gazette*, 21 July 1896.

"The Obeah Woman". *Oriental Observer*, 12 January 1833, 13.

Orwell, George. *The Collected Essays, Journalism and Letters of George Orwell*. Vol. 1. Edited by Susan Orwell and Ian Angus. Harmondsworth, UK: Penguin, 1968.

Paiewonsky, Isidor. *Eyewitness Accounts of Slavery in the Danish West Indies*. New York: Fordham University Press, 1989.

Palerne, Guillaume de. *The Ancient English Romance of William and the Werewolf*. London: Shakespeare Press, 1832.

Paton, Diana. "Obeah Acts: Producing and Policing the Boundaries of Religion in the Caribbean". *Small Axe* 28 (2009): 2–18.

Peake, Richard Brinsley. *Memoirs of the Colman Family*. Vol. 2. London: Richard Bentley, 1841.

Periodical Accounts Relating to the Missions of the Church of the United Brethren. London: Brethren's Society for the Furtherance of the Gospel, 1790–1889.

Phillippo, James M. *Jamaica: Its Past and Present State*. London: John Snow, 1843.

Phillips, Thomas. "A Journal of a Voyage from England to Barbadoes". In *A Collection of Voyages and Travels*, 173–239. London: Messrs Churchill, 1704.

Phillpotts, Eden. *In Sugar-Cane Land*. London: McClure, 1894.

———. "The Obi Man". *The Graphic*, 1 July 1893.

Poems Chiefly on the Superstition of Obeah. London: Gale and Fenner, 1816.

Powell, James. *Furibond; or, Harlequin Negro: A Grand Comic Pantomime*. London: J. Scales, 1807.

Powles, Louis Diston. *The Land of the Pink Pearl; or, Recollections of Life in the Bahamas*. London: Sampson Low, Marston, 1888.

Pullen-Burry, Bessie. *Jamaica As It Is*. London: T. Fisher Unwin, 1903.

Rampini, Charles. *Letters from Jamaica: The Land of Streams and Woods*. Edinburgh: Edmonston and Douglas, 1873.

Rankin, F. Harrison. *The White Man's Grave: A Visit to Sierra Leone in 1834*. 2 vols. London: Richard Bentley, 1836.

Renny, Robert. *An History of Jamaica*. London: J. Cawthorn, 1807.

Robb, Alex. *The Gospel to the Africans: A Narrative of the Life and Labours of the Rev. William Jameson in Jamaica and Old Calabar*. Edinburgh: Andrew Elliot, 1861.

Roberts, Alexander. *A Treatise of Witchcraft*. London: Samuel Man, 1620. http://www.gutenberg.org/files/17209/17209-h/17209-h.htm.

Roberts, Alexander, Matthew Hopkins and John William Brodie-Innes. *Witches and Witch-Hunters: A Reprint of a Treatise of Witchcraft*. Yorkshire: S.R. Publishers, 1971.

Robinson, May. "Obeah Worship in East and West Indies". *Folklore: A Quarterly Review of Myth, Tradition, Institution and Custom* 4 (1893): 207–18.

Robinson, William. "Trinidad and Its Capabilities and Prominent Products". *Journal of the Royal Colonial Institute* 10, no. 5 (1899).

Rose, George Henry. *A Letter on the Means and Importance of Converting the Slaves in the West Indies to Christianity*. London: John Murray, 1823.

Russell, Jeffrey Burton. *The Devil: Perceptions of Evil from Antiquity to Primitive Christianity*. Ithaca, NY: Cornell University Press, 1977.

———. *Satan: The Early Christian Tradition*. Ithaca, NY: Cornell University Press, 1981.

Sadie, Stanley, ed. *The New Grove Dictionary of Music and Musicians*. Vol. 1. London: Macmillan, 1980.

Sala, G.B. "The Outbreak in Jamaica: 'Vaudouism'". *Belfast Newsletter*, 22 November 1865.

Sargent, G.E. *The Jamaica Missionary: A Life of William Knibb*. London: Benjamin and Green, 1859.

Savage, John. "'Black Magic' and White Terror: Slave Poisoning and Colonial Society in Early 19th Century Martinique". *Journal of Social History* 40, no. 3 (2007): 635–62.

Schiebinger, Londa. *Plants and Empire: Colonial Prospecting in the Atlantic World*. Cambridge, MA: Harvard University Press, 2007.

[Scott, Michael]. *Tom Cringle's Log*. Edinburgh: William Blackwood and Sons, 1862.

Semmel, Bernard. *Jamaican Blood and Victorian Conscience: The Governor Eyre Controversy*. Westport, CT: Greenwood Press, 1962.

Shepard, Leslie. *The History of Street Literature*. London: David and Charles, 1973.

Shepherd, William. "The Negro Incantation". In *The Poetical Register, and Repository of Fugitive Poetry, for 1803*, 413–15. London: F. and C. Rivington, 1805.

Sheridan, Richard B. *Doctors and Slaves: A Medical and Demographic History of Slavery in the British West Indies, 1680–1834*. Cambridge: Cambridge University Press, 1985.

Sherlock, Philip M. *Three Finger Jack's Treasure*. Kingston: Jamaica Publishing, 1961.

Skey, Frederic Edward Guthrie. *The Obeah Tree: A Tale of the West Indies for Boys*. London: Thomas Nelson and Sons, 1932.

Sloane, Hans. *A Voyage to the Islands Madera, Barbados, Nieves, S Christophers and Jamaica.* 2 vols. London, 1725.

Smith, Charlotte Turner. "The Story of Henrietta". In *The Letters of a Solitary Wanderer: Containing Narratives of Various Descriptions.* London: Sampson Low, 1800.

Smith, G.W. *Conquests of Christ in the West Indies: A Short History of Evangelical Missions.* Jamaica: Evangelical Book Room, 1939.

Smith, Paul Jordan. *For the Love of Books: The Adventures of an Impecunious Collector.* Oxford: Oxford University Press, 1934; reprint, 1963.

Smith, Wilbur. *Warlock.* London: Macmillan, 2002.

Snelgrave, William. "A New Account of Some Parts of Guinea and the Slave Trade in 1730". In Astley, *New General Collection*, 2:485–519.

Southey, Thomas. *Chronological History of the West Indies.* London: Longman, Rees, Orme, Brown and Green, 1827.

Stacpoole, Henry De Vere. *The Intended: A Novel.* London: Richard Bentley and Son, 1894.

Stanford, Peter. *The Devil: A Biography.* London: Heinemann, 1996.

Starret, Vincent. "Haldane Macfall: Novelist". In *Buried Caesars: Essays in Literary Appreciation.* Chicago: Covivi-McGee, 1923.

Stearns, Raymond Phineas. *Science in the British Colonies of America.* Champaign: University of Illinois Press, 1970.

Stephens, James. *The Slavery of the British West India Colonies Delineated.* Vol. 1. London: Joseph Butterworth and Son, 1824.

Stephens, John Russell. "Kemble, Charles (1775–1854)". *Oxford Dictionary of National Biography*, edited by Lawrence Goldman. https://doi.org/10.1093/ref:odnb/15316.

Sturge, Joseph, and Thomas Harvey. *The West Indies in 1837.* London: Hamilton, Adams, 1838.

Sutherland, John. *The Longman Companion to Victorian Fiction.* 2nd ed. London: Pearson, 2009.

Tanna, Laura. *Jamaican Folk Tales and Oral Histories.* Kingston: Institute of Jamaica, 1984.

[Thomas, Richard Caddy]. *Letters from the Virgin Islands: Illustrating Life and Manners in the West Indies.* London: John Van Voorst, 1843.

Thompson, Thomas. *Memoirs of an English Missionary to the Coast of Guinea.* London: Shepperson and Reynolds, 1788.

Tokson, Elliot H. *The Popular Image of the Black Man in English Drama, 1550–1688.* Boston: G.K. Hall, 1982.

Trowbridge, William Rutherford Hayes. *Gossip of the Caribbees: Sketches of Anglo-West Indian Life.* London: T. Fisher Unwin, 1895.

Turner, Mary. *Slaves and Missionaries: The Disintegration of Jamaican Slave Society, 1787–1834.* Chicago: University of Illinois Press, 1982.

Underhill, Edward Dean. *The Tragedy of Morant Bay: A Narrative of the Disturbances in the Island of Jamaica in 1865.* London: Alexander and Shepheard, 1895.

United Kingdom. *British Parliamentary Papers*. 21 November 1826–2 July 1827. Vols. 25 and 26, *State Papers Relating to the Slave Population in the West Indies* [. . .].
———. *British Parliamentary Papers*. 1866. Vol. 31, *Report of the Jamaica Royal Commission*.
Vernon, Edward. *A New History of Jamaica: In Thirteen Letters from a Gentleman to His Friend*. London: J. Hodges, 1740.
Villault, Nicolas, Sieur de Bellefond. *A Relation of the Coasts of Africa Called Guinee*. London: The Mitre, 1670.
Virgin Islands. *The Revised Laws of the Virgin Islands*. 1904.
Walcott, Derek. *Poems in a Green Night, 1949–1960*. London: Jonathan Cape, 1962.
Waugh, Alec. "Change and Tradition in the Caribbean". *The Times*, 18 October 1952.
———. *Love and the Caribbean: Tales, Characters and Scenes of the West Indies*. 1930. Reprint, New York: Farrar, Straus and Cudahy, 1958.
Whitehead, Henry S. "Sweet Grass". *Weird Tales*, July 1929.
Wikipedia. "Nanny of the Maroons". http://en.wikipedia.org/wiki/Nanny_of_the_Maroons.
Wilberforce, William. *An Appeal to the Religion, Justice and Humanity of the Inhabitants of the British Empire in Behalf of the Negro Slaves in the West Indies*. London: J. Hatchard and Son, 1823.
Williams, Cynric R. *Hamel, the Obeah Man*. 2 vols. London: Hunt and Clarke, 1827.
———. *A Tour Through the Island of Jamaica from the Western to the Eastern End in the Year 1823*. London: Thomas Hurst, Edward Chance, 1827.
Williams, Joseph J. *Psychic Phenomena of Jamaica*. New York: Dial Press, 1934.
———. *Voodoos and Obeahs: Phases of West India Witchcraft*. London: George Allen and Unwin, 1933.
Williamson, Karina. "Mrs Carmichael: A Scotswoman in the West Indies, 1820–1826". *International Journal of Scottish Literature* 4 (Spring/Summer 2008). http://www.ijsl.stir.ac.uk/issue4/williamson.htm.
Work, Monroe N., ed. *The Negro Year Book: An Annual Encyclopedia of the Negro, 1931–1932*. Tuskegee, AL: Tuskegee Normal and Industrial Institute, 1931. http://www.archive.org/stream/negroyearbookana00workrich#page/n7/mode/2up.
Young, Everild, and Kjeld Helweg-Larsen. *The Pirates' Priest: The Life of Père Labat in the West Indies, 1693–1705*. London: Jarrolds, 1965.

PERIODICALS AND NEWSPAPERS

Baily's Magazine of Sports and Pastimes
Baptist Magazine
La Belle Assemblée, or Bell's Court and Fashionable Magazine
Big Budget

Blackwood's Edinburgh Magazine
Boys of the Empire
Boys' Own Paper
Caledonian Mercury
Chums
Church of England Magazine
Daily Gleaner (Jamaica)
Daily News (Great Britain)
Englishwoman's Domestic Magazine
Evangelical Magazine
The Examiner
Freeman's Journal and Daily Commercial Advertiser
Gazetteer and New Daily Advertiser
Glasgow Herald
The Graphic
Hull Packet and Original Weekly Commercial
John Bull
Lady's Monthly Museum
Literary Gazette; or Journal of Belles Lettres, Politics, and Fashion
Liverpool Mercury
London Magazine (New Series)
Manchester Guardian
Medical Times
Methodist Magazine
The Monthly Magazine, or British Register
Monthly Mirror
Morning Chronicle (Great Britain)
Morning Herald (Great Britain)
Morning Post (Great Britain)
National Register
Notes and Queries: A Medium of Communication for Literary Men, Artists, Antiquaries, Etc.
The Observer
Oriental Observer
Pall Mall Gazette
Penny Illustrated Paper and Illustrated Times
Peter Parley's Annual
Pluck: A High-Class Weekly of Adventure at Home and Abroad
Publisher's Circular and Bookseller's Record of British and Foreign Literature
Quarterly Review

Royal Gazette (Kingston, Jamaica)
The Satirist; or the Censor of the Times
The Spectator
Theatrical Inquisitor and Monthly Mirror
The Times (London)
Trewman's Exeter Flying Post
Universal Magazine
Westminster Review
Whitehall Evening Post
Young England: An Illustrated Magazine for Boys Throughout the English-Speaking World

Index

abolitionists and abolition, 62–63, 82–83, 158–59, 168, 170–72, 300, 307
Adam (Obeah man), 67–68
Africans: association with cannibalism, 26–29; association with devil worship, 22–24, 42; Shango dancers, 395; superstition, 31–37
Aldridge, Ira, 252
Allen, Grant 377–81. See also *Hobbling Mary*
Anglicans, 155, 163–64, 170–71, 176, 197–98, 300–301
Antigua, 98–99, 186–87
anti-Semitism, 280–83, 287–90, 292–95, 313
Atwood, Thomas, 82, 100, 112–13, 160

Bahamas, 56–57
Baker, Moses, 156. See also Baptists
Baptists, 42, 83–89, 132, 156–58, 168–69, 176
Barham, Henry, 77, 102
BBC Home Service, 221
Belinda, 258–63, 397
Bell, Hesketh, 46, 49, 54–56, 86, 90, 100–101, 140, 326–29, 397–98
Bible and key trial, 98. See also European superstitions
Big Budget, 359–62, 366–70,
blackness, 16–17
Blood of the Vampire, The, 335–43, 380
Boys of the Empire, 357–58, 360
Bridges, George, 83, 130, 137

Bryant, Jacob, 38–42, 47–48, 219, 234, 385
Burdett, William, 50, 54, 60–61, 232–36

Canot, Theodore, 28–29
Captain Clutterbuck's Champagne, 124, 271–76
Cathars, 22
Christianization, 161–64, 168, 174–75
Clarkson, Thomas, 25, 31–32, 34
Coromantyns, 126–30, 264, 317
Crisis, The, 353

Daily Gleaner, 151
Dancer, Thomas, 6, 52, 76–77, 104–5
Danish West Indies, 44, 65–66, 113–14
Devil: as a black man, 16–18
Dickens, Charles, 6–8, 135, 360
Discoverie of Witchcraft, 39
Dominica, 82, 112–13, 163, 396

Earle, William, 226–32. See also Three Fingered Jack
Edgeworth, Maria, 258–71, 313, 397
Edwards, Bryan, 33, 49, 53, 91, 169–71, 179–81
Ellis, Alexander (Obeah man), 150
European superstition, 10–20, 31

Falconbridge, Anna Maria, 21
Fawcett, John, 237, 242–43
Fermor, Patrick Leigh, 125

419

Fisher, William (Obeah man), 147. *See also* Obeah trials
Fuller, Stephen, 48–49, 53, 93–94, 116, 127–29, 149–50, 284, 388; Fuller report, 53, 93–94, 116, 127–29, 149, 229, 234, 261, 284
Furibond, A Grand Comic Pantomime, 204–7

Gardner, William J., 106, 112–13, 118–19, 121–22, 129–30, 142, 148, 193, 237
Gemmell, David, 372
Grainger, Dr James, 200–202
Graphic, 8, 373–77
Grateful Negro, The, 263–67
Grenada, 55, 104, 192, 326, 394–95
Guyana, 79

Hamel, the Obeah Man, 295–313, 372. *See also* Cynric Williams
Hamley, William George, 124, 271–76
Hearn, Lafcadio, 88, 114, 193–94, 223, 323–26
History and Adventures of Jack Mansong, The, 235–36
History Civil and Commercial, 49, 53, 267
History of Jamaica (Long) 6, 39–40, 102, 115, 118, 120–22, 127, 130, 155, 160
Hobbling Mary, 377–80
How We Caught the Obeah Man, 399–400
Hughes, Griffith, 43–44, 96–97, 111, 155

Igbo, 9
Illustrated London News, 133
Inn Album, 214
Intended, The, 329–35

John Canoe (junkanu), 116

Jones, William (Obeah man), 146–47. *See also* Obeah trials
Journal of the Royal Colonial Institute, 56

Kemble, Charles, 238–39, 243
Kingsley, Charles, 72–74, 79–80, 85–88, 151, 162, 194, 215, 360, 381–83, 402

Labat, Père Jean-Baptiste, 26, 66, 79–82, 159–60, 383
Letters from Jamaica, 389–93
Lewis, Matthew Monk, 66–71, 83, 86–87, 105, 119, 131, 142–43, 222, 384
Life and Exploits of Mansong, 232–35
Ligon, Richard, 101–2
Little Theatre, Haymarket, 237, 242
Long, Edward, 39–40, 48, 81, 94, 102, 115, 127, 154–55, 160–61, 177–79
Love and the Caribbean, 394–96
Lynch, Theodora Elizabeth, 61, 71–72, 84, 154. *See also Wonders of the West Indies*

MacFall, Haldane, 343
Madden, Richard, 41, 46–47, 50, 53–54, 79, 85, 98, 105, 116, 129, 141–42, 144–46, 189
Maldina (Obeah woman), 74–75
Malleus Maleficarum, 13–14, 34
Manchester Guardian, 5, 8, 42, 57, 63
Manm Robert (Obeah woman), 114
Marble, Andrew (Obeah man), 51, 98, 107–8, 112, 143.
Maroon, The, 276–95
Maroons, 4, 45, 47, 116, 125–26, 129, 149–50, 224, 245, 255–56, 303
Marryat, Florence, 335–43
Martinique, 14–15, 80, 153, 194, 324–26, 376, 395–96

Methodist, 163–68, 176, 275, 308, 311–13
Mokombo (Obeah man), 94–95
Mongo Maud (Obeah woman), 113–14
Montserrat, 140, 153–54, 194
Morant Bay Rebellion, 133, 148–50, 360, 363
Moravians, 50, 118, 120, 161, 187, 209
Morning Chronicle, 131–32, 143, 220, 245
Moseley, Benjamin, 40–41, 47–48, 52, 60, 81, 92, 131, 138, 223–25, 231–36, 244, 356
Mrs Carmichael, 46, 54
myal dance, 119–20
myalism, 115–25, 186, 278, 284, 287, 294, 393

Nanny (Obeah woman), 125–26, See also Maroons
"A Naval Officer's Yarn", 360–61
"The Negro Incantation", 202–4
Negro in the New World, The, 182–83
Neil, George (Obeah man), 123–24
Notes and Queries, 189, 217–21

Obeah: African susceptibility, 53; African words for, 1; association with deformity and ugliness, 60, 63, 229, 234, 236, 284–85, 345, 356–57; association with devil worship, 75–76, 175, 196, 199, 279, 299, 347–49, 392; association with serpents, 8, 38–39, 41–42, 175, 191, 331, 366, 385, 392; and blackness, 61, 65, 272; in boys' adventure papers, 355–70; catching criminals, 95, 100; causing illness, 108–12; as defined by Bryant, 38–39, 41–42; laws against, 44–45, 135–40; making of, 75, 81, 88, 91–92; necessary ingredients, 33, 45, 47–51, 58, 92, 94, 138, 150–51, 239, 240, 246, 273, 283, 296–97, 328, 349, 350, 374; and poisons, 54, 67, 76–90, 388; post-emancipation, 190, 193; power of, 53, 82, 99; prevention of robbery, 93–94, 96; profitability, 100; pulling illness, 111–12; and resistance, 45, 131–33; trials, 142–48, 165; used by whites, 94–96; uses of, 91–94, 100, 388; and wild dancing, 122, 362, 366; and the Witch of Endor, 39–41, 47, 219,
Obeah in English poetry, 13, 1, 162, 200–204, 207–9
Obeah Jack (Obeah man), 131–32
Obeah man (fictional), 228–32, 237, 278–79, 319, 345, 399–401;
Obeah practitioners, 45–48, 51, 55, 59–70, 72, 75–83, 85–86, 91–92, 94, 100–101, 113, 115, 120, 123, 127–29, 131, 133, 136, 138, 141–42, 148–49, 151, 153–54, 159, 162–63, 190, 197–98, 202, 214, 216–17, 219, 234, 237, 257, 272, 278, 286, 308–10, 316, 323, 326, 356, 364, 368–69, 371–72, 382, 393–94, 400, 402
Obeah Tree, The, 370–73
Obeah vs. Christianity, 188–89, 210, 299
Obeah woman (fictional), 123, 265–67, 316–28, 330–33, 335, 337, 341, 346, 348–50
Obi Man, The, 373–77
Orwell, George, 356, 358
Oxford Dictionary of National Biography, 204, 239

Pall Mall Gazette, 58, 335, 353–54, 399
Pardoner's Tale, The, 400–402
Peter Parley's Annual, 356, 357. See also Obeah: boys' adventure papers
Phillippo, James, 42, 46, 158

Phillpotts, Eden, 5, 373–77, 402–03
Phyllis (Obeah woman), 72–73
Plato (Obeah man), 69–72, 222, 225
Pluck, 356–57
Poems Chiefly on the Superstition of Obeah, 13, 162, 209–13
Poems on the Abolition of the Slave Trade, 81, 207–9
poisons, 76–90, 153, 326; fingernail poison, 74, 77, 80, 84, 98, 374
Pringle, Rachel, 338

Quakers, 62–63, 103, 184
Quarterly Review, 215, 270
Quassie (Obeah man), 68, 259

racist ideas, 3, 7, 58, 70, 137, 160, 169, 173–78, 180–85, 189–91, 194, 196, 216, 229–30, 242, 247, 251–53, 255, 258, 263, 267, 271, 278, 283, 285, 295, 308–9, 312, 320, 324, 333, 339–41, 347, 353, 356, 358, 362, 368, 372–73, 382, 390, 393, 398, 400, 402–3; desire for white women, 248, 250–51, 256–57, 262, 289, 293, 300, 306, 312, 360; justifying colonization, 182; justifying slavery, 178–80, 192; Charles Kingsley, 382; mulattoes, 67, 273–74, 276, 324–25, 332–33, 335, 337; of planters/slave owners, 177, 192
Rampini, Charles, 61–62, 64, 146–48, 187, 390, 391
Reeder, John, 223, 245
Reid, Mayne, 276–78, 313, 343
Renny, Robert, 53–54, 137
Roman Catholics, 11, 49, 55, 101, 160, 162–63, 370, 372

Secret of Grenville Towers, The, 357
Sharpe, Samuel, 132

Slaves' Fetish, 366–70
Sloane, Hans, 77–79, 90, 102–4
Smith, Charlotte Turner, 253–58
Smith, Wilbur, 372–73
Society for the Abolition of the Slave Trade, 204
St Lucia, 55, 159, 196, 219–20, 350
Stacpoole, Henry de Vere, 329–35
The Story of Henrietta, 253–58
Sub-Officers' Guide of Jamaica, 150–51
"The Sugar Cane", 200–202
Suriname, 51, 174–75, 259

Tacky's Rebellion, 45–46, 126–29, 202, 229
Three-Finger'd Jack, 222; in Moseley, 223–24, 231
Times, The, 90, 140, 143, 215, 221, 394, 397–98
Tom Cringle's Log, 215–16, 271
traditional healers, 103–7
traditional medicine, 1, 107
travel narratives, 9, 19, 121, 355, 381–84
Trinidad, 56, 72–73, 133, 140, 402
Trowbridge, William Rutherford, 8, 188, 196
Two Guardians, The, 267–71

Virgin Islands, 138–39
Voice from Jamaica in Reply to William Wilberforce, A, 171–72. See also George Bridges
Voice of Jubilee, The, 183

Waite, William (Obeah man), 61, 113, 217
Walduck, Thomas, 43–44, 163
Waugh, Alec, 394–96
Wellington, Arthur (Obeah man), 148–49. See also Obeah trials

white anxiety, 17–18, 90, 262
white Obeah, 189. *See also* Obeah vs Christianity,
Whitehall Evening Post, 244
Wilberforce, William, 82–83, 141, 159, 168, 170, 300, 307
Williams, Cynric, 70–71, 151–53, 163–64, 166, 181, 222, 225, 295. See also *Hamel, the Obeah Man*
Williams, Joseph, 39, 59, 121, 213–14

witch hunts, 12–14, 60
Witch's Legacy, A, 326–29. *See also* Hesketh Bell
Wonders of the West Indies, The, 62, 384–89
Wooings of Jezebel Pettyfer, The, 343–54, 399
World Went Very Well Then, The, 314–23

Youma, 323–26

www.ingramcontent.com/pod-product-compliance
Lightning Source LLC
Chambersburg PA
CBHW051241300426
44114CB00011B/845